Collaborative Search and Communities of Interest:
Trends in Knowledge Sharing and Assessment

Pascal Francq
Universite Libre de Bruxelles, Belgium

INFORMATION SCIENCE REFERENCE

Hershey · New York

Director of Editorial Content:	Kristin Klinger
Director of Book Publications:	Julia Mosemann
Acquisitions Editor:	Lindsay Johnston
Development Editor:	Christine Bufton
Publishing Assistant:	Sean Woznicki
Typesetter:	Casey Conapitski
Production Editor:	Jamie Snavely
Cover Design:	Lisa Tosheff
Printed at:	Lightning Source

Published in the United States of America by
Information Science Reference (an imprint of IGI Global)
701 E. Chocolate Avenue
Hershey PA 17033
Tel: 717-533-8845
Fax: 717-533-8661
E-mail: cust@igi-global.com
Web site: http://www.igi-global.com

Copyright © 2011 by IGI Global. All rights reserved. No part of this publication may be reproduced, stored or distributed in any form or by any means, electronic or mechanical, including photocopying, without written permission from the publisher. Product or company names used in this set are for identification purposes only. Inclusion of the names of the products or companies does not indicate a claim of ownership by IGI Global of the trademark or registered trademark.

Library of Congress Cataloging-in-Publication Data

Collaborative search and communities of interest : trends in knowledge sharing and assessment / Pascal Francq, editor.
    p. cm.
  Includes bibliographical references and index.
  Summary: "This book offers indepth analysis of the different forms of collaborations on the Internet presenting several dimensions including sociological, psychological, and technical perspectives"--Provided by publisher. ISBN 978-1-61520-841-8 (hbk.) -- ISBN 978-1-61520-842-5 (ebook) 1. Information behavior. 2. Internet searching. 3. Computer network resources. I. Francq, Pascal, 1971- ZA3075.C665 2010
  025.5'24--dc22
                                        2009048639

British Cataloguing in Publication Data
A Cataloguing in Publication record for this book is available from the British Library.

All work contributed to this book is new, previously-unpublished material. The views expressed in this book are those of the authors, but not necessarily of the publisher.

Editorial Advisory Board

Pascal Francq, *Paul Otlet Institute, Belgium & Université Catholique de Louvain, Belgium*
Marco Saerens, *Université Catholique de Louvain, Belgium*
François Lambotte, *Université Libre de Bruxelles, Belgium*
Dirk Kenis, *University College of Mechelen, Belgium*
Joan Francesc Fondevila, *Cable Studies Center, Spain*

Table of Contents

Detailed Table of Contents

Chapter 1

Pascal Francq, Paul Otlet Institute, Belgium & Université Catholique de Louvain, Belgium

This chapter proposes an introduction to the whole book. In section 2, I will briefly present the new knowledge sources emerging from the Web 2.0. This increasing amount of information is not manageable anymore on an individual basis: people need to benefit from searches and feedbacks from others (section 3) and increase their involvements in collectives (section 4). Section 5 proposes an overview of the next chapters. Nerveless, the new opportunities offered by Internet have several drawbacks highlighted in section 6. Finally, section 7 concludes this introduction.

Chapter 2

Christophe Lejeune, Université Libre de Bruxelles, Belgium

The lay notion of virtual community is not satisfactory because, strictly speaking, depicted phenomena (Internet-coordinated collectives) are neither communitarian nor virtual. Moreover, the idiom embraces a (too) large variety of situations. For these reasons, we propose the narrower notion of mediated collectives. Previous ethnographies of Debian, Open Directory and Wikipedia help to define the notion from empirical observation.

Chapter 3

François Fouss, Facultés Universitaires Catholiques de Mons (FUCaM), Belgium

Recommender systems try to provide people with recommendations of items they will appreciate, based on their past preferences, history of purchase, and demographic information. This chapter (1) introduces recommender systems, classifying them along four dimensions (i.e. the way the preferences are gathered, the used approach, the type of algorithm, and the way the results are provided) and describing recent work done in the area, and (2) provides more details about one such type of recommender systems, namely collaborative-recommendation systems. Such systems work by analyzing the items previously rated by all the users and are not based on the content of the items, as content-based systems.

Chapter 4

Nowadays Web users are facing the problems of information overload and drowning due to the significant and rapid growth in the amount of information and the large number of users. As a result, how to provide Web users more exactly needed information is becoming a critical issue in Web-based information retrieval and data management. In order to address the above difficulties, Web mining was proposed as an efficient means to discover the intrinsic relationships among Web data. In particular, Web usage mining is to discover Web usage patterns and utilize the discovered usage knowledge for constructing interest-oriented user communities, which could be, in turn, used for presenting Web users more personalized Web contents, i.e. Web recommendation. On the other hand, Latent Semantic Analysis (LSA) is one kind of approaches that is used to reveal the inherent correlation resided in co-occurrence activities, such as Web usage data. Moreover, LSA possesses the capability of capturing the hidden knowledge at semantic level that can't be achieved by traditional methods. In this chapter, we aim to address building user communities of interests via combining Web usage mining and latent semantic analysis. Meanwhile we also present the application of user communities for Web recommendation.

Chapter 5

Link analysis is a framework usually associated with fields such as graph mining, relational learning, Web mining, text mining, hyper-text mining, visualization of link structures. It provides and analyzes relationships and associations between many objects of various types that are not apparent from isolated pieces of information. This chapter shows how to apply various link-analysis algorithms exploiting the graph structure of databases on collaborative-recommendation tasks. More precisely, two kinds of link-analysis algorithms are applied to recommend items to users: random-walk based models and kernel-based models. These link-analysis based algorithms do not use any feature of the items in order to compute the recommendations, they first compute a matrix containing the links between persons and items, and then derive recommendations from this matrix or part of it.

Chapter 6

This chapter presents a genetic algorithm, called the Similarity-based Clustering Genetic Algorithm (SCGA), used to group users' profiles. This algorithm is integrated in an approach which allows to share documents among users browsing a collection of documents. The users are described in terms of profiles, with each profile corresponding to one area of interest. While browsing through the collection of documents, users' profiles are computed. These profiles are then grouped into communities of interests using the SCGA which is based on the Grouping Genetic Algorithm (GGA). In fact, the SCGA can solve other similar problems under certain circumstances. The approach is part of a more generic model to manage information called the GALILEI Framework. This framework, which provides promising results, has been developed in a software platform available under the GNU GPL license.

Chapter 7

Silvana Castano, Università degli Studi di Milano, Italy
Alfio Ferrara, Università degli Studi di Milano, Italy
Stefano Montanelli, Università degli Studi di Milano, Italy

In this chapter, we present a P2P coordination approach for setting up and exploiting collective peer knowledge provided by autonomously emerging semantic communities. This approach aims at providing a practical means for allowing a peer to move from a restricted peer knowledge space, where it is considered as a single agent with its personal knowledge, towards an intermediate collective knowledge space, where it is considered as a member of a community storing a part of the overall collective knowledge, up to a final collective peer-knowledge space, where the peer builds its personal and coordinated view of the collective knowledge of interest harvested from the underlying communities. In this respect, ontologies and Semantic matching techniques are exploited to set up collective knowledge and to effectively enforce distributed resource sharing.

Chapter 8

Nikolaos Nanas, Center for Research and Technology, Greece & University of Thessaly, Greece
Manolis Vavalis, Center for Research and Technology, Greece & University of Thessaly, Greece
Lefteris Kellis, Center for Research and Technology, Greece & University of Thessaly, Greece
Dimitris Koutsaftikis, Center for Research and Technology, Greece & University of Thessaly, Greece
Elias Houstis, Center for Research and Technology, Greece & University of Thessaly, Greece

Web observatories are becoming a common on-line practice. Their role is to compile, organize and convey information that serves the needs of a thematically focused Web community. So far they are typically following a centralized approach, with an editorial team being responsible for finding, collecting, editing and presenting the observatory's information content. We propose a new approach for the development of Web observatories based on Collective Information Filtering. Community profiles are used to capture the collective interests of community members and evaluate the relevance of information content accordingly. We can thus build Web observatories that can be dynamically enriched and can continuously adapt their content to the interests/needs of the observatory's community. This new approach not only reduces significantly the cost of developing and maintaining a Web observatory, but also, following the current Web trends, it is community driven. In this chapter, we discuss Collective Information Filtering and we describe the architecture for applying it to a Web Observatory. We also present a series of prototype Web Observatories that adopt the proposed approach.

Microblogging's explosion has provoked changes in the Blogosphere (now bloggers prefer to publish brief content in microblogs), and it has changed some roles in journalism too. Twitter is the most important tool in this phenomenon and it has served to keep connected sources, journalists and audiences. In recent years, media and news agencies are being characterized by an intensive use of microblogs. Journalists start to be collaborate within communities of interests trough microblogging, in particular Twitter. Facts like California fires are a clear example of Twitter coverages, which were started by users and gathered by journalists. This is more than a brief and fast tool for journalism, it is related with making connections with audiences, witnesses and sources of breaking news. In this sense, this chapter will show several examples in order to explain how Twitter is a new way to design collaborative coverages. Hence, it is not just a platform on fashion.

Chapter 10

An e-business new product development (NPD) knowledge articulation model is built from the interdisciplinary empirical and theoretical literature. The model is intended to facilitate a case study of a large multinational mobile communications services/products company (with team members in Europe, Asia and Australia). The NPD teams include subject matter experts that function as a community of practice, electronically collaborating in a virtual context. The knowledge created and shared in the NPD teams involve various unknown levels of tacit and explicit ideas, which are difficult to understand or assess. The goal of the research is to build a tacit knowledge articulation framework and measurement construct that can be used to understand how a successful (or unsuccessful) NPD team operates, in terms of knowledge innovation and productivity. Complex issues and controversies in knowledge management are examined to clarify terminology for future research.

Chapter 11

This paper discusses social software technologies and presents an integrated social software model that can be used to achieve collective goals. This model has grown out of a need among practitioners to identify useful social software functionalities and to find out what to do with them. As the number of social software technologies increases, the question increasingly remains what to do with them and how to apply them usefully. The model can be used within an organization, to guide it in attaining organizational goals, but it can also be used to support activities in a network of organizations or in a network of non-affiliated individuals. First, we discuss social software in general. Subsequently, we discuss a model for understanding social software data and functionality. Finally, two possible applications of the social software model are discussed: knowledge sharing and increasing social inclusion among youth.

Chapter 12

Wolfgang Prinz, Fraunhofer Institute for Applied Information Technology FIT, Germany
Sabine Kolvenbach, Fraunhofer Institute for Applied Information Technology FIT, Germany

In this chapter we present results of our research on a collaborative platform that enables employees of a global company to present themselves, their business and company site in a company-wide autograph book. For the content generation the employees received an innovative technology, an application running on an Ultra-Mobile Personal Computer (UMPC) that enables users to generate video, sound, simple text, drawings, and photos. Main goal of this applied research is to bridge the gap between the various company sites, to foster working relationships and to strengthen the common understanding that each employee is part of a people company. This chapter describes the application, it presents an analysis of the generated content, the evaluation of the users' acceptance of the UMPC application and the autograph book and finally an outlook on further research activities informed by these results.

Preface

Since the beginning of the 21st century, the Internet has become a widely used social platform. Web 2.0, in particular social software, again emphasizes the crucial role of social relations in knowledge production and diffusion. Net surfers collaborate more and more (implicitly and explicitly) to manage the available knowledge on the Internet. Among the various forms of collaborations, two of them receive increasing attention:

- **collaborative search** tools allowing net surfers to benefit from the searches done by others to access relevant information (for example collaborative filtering tools);
- **communities (of interest)** formed by a collective of net surfers with common interests where knowledge is produced collectively and shared (for example the *Open Directory Project*).

For many specialists, these two forms of collaborations are crucial to manage the large amount of accessible information on the Internet or in intranets. Despite their success in practice, several questions are raised. There are three types of open issues: (i) the different approaches for implementing these forms of collaborations, (ii) the possible ways to make them work in practice, and (iii) their impact on the environments in which they are deployed. The aim of this book is to propose some answers to these different questions.

The first chapter introduces the context of these two forms of collaborations, explains the main reasons for their success and their (mostly ignored) potential dangers, and details each specific contribution. The second chapter studies the concept of "community" as defined by sociologists and demonstrates that its use in the context of the Internet is not really adequate. It proposes the concept of "project-driven mediated collectives" to better describe this phenomenon in the future.

The first set of chapters is related to innovative technologies providing solutions to detect communities of interests and/or to share knowledge. Chapter 3 overviews the recommender systems (a particular type of collaborative search tools), their approaches, their preference indicators, the algorithms used and their predictions mechanisms. In chapter 4, a method is proposed to detect communities of net surfers sharing common access patterns based on latent semantic analysis, and then to recommend Web pages. Another approach to make recommendations is described in chapter 5, where link analysis models that exploit the graph formed by the users and items they rated, are enumerated. Chapter 6 describes an algorithm that detects communities of interests based on the relevance of the documents read by the users. Chapter 7 reviews a P2P system that collectively organizes knowledge. The specific coordination mechanism used to allow different peers to find other peers sharing similar knowledge perspectives is detailed. Chapter 8 introduces a novel algorithm to filter relevant information for a community and shows how it can be integrated in Web observatories.

A second set of chapters studies how tools, communities of interest and knowledge sharing impact the environment in which they are used. Chapter 9 shows how Twitter may change the practices of journalism since the journalists, their sources and their audiences can now be directly connected through microblogging. Two generic theoretical frameworks are then analyzed. In chapter 10, a framework examines the important (and rarely understood) problem of tacit knowledge sharing. The framework introduced in chapter 11 studies how social software can be deployed in organizations or directly on the Internet. Finally, chapter 12 reports an interesting approach that helps members of a large community to better know each other (an important issue for trust building): an autograph book built by the different members and based on a collaborative platform.

Every researcher involved in studying collaboration on the Internet should be interested in this book. The concepts of *communities of practice* and *collaborative search* are defined and their theoretical and practical limits studied. The "technical" chapters describe several technologies and algorithms used to solve these problems. The researcher can not only find useful models for his or her own needs, but also an overview of the kind of information exploited by computer programs. The latter is important to understand the hypothesis behind the different approaches, and the inputs and outputs for the users. The "applications" chapters propose several examples of the impacts of communities of practice and collaborative search in real life. It is of course impossible to cover every possible impact, but the diversity of the examples is large enough to inspect the main elements.

This book outlines that studying the different forms of collaborations on the Internet has several dimensions (sociological, psychological, technical, etc.). While there are a lot of works about these different aspects, they are mostly published in different journals and books, and diffused in separate research communities. By treating these dimensions in a same book, the authors hope to build a bridge between these research communities and to initiate fruitful discussions between them.

I thank the authors for their contribution as well as the reviewers for their work and numerous interesting remarks. I will also thank Emilie Vossen for her help to finalize this book.

Dr. Ir. Pascal Francq
November 2009

Chapter 1
Internet, Collaborative Search, and Communities of Interests

Pascal Francq
Paul Otlet Institute, Belgium & Université Catholique de Louvain, Belgium

CONTEXT

With the arrival of the XXIst Century, some say that we now live in a *knowledge society* characterized by knowledge, expertise, creativity and innovation. For many economists, it becomes more and more crucial for our modern societies to produce, spread and share knowledge (David & Foray, 2003). For organizations, information is considered as the third factor of production (Schreyer, 1999), and many specialists have pointed the importance of competitive intelligence for an organization's strategy (Kahaner, 1997). Nowadays, everybody agrees on the fact that knowledge production and sharing are the key elements for human emancipation.

From the philosophical schools in the Antic Greece to the academical world, the production and the share of knowledge were, and still are, based on collaboration between individuals. As stated by Aristotle in his *Metaphysics*, "the total is more than the sum of the parts". With the widespread of Internet, and the availability of large amounts of information, many people claim that it will transform radically the way knowledge is produced. Several intellectuals, such as Lévy (1994), believe that a sort of *collective intelligence* will emerge from the cyberspace. Such hopes were reinforced while the Internet was transformed in something that many people call the *Web 2.0* (O'Reilly, 2005). Without discussing the different existing definitions for this term, I want to stress the new role of the net surfers: from passive information consumers, they become active information producers.

This chapter proposes an introduction to the whole book. In section 2, I will briefly present the new knowledge sources emerging from the Web 2.0. This increasing amount of information is not manageable anymore on an individual basis: people need to benefit from searches and feedbacks from others (section 3) and increase their involvements in *collectives* (section 4). Section 5 proposes an overview of the next chapters. Nerveless, the new opportunities offered by Internet have several drawbacks highlighted in section 6. Finally, section 7 concludes this introduction.

DOI: 10.4018/978-1-61520-841-8.ch001

Copyright © 2011, IGI Global. Copying or distributing in print or electronic forms without written permission of IGI Global is prohibited.

NEW KNOWLEDGE SOURCES

Until the end of the XXth Century, the traffic on the Web was largely monopolized by a "few" sites (the main portals, several media, big companies and major universities). But, since the Web 2.0 phenomenon, the number of alternative knowledge sources has exploded. My concern is not to enumerate all these sources, but to emphasize some typical examples.

It is impossible to speak about these alternative knowledge sources without citing the free on-line encyclopedia Wikipedia and its 13,7 millions notices (in August 2009). In fact, several studies have shown that Wikipedia is not considered as an alternative source anymore, but as a reference for many net surfers. Its increasing use in students' works illustrates its importance for the younger generations. Without detailing how Wikipedia works, it is important to underline the fact that the notices are written by many non-payed contributors, some of them being anonymous, and that the encyclopedia tries to ensure a given neutrality in the positions presented (at least for controversial subjects). Many notices are written by several contributors, so it makes perfect sense to present Wikipedia as a product of different collectives, each one editing several notices related to the corresponding interest.

The blogs are another important trend today on the Web. On the technical side, it is nothing more than a Web site working with technologies existing since the nineties. But, in reality, their authors share several practices, the most important being the massive use of hyperlinks (in particular to other blogs). These interconnections between blogs make them build a world of their own called the blogosphere. Authors such as Gillmor (2004) claim that they propose a new way for journalism where citizens write for citizens. The recent emergence of micro-blogs (where the size of the messages posted is limited to a fixed number of characters, usually 140), such as Twitter, has reinforced the role of blogging as a process of informing. Here also, it is possible to consider that the blogosphere is formed by different collectives, each one consulting and editing a specific cluster of blogs.

Other emerging sources of knowledge are social software, in particular those devoted to information sharing. Since the beginning of the Internet, the earlier communication tools (a particular type of social software) were heavily used by net surfers to discuss and share information. For several domains, Usenet is still today an interesting information source. But, the Web 2.0 has produced new softwares to share on-line resources: bookmarks (Delicious), scientific publications (CiteULike), pictures (Flickr), music (Last.fm) or videos (YouTube). All these applications implement the same approach: each user associates to a resource he or she founds interesting some tags. Since the tagging is public, everyone can see which are the resources associated with which tags. Since these resources are supposed to be relevant in a way or another (because someone has taken time to tag them), these software are powerful tools to access knowledge. Some researchers have shown that it is possible to cluster the net surfers into clusters based on the keywords they used to tag resources (Paolillo, & Penumarthy, 2007).

The important point is that the Internet provides a large amount of information written by different net surfers having different goals, origins, points of view, backgrounds, etc. Several people claim that the Internet will renew our democracies by making citizens aware of the fact that they are part of a "global village" to use the concept proposed by McLuhan (1967).

COLLABORATIVE SEARCH

These multiple knowledge sources provide an increasing number of information and it becomes impossible for the net surfers to manage them by themselves. More and more, people have to face the *information overload* in his or her everyday life.

In a now famous article of 2004 in the magazine *Wired*, Anderson has described this new situation (Anderson, 2004). To make it short, he explains that the market is usually characterized by a classical Pareto law: 80% of the sells are made by 20% of the products. But now, with Internet and the immateriality of the products (such as books or music), the remaining 80% of the products (the *long tail* of the selling curve) are available for the net surfers. Let us apply this theory to the access to information. Before the Web 2.0, only a few actors (the media groups) were diffusion channels for information. But now, it is possible for millions of actors to become these channels (individual, non-profit organizations, etc.). Information that was previously not published (because there was no "market" for it) can now be put on-line. For Anderson, this multiplies the niches (small players providing information for a very small number of people) and makes them viable.

Of course, Anderson knows that a lot of this information is not interesting at all, but he believes that collaborative filtering tools will help people to find the information they are interested in. Basically, these systems recommend some resources (information, books, music, etc.) to net surfers based on their preferences and those of other net surfers. Typically, if you buy the album "Machine Head" of Deep Purple on a commercial Web site, it will suggest you the album "In Rock" (since both albums are considered by many fans of Deep Purple as their two best ones).

In fact, recommendations systems are a particular type of *collaborate search* tools. Other similar tools include social software sharing resources (described above), collective knowledge coordination, adaptive information filtering or collective information filtering. The central point is that, when net surfers search for resources, in particular for relevant information, they benefit from the experiences of others and make others benefit from their own experiences. In other words:

if it is impossible to manage the whole information available on the Internet alone, let us try to handle it together.

COMMUNITIES OF INTERESTS

Many studies have shown how powerful social networks are for knowledge sharing. In his work on people sharing a common practice (forming so called "communities of practice"), Wenger (1998) has described how shared experiences help to define best practices and optimize the working environment of people. Another well known work is the one of Rheingold (2000) on on-line social networks (he called "virtual communities") where he testified of the new forms of relationships between individuals through communication mediated by computers. Whatever they are called, it is now evident that social networks are powerful tools to share information across organizational and geographical boundaries. In particular, they are crucial to share *tacit knowledge* that can with difficulty be formalized through (numeric) documents.

In this book, we are talking about *communities of interests*. Conscious that it is a lazy idiom, I define them as collectives of net surfers sharing a common interest, a common behavior or a common practice. In particular, the book focuses on resources (items or people): the Internet or intranets give access to many on-line resources, and sub-sets of them are relevant for different communities of interests. Of course, a given resource can be relevant for multiple communities, and a given user can be involved in several communities. A community is not only a gateway to interesting resources, but also a place where people can collaborate (if the members of a given community are brought into contact). There are also links between the different "kinds of communities". For example, a community of practice can be seen as a community of interest, the interest being the shared practice. A virtual community may be also considered as a community of interest, the interest being the use of a common communication tool.

Nevertheless, to identify who must collaborate with whom and on which topic is still an essential issue in the development of these communities of interests. The identification of their members can be done "manually". For example, a "community manager" studies the profiles of a set of individuals to discover those interested by the same kind of things, and contacts them to initialize a collaboration (for example by creating a virtual space in an intranet). But, this is only possible within an organization and is most of the time costly since someone has to "walk around" in the organization to learn people's interests. People can also search among themselves to find other ones with similar interests. Social networking software (for example Facebook or LinkedIn) are developed to facilitate this task: based on different criteria, it is possible to search for groups of people and consequently to join them. Another possibility is to use search tools to identify resources acting as focal points for a community (such as a blog, a forum, a set of tags, etc.).

The main drawback of manual approaches to detect communities of interests is that they are impractical when the number of potential members increases. In such cases, only automatic solutions can be of little help. To detect people forming a potential community of interests, these solutions need some information on what people are interested in. This feedback can be implicit (for example on Amazon.com when a net surfer buys a good, it is supposed that this good is considered as interesting by him or her) and/or explicit (the people are asked to provide an assessment on a resource). Once this data is collected, algorithms can use it to detect people sharing similar contents and/or feedbacks (using the content if available, using the links between different feedbacks on common resources, or both). The solutions of these algorithms evolute in a way or another: when new feedbacks are gathered, they are used

to update the communities of interests detected.

In practice, it is impossible to develop algorithms that really "understand" people interests. Therefore, it is important to understand the characteristics of the different solutions, such as how they work and which data they use.

PRESENTATION OF THE BOOK

The chapters published in this book propose several approaches related to collaborative search and communities of interests. Through these chapters, the reader may find elements to respond to several open questions related to on-line collectives of net surfers and possible forms of collaborations.

2. **From Virtual Communities to Project-driven Mediated Collectives Debian, Wikipedia and the Open Directory Project Compared.** As explained in the previous section, several idioms are used by researchers to deal with "groups of net surfers" (communities of interests, virtual communities, Web-based communities, etc.). Lejeune reminds us that these idioms recover so many different realities, that an increasing number of sociologists criticize them. In particular, for sociology, a common feature (such as a common interest) is not sufficient to speak of community. He introduces therefore the idiom of "mediated collectives" to skip the problematic concept of "community". Moreover, Lejeune proposes that they are "project-driven" when they collaborate for the realization of a common production (such as an encyclopedia). Using studies about Wikipedia, the Open Directory Project and Debian, he illustrates this new concept of *project-driven mediated collectives*.

A first set of chapters is dedicated to technologies (algorithms and/or systems) that help in detecting communities of interests and/or sharing knowledge (items, information, documents and semantical representation of interests).

3.   **Introduction to Recommender Systems**. Recommender systems are one of the main collaborative search tools. Fouss proposes a general introduction on these systems, and goes in details for the collaborative-recommendation systems which are based on explicit feedbacks: items rated by people. He analyzes the underlying algorithms with regards to four dimensions: the preference indicators, the global approach (content-based or item-based), the type of algorithms and how the predictions are done.

4.   **Building User Communities of Interests by Using Latent Semantic Analysis**. Xu describes recommendation algorithms that exploit the data provided by log files of Web sites (indicating which net surfer has visited which Web pages during a given session) in order to define navigation and access patterns. This is an important problem since the Web traffic can help to identify how net surfers deal with a given Web site. In practice, he proposes to first build communities of interests and then to address Web recommendations. Based on an *usage matrix* (where the rows represent the Web pages and the columns the users), he uses *latent semantic analysis* to reduce the complexity of the problem by reducing the dimensions of the search space. Using two different algorithms, Xu finds then in the dimension-reduced latent space, communities of interests by clustering the vectors representing the users behaviors. With the obtained clustering, he suggests a recommendation algorithm for Web pages for these communities.

5.   **Collaborative-recommendation systems and link Analysis**. Fouss describes different collaborative-recommendation algorithms based on a graph connecting users and items

rated by these users. One advantage of his approach is that no content of the items is necessary to make recommendations. He studies two kinds of algorithms: *random-walk based models* and *kernel-based models*. Random-walk models are based on a Markov-chain model where a virtual random walker goes through the graph. Different measures on this walk are computed to identify how "close" items and users are (the neighbor items being recommended to the users). These models are applied on a database of movies recommendation. The kernel-based models propose to use a kernel function to compute similarities between the points in a data space. In his chapter, Fouss analyses nine different kernels, i.e. the exponential diffusion kernel, the Laplacian exponential diffusion kernel, the von Neumann diffusion kernel, the regularized Laplacian kernel, the commute-time kernel, the Markov diffusion kernel, the cross-entropy diffusion matrix, the random-walk-with-restart similarity matrix, and the regularized commute-time kernel.

6.   **A Semi-Supervised Algorithm to Manage Communities of Interests**. This chapter proposes an algorithm to cluster users profiles into communities of interests. The approach is to ask the users to assess the documents they read (as relevant, fuzzy relevant or irrelevant) with regards with their different profiles (a profile being a given interest). The genetic algorithm proposed, called the *Similarity-based Clustering Genetic Algorithm (SCGA)*, exploits both the content of the documents and the explicit feedbacks of the users to identify similar profiles. Different tests show that this algorithm is efficient and performs better than several classical approaches. The algorithm is part of the *GALILEI Framework*. In particular, once the communities are detected, recommendations can be done: the documents

assessed as relevant are shared within the communities.

7. **P2P Semantic Coordination for Collective Knowledge Organization**. The increasing amount of available on-line information requires more efficient technologies. Since the 1990, the XML technologies are developed to better structure this information and to build a *Semantic Web* (Berners-Lee, et al., 2001). In this context, Castano, Ferrara & Montanelli describe a P2P system to organize collectively knowledge. Their approach supposes that single agents (each one being a peer in the system) have their own knowledge perspective (they are called a *peer ontology*) and use a *coordination mechanism* to launch queries to other peers to find those having similar perspectives. In this approach, the communities of interests are semantically expressed. Castano, Ferrara & Montanelli define the notion of *knowledge chunk* as the basis of the exchange between peers. These chunks are used to form the *community manifesto*, i.e. the description of the interest of a community. This chapter focuses on the particular coordination mechanism used.

8. **Collective Information Filtering for Web Observatories**. Within the different approaches used to share knowledge between people, *Web Observatories* (WOs) are a recent trend. Basically, WOs are Web sites built around a given community and providing information. Nanas, Vavalis, Kellis, Koutsaftikis & Houstis propose a general framework for WOs. Their solution is based on *Collective Information Filtering* (CIF) where a profile is defined for the whole community in order to filter relevant information. Based on user feedbacks on documents, a community profile is computed and the news are ranked according to this profile. They created *Nootropia*, a profiling model based on the exploitation of a weighted graph where

the vertices are the features extracted from documents, and the edges represent correlations between features co-occurring in the same context. They propose an architecture for a collective Web observatory integrating Nootropia, as well as a design based on a Web page containing several widgets. Several WOs are already available and are described in their chapter.

A second set of chapters treats the impacts of tools, communities of interests and knowledge sharing in organizations, the professional sphere of journalism and the society in general.

9. **Managing brief data from users to professionals: Collaborative trends around microblogging for journalism.** Noguera studies the influence of the microblogging site Twitter for journalism. He claims that this new practice of blogging creates new forms of relationships between journalists, sources and audiences. He studies eight case studies (including an earthquake in China and California fires) to show how microblogging is changing the work of journalists, in particular regarding the access to local information. The social aspect of microblogging embodies the journalists in communities with their readers, and Noguera argues that this will affect the practices of journalism.

10. **Articulating tacit knowledge in multinational e-collaboration on new product designs.** As pointed out in the previous section, communities of interests are crucial regarding tacit knowledge sharing. Tacit knowledge is a important aspect for organizations to ensure creativity, in particular in the design of new products/services. Strang proposes a generic theoretical framework for tacit knowledge sharing. Combining a review of the literature and his experience on new product designs in a large multinational

company, he describes the different aspects of his model. He also comments several problems and controversies in this field.

11. **Applications of a social software model**. Section 2 has indicated that social software are powerful tools to share knowledge. More and more, organizations deploy social software internally in the context of knowledge management since social interactions are crucial for knowledge sharing. Coenen & Van den Bosch propose a model to understand how social software can be deployed. Their model is based on two layers. The first layer is formed by the different kinds of data that social softwares manage (user generated content, identity, etc.). The second layer is related to the functionalities of such systems (search, recommendation, reputation etc.)[1]. After a description of their model, they applied it (a) to knowledge sharing in organizations, and (b) to fight social exclusion at the societal level (in particular the exclusion of the youth).

12. **People Company - Be Part of It**. An importance aspect of communities of interests is the trust between their members. In particular, this a tricky problem for large communities where people do not know *a priori* themselves. In fact, this is also a problem for large companies which have several sites all around the world. Prinz & Kolvenbach describe a particular approach to tackle this problem: a company-wide autograph book built to present the different employees. To gather the information, they develop a collaborative platform based on a *baton application* (an ultra-mobile personal computer) that walks through the different sites. Each employee could use this baton application to add text, pictures and/or movies to describe him- or herself, all the data being centralized by the autograph book.

POTENTIAL DANGERS

There is no doubt that without new technologies, it will be impossible to browse through the Internet to find relevant knowledge and people with which we may form some collective intelligence. But, despite the important influence of these technologies on our societies, it is important not to fall in an utopian's view. Many specialists have shown that the triumph of the Internet in general, and the Web 2.0 paradigm in particular, implies several drawbacks.

The first drawback is of course the *digital divide*: the fact that most people on earth have no access to the Internet. This divide is not only geographical (only 3.5% of the Africans have the Internet in 2009 while they represent more than 15% of the global population), it is also a socio-economical one. Many people in the occidental societies are excluded from the Internet: either because they have no access at all, or because they do not master the necessary tools for a full membership. Therefore, thinking that Internet and its technologies are an universal solution for human emancipation is completely wrong. They may contribute to it, but many other initiatives are more important (in particular education).

The Web 2.0 phenomenon allows everyone to contribute to the content of the Internet. The heavy use of hyperlinks builds clusters of related relevant information (at least if it is supposed that a hyperlink represents a quality assessment on the page pointed). Since search engines and collaborative search tools are using these hyperlinks and the users preferences to rank documents (Brin & Page, 1998), the net surfers decide which content will become the references. Keen (2007) has shown that there is a risk of a gradual disqualification of the expertise. If an amateur can influence which information is the best ranked (so the best one in quality for most net surfers), is there not a danger that expertise will disappear? One of the examples he gives is the one of the encyclopedia: while Wikipedia saw its content increase, Encyclopædia

Britannica (the reference in the English-speaking world) was disbanding a hundred contributors. Despite the numerous advantages of Wikipedia (including a lot of high quality notices), the possible disappearance of a classical encyclopedia with a clear editor's project and well-defined contributors raises questions.

Another problem emerging from the increasing use of collaborative filtering tools was pointed out by Sunstein (2007). He claims that democracy and freedom of speech rely not only on the free expression, but also on the confrontation of different points of view. He believes that, when people are able to choose precisely what they want to read or view and what not, there is a danger that this necessary confrontation of opinions may disappear for some citizens. He comments studies showing that most blogs point to other blogs reinforcing their own views, with the risk that some net surfers will completely ignore the arguments of others. He is worried that people radicalize themselves (he calls it the *polarization*) which can lead to the potential destruction of the necessary common social base needed by any democratic project.

CONCLUSION

With the widespread of the Internet, the amount of information has exploded. In the context of the knowledge society, the production and the spread of knowledge are crucial development factors. Internet, in particular since its Web 2.0 era, proposes an access to an increasing number of knowledge sources (Wikipedia, blogs, social software, etc.).

To manage this enormous sum of available knowledge, net surfers cannot act anymore alone. It is necessary to collaborate with others. This collaboration can be implicit with collaborative search tools (people benefit from recommendations from unknown net surfers) or explicit with the memberships to communities of interests. An overview of the next chapters showed that each one of them proposes a particular contribution to a better understanding of collaborative search and/or communities of interests.

Despite the success of the different approaches, they do not solve all the problems. Neither Keen (2007) nor Sunstein (2007) say that the Internet and its technologies are usefulness, their concern is that there are several drawbacks and dangers that citizens should be warned of. Decision makers and researchers promoting these technologies should always be aware of these risks. Finally, readers of this book must conserve their critical thinking throughout their reading.

REFERENCES

Anderson, C. (2004). The Long Tail. *Wired, 12*(10).

Berners-Lee, T., Hendler, J., & Lassila, O. (2001). *The Semantic Web*. Scientific American.

Brin, S., & Page, L. (1998). The anatomy of a large-scale hypertextual Web search engine. *Computer Networks and ISDN Systems*, (33): 107–135. doi:10.1016/S0169-7552(98)00110-X

David, P. A., & Foray, D. (2003). Economic Fundamentals of the Knowledge Society. *Policy Futures in Education, 1*(1), 20–49. doi:10.2304/pfie.2003.1.1.7

Gillmor, D. (2004). *We the Media: Grassroots Journalism by the People, for the People*. O'Reilly.

Kahaner, L. (1997). *Competitive Intelligence: How to gather, analyze and use information to move your business to the top*. Touchstone.

Keen, A. (2007). *The Cult of the Amateur: How Today's Internet is Killing our Culture*. Currency.

Lévy, P. (1994). *L'intelligence collective. Pour une anthropologie du cyberespace*. Paris: La Découverte.

O'Reilly, T. (2005). *What is Web 2.0: Design Patterns and Business Models for the Next Generation of Software.*

Paolillo, J. C., & Penumarthy, S. (2007). The Social Structure of Tagging Internet Video on del. icio. us. *HICSS 2007. 40th Annual Hawaii International Conference on System Sciences* (p. 85).

Rheingold, H. (2000). *The Virtual Community: Homesteading on the Electronic Frontier.* MIT Press.

Schreyer, P. (1999). The Contribution of Information and Communication Technology to Output Growth. *Statistical Working Party, 99*(4).

Sunstein, C. R. (2007). *Republic.com 2.0.* Princeton, NJ: Princeton Univ Press.

Wenger, E. (1998). *Communities of Practice: Learning, Meaning, and Identity.* Cambridge University Press.

ENDNOTE

[1] They added to these two layers, single signon mechanisms allowing interactions between different social software.

Chapter 2
From Virtual Communities to Project–Driven Mediated Collectives:
A Comparison of Debian, Wikipedia and the Open Directory Project

Christophe Lejeune
Université Libre de Bruxelles, Belgium

ABSTRACT

The lay notion of a virtual community is not satisfactory as, strictly speaking, depicted phenomena (Internet-coordinated collectives) are neither communitarian nor virtual. Moreover, the idiom embraces too wide a range of situations. For these reasons, we propose the narrower notion of mediated collectives. Previous ethnographies of Debian, Open Directory and Wikipedia help to define the notion based on empirical observation.

PHENOMENA

Lay Internet users, newspapers, commentators and politicians speak of *virtual communities*[1]. Intuitively, we all understand quite clearly what this idiom refers to. This huge interest is not merely a passing fashion. According to some of the best-known software programmers (Torvalds, 2001; Raymond, 2001), The Internet was more of a social phenomenon than a technical innovation. It therefore comes as no surprise that even social researchers are busy with *virtual communities*. But, as stated by some of them (Proulx & Latzko-

Toth, 2005), the notion lacks conceptualization. We propose here to help clarify these issues.

CONCEPT

The notion of *virtual community* was not created by researchers. It came from the relevant actors, in other words the people actually involved. Such a vernacular idiom has to be defined before it can be embodied in scientific concepts (Pareto, 1935; Mounin, 1995). This can be achieved in two ways. Either it is considered a vernacular label[2]. This implies that the researcher must describe precisely how the actors define the notion; this way

DOI: 10.4018/978-1-61520-841-8.ch002

Copyright © 2011, IGI Global. Copying or distributing in print or electronic forms without written permission of IGI Global is prohibited.

of defining a notion is specific to social sciences (whose subjects include languages and cultures). Otherwise the notion becomes a professional concept, whose content is defined by the researcher[3]. The terms alone are not enough. In the case of *virtual communities*, no such terminological task has yet been achieved.

The following sections deal with the two separate terms that make up the idiom.

Virtual

The term *virtual* was coined by IBM when it introduced a virtual memory device. This subsequently led to the creation of such idioms as *virtual reality* and *virtual community* (Rheingold, 1991; Rheingold, 1993).

Virtual communities are social aggregations that emerge from the Net when enough people carry on those public discussions long enough, with sufficient human feeling, to form webs of personal relationships in [...] the conceptual space where words, human relationships, data, wealth, and power are manifested by people using CMC [computer mediated communication] technology. (Rheingold, 1993)

Despite this original definition, the notion remains vague. One of its common sense meanings is similar to simulation. According to this meaning, the virtual is opposed to the reality. A second meaning describes how, with cognitive artifacts, information is no longer attached to a support; the virtual then refers to disembodiment, as opposed to materiality. A third (philosophical) meaning defines the virtual as what could be actualized. As a matter of possibilities and becomings, the virtual is then opposed to the actual (Deleuze & Parnet, 2002).

Some Internet analysts oppose the virtual to categories. According to them (Lévy, 1998; Lévy, 2000), categories are about frontiers, whereas the virtual is about crossing barriers. Categories thus resemble clear-cut and impermeable containers or classes that delimit, divide or enclose. Inherited from the past, they are structures that determine history once and for all. Reticular ideology (Parrochia, 1993) breaks with such a tradition: interactions are more likely to actualize on-line, in an open, liberated way, similar to the horizontal, immanent, continuously moving relations enabled by hypertext.

Community

Community forms part of the classical set of sociological notions: most of the founders of social sciences refer to community: Durkheim, Weber, Marx, Simmel, Le Play (Nisbet, 1993, quoted by Guerin, 2004). The etymological and semantic roots of *community* refer to "what is in common" (Winkin, 1981; Proulx & Latzko-Toth, 2005).

Traditionally, community is opposed to society. The former refers to traditions, belief, trust, value, kinship, village and family while the latter concerns innovation, rationality, interest, interaction, city and industry (Weber, 1980). The epistemological background of this classical opposition by Tönnies betrays a nostalgia for the Ancien Régime, which values *community* to the detriment of *society*. Many attempts have so far been made to scientifically define this notion (Moreau de Bellaing, 1990, quoted by Guerin, 2004). George Hillery made an inventory of 94 definitions without any common feature (Hillery, quoted by Guerin, 2004). This ambiguity can be seen as the root of the problem (Geiger, 1959; König, 1972; Minar & Greer, 1979; Poplin, 1972; Sherer, 1972, quoted by Guerin, 2004) but it also explains why the term has become so popular.

As the virtual, community can be compared to category. Both include affiliated elements called *members* (in the field of social sciences, these members are known as actors). Both community and category are membership devices. But membership is declared differently. The members of a community themselves declare that they belong

Figure 1. Mutual constitution of community and members

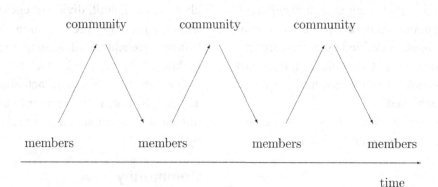

this community. Community membership can be declared, claimed or refuted, but cannot be imposed by someone else. It requires members to feel deep down that they belong. For categories, things work differently. A category can be attributed. It is commonly achieved in social surveys (through socio-professional groups), ordinary judgment or everyday conversation (Sacks, 1992; Hester, 1997).

What category and community have in common is that the relationship with their members is not deterministic: members do not unilaterally define the device no more than the device determines what the members are (or do). Members and community (or category) are mutually constituted. The involved phenomena are numerous and complex: membership motivated by the assignment of labels, everyday normalization and normativeness inside a community (Tajfel, 1972; Moscovici, 1984), strategical, programmatic or performative definition - by members - of a new class identity (Boltanski, 1987). Relations between members and community (or category) are complex and reciprocal. However, contrary to the diagnostic by Simmel (1908), mutual constitution is not circular, namely because it evolves with time (see Figure 1). A community (or category) can grow or dwindle; the role a member occupies can move from centrality to periphery. For community, the limit extends to the whole of humanity (which implies that the notion looses

its distinctive feature). For a member, the limits are central authority or departure (which imply losing membership).

COMMUNITY COMPOSED IDIOMS

Proposed Solutions

In the previous section, we underlined existing comments on relations between the category, on one hand, and the virtual and the community, on the other hand. The category resembles the community in terms of membership but is opposed to the virtual in relation to boundaries. These remarks should not lead us to conclude that *virtual community* is an oxymoron, because the tension is based on two different aspects (membership and boundaries). The former concerns the 'vertical' affiliation of members and community, while the latter is about the permeability of the "membrane" (between inside and outside the community). However, these dimensions are neither orthogonal nor independent of each other: according to specific internal rules, some memberships facilitate connections with the outside, while others hinder them.

Sensitive to ambiguities and difficulties raised by the virtual characterization, a range of researchers propose concepts such as *on-line communities*, *Web-based communities*, *communities of inter-*

*ests, communities of practices (*Wenger, 1998) or *epistemic communities* (Haas, 1992; Cowan, et al., 2000; Conein, 2004).

These proposals all aim to keep the notion of a community, which is combined with another dimension (on-line, Web-based interest, practices, epistemic). In a way, such proposals assume a relevant intuition (that the phenomenon is not accurately depicted by the sole invocation of *community*). From an analytical point of view, these community-composed idioms, however, complicate the issue, by introducing conceptual tensions. For instance, *community of interests* refers both to "hot" communitarian features (deep feelings, values, trust) and "cold" societal features (strategies, calculus and rationalities).

An Unresolved Problem

These idioms tend, moreover, to underestimate the differences between various meanings of *community*. There are at least two (a weak and a strong) meanings of community. In its minimal, weakest sense, community expresses that members have something in common (it is then close to category, in its broader sense). In its strong meaning, community refers to a conscious gathering of persons interacting with each other.

While "identifying communities of interest", computer sciences rely on similar traces of activities such as logs, common hyperlinks (URL), shared documents and the like. Such a "identified community" matches the minimal meaning of the concept. Indeed, even people that do not interact at all can be said to constitute a community of interest provided they share a common interest, common behavior or common practices. For social sciences, however, a common feature is not sufficient in order to refer to community (Weber, 1980). Indeed, social sciences communities are closer to the strong definition of *community*. Idioms such as political community, cultural community or anthropological community describe a range of people interacting (and socializing)

with each other, independently of their interests in common features. Such communities (as described by Tönnies) correspond to the stronger notion of community. Anyway, in a number of social researches, *community* is also used in an intermediate meaning. In this later (intermediate) variation, *community* is considered a relevant contribution to members' socialization (even if no direct interactions occur). Being a member of a political community implies acting consistently with what members acknowledge to be politically-oriented behavior.

Interdisciplinary Collaboration

According to the scientific orientation (computer or social sciences), the term *community* does not designate the same phenomena. In the former case, the researcher collects similar traces of activity; he himself determines how people are brought together, independently of people's perceived identities. In a way, the community results from these scientific investigations. In the latter case, people gather by themselves, deliberately, while the researcher diagnoses this social gathering. The community thus "preexists" the social research.

Although the depicted phenomena (the minimal and strong senses of the community) are not exactly the same, they are, however, not incompatible. Identifying similar on-line practices and analyzing social mediated interactions are complimentary research programs. We furthermore argue that such a collaboration between computer sciences and social sciences can be fruitful. However, for successful interdisciplinary work, we need a precise definition of the concepts used. Basing the collective scientific effort on shared concepts without elucidating their differences would be misleading. The present argument is thus far from condemning interdisciplinary research. On the contrary, it aims to establish strong foundations to such interdisciplinary researches by shedding light on the difference between the definitions of (and phenomena designated by) the community, before proposing an alternative free from unfounded assumptions.

MEDIATED COLLECTIVES

From Community to Collective

As we have seen with the compounds discussed above, the adjunct of a supplementary dimension to community can be misleading. Firstly, *community* introduces ambiguity, as it is understood differently according to various disciplines. Secondly, *community* assumes a bundle of traditional features (also misleading). For instance, community assumes trust among members. However, in many situations, members do cooperate through on-line interactions because it is in their interest to do so, knowing that it is in the interest of other members not to violate such a tacit contract. Resting on encapsulated interests, such behaviors are about trust, but a kind of (societal) trust - sometimes called confidence - that has nothing to do the (communitarian) trust shown to friends or family members (Lejeune, 2009).

More generally, there is nothing to indicate that on-line social interactions are communitarian. With reference to ethnographic elements collected on the subject of on-line cooperation (see below for further information), we therefore argue that there is no reason to assume that these phenomena have more to do with community than society. The adjunct of a supplementary dimension is thus not sufficient to deal with problems linked to these communitarian assumptions. From a sociological perspective, *community* is thus too narrow a concept. For these reasons, we propose abandoning the notion of community. It would appear more accurate to speak of a *collective*. A collective can be made up of either community or society-style relationships.

From Virtual to Mediateness

A common feature of collectives that have been the focus of current research is that they are Internet-based. It is precisely for this reason that they are said to be *virtual*. It must be stressed that the virtual is considered synonymous with becomings (as opposed to actual), simulations (opposed to reality) and disembodiment (opposed to materiality). Unfortunately, none of the meanings of *virtual* help to describe the specific phenomena of Internet-based collectives.

The former (philosophical) meaning is quite easy to dismiss. If Web-based collectives involve becomings, they would generate only likely, *possible* interactions. Such becomings would have a chance of actualizing in another space and time. Arguing that social initiatives can be catalyzed through on-line mobilization, this meaning provides fruitful metaphors for political discussion (Lévy, 1998). But, despite this analogical virtue, such an argument simply fails to make sense: some events, encounters and mobilizations do occur on-line, it is not just about becomings.

In the scope of Internet-based collectives, the second meaning sounds equally strange. On-line collectives do not simulate off-line socialization. Even if critics of the Internet might argue that computer-supported interactions are less real that face-to-face conversation, this argument is insufficient to conclude that Internet-based collectives work at building *unreal* interactions. Their number and strength testify that these interactions (though perhaps specific) are real.

Considered as the prototype of interactions, face-to-face conversations are embodied. Compared to such co-present relations, on-line interactions are disembodied. The lack of visual feedback conflicts with mutual regulations. Inside such collectives, people indeed interact (on discussion forums, via email or instant messaging) mostly though language without any direct visual contact. When non-co-present people interact remotely, they are likely to adopt a rather specific language, which is free of non-verbal expression. Thus, as shown by a range of studies (Herring, 1996; Yates, 2001), on-line communication is rather specific.

While there is no sociological reason to distinguish on-line interactions (as not-yet-actualized or unreal), there are thus strong communication reasons to isolate on-line interactions as *mediated*. From a communication perspective, it would therefore be more accurate to speak of *mediateness* than *virtual*. For this reason, we speak of *mediated collectives*.

PRODUCTION ORIENTED MEDIATED COLLECTIVES

A mediated collective is therefore a collective. It is actually composed of interdependent relations between people. A collective is indeed the result of multiple mutually-oriented interactions (Weber, 1980). One single accurately accomplished interaction is thus not sufficient.

When the main channel for such relevant, mutually fine-tuned interactions differs from face-to-face conversation, the collective is mediated. Mediated collectives are thus defined as sets of mutually-oriented interactions using technology-mediated communication. This definition is indeed close to the definition that Howard Rheingold (1993) originally gave to *virtual community* (see above quotation). Our definition, however, avoids the confusion associated with these terms.

Based on this definition, while CB radio collectives and the free software movement differ from a communication perspective, this is not necessarily the case from a sociological perspective. As we have already discussed, mediated collectives can be either communitarian or societarian.

While the notion of *mediated collectives* more accurately describes the Internet-based social phenomenon, it could, however, potentially cover a range of phenomena as broad as *virtual community*, including, for instance, dating clubs, programmer teams, groups of cookery fans or gatherings of martial arts practitioners.

Most of these collectives are on-line spaces where meetings and discussions take place or tips can be exchanged. Only a few collectives provide deeper social collaboration. The former focus on communication while the latter bring together people who focus their efforts on the realization of a common production. Although such collaborative practices do not constitute a *community*, they still constitute a relevant factor for the isolation of a class of project-driven mediated collectives. Pursuing a common purpose, these collectives imply collaboration on a collective production. Most of the time, these specific mediated collectives require their members to purposely interact.

Free software initiatives are instances of such project-driven mediated collectives. But free software is not the only possible product of Internet-based collaboration: literary, content or editorial works can also be collectively achieved through Internet. In the following sections, empirical elements from ethnographic investigations of such initiatives will help to further specify the notion of project-driven mediated collectives.

EMPIRICAL GROUNDS

The fact that analysts still speak of *virtual communities* in a wide range of situations has helped to under-determine it: the notion qualifies discussion forums, dating sites, social networks, multiplayer on-line games or collaborative projects. But case studies - in linguistics, anthropology and communication - show that these configurations are radically heterogeneous. Underspecification thus had the advantage of encouraging numerous detailed ethnographies, helping to better understand various concrete phenomenal realities than a disembodied concept.

We propose to take advantage of these studies (including our own investigations) in order to give content to the specific notion of *project-driven mediated collectives*. We start from descriptions of Debian, Open Directory Project and Wikipedia collectives. These empirical ethnographic elements help to establish the common ground of collectives involved in free software or free content elaboration.

Targeted Productions

Common Features

All studied initiatives have the purpose of releasing a collective production. The Debian collective designs software, which forms part of an operating system. Members of the Open Directory Project work on the collation, description and organization of web site addresses into a hierarchical thematic directory. Wikipedia contributors prepare articles for a generalist encyclopedia.

These collective productions have a high degree of dematerialization and largely consist of computer files. Moreover, due to their low finiteness, they require regular maintenance and are never completed.

Differences

Historically, people gathered on-line in order to collectively produce software before content: the GNU operating system project was launched by Richard Stallman in 1983 and Linus Torvalds launched Linux kernel in 1994. When the Open Directory Project was launched in 1998, the model for such a collaborative project moved from software design to the sphere of content edition. GnuHoo, the first name given to the directory makes this inspiration explicit. Since then, similar initiatives unite people (who are not computer specialists) for the realization of language resources (such as dictionaries - FreeDict - or thesauri - WordNet) or cultural information (such as an encyclopedia - Wikipedia - or a directory - Open Directory Project).

Contributors

Common Features

Those taking part in the initiative are mainly volunteers; they contribute either occasionally or on a regular basis. Users participate occasionally (which means that many users are involved). Moreover, such user contributions take a variety of forms. They can consist of bug reports (when the targeted production is software) or reference submissions (for a directory) or the correction of typographic misprints (in the case of an encyclopedia).

In order to contribute on a regular basis, users are encouraged to apply spontaneously. Most of the time, applications focus on a part of the targeted production: a software feature (or package), a directory rubric (Lazaro, 2008; Lejeune, 2006). If the application is accepted, the contributor becomes accountable for the dedicated part and becomes a member of the collective (such as Open Directory *editors* or Debian *developers*). Such a division of labor implies that any member is not allowed to work directly on any part of the production. Initiatives (such as Wikipedia) where any member can work on any part without any prior application are thus marginal.

In selected cases, supplementary prerogatives are added to membership, such as - typically - the ability to work on any (not necessarily explicitly entrusted) part of the product. Wikipedia's *administrators* and Open Directory *meta-editors* are instances of such a position. As membership, such supplementary responsibilities are delegated on a voluntary and meritocratic basis and usually attributed though a co-opting procedure (Auray, 2003a).

Differences

The voluntary character of the commitment can be variable (in selected cases, contributors may be salaried). Company initiatives (such as StarOffice, initiated by Sun MicroSystem) often involve salaried contributors. In other cases, collectives are initiated by individuals and ask companies for support at a later stage (these companies may then assign some of their staff to this project - as America Online did for the Open Directory Project or Andover for Slashdot). Other successful initiatives (such as Wikipedia) also secure sufficient funding to hire some of their contributors. Very different configurations may follow within the same project. For instance, a software suite first initiated by a company (Netscape) was later released as a community-driven open source project (under the Mozilla name), which gained a huge number of volunteers and subsequently created an eponymous foundation (owning the Firefox and Thunderbird trademarks), which now hires some of its contributors.

Regulation

Common Features

Given that targeted productions are dematerialized, contributors can be coordinated through on-line communication devices (in particular, Usenet groups, instant messaging, discussion forums and emails). Modalities of regulation are similar to direct democracy: any member is invited to take part in every discussion inside the project (Lejeune, 2002).

Differences

When the ability to close the discussion happens to be reserved to some members (Lejeune, 2010), the role distinctions bear some similarity to a hierarchy (Lazaro, 2008; Lejeune, 2006). Contrary to what has been said by some early commentators on on-line phenomena (Lévy, 1997), collective phenomena are thus not necessarily less structured, organized and hierarchical because they are *virtual*.

Peak Moments

Common Features

Mediated collectives are punctuated by peak moments (Boltanski, 2006). Such events have a limited duration (an evening, a couple of days or a week). During such an event, contributors are encouraged to combine their efforts in order to correct any remaining imperfections in their collective production. Such defects can result from lack of time from the members responsible for the concerned part or from particularly difficult problems. By reallocating the remaining tasks, peak moments provide solutions to these situations.

In the Open Directory Project, members inspect all references submitted by users that are not yet edited so that these submissions can be included in the public directory. Given that the editor interface features submitted references as green hyperlinks, the peak moments are known as *greenbuster* parties. Thanks to these parties, the directory is as up-to-date and as user-concerned as possible.

In software programmer collectives, members are invited to correct defects (known as bugs) existing in software (Auray, 2003a). The *bug squashing parties* stands for these peak moments. These parties ensure that the distributed software is as bug-free as possible.

In both cases, peak moments provide an opportunity for active members to intervene on parts that are not necessarily assigned to them. Peak moments thus interrupt the ordinary division of labor described above. For members going beyond their usual sphere of activities, peak moments therefore represent an opportunity to demonstrate that they are ready to apply for further responsibilities in the collective.

Differences

In some cases, the peak moments are motivated by a major release. Motivated by a quality concern, collectives dedicated to software programming aim to ensure that there are as few errors as possible in the product that they distribute to the vast majority of users. For this reason, they do not distribute the continuously contributed (and thus modified) version of their work but, instead, a double-checked, error-free version. At least two different versions can thus be distinguished: a development version (with ongoing modifications) and a production version (distributed to users)[4]. Before releases, the latter version is widely tested, improved and corrected, precisely through peak moments such as bug squashing parties.

Unlike free software development, collectives involved in free content development (such as Wikipedia and the Open Directory Project) continuously provide each user with the one and only v of their production (no development version exists). In these cases, development is thus not punctuated by releases.

However, there are even some differences between content production collectives. Under Wikipedia, user contributions are publicly available as soon as they are submitted. The configuration of the Open Directory Project is somewhat intermediate: although there is no development version, user contributions are, however, not directly available to the public. They are first submitted to a private space, for approval by an editor (through the above-mentioned appearance of green hyperlinks). Although there is only one version of the directory (as for Wikipedia), user-contributions are first examined before being distributed as a reliable production (which is also true of Debian).

CONCLUSION

Fruitful interdisciplinary researches cannot be based on loose definitions. In the first part of this chapter, our discussion of academic literature showed the implications of terms like *community* or *virtual*. In order to identify what each discipline

can contribute, we have explicitly isolated the phenomena investigated under these terms. This exploration reveals inaccurate assumptions. In order to avoid these undesired assumptions, we propose the notion of mediated collectives.

The ethnographies of the Open Directory, Debian and Wikipedia therefore suggest a class of these mediated collectives. Such project-driven mediated collectives belong to collective apparatuses, whose members are involved in the concrete production of content or software. Each voluntary member of the collective applies to become responsible for one part of the overall production. Coordination is based on discussions, but regulation is not strictly based on direct democracy, given that more committed members can be entrusted with some decision-making prerogatives.

As showed by these empirical elements, the social organization of mediated collectives is not necessarily communitarian, in the strong sense typically used in the social sciences. This, however, does not prevent us from identifying traces of activities (logs, for example) from this social collaborative distribution of on-line labor. These clarifications aim to provide solid foundations for collaboration between computer and social sciences within the scope of the scientific study of mediated collectives.

REFERENCES

Auray, N. (2003a). La régulation de la connaissance: arbitrage sur la taille et gestion aux frontières dans la communauté Debian. *Revue d'Economie Politique, 113*, 161–182.

Auray, N. (2003b). Le sens du juste dans un noyau d'experts: Debian et le puritanisme civique. In S. Proulx, F. Massit-Foléa, & B. Conein (Eds.), Internet, une utopie limitée: nouvelles régulations, nouvelles solidarités (pp. 71-94). Laval: Presses de l'Université de Laval.

Boltanski, L. (1987). *The Making of a Class: Cadres in French Society*. Cambridge: Cambridge University Press.

Boltanski, L., & Thévenot, L. (2006). *On Justification. Economies of Worth*. Princeton, NJ: Princeton University Press.

Conein, B. (2004). Communautés épistémiques et réseaux cognitifs: coopération et cognition distribuée. *Revue d'Economie Politique, 113*, 141–159.

Cowan, R., David, P. A., & Foray, D. (2000). The explicit economics of knowledge: Codifcation and tacitness. *Industrial and Corporate Change, 9*(2), 211–253. doi:10.1093/icc/9.2.211

Deleuze, G., & Parnet, C. (2002). *Dialogues II*. New York: Columbia University Press.

Guérin, F. (2004). Le concept de communauté: une illustration exemplaire de la production des concepts en sciences sociales ? *13ème conférence de l'association internationale de management stratégique*, 13, 1-30.

Haas, P. (1992). Introduction: Epistemic communities and international policy coordination. *International Organization, 46*, 1–37. doi:10.1017/S0020818300001442

Herring, S. (Ed.). (1996). *Computer-Mediated Communication. Linguistic, Social and Cross-Cultural Perspectives*. Amsterdam: John Benjamins.

Hester, S., & Eglin, P. (Eds.). (1997). *Culture in Action. Studies in Membership Categorization Analysis*. Washington: International Institute for Ethnomethodology and Conversation Analysis & University Press of America.

Lazaro, C. (2008). *La liberté logicielle. Une ethnographie des pratiques d'échange et de coopération au sein de la communauté Debian*. Louvain-la-Neuve: Academia Bruylant.

Lejeune, C. (2002). Indexation et organisation de la connaissance. La régulation des décisions sur un forum de discussion. *Cahiers du numérique, 3*(2), 129-144.

Lejeune, C. (2006). D'un annuaire de sites Internet à l'organisation documentaire. Une sociologie des relations sémantiques. *Cahiers de la Documentation, 3*, 12–22.

Lejeune, C. (2008). Quand le lézard s'en mêle... Ethnographie de l'indexation collective de sites Internet. *Science and Society, 75*, 101–114.

Lejeune, C. (2009). La confiance au sein des collectifs médiatisés. Une entrée par les catégorisations. *Cahiers d'ethnométhodologie, 3*.

Lejeune, C. (2010). L'organisation socio-politique des collectifs médiatisés. De quelques controverses internes à l'Open Directory Project. In Jacquemain, M., & Delwit, P. (Eds.), *Engagements actuels, actualité des engagements*, Louvain-la-Neuve: Académia Bruylant.

Lévy, P. (1997). *Collective Intelligence: Mankind's Emerging World in Cyberspace*. Cambridge, MA: Perseus.

Lévy, P. (1998). *Becoming Virtual: Reality in the Digital Age*. Da Capo Press.

Lévy, P. (2000). Question de caractère. *Buddhaline*. Retrieved June 7, 2009, from http://www.buddhaline.net/spip.php?article322

Moscovici, S. (Ed.). (1984). *Psychologie sociale*. Paris: PUF.

Mounin, G. (1995). Introduction au problème terminologique. In *Dictionnaire de la linguistique*. Paris: PUF.

Pareto, V. (1935). The Mind and Society: A Treatise on General Sociology. New York: Harcourt Brace [1916].

Parrochia, D. (1993). *Philosophie des réseaux*. Paris: PUF.

Proulx, S., & Latzko-Toth, G. (2005). Mapping the virtual in social sciences: On the category of 'virtual community'. *The Journal of Community Informatics*, *2*(1).

Raymond, E. S. (2001). *The cathedral & the Bazaar. Musings on Linux and Open Source by an Accidental Revolutionary*. Sebastopol: O'Reilly.

Rheingold, H. (1991). *Virtual Reality. The Revolutionary Technology of Computer-Generated Artificial Worlds – And How It Promises to Transform Society*. New York: Simon & Schuster.

Rheingold, H. (1993). *The Virtual Community. Homesteading on the Electronic Frontier*. Boston, MA: Addison-Wesley.

Rose, E. (1960). The English record of a natural sociology. *American Sociological Review*, *25*(2), 193–208. doi:10.2307/2092625

Sacks, H. (1992). *Lectures on Conversation*. Oxford: Blackwell.

Simmel, G. (1908). *Soziologie. Untersuchungen über die Formen der Vergesellschaftung*. Berlin: Duncker & Humblot.

Tajfel, H. (1972). La catégorisation sociale. In Moscovici, S. (Ed.), *Introduction à la psychologie sociale* (*Vol. 1*). Paris: Larousse.

Torvalds, L. B., & Diamond, D. (2001). *Just for Fun: The Story of an Accidental Revolutionary*. New York: Harper Business.

Weber, M. (1980). *Wirtschaft und Gesellschaft. Grundriß der verstehenden Soziologie*. Tübingen: Mohr.

Wenger, E. (1998). Communities of practice. Learning as a social system. *Systems Thinker, 9*(5).

Winkin, Y. (1981). *La nouvelle communication*. Paris: Seuil.

Yates, S. (2001). Researching Internet Interaction: Sociolinguistics and Corpus Analysis. In Wetherell, M., Taylor, S., & Yates, S. (Eds.), *Discourse as Data. A Guide for Analysis* (pp. 93–146). London: The Open University.

ENDNOTES

[1] The author is thankful to Yana Breindl and Pascal Francq for their comments to a preliminary version of this chapter. Thanks to David Ward for helping to revise the preliminary version and correct the English text.

[2] Importing common sense notions into scientific terminology is nothing but usual, while researchers share language and culture with lay members (Rose, 1960).

[3] In such a case, the definition is thus conventional.

[4] In many case, the situation is even more complex. For instance, the Debian Project provides an experimental stage, a development version, a testing version and a stable (production) version (Lazaro, 2008).

Chapter 3
Introduction to Recommender Systems

François Fouss
Facultés Universitaires Catholiques de Mons (FUCaM), Belgium

ABSTRACT

Recommender systems try to provide people with recommendations of items they will appreciate, based on their past preferences, history of purchase, and demographic information. This chapter (1) introduces recommender systems, classifying them along four dimensions (i.e. the way the preferences are gathered, the used approach, the type of algorithm, and the way the results are provided) and describing recent work done in the area, and (2) provides more details about one such type of recommender systems, namely collaborative-recommendation systems. Such systems work by analyzing the items previously rated by all the users and are not based on the content of the items, as content-based systems.

INTRODUCTION

Recommender systems try to provide people with recommendations of items they will appreciate, based on their past preferences, history of purchase, and demographic information. Recommender systems have their origin (see the survey of the state-of-the-art of Adomavicius and Tuzhilin (2005) for more details) in the work done in, mainly, machine learning, information retrieval (Salton, 1989), cognitive science (Rich, 1979), forecasting theories (Armstrong, 2001), marketing (Lilien, Smith & Moorthy, 1992), management (Murthi & Sarkar, 2003), and emerged as an independent research area in the mid-1990s, with the first papers on collaborative filtering (Hill, Stead, Rosenstein & Furnas, 1995; Resnick, Neophytos, Mitesh, Bergstrom & Riedl, 1994; Shardanand & Maes, 1995).

Three steps usually are common to the functioning of recommender systems:

1. Gather valuable information on the users (past preferences, demographic information, etc.) and on the items (description, keywords, etc.).

DOI: 10.4018/978-1-61520-841-8.ch003

Copyright © 2011, IGI Global. Copying or distributing in print or electronic forms without written permission of IGI Global is prohibited.

2. Determine patterns from these historical data.
3. Suggest items to people.

TYPOLOGY OF RECOMMENDER SYSTEMS

Many different ways have been developed to achieve the final goal of making recommendations to persons. This section reviews the main features of recommender systems:

1. Related to the first step, the way the preferences are gathered is described in the Section "Preference Indicators".
2. Related to the second step, various ways developed to extract new information from data are analyzed. Finding new information depends on two axes, the first one describing the global approach (content-based or collaborative approaches in the Section "Filtering Approach"), while the second one describes the type of algorithm (memory-based or model-based algorithms in the Section "Recommendation Algorithm").
3. Related to the third step, the two possibilities existing for providing results to a user are introduced in the Section "Prediction or Recommendation".

Preference Indicators

The goal of a recommender system is to suggest new items or to predict the degree of linking of a particular item to a specific user, based on historical information (about both users and items). In a typical recommender system, each user has a list of items about which he/she has expressed opinions. The main types of preference indicators expressing user opinions (see (Marlin, 2004) for more details) are numerical rating triplets and co-occurrence pairs:

- a rating triplet has the form (u,i,r) where u corresponds to a particular user, i to a particular item, and r to the rating provided by the user u to the item i (e.g. on a scale from 1 to 5);
- a co-occurrence pair has the form (u,i) where, again, u corresponds to a particular user and i to a particular item. The occurrence of the pair (u,i) means that user u rated, liked, viewed, or purchased item i.

Another distinction about preference indicators, highlighted in several works such as (Marlin, 2004), is whether they are explicitly provided by the user (usually a rating following a predefined scale) or implicitly gathered when the user performs specific tasks such as browsing an Internet site (by analyzing timing logs, by mining Web hyperlinks, etc.).

Explicit preference indicators are, for example, obtained by:

- asking a person to rate an item on a predefined scale;
- asking a person to rank a set of items (his or her favorite is ranked first, his/her least preferred is ranked last);
- asking a person to choose the item he or she prefers when showing him/her two or more items;
- asking a person to list items he or she likes.

Implicit preference indicators are, for example, obtained by:

- observing the items that a person views in on-line shopping;
- saving details about the items a person liked in on-line shopping;
- saving a list of items that a person has listened to or watched on his or her computer.

Claypool, et al. (2001) suggest that a more clever method than using explicit ratings should be to use implicit ratings, showing that implicit indicators have many advantages, including removing the cost of the user rating, arguing that every user interaction with the recommender system (and sometimes, the absence of interaction) can contribute to an implicit indicator that should be considered as information on the user. Their results showed, for example, that the time spent on a Web page is a good implicit indicator and that mouse clicks are ineffective implicit indicators. Notice however that most actual recommender-systems algorithms are based on explicit ratings (sometimes together with implicit ratings).

A last point about preference indicators concerns the variability of user preferences. As mentioned by Marlin (2004), very few recommendation algorithms take into account the sequence in which the preferences are collected. Preferences are usually seen as a "static" view of user opinion. However, over long periods of time, or in areas where user preferences change very often, older preferences can rapidly become inaccurate. This problem especially arises with implicit indicators because the user has no means to update past preference indicators. Some authors suggested approaches to generate recommendations in the context of dynamic data. Uchyigit, et al. (2003) introduced an agent-based approach to collaborative filtering where agents work on behalf of their users to form shared interest groups. These groups are dynamically updated to reflect the evolution of user interests over time. In his work, Pavlov introduced algorithms dealing with dynamic preferences; for example, Pavlov & Pennock (2002) explicitly modeled the data as a time series and developed a complex maximum-entropy approach to recommend documents to users.

Filtering Approach

When considering the approach followed to suggest items to persons, recommender systems can be classified into three categories:

- **Content-based approaches**. A user will be recommended items similar to the ones he/she preferred in the past, depending on the features of the items.
- **Collaborative approaches**. A user will be recommended items that people with similar tastes and preferences have liked or items similar to the ones the user has preferred, depending on the links between items and persons, rather than on the features of items.
- **Hybrid approaches**. These approaches combine collaborative and content-based filtering approaches.

Content-Based Approaches

A content-based recommender system tries to discover patterns among the items the active person has consumed in the past (e.g. a movie recommender system tries to find patterns among features such as directors, actors, subject, or categories of the movies). The second step is then to find items having a high degree of similarity with those patterns (Adomavicius & Tuzhilin, 2005).

The content-based approach to recommendation has its roots in the information-retrieval (Baeza-Yates & Ribeiro-Neto, 1999) and information-filtering communities (Belkin & Croft, 1992), using many of the same techniques. As for information filtering and information retrieval, content-based approaches primarily deal with textual information and with large amounts of data (documents, Web sites, news messages, etc.). The improvement over the traditional information-retrieval approaches lies in the analysis of user profiles. These profiles are established using historical data and contain information about people tastes, preferences, and needs. Various algorithms (Bayesian classifiers, clustering, decision trees, artificial neural networks, etc.) have been developed to analyze the content of text documents and to find patterns (regularities) that can serve as a basis to make appropriate recommendations. For example, Balabanovic & Shoham (1997) represent a document in terms of the 100 words with the highest Term Frequency-Inverse Document Frequency (*tf* and *idf* factors) weights (i.e. the words occurring more frequently than the average) and Pazzani & Billsus (1997) represent documents by the 128 most informative words.

As observed in (Adomavicius & Tuzhilin, 2005; Balabanovic & Shoham, 1997), content-based approaches have several shortcomings:

1. Content-based approaches are limited by the features associated with the items recommended by the system. Usually, only a shallow analysis of certain kinds of content is available in domains such as movies, music, restaurants, etc. Another related issue comes from the fact that two different items described by the same set of attributes are indistinguishable. Thus, it is, for example, hard to distinguish a well-written article from a badly written one containing both the same terms or keywords.

2. Overspecialization can also arise using content-based systems. When a system can only recommend items highly correlated to a user profile, the user is limited to being recommended items similar to those already rated. This issue is often addressed by introducing a degree of randomness.

3. Finally, as for collaborative systems, it is difficult for content-based systems to deal with new users. In order to make accurate recommendations, the system has first to learn from users. Notice that several techniques (based on item popularity, item entropy, user personalization, and combination of them) are explored for determining the best items for a new user to rate (see for example Rashid, et al. (2002)). Hybrid approaches are also often introduced to overcome this problem.

Collaborative Approaches

Collaborative approaches recommend items to the active user based on the items previously rated by all the users. Remember that content-based approaches try to discover patterns among the items using mainly textual information providing details on the items. Recommending items by collaborative approaches can be achieved directly or by finding neighbors either of the active user or of the items that the active user has rated.

Many collaborative-filtering systems have been developed in the last decades, and, as stated by Herlocker, et al. (1999), collaborative approaches provide three key additional advantages to information filtering that are not provided by content-based approaches: (i) support for filtering any type of content, (ii) the ability to filter items based on dimensions that are hard to represent, and (iii) the ability to make good, but unexpected recommendations.

First of all, filtering can be performed on items that are hard to analyze with automated processes, such as movies, ideas, feelings, people, jokes, etc. Indeed, only links are needed while information about the contents of such items are not needed. Second, collaborative-filtering systems can enhance content-based filtering systems by measuring, in dimensions beyond that of simple content, how well an item meets a user's need or interests. Humans are able to incorporate dimensions such as quality or taste, which are very hard to analyze for computer algorithms. Finally, collaborative-filtering systems can recommend items in which a person is very interested, but which do not contain content that the person was expecting (e.g. in a collaborative-recommendation system, a user can be recommended a drama movie even if he or she has watched only comedy movies by now). Herlocker, et al. (1999) explain that such recommendations occur frequently in cultural domains.

The main shortcomings of collaborative-recommendation systems (i.e. the main focus of this chapter) are described in Section 3.

Hybrid Approaches

The potential for collaborative filtering to enhance content-based filtering tools is great. However, to reach the full potential, it must be combined with existing content-based information filtering technology. Collaborative filtering by itself performs well predicting items that meet a user's interests or tastes, but is not well-suited to locating information for a specific content information need. Collaborative-filtering approaches do not necessarily compete with content-based ones. In most cases, they can be integrated to provide a powerful hybrid filtering solution.

Several recommendation systems use a hybrid approach by combining collaborative and content-based approaches. For example, Balabanovic & Shoham (1997) explain how their hybrid system, *Fab*, can eliminate many of the shortcomings of the pure versions of either approach. *Fab* is a distributed implementation of a hybrid system which contains three main components (collection agents that find pages for a specific topic, selection agents that find pages for a specific user, and central router that collect pages found by the collection agents and forward them to users whose profiles match) in order to find Web pages for a specific topic or for a specific user. Another example is proposed by Basu, et al. (1998): they use content-based and collaborative features (e.g. the age of the user or the category of the movie) in a single rule-based classifier. Notice also the unified approach suggested by Basilico & Hofmann (2004) who propose a novel approach (combining various kernel-based methods and applying perceptron learning) that systematically integrates all available training information such as past user-item ratings as well as attributes of items or users to learn a prediction function (resulting in an on-line algorithm, *JRank*).

These examples illustrate the various methods existing to combine collaborative and content-based filtering approaches into a hybrid recommender system:

- develop collaborative and content-based systems independently and combining their predictions;
- insert some content-based features into a collaborative approach;
- insert some collaborative features into a content-based approach;
- develop an integrated system including both collaborative and content-based features.

Several works (Balabanovic & Shoham, 1997; Pazzani & Billsus, 1997; Soboroff & Nicholas, 1999) compared the performance of their hybrid system with pure collaborative and content-based systems. The results show that the hybrid systems provide more accurate recommendations than pure systems. For example, Soboroff & Nicholas (1999) show a way to compare user profiles and documents in a unified model (using latent semantic indexing to rearrange a collection of user profiles, so that their commonalities are exploited in the filtering task itself), which derives relationships between users' interests; results provide by this model lead to the conclusion that lending a collaborative view to content filtering can increase performance.

Recommendation Algorithm

Researchers have developed various recommendation algorithms that can be classified into two main categories:

1. Memory-based algorithms use the entire user-item dataset to make recommendations.
2. Model-based algorithms try to develop first a model of user ratings which is then applied on new information to make recommendations.

The latest developments include approaches combining the memory-based and model-based algorithms (see, for example, (Yu, et al., 2004) where a probabilistic active learning method is used to actively query the user, thereby solving the new-user problem).

Memory-Based Algorithms

Traditionally, these algorithms use various statistical techniques to determine a set of persons, often referred to as the neighbors, who are most similar to the active user, depending on their historical behavior (they rate various items in a similar way or they often buy similar items or set of items). In most existing approaches, the similarity between two users is computed on the items that both users (i.e. the active user for which the algorithm is looking for neighbors and another user, potentially a nearest neighbor) have rated. The most popular approaches (Herlocker, et al., 2002) use the Pearson correlation coefficient, the Spearman rank correlation coefficient, and the cosine correlation as measure of similarity. Another recent memory-based approach is based on the definition of kernels on a graph derived from the database (see chapter 5 in this book for details). Many modifications trying to improve performance of these systems have been proposed as extensions to the classical correlation-based and cosine-based techniques. Here are some examples:

- **Default rating**. The idea is to give some default value to items for which the system has no explicit ratings, in order to enlarge the size of the intersection of the items both individuals have rated since many algorithms work on this intersection (Breese, Heckerman & Kadie, 1998).
- **Inverse user frequency**. The idea is that universally liked items are not as useful in capturing similarity as less common items (Breese, Heckerman & Kadie, 1998).
- **Case amplification**. The idea is to apply a transformation to the weights used for collaborative recommendation in order to emphasize some weights and to punish other ones (Breese, Heckerman & Kadie, 1998).

- **Weighted-majority prediction**. The idea is to combine memory-based algorithms and on-line learning models (continuous and interactive process), in which there is a pool of algorithms each of which is considered to be an "expert predictor" and is given a weight used to measure its confidence on the recommendation task (Delgado & Ishii, 1999; Nakamura & Abe, 1998).

To combine the preferences (i.e. to aggregate the ratings) of the found neighbors, memory-based algorithms use various ways (the average in the simplest case, but more frequently a weighted sum or an adjusted weighted sum) in order to provide the active user with recommendations. The above algorithms have traditionally been applied to, firstly, compute similarities between users. Notice that Karypis and Deshpande suggest in (Deshpande & Karypis, 2004; Karypis, 2001) to compute similarities between items and to proceed from there to provide recommendations to users. More precisely, three methods are defined to determine which items to suggest to a particular person based on computing proximity measures: the *direct method*, the *user-based indirect method*, and the *item-based indirect method*. Both indirect methods using a nearest-neighbor technique which requires a measure of "closeness" or "similarity".

When using the *user-based indirect method*, recommender systems usually suggest items by applying a two-step process:

1. Look for users sharing the same rating patterns with the active user (the user who wants to receive recommendation).
2. Use the ratings from those users (close to the active user) to compute recommendations.

Alternatively, the *item-based indirect method* works in another manner:

1. First determine a set of neighbors for each item.

2. Use these neighbors and the ratings of the active user to compute recommendations.

These *indirect methods* both look for neighbors and proceed from there. The nearest-neighbor scoring algorithm is one of the simplest and oldest methods for performing general classification tasks (Duda, Hart & Stork, 2001). It can be represented by the following rule: to classify an unknown pattern, choose the class of the nearest example in the dataset as measured by a similarity metric. When choosing the k nearest examples to classify the unknown pattern, one speaks about k nearest neighbors techniques.

Model-Based Algorithms

This section describes the most frequent model-based algorithms, aiming at developing a model of user ratings which is then applied on new information to make recommendations:

- **Cluster models**. Such models use existing data-partitioning and clustering algorithms to partition the set of items (O'Connor & Herlocker, 2001) or to group people into clusters (Ungar & Foster, 1998) based on user rating data. Predictions (i.e. classify unseen items into two or more classes, for example *like* and *dislike*) are then computed independently within each partition. Experimental results (Ungar & Foster, 1998; O'Connor & Herlocker, 2001) suggest that partitioning algorithms can greatly increase the scalability, but the accuracy is not improved when working with partitions rather than working with the base unpartitioned dataset. Chapter 6 introduces another clustering algorithm (the similarity-based clustering genetic algorithm) aiming at grouping users into communities of interests.
- **Bayesian networks**. Bayesian networks contains a node for each item in the data-

set (Breese, Heckerman & Kadie, 1998; Ji, Liu, Yan & Zhong, 2004). The states of each node correspond to the possible rating values for each item and the learning algorithm searches over various model structures in terms of dependencies for each item. In the resulting network used to compute recommendations, each item has a set of parent items that are the best predictors of its ratings. Experimental results (Breese, Heckerman & Kadie, 1998; Ji, Liu, Yan & Zhong, 2004) comparing Bayesian networks and memory-based algorithms (i.e. Pearson correlation and cosine coefficients) show that the best algorithm depends on the nature of the dataset and on the availability of ratings considered to recommend items.

- **Neural networks**. For example, Billsus & Pazzani (1998) apply, after computing a singular-value decomposition to represent rated items in k dimensions, an artificial neural network, taking real-valued feature vectors as inputs and learns a function that either predicts class membership or computes a score a user would assign to an item. Experimental results (Billsus & Pazzani, 1998) comparing such model-based and memory-based algorithms (i.e. Pearson correlation and cosine coefficients) show that the best results, in terms of the *F-measure* (i.e. a combination of recall and precision measures), are obtained by the suggested neural-network algorithm.
- **Linear regression**. Such an approach (see, for example, Sarwar, Karypis, Konstan & Riedl (2001)) of computing the predicted value is similar to a weighted-sum method but instead of directly using the ratings of similar items, it uses an approximation of the ratings based on a regression model. Experimental results (when, again, comparing with Pearson correlation and cosine coefficients) show that regression-based

algorithms perform better with very sparse data set, but as more data are added the quality decreases.

- **Maximum-entropy models**. Pavlov & Pennock (2002) developed a maximum-entropy approach to generate recommendations in the context of a user's current navigation stream, suitable for environments where data is sparse, high-dimensional, and dynamic. In their model, each user is associated with a set of sessions, and each session is modeled as a time sequence of document accesses. The model estimates the probability of the next visited document given the most recently visited documents. It is shown that this maximum-entropy model outperforms several competing algorithms in off-line tests simulating the recommendation of documents to users.
- **Latent-class models**. Hofmann & Puzicha (1999) introduce a latent-variable model, called "latent-class model", in the context of collaborative filtering. It is a clustering model assuming that the preferences of a user are established through a latent variable. In this model, a latent-class variable z is associated with each observation (x,y) where variable x represents a user and variable y represents an item. The key assumption made is that x and y are independent, conditioned on z. Hofmann & Puzicha (1999) also specify that it is neither assumed that persons form "groups", nor is stipulated that items can be partitioned into "clusters", offering a high degree of flexibility in modeling preference behavior: persons may have various specific interests, some of them being shared with some people, some with others. This flexibility as well as very interesting experimental results are shown in (Hofmann & Puzicha, 1999), leading to the application of this model for comparison with other scoring

algorithms developed in our work. Latent-class models are also used for clustering tasks as explained in Chapter 4 which aims to address building user communities of interests via Web usage mining and latent-class models. Chapter 4 also presents the application of user communities for Web recommendation.

- **Random-walk models**. A random-walk model through the database (i.e. a dataset of links) is defined by assigning a transition probability to each link existing between the elements of the database. Thus, a virtual random walker can jump from element to element and each element therefore represents a state of a Markov chain. From this random-walk model, quantities such as the average commute time, the average first-passage time, the average first-passage cost, and the pseudoinverse of the Laplacian matrix of the graph can be defined and used for recommendations (see (Fouss, Pirotte, Renders & Saerens, 2005; Fouss, Pirotte, Renders & Saerens, 2007) for details on this approach).
- **Support-vector machines**. These works (Grcar, et al., 2005; Maritza, et al., 2004; Schmidt-Thieme, 2005) view the recommendation task as a classification task, classes being different rating values. In this framework, any supervised learning algorithm can be applied to perform classification. For each user, a separate classifier is trained. To predict a rating, it is needed to classify the item into one of the classes representing rating values. Experimental results comparing memory-based algorithms (i.e. Pearson correlation and cosine coefficients) with support-vector machines classifier show that a standard algorithm is dominant on some datasets while support-vector machines provide better results when applied to a real-life corporate dataset with high level of sparsity (the accu-

racy of support-vector machines seems to depend on the characteristics of the input data).

- **Generalized linear models**. Delannay & Verleysen (2007) develop an approach based on a factorization of the ratings matrix, using probabilistic modeling to represent uncertainty in the ratings. The advantage of the approach is that different configurations, encoding different intuitions about the rating process, can be easily tested while keeping the same learning procedure. Experimental results show that this generalized linear model can be applied on large datasets and performs comparably to other state-of-the-art algorithms.

Prediction and Recommendation

In addition to recommender systems that predict the absolute values of ratings that individual users would give to the yet unrated items (called *prediction*), there has been work done on preference-based filtering, i.e. predicting the relative preferences of users (see, for example, Cohen, Schapire & Singer (1999) and Jin, Si, Zhai & Callan (2003)). These techniques (called *recommendation*) focus on predicting the correct relative order of the items rather than their individual ratings. Notice that this relatively nascent "learning to rank" issue (i.e. construct a model or a function for ranking objects) is a central matter in many recent applications (including document retrieval, collaborative recommendation, expert finding, etc. - see, for example, Agarwal & Chakrabarti (2007), Cao, Qin, Liu, Tsai & Li (2007), and Cortes, Mohri & Rastogi (2007)).

A definition can be adopted for both concepts:

- a *prediction* is a numerical value expressing the predicted likelihood that a user will "like" an item;
- a *recommendation* is a list (ranked or not) of items, provided by a particular algorithm, that a user will "like" the most, according to the algorithm.

COLLABORATIVE RECOMMENDATION SYSTEMS

Collaborative filtering is first mentioned by Goldberg, et al. (1992) who were the first to publish an account of using collaborative-filtering techniques for the filtering of information. Their system, called *Tapestry*, was used to filter e-mails, allowing users to express their opinions in the form of text messages. These messages became accessible as virtual fields of the e-mail, and users could construct filtering queries accessing those fields. *Tapestry* relied on the explicit opinions of people from a small community, such as an office workgroup. However, recommender systems for large communities cannot be based on the assumption that each person knows all the other persons. Later, several ratings-based automated recommender systems were developed. *GroupLens* (Konstan, et al., 1997; Resnick, et al., 1994) introduced an automated collaborative-filtering system using a neighborhood-based algorithm. They provided personalized predictions for *Usenet* news articles by (1) using Pearson correlation coefficient to weight user similarity, (2) using all available correlated neighbors, and (3) computing a final prediction thanks to a weighted average.

The *Ringo* music recommender (Shardanand & Maes, 1995) and the *Bellcore* video recommender (Hill, et al., 1995) improved the original *GroupLens* system by computing similarity weights using a constrained Pearson correlation coefficient. *Ringo*, claiming better performance, limited neighborhood by only retaining the neighbors whose correlation was greater than a fixed threshold, with higher thresholds resulting in greater accuracy. Notice however that this improvement reduced the number of items for which the system was able to generate predictions. To generate predictions, *Ringo* computed a weighted average of ratings from all the pre-selected neighbors. *Bellcore* used Pearson correlation to weight a random sample of neighbors, selected the best neighbors, and performed a full multiple regression on them to create a prediction.

Various work has been done in the field of collaborative recommendation since the introduction of these first systems. This section lists various real systems using collaborative-recommendation algorithms, introduces the main limitations and the main errors of collaborative-recommendation systems, and provides some indications about the various criteria that are traditionally used for evaluating the performance of such systems.

Real Systems

Sites that implement collaborative-recommendation systems include:

- *Amazon* was one of the first major companies to sell goods over the Internet;
- *Half.com[1]* is a subsidiary of *eBay*, in which sellers offer items at fixed prices;
- *Hollywood Video[2]* is the second largest movie and game rental company in the United States;
- *Netflix[3]* is the largest on-line dvd rental service;
- *AmphetaRate[4]* is an open-source recommendation server recommending articles;
- *StumbleUpon[5]* combines collaborative human opinions with machine learning of personal preference to create virtual communities containing similar Web users;
- *Jester[6]* uses a collaborative-filtering algorithm called *EigenTaste* to recommend jokes based on the ratings of users on a set of sample jokes;
- *WikiLens[7]* provides recommendations on various items including movies, books, albums, restaurants, beers, etc.

Main Limitations

Even if collaborative-recommendation systems have achieved great success in research, they are not widely used in practice. Actually, many issues still have to be addressed.

The first challenge is to improve the capacity of these algorithms. They are now able to look for thousands of potential neighbors in real-time but demands for this kind of systems are rather to look for millions of potential neighbors as fast as possible.

The second challenge is to improve the quality of the recommendations. Indeed, the users need recommendations that they can trust and will not hesitate to go somewhere else if the recommendation system is not as accurate as they want.

From one side, one can think that these two challenges are complete opposite for most real-time applications since more accurate recommendations often result in slower algorithms, therefore leading to a reduction in the capacity of the algorithms that have to be applied on-line. It is therefore important to tackle these two issues simultaneously.

Besides these two major challenges, other issues have to be mentioned:

1. Collaborative-recommendation systems assume that similar persons behave in a similar way. However, even for music or movies (areas in which these systems are the most used nowadays), tastes of people are still a complex phenomenon. It's a great challenge, for an automatic algorithm, to take into account the special nature of each individual.
2. Collaborative-recommendation systems need, in most cases, an important active participation from users. They continually have to fill in questionnaires or to evaluate various items. This process can become heavy for users of such systems.

3. It is difficult, for collaborative-recommendation systems, to take new information (new users or new items) into account. Indeed, such systems encounter difficulties when trying to provide recommendations to a user about whom no information (ratings on items, etc.) is available or on an item that has not been rated yet.

4. In recommender systems, the number of available ratings is usually very small compared to the number of ratings to be predicted. This could lead to difficulties in recommendations if, for example, there are many items that have been rated by only a few people, leading to rare recommendations of these items.

Main Errors

If we do not consider recommendation errors (arising when the developed algorithm has not well integrated user preferences and provides inaccurate recommendations), the main errors come from problems in the data available to make recommendations. Data errors can be classified into three main categories: too sparse data, false or of poor-quality data, and highly variable data:

1. Sparse data and missing values are two important issues (especially when considering new items or new users) in the computations needed by collaborative-recommendation algorithms.

2. Even if the dataset contains a lot of data on users and items, it can be of poor quality resulting in poor recommendations. Poor quality data come, for example, from a badly defined method for gathering data or from intentional/non-intentional mistakes of users.

3. Highly variable data should not be necessarily considered as bad data but they can result in poor recommendations. If, for example, from all the nearest neighbors of a particular user, half of them gave a very bad rating to an item while the other half gave a very good rating to the same item, the "true" prediction should not be the means of the ratings of the nearest neighbors of the user, even if the algorithm will probably provide this kind of prediction.

These data errors bring us to investigate the robustness of collaborative-recommendation systems. The next paragraph is inspired by the work developed in (O'Mahony, et al., 2004). Using this definition, robustness "*measures the ability of the algorithm to make good predictions in the presence of noisy data*". For (Groot, et al., 2000), robustness is "*the degree to which a system or component can function correctly in the presence of invalid inputs or stressful environmental conditions*". There are two aspects in robustness: *accuracy* (does the system recommend, after an external intentional or non-intentional attempt to alter recommendations, items that are actually liked) and *stability* (does the system recommend different items after an external intentional or non-intentional attempt to alter recommendations). Notice that, even if stability and accuracy are distinct, they are not independent.

Collaborative-recommendation systems update their data when users enter new ratings, but there is no guarantee that these ratings reflect the user's true preferences. Indeed, since rating entry can be a long process, users may be careless and inaccuracies in the data can be expected. It is also possible to imagine scenarios in which malicious users may be motivated to deliberately attack the recommendation system to cause it to malfunction. For example, a publisher may wish to promote his own work by encouraging a recommendation system to output artificially high ratings for his publications. Usually, the cost of perturbing the recommendations is prohibitive; however, many collaborative recommender's are open (Web) services that malicious agents could easily attack. Figure 1, inspired by (O'Mahony, et al., 2004),

Figure 1. Example of an attack (i.e. an attempt to alter recommendations) on a particular item

	I1	I2	I3	I4	I5	I6	I7
P1	x	x		✓	✓		✓
P2	x	x	✓		✓		✓
P3	✓	x	✓		x	x	
P4	x	✓	✓	x			x
P5	x		x	x	x		x
P6	✓	✓	x	✓	x		✓
P7		x	✓	✓	x	x	✓
P8	x	x	✓	✓	✓		?
P9	✓	x	✓		x	x	x
P10	x	✓	✓	x			x
P11	x		x	x	x		x
P12	x	x	✓	✓	✓		x
P13		x	✓	✓	x	x	x

illustrates the concepts of attacks and robustness: each row represents a person (from *P1* to *P13*) while each column represents an item (from *I1* to *I7*), the symbol "√" in the ith row and jth column represents the fact that person Pi has liked item Ij, the symbol "×" in the ith row and jth column represents the fact that person Pi disliked item Ij, and a blank cell in the ith row and jth column means that person Pi has, at this time, no advice on item Ij.

(Figure 1) shows, for example, that user (person) $P2$ likes items $I3, I5$ and $I7$, and dislikes items $I1$, and $I2$ (while having no advice on items $I4$ and $I6$). Suppose the system wants to predict whether active user $P8$ will like item $I7$. In order to achieve its goal, the system compares the profile of user $P8$ with the profiles of all the other users (assuming that the system applies the *user-based indirect method*). For now, consider only the top portion of the matrix, users $P1$ to $P8$. The details of the computations obviously depend on the similarity measure used, but presumably the system would conclude that users $P1$ and $P2$ are similar to user $P8$, since they tend to agree on the items they have rated in common. Recommender systems will provide a recommendation for $P8$ based on the ratings given by its most similar users (i.e. $P1$ and $P2$). In this case, we suppose that the system

predicts that the active user $P8$ will like item $I7$. Now, suppose that a competitor to item $I7$ wants to influence the recommendations of the system so that item $I7$ is rarely recommended. In order to achieve his goal, this competitor introduces various fake users, $P9$ to $P13$. What ratings should the competitor give to these fake users in order to decrease the rating for item $I7$. Clearly, none of the fake users should like item $I7$ (as shown in the last column of rows $P9$ to $P13$). It is clear, by observing the ratings of all users, that user $P12$ and $P13$ badly influence the recommender system so that item $I7$ will probably not be predicted any more as an item that user $P8$ will like. Indeed, users $P12$ and $P13$ are now highly similar to the active user, which may lead the recommender system to switch its prediction from like to dislike.

This lack of robustness could be quantified, in general, in two ways. Firstly, we can measure the accuracy of the recommendations by looking at the performance obtained by the system after such changes in the environment. Secondly, we can measure the stability of the system (i.e. the fact that the recommender system switched its prediction) by comparing the recommendations provided by the system before and after such changes in the environment. In theory, a malicious user could clearly force a recommender system to behave in an arbitrary fashion, by adding to the ratings matrix enough errors to completely dilute the preferences of the real users. Notice however that such a behavior could be very expensive, even assuming an open system.

Moreover, the utility of a recommendation depends on the perspective of the parties involved. In recommender systems, three distinct parties can be identified:

- **End users**. They receive the recommendations. From this perspective, the utility depends on how well the recommender system follows their personal tastes.
- **Database owner**. He is primarily interested in the output of the system as measured by the total number of transactions. From this perspective, the recommender system does not need to be accurate, so long as it attracts customers to the service.
- **External parties**. They have an indirect interest in the transactions. For a book recommendation system, such a party might be the author of some of the books that are being recommended. These parties have an interest in the recommendations that are made for their product, but do not have direct access to the recommendation system.

Performance Evaluation

Most of the works done in the field of recommender system use *accuracy* to evaluate various systems. It is therefore assumed that every user provides a preference score for all the rated items. The accuracy measure evaluates either the correspondence between the ranking provided by the user and the ranking provided by the recommender system or the difference between the rating values provided by the user and the recommender system. Moreover, even if two recommender systems provide similar accuracies, it could be very informative to compare the rankings provided to the user, in-

troducing a *ranking-comparison* measure, applied to compute a distance between two ranked lists.

Good recommendation (in terms of accuracy) has, however, to be coupled with other considerations. A recommender system providing good accuracy results, only if the items are easy to predict, or a recommender system systematically recommending the best-sellers are not very interesting. Another important consideration is the *robustness* of the system. Moreover, Herlocker, et al. (2004) suggest to use, besides accuracy, the suitability of the recommendations to users. Suitability includes, in Herlocker's work, "*coverage*" (the proportion of items for which the recommender system could provide a ranking or a prediction), "*confidence*" (to help user to make his decisions), the "*computing time*" (the time needed by a recommender system to provide recommendations or predictions), and a "*novelty/serendipity*" aspect (is a recommendation a novel, original, possibility for a user or not). Recent work done in the evaluation of collaborative-recommendation systems includes (Carenini, 2005; Fouss & Saerens, 2008; Herlocker, et al., 2004; McNee et al., 2006; Schein et al., 2005).

CONCLUSION

After a brief introduction to recommender systems, we proposed a typology of recommender systems, based on four features (preference indicator, recommendation approach, filtering algorithm, and prediction vs recommendation). The second part of this chapter is devoted to collaborative-recommendation systems, providing some historical considerations, a list of real well-known collaborative systems, a discussion about the main limitations and the main errors encountered in such systems, as well as a brief introduction on the evaluation of the performance of collaborative systems.

REFERENCES

Adomavicius, G., & Tuzhilin, A. (2005). Toward the next generation of recommender systems: A survey of the state-of-the-art and possible extensions. *IEEE Transactions on Knowledge and Data Engineering*, 734–749. doi:10.1109/TKDE.2005.99

Agarwal, A., & Chakrabarti, S. (2007). Learning random walks to rank nodes in graphs. In *Proceedings of the 24th International Conference on Machine Learning* (pp. 9–16).

Armstrong, J. (2001). *Principles of Forecasting, A Handbook for Researchers and Practitioners*. Kluwer Academic.

Baeza-Yates, R., & Ribeiro-Neto, B. (1999). *Modern information retrieval*. Addison-Wesley.

Balabanovic, M., & Shoham, Y. (1997). Fab: Contentbased, collaborative recommendation. *Communications of the ACM, 40*, 66–72. doi:10.1145/245108.245124

Basilico, J., & Hofmann, T. (2004). Unifying collaborative and content-based filtering. In *Proceedings of the Twenty-first International Conference on Machine Learning* (pp. 65–72).

Basu, C., Hirsh, H., & Cohen, W. (1998). Recommendation as classification: Using social and content-based information in recommendation. *Recommender System Workshop, 98*, 11–15.

Belkin, N. J., & Croft, W. B. (1992). Information filtering and information retrieval: Two sides of the same coin. *Communications of the ACM, 35*(12), 29–38. doi:10.1145/138859.138861

Billsus, D., & Pazzani, M. J. (1998). Learning collaborative information filters. In *Proceedings of the 15th International Conference on Machine Learning* (pp. 46–54).

Breese, J., Heckerman, D., & Kadie, C. (1998). Empirical analysis of predictive algorithms for collaborative filtering. In *Proceedings of the 14th Conference on Uncertainty in Artificial Intelligence*.

Cao, Z., Qin, T., Liu, T.-Y., Tsai, M.-F., & Li, H. (2007). Learning to rank: From pairwise approach to listwise approach. In *Proceedings of the 24th International Conference on Machine Learning* (pp. 129–136).

Carenini, G. (2005). User-specific decision-theoretic accuracy metrics for collaborative filtering. In *Proceedings of the Intelligent User Interface Conference (IUI'05)*.

Claypool, M., Le, P., Waseda, M., & Brown, D. (2001). Implicit interest indicators. In *Proceedings of the ACM Intelligent User Interfaces Conference* (pp. 33–40).

Cohen, W., Schapire, R., & Singer, Y. (1999). Learning to order things. *Journal of Artificial Intelligence Research, 10*, 243–270.

Cortes, C., Mohri, M., & Rastogi, A. (2007). Magnitude-preserving ranking algorithms. In *Proceedings of the 24th International Conference on Machine Learning* (pp. 169–176).

Delannay, N., & Verleysen, M. (2007). Collaborative filtering with interlaced generalized linear models. *European Symposium on Artificial Neural Networks*.

Delgado, J., & Ishii, N. (1999). Memory-based weighted-majority prediction for recommender systems. In *Proceedings of the ACM SIGIR '99 Workshop Recommender Systems: Algorithms and Evaluation*.

Deshpande, M., & Karypis, G. (2004). Item-based top-n recommendation algorithms. *ACM Transactions on Information Systems, 22*(1), 143–177. doi:10.1145/963770.963776

Duda, R. O., Hart, P. E., & Stork, D. G. (2001). *Pattern classification* (2nd ed.). John Wiley & Sons.

Fouss, F., Pirotte, A., Renders, J.-M., & Saerens, M. (2005). A novel way of computing similarities between nodes of a graph, with application to collaborative recommendation. In *Proceedings of the 2005 IEEE/WIC/ACM International Joint Conference on Web Intelligence* (pp. 550–556).

Fouss, F., Pirotte, A., Renders, J.-M., & Saerens, M. (2007). Random walk computation of similarities between nodes of a graph, with application to collaborative recommendation. *IEEE Transactions on Knowledge and Data Engineering, 19*(3), 355–369. doi:10.1109/TKDE.2007.46

Fouss, F., & Saerens, M. (2008). Evaluating performance of recommender systems: An experimental comparison. In *Proceedings of the 2008 IEEE/WIC/ACM International Joint Conference on Web Intelligence* (pp. 735–738).

Goldberg, K., Nichols, D., Oki, B. M., & Terry, D. (1992). Using collaborative filtering to weave an information tapestry. *Communications of the ACM, 35*(12), 61–70. doi:10.1145/138859.138867

Grcar, M., & Fortuna, B. Mladenic, D., & Grobelnik, M. (2005). knn versus svm in the collaborative filtering framework. In *Proceedings of the 2005 KDD Workshop on Web Mining and Web Usage Analysis*.

Groot, P., van Harmelen, F., & ten Teije, A. (2000). Torture tests: a quantitative analysis for the robustness of knowledge-based systems. In *Proceedings of the European Workshop on Knowledge Acquisition, Modelling and Management (EKAW 00), LNAI Springer-Verlag* (pp. 403–418).

Herlocker, J., Konstan, J., Borchers, A., & Riedl, J. (1999). An algorithmic framework for performing collaborative filtering. In *Proceedings of the international ACM SIGIR Conference on Research and Development in Information Retrieval* (pp. 230–237).

Herlocker, J., Konstan, J., & Riedl, J. (2002). An empirical analysis of design choices in neighborhood-based collaborative filtering algorithms. *Information Retrieval, 5*, 287–310. doi:10.1023/A:1020443909834

Herlocker, J., Konstan, J., Terveen, L., & Riedl, J. (2004). Evaluating collaborative filtering recommender systems. *ACM Transactions on Information Systems, 22*(1), 5–53. doi:10.1145/963770.963772

Hill, W., Stead, L., Rosenstein, M., & Furnas, G. (1995). Recommending and evaluating choices in a virtual community of use. In *Proceedings of ACM CHI'95 Conference on Human Factors in Computing Systems* (pp. 194–201).

Hofmann, T., & Puzicha, J. (1999). Latent class models for collaborative filtering. In *Proceedings of the sixteenth International Joint Conference on Artificial Intelligence* (pp. 688–693).

Ji, J., Liu, C., Yan, J., & Zhong, N. (2004). Bayesian networks structure learning and its application to personalized recommendation in a b2c portal. In *Proceedings of the IEEE/WIC/ACM International Conference on Web Intelligence*.

Jin, R., Si, L., Zhai, C., & Callan, J. (2003). Collaborative filtering with decoupled models for preferences and ratings. In *Proceedings of the 12th International Conference on Information and Knowledge Management* (pp. 309–316).

Karypis, G. (2001). Evaluation of item-based top-n recommendation algorithms. In *Proceedings of the tenth International Conference on Information and Knowledge Management* (pp. 247–254).

Konstan, J., Miller, B., Maltz, D., Herlocker, J., Gordon, L., & Riedl, J. (1997). Grouplens: Applying collaborative filtering to usenet news. *Communications of the ACM, 40*(3), 77–87. doi:10.1145/245108.245126

Lilien, G., Smith, B., & Moorthy, K. (1992). *Marketing Models*. Prentice Hall.

Maritza, L., Cristina, N., Perez-Alcazar, J., Garcia-Diaz, J., & Delgado, J. (2004). A comparison of several predictive algorithms for collaborative filtering on multivalued ratings. *ACM Symposium on Applied Computing* (pp. 1033–1039).

Marlin, B. (2004). *Collaborative Filtering: A Machine Learning Perspective*. University of Toronto.

McNee, S. M., Riedl, J., & Konstan, J. A. (2006). Being accurate is not enough: how accuracy metrics have hurt recommender systems. In *Proceedings of the Conference on Human Factors in Computing Systems (CHI'06)* (pp. 1097–1101).

Murthi, B., & Sarkar, S. (2003). The role of the management sciences in research on personalization. *Management Science, 49*(10), 1344–1362. doi:10.1287/mnsc.49.10.1344.17313

Nakamura, A., & Abe, N. (1998). Collaborative filtering using weighted majority prediction algorithms. In *Proceedings of the 15th International Conference on Machine Learning*.

O'Connor, M., & Herlocker, J. (2001). Clustering items for collaborative filtering. In *Proceedings of the SIGIR-2001 International Workshop on Recommender Systems*.

O'Mahony, M., Hurley, N., Kushmerick, N., & Silvestre, G. (2004). Collaborative recommendation: A robustness analysis. *ACM Transactions on Internet Technology, 4*(4), 344–377.

Pavlov, D. X., & Pennock, D. M. (2002). A maximum entropy approach to collaborative filtering in dynamics, sparse, high-dimensional domains. In Proceedings of Neural Information Processing Systems, (pp. 1441–1448).

Pazzani, M., & Billsus, D. (1997). Learning and revising user profiles: The identification of interesting web sites. *Machine Learning, 27*, 313–331. doi:10.1023/A:1007369909943

Rashid, M., Albert, I., Cosley, D., Lam, S., Mc-Nee, S., Konstan, J., & Riedl, J. (2002). Getting to know you: Learning new user preferences in recommender systems. In *Proceedings of the 7th International Conference on Intelligence User Interfaces* (pp. 127–134).

Resnick, P., Neophytos, I., Mitesh, S., Bergstrom, P., & Riedl, J. (1994). GroupLens: An open architecture for collaborative filtering of netnews. In *Proceedings of the Conference on Computer Supported Cooperative Work* (pp. 175–186).

Rich, E. (1979). User modeling via stereotypes. *Cognitive Science, 3*(4), 329–354. doi:10.1207/s15516709cog0304_3

Salton, G. (1989). *Automatic Text Processing*. Addison-Wesley.

Sarwar, B., Karypis, G., Konstan, J., & Riedl, J. (2001). Item-based collaborative filtering recommendation algorithms. In *Proceedings of the International World Wide Web Conference* (pp. 285–295).

Schein, A. I., Popescul, A., Ungar, L. H., & Pennock, D. M. (2005). CROC: A new evaluation criterion for recommender systems: World wide web electronic commerce, security and privacy. *Electronic Commerce Research, 1*(5), 51. doi:10.1023/B:ELEC.0000045973.51289.8c

Schmidt-Thieme, L. (2005). Compound classification models for recommender systems. In *Proceedings of the Fifth IEEE International Conference on Data Mining* (pp. 378–385).

Shardanand, U., & Maes, P. (1995). Social information filtering: Algorithms for automating 'word of mouth'. *Proceedings of the Conference on Human Factors in Computing Systems* (pp. 210–217).

Soboroff, I., & Nicholas, C. (1999). Combining content and collaboration in text filtering. In *Proceedings of the IJCAI'99 Workshop on Machine Learning in Information Filtering* (pp. 86–91).

Uchyigit, G., & Clark, K. (2003). A multi-agent architecture for dynamic collaborative filtering. In *Proceedings of the 5th International Conference on Enterprise Information Systems*, 4, 363–368.

Ungar, L. H., & Foster, D. P. (1998). Clustering methods for collaborative filtering. In *Proceedings of the Workshop on Recommendation Systems*.

Yu, K., Schwaighofer, A., Tresp, V., Xu, X., & Kriegel, H.-P. (2004). Probabilistic memory-based collaborative filtering. *IEEE Transactions on Knowledge and Data Engineering, 16*(5), 56–69.

ENDNOTES

1. http://www.half.ebay.com
2. http://www.hollywoodvideo.com
3. http://www.netflix.com
4. http://sourceforge.net/projects/amphetarate
5. http://www.stumbleupon.com
6. http://shawdow.ieor.berkeley.edu/humor
7. http://www.wikilens.org

Chapter 4
Building User Communities of Interests by Using Latent Semantic Analysis

Guandong Xu
Victoria University, Australia

ABSTRACT

Nowadays Web users are facing the problems of information overload and drowning due to the significant and rapid growth in the amount of information and the large number of users. As a result, how to provide Web users more exactly needed information is becoming a critical issue in Web-based information retrieval and data management. In order to address the above difficulties, Web mining was proposed as an efficient means to discover the intrinsic relationships among Web data. In particular, Web usage mining is to discover Web usage patterns and utilize the discovered usage knowledge for constructing interest-oriented user communities, which could be, in turn, used for presenting Web users more personalized Web contents, i.e. Web recommendation. On the other hand, Latent Semantic Analysis (LSA) is one kind of approaches that is used to reveal the inherent correlation resided in co-occurrence activities, such as Web usage data. Moreover, LSA possesses the capability of capturing the hidden knowledge at semantic level that can't be achieved by traditional methods. In this chapter, we aim to address building user communities of interests via combining Web usage mining and latent semantic analysis. Meanwhile we also present the application of user communities for Web recommendation.

INTRODUCTION

Background

Nowadays Web users are facing the problems of information overload and drowning due to the significant and rapid growth in the amount of information and the large number of users. As a result, how to provide Web users more exactly needed information is becoming a critical issue in Web-based information retrieval and data management. There are a variety of ways that can address the above challenge based on various technical solutions. Among these proposed techniques, Web

DOI: 10.4018/978-1-61520-841-8.ch004

Copyright © 2011, IGI Global. Copying or distributing in print or electronic forms without written permission of IGI Global is prohibited.

data mining is devised as an efficient means to discover organizational structure of Web contents, interest-oriented user navigational behaviors and underlying interactions between Web users and Web contents in depth. Web communities are termed as the gathering of Web objects, and could be categorized into Web page community and Web user community dependent on the types of Web objects. The former reflects the functional inherence of Web pages serving, whereas the latter reveals the navigational interest of users, i.e. user community of interest. In this chapter, we mainly aim to address modeling user navigational behaviors (i.e. user communities of interests) and revealing the navigational task space at a semantic level via Web data mining and latent semantic analysis. The proposed chapter will covers a broad range of contents from theoretical aspects such as mathematical models and algorithmic descriptions to experimental investigations including result interpretations, evaluations and comparisons along with an application case study.

Web data mining is a process that discovers the intrinsic relationships among Web data, which are expressed in the forms of textual, linkage or usage information, via analyzing the features of the Web data using data mining techniques. Dependent on the implemented targets, Web data mining consists of Web content mining, Web linkage mining as well as Web usage mining. Particularly, in this chapter we only concentrate our study on discovering Web usage patterns via Web usage mining, and then utilize the discovered usage knowledge for constructing interest-oriented user communities, which could be, in turn, used for presenting Web users more personalized Web contents, i.e. Web recommendation.

Latent Semantic Analysis (LSA) is first proposed in text processing by Deerwester to efficiently tackle the linguistic phenomenon such as synonymy and polysemy. The intuition behind LSA is the concept of "hidden topic", which is deemed to govern the certainty of co-occurrence of words within the corpus. Recently LSA has been successfully introduced into Web usage mining and has achieved great successes in many related studies e.g. user modeling, collaborative filtering and Web personalization.

In this chapter, we aim to address building user communities of interests via Web usage mining and latent semantic analysis. Meanwhile we also present the application of user communities for Web recommendation.

Structure of This Chapter

This chapter is organized as follows:

Foundation of Web Usage Mining and Latent Semantic Analysis describes the basic concepts and techniques necessary for Web usage mining, latent semantic analysis and Web recommendation. A mathematical usage data model (matrix) is presented in this section, and the related mathematical knowledge and backgrounds are provided for better understanding the algorithms and techniques developed in this chapter as well. The engaged algorithms and techniques for Web usage mining, latent semantic analysis and Web recommendation are also reviewed and discussed. This section provides a foundation for further study of Web usage mining and Web recommendation described in the following sections.

In Modeling User Communities of Interests Based on Latent Semantic Indexing, we address Web usage mining by employing the traditional latent semantic indexing approach. A LUI algorithm is proposed to extract the latent semantic knowledge from usage data via computing the singular values of the original usage data, which approximates the original semantics hidden in the usage matrix. Different from other algorithms, such as (Mobasher, Dai, Nakagawa, & Luo, 2002), that employed a standard clustering algorithm on the usage data directly to find the aggregates of user sessions, we develop another algorithm that performs clustering on the transformed usage space to improve the quality of Web usage mining. In this algorithm, each user session is represented by a dimensionality-reduced page vector, which conveys the latent relationships among the Web objects in the usage data model. From the revealed relationships, user session aggregates that contain a highly semantic similarity are eventually generated. Experiments are conducted to demonstrate the effectiveness of the algorithm for usage pattern mining.

Modeling User Communities of Interests Using Probablisitic Latent Semantic Analysis Model presents another latent semantic analysis model, PLSA model. In contrast to the tradition LSI approaches, PLSA model is based on a more solid foundation of statistical analysis. It is capable of discovering latent semantic factor space associated with the usage patterns in addition to the latent semantic analysis. In this section, a series of equations are formulated based on the Bayesian and uncertainty theory, which characterize the associations between Web objects (i.e. Web pages and user sessions) and latent semantic factors. Meanwhile, an EM algorithm is developed to estimate the parameters of PLSA model that leads to maximizing the likelihood of usage data. The parameters of PLSA model are termed as conditional probabilities of Web pages or user sessions over the latent semantic factors, which convey the intrinsic aggregation property of Web objects. We then utilize these kinds of factor-based feature vectors to group the Web pages and user sessions as well as identify the latent semantic factor space via a probability inference approach. The algorithms are evaluated by a series of experiments.

We turn to address Web recommendation as an application of building user communities of interests in Applications of User Profiling by using the discovered usage knowledge based on the above analytical models. We introduce a top-N collaborative Web recommendation algorithm, which is to compute the recommendation score of each page based on the probability weight. This section concentrates on the study of employing user profiling approach for Web recommendation.

In this section, we utilize the proposed user profile approach to deal with Web recommendation based on PLSA model. The user profiles are then applied into the collaborative recommendation algorithm to select the most matched usage pattern and predict the most potentially interested pages by referring to the visiting histories of other users who exhibit similar navigation preference. Experimental results on two Web log files show the effectiveness of the proposed algorithms in terms of recommendation accuracy.

We summarize this chapter and outline future research directions in Future Research Directions.

FOUNDATION OF WEB USAGE MINING AND LATENT SEMANTIC ANALYSIS

Research Problems

It is well known that the Internet has become a very popular and powerful platform to store, disseminate and retrieve information as well as a data repository for knowledge discovery. However, Web users always suffer the problems of information overload and drowning due to the significant and rapid growth in amount of information and the number of users. The problems of low precision and low recall rate caused by the above reasons are two major concerns that users have to deal with while searching for the needed information over the Internet. On the other hand, the huge amount of data/information residing over the Internet contains very valuable informative knowledge that could be discovered via using advanced data mining approaches. It is believed that mining this kind of knowledge will greatly benefit Web site designs and Web application developments, and promote other related applications, such as business intelligence, e-commerce, and entertainment broadcast, etc. Thus, the emerging of Web has put forward a great deal of challenges of Web-based information management and retrieval to Web researchers and engineers, who are requested to develop more efficient and effective techniques to satisfy the demands of various Web users.

Web data mining is one kind of these techniques that efficiently handles the tasks of searching the needed information from the Internet, for Web site structure designs, Internet service quality improvements, and informative knowledge discovery and better advanced Web applications. In principle, Web mining techniques are the means of utilizing data mining methods to induce and extract the useful information from Web applications. Web mining research has attracted a variety of academics and researchers from database management, information retrieval, artificial intelligence research areas especially from knowledge discovery and machine learning, and many research communities have addressed this topic in recent years due to the tremendous growth of data contents available on the Internet and urgent needs of e-commerce applications especially. Dependent on various mining targets, Web data mining could be categorized into three types, i.e. Web content, Web structure and Web usage mining. However in this chapter, we mainly focus on Web usage mining, i.e. discovering user communities of interests that represented by various access patterns from Web log files, which contain the historic visiting records of different users on the website. The discovered usage knowledge makes it possible for Web designers and developers to better understand user navigational behaviors, which will not only provide them helps in re-structuring Web site, but also in improving Web presentation.

Web recommendation or personalization is a process that utilizes the informative knowledge learned from Web data mining as a knowledge base, then predicts user potential access preference, and recommends the customized Web contents by referring to the knowledge base. The knowledge base can be made up of content, linkage, usage and semantic information. Recommender systems are well studied in the context of artificial intelligence

and information retrieval. To-date, there are two kinds of approaches and techniques commonly used in recommender systems, namely content-based filtering and collaborative filtering systems (Dunja, 1996; Herlocker, Konstan, Terveen, & Riedl, 2004a). Recently the collaborative filtering approaches have been extensively used in Web recommendation applications and have achieved great successes as well (Herlocker, Konstan, Borchers, & Riedl, 1999; Konstan, et al., 1997; Shardanand & Maes, 1995). Meanwhile, with the progress of Web usage mining research, Web researchers intend to combine the usage pattern knowledge into recommendation to reinforce Web recommendation systems. Using the usage knowledge as a collaborative information source will dramatically improve the recommendation performance and on-line response efficiency. With the benefit of the great progress in data mining research community, many data mining techniques, such as collaborative filtering based on the k-Nearest Neighbour algorithm (kNN) (Herlocker, et al., 1999; Konstan, et al., 1997; Shardanand & Maes, 1995), Web user or page clustering (Han, Karypis, Kumar, & Mobasher, 1998; Mobasher, et al., 2002; Perkowitz & Etzioni, 1998), association rule mining (Agarwal, Aggarwal, & Prasad, 1999; Agrawal & Srikant, 1994) and sequential pattern mining technique (Agrawal & Srikant, 1995) have been adopted in current Web usage mining methods.

To implement Web usage mining efficiently, it is essential to first introduce a solid mathematical framework, on which the data mining/analysis is performed. There are many types of data expressions that could be used to model the co-occurrence of Web user behavior, such as matrix, directed graph and click sequence and so on. Different data expression models have different mathematical and theoretical backgrounds. In particular, here we aim to adopt the commonly used matrix expression. In this framework, the user navigational behavior is modeled by a usage matrix, in the

Figure 1. Scheme of Web usage mining and Web recommendation

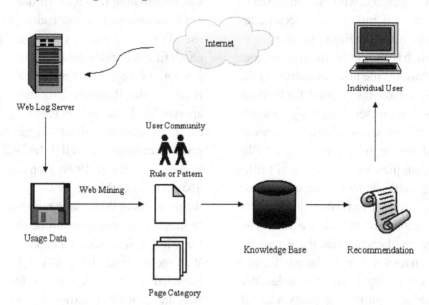

form of session-page vector. Based on the proposed mathematical framework, a variety of data mining and analysis methods could be employed to conduct Web usage mining. Amongst the approaches, Web clustering algorithm is a common analytical approach used in this work, which is to partition Web objects into various groups based on their mutual distance. On the other hand, latent semantic analysis model is another interesting topic for Web usage mining, which is able to discover the underlying relationships among the Web objects. We present these basic descriptions to these concepts and techniques in this section.

In the context of Web recommendation, there are several algorithms and techniques, which have been studied and developed in conventional recommender systems. In this section, we also review and discuss the background knowledge involved in Web recommendation. All these fundamentals prepare us a necessary knowledge base for better understanding the studies addressed. (Figure 1) outline a schematic description of the above techniques.

Web Data Analysis Models

For efficient Web data management, the issue of Web data model is essential and crucial, on which a variety of data mining and machine learning techniques are employed. To achieve the desired mining tasks discussed above, there are different Web data models in the forms of feature vectors, engaged in pattern discovery and knowledge applications. According to the three identified categories of Web mining, three types of Web data/sources, namely content data, structure data and usage data, are mostly considered in the context of Web mining. Before we start to propose the Web usage data model, we first give a brief discussion on these three data types in the following parts.

Web content data is a collection of objects used to convey content information of Web pages to users. In most cases, it is comprised of textural material and other types of multimedia content, which include static HTML/XML pages, images, sound and video files, and dynamic pages generated from scripts and databases. The content data also includes semantic or structured meta-data embedded within the site or individual page. In addition, the domain ontology might be considered as a complementary type of content data hidden in the site implicitly or explicitly. The underlying domain knowledge could be incorporated into Web site design in an implicit manner, or be represented in some explicit forms. The explicit form of domain ontology can be conceptual hierarchy e.g. product category, and structural hierarchy such as yahoo directory (Pierrakos, Paliouras, Papatheodorou, Karkaletsis, & Dikaiakos, 2003).

Web structure data is a representation of linking relationship between Web pages, which reflects the organization concept of a site from the viewing point of the designer (Hou & Zhang, 2002). It is normally captured by the inter-page linkage structure within the site, thus, is called linkage data. Particularly, the structure data of a site is usually represented by a specific Web component, called "site map", which is generated automatically when the site is completed. For dynamically generated pages, the site mapping is becoming more complicated to perform since more techniques are required to deal with the dynamic environment.

Web usage data is mainly sourced from Web log files, which include Web server access logs and application server logs (Otsuka, Toyoda, Hirai, & Kitsuregawa, 2004; Srivastava, Cooley, Deshpande, & Tan, 2000). The log data collected at Web access or application servers reflects the navigational behavior knowledge of users in terms of access patterns. In the context of Web usage mining, the usage data that we need to deal with is transformed and abstracted at different levels of aggregations, namely Web page set and user session collection. Web page is a basic unit of Web site organization, which contains a number of meaningful units serving for the main functionality of the page. Physically, a page is a collection of Web items, generated statically or dynamically, contributing to the display of the results in response to a user action. A page set is a collection of whole pages within a site. User session is a sequence of Web pages clicked by a single user during a specific period. A user session is usually dominated by one specific navigational task, which is exhibited through a set of visited relevant pages that contribute greatly to the task conceptually. The navigational interest/preference on one particular page is represented by its significant weight value, which is dependent on user visiting duration or click number. The user sessions (or called usage data), which are mainly collected in the server logs, can be transformed into a processed data format for the purpose of analysis via data preparing and cleaning process. In one word, the usage data is a collection of user session, which is in the form of weight distribution over the page space.

Matrix expression has been widely used to model the co-occurrence activities like Web data. The illustration of a matrix expression for Web data is shown in (Figure 2). In this scheme, rows and columns correspond to various Web objects which are dependent on various Web data mining tasks. In the context of Web content mining, the relationships between a set of documents and a set of keyword could be represented by a document-keyword co-occurrence matrix, where the rows of the matrix represent the documents, while the columns of the matrix correspond to the keywords. The intersection value of the matrix indicates the occurrence frequency of a specific keyword appeared in a particular document, i.e. if a keyword is appeared in a document, the corresponding matrix element value is 1, otherwise 0. Of course, the element value could also be a precise weight rather than 1 or 0 only, which exactly reflects the occurrence degree of two concerned objects of document and keyword. For example, the element value could represent the frequent rate of a specific keyword in a specific document. Likewise, to model the linkage information of a Web site, an adjacent matrix is used to represent the relationships between pages via their hyperlinks. And usually the element of the adjacent matrix is defined by the hyperlink linking

Figure 2. The illustration of Web data model

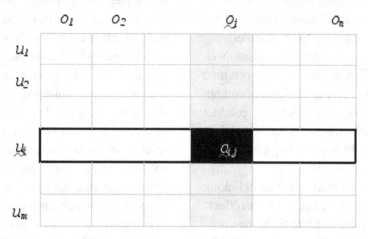

two pages, that is, if there is a hyperlink from page i to page j ($i \neq j$), then the value of the element a_{ij} is 1, otherwise 0. Since the linking relationship is directional, i.e. given a hyperlink directed from page i to page j, then the link is an out-link for i, while an in-link for j, and vice versa. In this case, the ith row of the adjacent matrix, which is a page vector, represents the out-link relationships from page i to other pages; the jth column of the matrix represents the in-link relationships linked to page i from other pages.

In Web usage mining, we can model one user session as a page vector in a similar way. As the exhibited user access interest may be reflected by the varying degrees of visits on different Web pages during one session. Thus, we can represent a user session as a collection of pages visited in the period along with their significant weights. The total collection of user sessions can, then, be expressed a usage matrix, where the ith row is the sequence of pages visited by user i during this period; and the jth column of the matrix represents the fact which users have clicked this page j. The element value of the matrix, a_{ij}, reflects the access interest exhibited by user i on page j, which could be used to derive the underlying access pattern of users.

Web Clustering

Web clustering analysis is a widely used data mining algorithm for many data management applications. Clustering is a process of partitioning a set of data objects into a number of object clusters, where each data object shares high similarity with the other objects within same cluster but is quite dissimilar to objects in other clusters. Different from classification algorithm that assigns a set of data objects with various labels previously defined via a supervised learning process, clustering analysis is to partition data objects objectively based on measuring the mutual similarity between data objects, i.e. via a unsupervised learning process. Due to the fact that the class labels are often not known before data analysis, for example, it is sometimes hard and unlike to pre-define explicit and meaningful class labels and assign them to the training data especially in large databases, clustering analysis is thus, sometimes an efficient approach for analyzing such kind of data. To perform clustering analysis, similarity measures are often utilized to assess the distance between a pair of data objects based on the feature vectors describing the objects, in turn, to help assign them into different object classes/clusters. There are a variety of distance functions used in different scenarios, which are really dependent on the application background. For example, Cosine function and Euclidean distance function are two commonly used distance functions in information retrieval and pattern recognition (Baeza-Yates & Ribeiro-Neto, 1999). On the other hand, assignment strategy is another important point involved in partitioning the data objects. Therefore, distance function and assignment algorithm are two core research focuses that attract a lot of efforts contributed by various research domain experts, such as from database, data mining, statistics, business intelligence and machine learning, etc.

The main data type typically used in clustering analysis is the matrix expression of data. Suppose that a data object is represented by a sequence of attributes/features with corresponding weights, for example, in the context of Web usage mining, a usage data piece (i.e. user session) is modeled as a weighted page sequence. Like what we discussed above, this data structure is in the form of object-by-attribute structure, or $n \times m$ matrix where n denotes the number of data objects and m represents the number of attributes. In addition to data matrix, similarity matrix where the element value reflects the similarity between two objects is also used for clustering analysis. In this case, the similarity matrix is expressed by an n-by-n table. For example, an adjacent matrix addressed in the Web linkage analysis is actually a similarity/relevance matrix. In this chapter, we are only interested in the first data expression, i.e. data matrix to address Web usage mining and Web recommendation.

To date, there are a large number of approaches and algorithms have been developed for clustering analysis in the literature (Broder, Glassman, Manasse, & Zweig, 1997; Flake, Tarjan, & Tsioutsiouliklis, 2004; Han, et al., 1998; Han & Kamber, 2007; Hou & Zhang, 2003b; Mobasher, et al., 2002; O'Conner & Herlocker, 1999; Wang & Kitsuregawa, 2001; Xiao, Zhang, Jia, & Li, 2001; Zhang, Yu, & Hou, 2006). Based on the operation targets and procedures, the major clustering meth-

ods can be categorized as: partitioning methods, hierarchical methods, density-based methods, grid-based methods, model-based methods, high-dimensional clustering and constraint-based clustering (Han & Kamber, 2007).

Latent Semantic Analysis

Different from the conventional information processing algorithms, *Latent Semantic Analysis* (LSA) model is one kind of statistical data analytical models, which is to perform analysis on a so-called latent semantic space rather than on the original data matrix. The latent semantic space is usually a transformed data space derived from the original input space, which can convey semantic information in some senses. *Latent Semantic Indexing* (LSI), one kind of LSA models, was firstly proposed to address finding semantic relevance in the context of information retrieval and digital library. Researchers utilized it to identify the semantic themes hidden in a large amount of document collection. LSI algorithm has achieved great successes in text mining and has been extended to other related applications (Hou & Zhang, 2003a). The standard LSI algorithm is based on SVD operation. The SVD definition of a matrix is illustrated as follows (Datta, 1995): For a real matrix $\mathbf{A}=[a_{ij}]_{m \times n}$, without loss of generality, suppose $m \geq n$ and there exists a SVD of A (shown in Figure 3):

$$\mathbf{A} = \mathbf{U}\begin{pmatrix}\Sigma_1 \\ 0\end{pmatrix}\mathbf{V}^T = \mathbf{U}_{m \times m}\sum\nolimits_{m \times n}\mathbf{V}^T_{n \times n} \qquad (1)$$

where $\mathbf{U}$ and $\mathbf{V}$ are orthogonal matrices $\mathbf{U}^T\mathbf{U}=\mathbf{I}_m$, $\mathbf{V}^T\mathbf{V}=\mathbf{I}_n$. Matrices $\mathbf{U}$ and $\mathbf{V}$ can be respectively denoted as $\mathbf{U}_{m \times m}=[\mathbf{u}_1,\mathbf{u}_2,\ldots,\mathbf{u}_m]_{m \times n}$ and $\mathbf{V}_{n \times m}=[\mathbf{v}_1,\mathbf{v}_2,\ldots,\mathbf{v}_n]_{n \times m}$, where $\mathbf{u}_i$, $(i=1,\ldots,m)$ is a m-dimensional vector $\mathbf{u}_i=(u_{1i},u_{2i},\ldots,u_{mi})^T$ and $\mathbf{v}_j$, $(j=1,\ldots,n)$ is a n-dimensional vector $\mathbf{v}_j=(v_{1j},v_{2j},\ldots,v_{nj})^T$.

The rank of $\mathbf{A}$ indicates the maximal number of independent rows or columns of $\mathbf{A}$. Equation

Figure 3. Illustration of SVD approximation

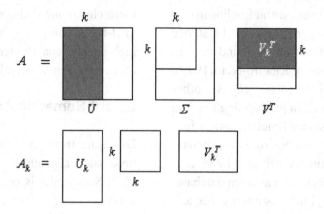

(1) is called the singular value decomposition of matrix A. The singular values of $\mathbf{A}$ are diagonal elements of Σ (i.e. $\sigma_1,\ldots,\sigma_n$). The columns of $\mathbf{U}$ are called left singular vectors and those of $\mathbf{V}$ are called right singular vectors. Since the singular values of $\mathbf{A}$ are in a non-increasing order, it is possible to choose a proper parameter k such that the last r-k singular values are much smaller than the first k singular values and these c singular values dominate the decomposition. The next theorem reveals this fact.

Theorem [Eckart and Young]. Let the SVD of $\mathbf{A}$ be given by equation (1), $rank(\mathbf{A})=r$, and $\mathbf{U}=[\mathbf{u}_1,\mathbf{u}_2,\ldots,\mathbf{u}_m]$, $V=[\mathbf{v}_1,\mathbf{v}_2,\ldots,\mathbf{v}_n]$ with $0<r=rank(\mathbf{A})\leq min(m,n)$, where $\mathbf{u}_i$, $(i=1,\ldots,m)$ is an m-vector, $\mathbf{v}_j$, $(j=1,\ldots,n)$ is an n-vector, and suppose the single values of $\mathbf{A}$ are the diagonal elements of Σ as follows:

$$\Sigma = \begin{bmatrix} \sigma_1 & 0 & \ldots & 0 \\ 0 & \sigma_2 & \ddots & \vdots \\ \vdots & \ddots & \ddots & 0 \\ 0 & \ldots & 0 & \sigma_n \end{bmatrix} = diag\left(\sigma_1,\sigma_2,\ldots\sigma_m\right)$$

where $\sigma_i \geq \sigma_{i+1} > 0$, for $1 \leq i \leq r$-1; $\sigma_j = 0$, for $j \geq r+1$, that is: $\sigma_1 \geq \sigma_2 \geq \ldots \sigma_r \geq \sigma_{r+1} = \ldots = \sigma_n = 0$

Let $k \leq r$ and define $\mathbf{A}_k = \sum_{i=1}^{k} \mathbf{u}_i \cdot \sigma_i \cdot \mathbf{v}_i^T$ then $rank(\mathbf{A})=k$:

$$\min_{rank(\mathbf{B})=k} \| \mathbf{A} - \mathbf{B} \|_F^2 = \| \mathbf{A} - \mathbf{A}_k \|_F^2 = \sigma_{k+1}^2 + \ldots + \sigma_r^2$$

$$\min_{rank(\mathbf{B})=k} \| \mathbf{A} - \mathbf{B} \|_2 = \| \mathbf{A} - \mathbf{A}_k \|_2 = \sigma_{k+1}$$

where: $\| \mathbf{A} \|_F^2 = \sum_{j=1}^{n} \sum_{i=1}^{m} | a_{ij} |^2$

and $\|\mathbf{A}\|_2^2 = max$(eigenvalues of $\mathbf{A}^T\mathbf{A}$) are measurements of matrix $\mathbf{A}$. The proof can be found in (Datta, 1995).

In real implementation of SVD, it works as follows: for a given threshold ε ($0<\varepsilon<1$), choose a parameter k such that $(\sigma_k$-$\sigma_{k+1})/\sigma_k \geq \varepsilon$. Then, denote $\mathbf{U}_k=[\mathbf{u}_1,\mathbf{u}_2,\ldots,\mathbf{u}_k]_{m \times k}$, $\mathbf{V}_k=[\mathbf{v}_1,\mathbf{v}_2,\ldots,\mathbf{v}_k]_{n \times k}$, $\Sigma_k=diag(\sigma_1,\sigma_2,\ldots,\sigma_k)$, and $\mathbf{A}_k=\mathbf{U}_k\Sigma_k\mathbf{V}_k^T$.

Thus, $\mathbf{A}_k$ is the best approximation matrix to $\mathbf{A}$ and conveys the maximum latent information among the processed data. This property makes it possible to find out the underlying semantic association from original feature space with a dimensionality-reduced computational cost, in turn, is able to be used for latent semantic analysis.

While SVD algorithm is usually used in the conventional latent semantic indexing techniques, some variants of the LSA have been proposed recently in the context of Web information processing and text mining. Apart from the difference at theoretical formulation, the common characteristics of these methods are to map the original feature space into a new transformed feature space, and maintain the maximum approximation of the original feature space. For example, PLSA and LDA model are two representative of such kinds of approaches (Blei, Ng, & Jordan, 2003; Hofmann, 2004). In particular, we propose a Web usage mining approach based on PLSA in the following section.

Web Recommendation Algorithms

As discussed in the introduction part, the ultimate aim of Web usage mining is to discover the usage knowledge, identify the navigational access pattern of the current active user, and recommend a list of pages that user might be interested in, via referring to the visiting preference of other like-minded users. To perform recommendation efficiently and effectively, there are a variety of data mining and machine learning algorithms that have been well studied and developed, and can be used in Web recommendation. In this section, we simply review several related algorithms that are often used in the recommendation process.

k-Nearest Neighbor Algorithm

K-Nearest-Neighbor (*kNN*) approach is the most often used recommendation scoring algorithm in many recommender systems, which is to compare the current user activity with the historic records of other users for finding the top *k* users who share the most similar behaviors to the current one. In conventional recommender systems, finding *k* nearest neighbors is usually accomplished by measuring the similarity in rating of items or visiting on Web pages between current user and others. The found neighboring users are then used to produce a prediction of items that are potentially rated or

visited but not done yet by the current active user via collaborative filtering approaches. Therefore, the core component of the *kNN* algorithm is the similarity function that is used to measure the similarity or correlation between users in terms of attribute vectors, on which each user activity is characterized as a sequence of attributes associated with corresponding weights.

A variety of similarity functions can be used as measuring metrics. Among these measures, cosine similarity is one of the well-known and widely used similarity functions in recommender systems (Sarwar, Karypis, Konstan, & Riedl, 2001).

The cosine coefficient can be calculated by the ratio of the dot product of two vectors with respect to their vector norms. Given two vectors **A** and **B**, the Cosine coefficient is defined as:

$$sim(\mathbf{A}, \mathbf{B}) = \cos(\mathbf{A}, \mathbf{B}) = \frac{\mathbf{A} \cdot \mathbf{B}}{|\mathbf{A}| \times |\mathbf{B}|} \qquad (2)$$

where "·" denotes the dot operation and "×" denotes the norm form.

Content-Based Recommendation

Content-based recommendation is a textual information filtering approach based on user's historic ratings on items. In a content-based recommendation, a user is associated with the attributes of the items that rated, and a user profile is learned from the attributes of the items to model the interest of the user. The recommendation score is computed by measuring the similarity of the attributes the user rated with those of not being rated, to determine which attributes might be potentially rated by the same user. As a result of attribute similarity comparison, this method is actually a conventional information processing approach in the case of recommendation. The learned user profile reflects the long-time preference of a user within a period, and could be updated as more different rated attributes representing user's interest. Content-based recommendation is helpful for predicting individual's preference since it is on a basis of referring the individual's historic rating data rather than taking other's preference into consideration.

Collaborative Filtering Recommendation

Collaborative filtering recommendation is probably the most commonly and widely used technique that has been well developed for recommender systems. As the name indicated, collaborative recommender systems work in a collaborative referring way that is to gather ratings or preferences on items, discover user profiles/patterns via learning from users' historic rating records, and generate new recommendations on a basis of inter-pattern comparison. A typical user profile in recommender systems is expressed as a vector of the ratings on different items. The rating values could be either binary (like/dislike) or analogous-valued indicating the degree of preference, which is dependent on the application scenarios. In the context of collaborative filtering recommendation, there are two major kinds of collaborative filtering algorithms mentioned in literature, namely memory-based and model-based collaborative filtering algorithm (Herlocker, Konstan, Terveen, & Riedl, 2004b; O'Conner & Herlocker, 1999; Sarwar, et al., 2001).

Memory-based algorithms use the total ratings of users in the training database while computing recommendations. These systems can also be classified into two sub-categories: user-based and item-based algorithms (Sarwar, et al., 2001). A model-based collaborative filtering algorithm is to derive a model from the historic rating data, and in turn, uses it for making recommendations. To derive the hidden model, a variety of statistical machine learning algorithms can be employed on the training database, such as Bayesian networks, neural networks, clustering and latent semantic

analysis and so on. For example, in a model-based recommender system, a clustering algorithm named Profile Aggregations based on Clustering Transaction (PACT) (Mobasher, et al., 2002), was employed to generate aggregations of user sessions, which are viewed as profiles via grouping users with similar access taste into various clusters. The centroids[1] of the user session clusters can be considered as access patterns/models learned from the Web usage data, in turn, used to make recommendations via referring to the Web objects visited by other users who share the most similar access task to the current target user.

Although the existence of different recommendation algorithms in recommender systems, however, it is easily found that these algorithms are both executing in a collaborative manner, and the recommendation score is dependent on the significant weight of engaged objects. In the following parts, we adopt these findings into our work.

MODELING USER COMMUNITIES OF INTERESTS BASED ON LATENT SEMANTIC INDEXING

Web clustering is one of the mostly used techniques in the context of Web mining, which is to aggregate similar Web objects, such as Web page or user session, into a number of object groups via measuring their mutual vector distance. Basically, clustering can be performed upon these two types of Web objects, which results in clustering Web users or Web pages, respectively. The resulting Web user session groups are considered as user communities of interests represented by user navigational behavior patterns, while Web page clusters are used for generating task-oriented functionality aggregations of Web organization. Moreover, the mined usage knowledge in terms of Web usage pattern and page aggregate property can be utilized to improve Web site structure design or Internet service quality provided.

There has been a considerable amount of work on the applications of Web usage mining and recommender systems. For example, Mobasher, et al. (2002) proposed an aggregate usage profile technique to cluster Web user transactions into various usage groups by using standard clustering algorithms, such as *k*-means clustering algorithm. On the other hand, an algorithm called PageGather was proposed by Perkowith & Etzioni (1999) to discover significant page segments, which were used to help Web designer to add an additional index page not existed before to facilitate Web users locate their interested content quickly, by using the Clique (complete link) clustering algorithm.

In the context of clustering, the computational cost is a major concerned issue suffering researchers due to the particular characteristics of Web data, e.g. the problems of high-dimension and sparsity nature of Web data. For example, it is difficult, sometimes, to simply apply a standard clustering algorithm on the Web usage data with millions of user sessions to derive a collection of Web pages, which is resulting in a tough computational task. The reason is that instead of using pages as dimensions, the user sessions must be treated as dimensions and clustering is performed on this very high-dimensional space. To address there issues, dimensionality reduction techniques and alternative clustering algorithms are explored. Amongst these, *Latent Semantic Analysis* (LSA) is considered as an efficient dimensionality reduction algorithm with latent semantic analysis capability, that is, the capability of discovering the hidden knowledge from Web data by taking the semantic property of data into consideration.

Latent Semantic Indexing (LSI), one kind of traditional LSA algorithms, is a statistical method, which is to reconstruct the co-occurrence observation space into a dimension-reduced latent space that keeps the maximum approximation of the original space by using mathematical transformation procedures such as *Single Value Decomposition* (SVD). With the reduced dimensionality of the transformed data expression, the computational cost is significantly decreased accordingly, and the problem of sparsity of data is also well handled. Besides, LSI based techniques are capable of capturing the semantic knowledge from the observation data, while the conventional statistical analysis approaches such as clustering or classification lack in finding underlying association among the observed co-occurrence. In the past decades, LSI is extensively adopted in the applications of information retrieval, image processing, Web research and data mining, and a great deal of successes have been achieved. In this section, we aim to integrate LSI analysis with Web clustering process, to discover Web user communities of interests with better clustering quality, in other words, this techniques is on the basis of the combination of latent semantic analysis with Web usage mining.

Representations of User Sessions in a Latent Semantic Space

As we discussed in Foundation of Web Usage Mining and Latent Semantic Analysis, we can employ a SVD operation to conduct latent semantic analysis on Web usage data. Given a real usage matrix $\mathbf{A} = [a_{ij}]_{m \times n}$, the implementation of SVD results in $\mathbf{A}_k = \mathbf{U}_k \Sigma_k \mathbf{V}_k^{\mathrm{T}}$, where $\mathbf{A}_k$ is the best approximation matrix to $\mathbf{A}$ and conveys the maximum latent information among the processed data, and $\mathbf{U}_k$ and $\mathbf{V}_k$ are the principal components of row and column vectors. Once SVD implementation is completed, we may rewrite user sessions with the obtained approximation matrix $\mathbf{U}_k$, Σ_k and $\mathbf{V}_k$ by mapping them into another *k*-dimensional latent semantic space. For a given session s_i, it is represented as a coordinate vector with respect to pages, $\mathbf{s}_i = \{a_{i1}, a_{i2}, \ldots, a_{im}\}$. The projection of coordinate vector $\mathbf{s}_i$ in the *k*-dimensional latent semantic subspace is re-parameterized as:

$$\mathbf{s}_i' = \mathbf{s}_i \mathbf{V}_k \sum\nolimits_k = (t_{i1}, t_{i2}, \ldots, t_{ik}) \qquad (3)$$

where $t_{ij} = \sum_{k=1}^{n} a_{ik} v_{kj} \sigma_j, j = 1, 2, \ldots, k$.

Thus, to a given session s_i (represented by a vector $\mathbf{s}_i$) correspond in the k-dimensional latent semantic subspace a session s'_i (represented by vector $\mathbf{s}'_i$).

For the similarity measure, we adopt the traditional cosine function to capture the common interests shared by user sessions, i.e. for two vectors $\mathbf{x}=(x_1,x_2,\ldots,x_k)$ and $\mathbf{y}=(y_1,y_2,\ldots,y_k)$ in a k-dimensional space, the similarity between them is defined as:

$$sim(\mathbf{x}, \mathbf{y}) = \left(\mathbf{x} \cdot \mathbf{y}\right) \Big/ \left(\|\mathbf{x}\|_2 \|\mathbf{y}\|_2\right)$$

where $\mathbf{x} \cdot \mathbf{y} = \sum_{i=1}^{k} x_i y_i$, $\|\mathbf{x}\|_2 = \sqrt{\sum_{i=1}^{k} x_i^2}$.

In this manner, the similarity between two transformed user sessions is defined as the cosine between their vectors:

$$sim(\mathbf{s}'_i, \mathbf{s}'_j) = \left(\mathbf{s}'_i \cdot \mathbf{s}'_j\right) \Big/ \|\mathbf{s}'_i\|_2 \|\mathbf{s}'_j\|_2$$

Algorithms for Building User Communities of Interests

In this section, we present an algorithm called *Latent Usage Information* (LUI) (Xu, Zhang, & Zhou, 2005) for clustering Web sessions and generating user communities in the forms of user profiles based on the discovered clusters. This algorithm consists of two steps, the first step is a clustering algorithm, which is to cluster the converted latent usage data into a number of session groups; and the next step is about generating a set of user profiles, which are derived from calculating the centroids of the discovered session clusters.

Clustering User Sessions by LUI

Here we adopt a variant of k-means clustering algorithm, named MK-means clustering, to partition user sessions based on the transformed usage data matrix over the latent k-dimensional space. This algorithm does not need to predefine parameter k and k initial centroids, whereas the standard k-means has to do so to start clustering. The algorithm is described as follows.

Algorithm 1. *MK*-means clustering

Input: A converted usage matrix **SP** and a similarity threshold ε.

Output: A set of user session clusters $SCL=\{SCL_i\}$ and corresponding centroids $Cid=\{Cid_i\}$ (represented by the vectors $\{\mathbf{Cid}_i\}$).

1. Choose the first user session s_i' as the initial cluster SCL_1 and the centroid of this cluster, i.e. $SCL_1=\{s_i'\}$ and $Cid_1=s_i'$.

2. For each session s_i', calculate the similarity between s_i' and the centroids of other existing cluster $sim(s_i',Cid_j)$.

3. If $sim(s_i',Cid_k)=max_j(sim(s_i',Cid_j))>\varepsilon$, then allocate s_i' into SCL_k and recalculate the centroid of cluster SCL_k. Otherwise, let it construct a new cluster and be the centroid of this cluster.

4. Repeat step 2 to 4 until all user sessions are processed and all centroids do not update any more.

Building User Profiles

As we mentioned above, each user session is represented as a weight-based page vector. In this way, it is reasonable to derive the centroid of the cluster obtained by the described clustering algorithm as a user profile. In this work, we compute the mean vector to represent the centroid. For each session cluster $SCL_i \in SCL$, the mean page vector of all sessions in the cluster (i.e. centroid), is determined by the ratio of the sum of page weights in SCL_i to the number of sessions in the cluster. In order to eliminate the impact of difference in visiting time or click number of each session, the weights are normalized while calculating the centroid of cluster. That is, the maximum weight in the constructed user profile is tuned to be 1, whereas other page weights are divided by the maximum weigh accordingly. Meanwhile, some less-contributed pages (i.e. those with mean weights being less than one certain limit) are filtered out. The algorithm for constructing user profile is as follows.

Algorithm 2. Building user profiles based on LSI

Input: A set of user session cluster $SCL=\{SCL_k\}$.

Output: A set of user profile $UP=\{up_k\}$ represented by the vectors $\{\mathbf{up}_k\}$.

1. For each page p in the cluster SCL_k, we compute the mean weight value of page:

$$wt(p, SCL_k) = 1/|SCL_k| \sum_{s \in SCL_k} w(p,s) \qquad (5)$$

where $w(p,s)$ is the weight of page p in the session $s \in SCL_k$, and $|SCL_k|$ denotes the session number in the cluster SCL_k.

2. For each cluster, furthermore, we calculate its mean vector (i.e. centroid) as:

$$\mathbf{mv}_C = \{< p, wt(p, SCL_k) > \big| p \in P\} \qquad (6)$$

3. For each page within the cluster, if the value is less than the threshold μ, the corresponding page will be filtered out, otherwise keep it left.

4. Sort the pages with their weights in a descending order and output the mean vector as the user profile:

$$up_k = \{< p_{1k}, wt(p_{1k}, SCL_k) >,$$
$$< p_{2k}, wt(p_{2k}, SCL_k) > ..., < p_{tk}, wt(p_{tk}, SCL_k)\} \qquad (7)$$

where $wt(p_{1k}, SCL_k) > wt(p_{2k}, SCL_k) > ... > wt(p_{tk}, SCL_k) > \mu$.

5. Repeat step 1 to 4 until all session clusters are processed, output the user profiles.

Experiments and Discussions

In order to evaluate the effectiveness of the proposed LUI algorithm, which consists of the Web clustering algorithm and user profile generating algorithm, and evaluate the discovered user access patterns, we conduct experiments on two real world data sets and make comparisons with the previous work.

Experimental Design and Data Sets

We take one Web log file, which is public to access from KDDCUP[2] for the purpose of research, as the usage data for experiments. The data set is a commonly-used data source provided to test and compare knowledge discovery methods (prediction algorithm, clustering approaches, etc.) for the data mining purpose. Data pre-processing is needed to perform on the raw data set since there are some short user sessions existing in the data set, which means they are of less contribution for data mining. Support filtering technique is used to eliminate these user sessions, leaving only sessions with at least four pages. After data preparation, we have setup a data set including 9308 user sessions and 69 pages, where every session consists of 11.88 pages in average. We refer this data set as "KDDCUP data". In this data set, the entries in session-page matrix associated with the specific page in the given session are determined by the numbers of Web page hits by a given user.

The whole experiment design is structured as follows. We use the constructed usage data in the form of matrix as input data source, and apply appropriate data mining or analysis algorithms on it to extract usage knowledge and latent semantic relationship, which is formed as an informative

Table 1. Two examples of the generated user profiles from KDD dataset

Page #	Page content	weight
29	Main-shopping_cart	1.00
4	Products-productDetailleagwear	0.86
27	Main-Login2	0.67
8	Main-home	0.53
44	Check-express_Checkout	0.38
65	Main-welcome	0.33
32	Main-registration	0.32
45	Checkout-confirm_order	0.26
Page #	Page content	weight
11	Main-vendor2	1.00
8	Main-home	0.40
12	Articles-dpt_about	0.34
13	Articles-dpt_about_mgmtteam	0.15
14	Articles-dpt_about_broadofdirectors	0.11

knowledge base. To assess the employed algorithms and data analytical models, we introduce some evaluation metrics and carry out comparisons with other related studies. The experimental results are presented in the following parts.

Results of User Profiles

We first utilize the LUI algorithm to conduct Web usage mining on the selected two usage datasets respectively. We tabulate some results in below (Table 1). In the table, each user profile is represented by a sequence of significant pages together with corresponding weights. As we indicate before, the calculated weight is expressed in a normalized form, that is, the biggest value of them is set to be 1 while others are the relatively proportional values, which are always less than 1.

(Table 1) depicts 2 user profiles generated from KDD dataset using LUI approach. Each user profile is listed in an ordered page sequence with corresponding weights, which means the greater weight a pageview contributes, the more likely it is to be visited. The first profile in (Table 1) represents the activities involved in on-line

shopping behavior, such as login, shopping cart, and checkout operation, etc., especially occurred in purchasing leg-wear products, whereas the second user profile reflects customers' concern focused on the interests with regard to department store itself. Looking at the generated user profile examples, it is shown that most of them do reflect one specific navigational intention, but some may represent more than one access themes.

Quality Evaluation of User Session Clusters

When the user session clustering is accomplished, we obtain a number of session clusters. However, how to assess the quality of the obtained clusters is another big concern for us in Web usage mining. A better clustering result should be that the sessions within same cluster aggregate closely enough but keeping far from other clusters enough. After completing user session clustering, the next goal is to evaluate the quality of the generated clusters.

In order to evaluate the quality of clusters derived from LUI approach, we adopt one specific metric, named the *Weighted Average Visit*

Percentage (WAVP) (Mobasher, et al., 2002). This evaluation method is based on assessing each user profile individually according to the likelihood that a user session which contains any pages in the session cluster will include the rest pages in the cluster during the same session. The calculating procedure of WAVP metric is discussed as follows: suppose T is one of the transaction sets within the evaluation set, and for a specific cluster C (represented by a vector $\mathbf{C}$), let Tc denote a subset of T whose elements contain at least one pageview from C. Moreover, the weighted average visit percentage of Tc may conceptually be determined by the similarity between Tc and the cluster C if we consider the Tc and C as in the form of pageview vector. Therefore, the WAVP is computed as:

$$WAVP = \frac{\sum_{t \in T_c} \frac{\mathbf{t} \cdot \mathbf{C}}{|T_c|}}{\sum_{p \in Pf} wt(p, pf)} \qquad (8)$$

From the definition of WAVP, it is known that the higher WAVP value is, the better quality of obtained session cluster possesses.

To compare the effectiveness and efficiency of the proposed algorithm with existing algorithms, here we use a page clustering algorithm, named Page Aggregate Clustering Technique (PACT) (Mobasher, et al., 2002). We conduct data simulations upon two real world datasets by using these two approaches. (Figure 4) depicts the comparison results in terms of WAVP values for KDD datasets with PACT respectively. In the figure, the obtained user profiles are arrayed in the descending rank according to their WAVP values, which reflect the quality of various clustering algorithms. From these two curves, it is easily concluded that the proposed LUI-based technique overweighs the standard k-means based algorithm in term of WAVP parameter. This is mainly due to the distinct latent analysis capability of LUI algorithm. In

other words, LUI approach is capable of capturing the latent relationships among Web transaction and discovering user profiles representing the actual navigational patterns more effectively and accurately.

MODELING USER COMMUNITIES OF INTERESTS USING PROBABILISTIC LATENT SEMANTIC ANALYSIS MODEL

In this section we aim to introduce *Probabilistic Latent Semantic Analysis* (PLSA) model into Web usage mining, to generate Web user groups and Web page clusters based on latent usage analysis (Xu, Zhang, & Zhou, 2005). The reminder of this section is structured as follows: we first introduce the theoretical background of PLSA model in Probabilistic Latent Semantic Analysis Model, then propose the algorithms for discovering the user access patterns and the latent factor space based on PLSA model in Constructing User Communities of Interests and Identifying Latent Factors with PLSA Model, experiments and analysis are carried out to demonstrate the effectiveness of the proposed approaches in terms of the derived usage knowledge as well as the latent task space in Experiments and Results.

Probabilistic Latent Semantic Analysis Model

The PLSA model has been firstly presented and successfully applied in text mining by (Hofmann, 1999). In contrast to the standard LSI algorithms, which utilize the Frobenius norm as an optimization criterion, PLSA model is based on a maximum likelihood principle, which is derived from the uncertainty theory in statistics.

Basically, PLSA model is based on a statistic model called aspect model, which can be utilized to identify the hidden semantic relationships among general co-occurrence activities. Theoretically,

Figure 4. User cluster quality analysis results in terms of WAVP for KDD dataset.

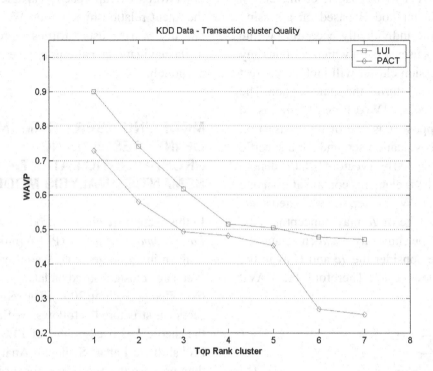

we can conceptually view the user sessions over Web pages space as co-occurrence activities in the context of Web usage mining, to infer the latent usage pattern. Given the aspect model over user access pattern in the context of Web usage mining, it is first assumed that there is a latent factor space $Z=\{z_1,z_2,...,z_k\}$, and each co-occurrence observation data (s_i,p_j) (i.e. the visit of page p_j in user session s_i) is associated with the factor $z_k \in Z$ by a varying degree to z_k. According to the viewpoint of the aspect model, it can be inferred that there do exist different relationships among Web users or pages corresponding to different factors. Furthermore, the different factors can be considered to represent the corresponding user access pattern. For example, during a Web usage mining process on an e-commerce Web site, we can define that there exist k latent factors associated with k kinds of navigational behavior patterns, such as z_1 factor standing for having interests in sports-specific product category, z_2 for sale prod-

uct interest, z_3 for browsing through a variety of product pages in different categories, etc. In this manner, each co-occurrence observation data z_k may convey user navigational interest by mapping the observation data into the k-dimensional latent factor space. The degree, to which such relationships are "explained" by each factors, is derived by a conditional probability distribution associated with the Web usage data. Thus, the goal of employing PLSA model, therefore, is to determine the conditional probability distribution, in turn, to reveal the intrinsic relationships among Web users or pages based on a probability inference approach. In one word, the goal of PLSA model is to model and infer user navigational behavior in a latent semantic space, and identify the latent factor associated. Before we propose a PLSA based algorithm for Web usage mining, it is necessary to introduce the mathematical background of PLSA model, and the algorithm which is used to estimate the conditional probability distribution.

Firstly, let's introduce the following probability definitions:

- $P(s_i)$ denotes the probability that a particular user session s_i will be observed in the occurrences data,
- $P(z_k|s_i)$ denotes a user session-specific probability distribution on the latent class factor z_k,
- $P(p_j|z_k)$ denotes the class-conditional probability distribution of pages over a specific latent variable z_k.

Based on these definitions, the probabilistic latent semantic model can be expressed in following way:

- select a user session s_i with probability $P(s_i)$,
- pick a hidden factor z_k with probability $P(z_k|s_i)$,
- generate a page p_j with probability $P(p_j|z_k)$.

As a result, we can obtain an occurrence probability of an observed pair z_k by adopting the latent factor variable z_k. Translating this process into a probability model results in the expression:

$$P(s_i, p_j) = P(s_i) \cdot P(p_j \mid s_i) \qquad (9)$$

where: $P(p_j \mid s_i) = \sum_{z \in Z} P(p_j \mid z) \cdot P(z \mid s_i)$

$$(10)$$

By applying Bayesian rule, a re-parameterized version will be transformed based on equations (9) and (10) as:

$$P(s_i, p_j) = \sum_{z \in Z} P(z) \cdot P(s_i \mid z) \cdot P(p_j \mid z) \qquad (11)$$

Following the likelihood principle, we can determine the total likelihood Li of the observation as:

$$Li = \sum_{s_i \in S, p_j \in P} m(s_i, p_j) \cdot \log P(s_i, p_j) \qquad (12)$$

where $m(s_i, p_j)$ corresponds to the entry of the session-page matrix associated with session s_i and pageview p_j, which is discussed in the Web usage data model in Foundation of Web Usage Mining and Latent Semantic Analysis.

In order to maximize the total likelihood, we need to repeatedly generate the conditional probabilities of $P(z)$, $P(s_i|z)$ and $P(p_j|z)$ by utilizing the usage observation data. Known from statistics, *Expectation Maximization* (EM) algorithm is an efficient procedure to perform maximum likelihood estimation in latent variable model (Dempster, Laird, & Rubin, 1977). Generally, two steps are needed to implement the procedure and alternately executed: (1) Expectation (E) step where posterior probabilities are calculated for the latent factors based on the current estimates of conditional probability, and (2) Maximization (M) step, where the estimated conditional probabilities are updated and used to maximize the likelihood based on the posterior probabilities computed in the previous E step.

We now discuss the whole procedure in details as follows:

1. Let us define the randomized initial values of $P(z)$, $P(s_i|z)$ and $P(p_j|z)$.
2. In the E-step, we can simply apply Bayesian formula to generate the following variable based on the usage observation:

$$P(z_k \mid s_i, p_j) = \frac{P(z_k) \cdot P(s_i \mid z_k) \cdot P(p_j \mid z_k)}{\sum_{z_k \in Z} P(z_k) \cdot P(s_i \mid z_k) \cdot P(p_j \mid z_k)}$$

$$(13)$$

3. Furthermore, in M-step, we can compute:

$$P(p_j \mid z_k) = \frac{\sum_{s_i \in S} m(s_i, p_j) \cdot P(z_k \mid s_i, p_j)}{\sum_{s_i \in S, p_j' \in P} m(s_i, p_j') \cdot P(z_k \mid s_i, p_j')}$$

$$(14)$$

$$P(s_i \mid z_k) = \frac{\sum_{p_{j \in P}} m(s_i, p_j) \cdot P(z_k \mid s_i, p_j)}{\sum_{s_i' \in S, p_j \in P} m(s_i', p_j) \cdot P(z_k \mid s_i', p_j)}$$

$$(15)$$

$$P(z_k) = \frac{1}{R} \sum_{s_i \in S, p_j \in P} m(s_i, p_j) \cdot P(z_k \mid s_i, p_j)$$

$$(16)$$

$$\text{where: } R = \sum_{s_i \in S, p_j \in P} m(s_i, p_j) \qquad (17)$$

Basically, substituting equations (14)-(16) into (11) and (12) will result in the monotonically increasing of total likelihood L_i of the observation data. The iterative implementation of the E-step and M-step is repeating until L_i is converging to a local optimal limit, which means the calculated results can represent the optimal probability estimates of the usage observation data. From the previous formulation, it is easily found that the computational complexity of PLSA model is $O(mnk)$, where m, n and k denote the number of user sessions, Web pages and latent factors, respectively.

By now, we have obtained the conditional probability distribution of $P(z)$, $P(s_i|z)$ and $P(p_j|z)$ by performing the E and M step iteratively. The estimated probability distribution which is corresponding to the local maximum likelihood Li contains the useful information for inferring semantic usage factors, performing Web user sessions clustering and generating the aggregated user profiles which are described in next sections.

Constructing User Communities of Interests and Identifying Latent Factors with PLSA Model

As discussed in Probabilistic Latent Semantic Analysis Model, note that each latent factor z_k do really represent a specific aspect associated with the usage co-occurrence activities in nature. In other words, for each factor, there might be a task-oriented user access pattern corresponding to it. We, thus, can utilize the class-conditional probability estimates generated by PLSA model to produce the aggregated user profiles for characterizing user communities of interests. Conceptually, each aggregated user profile will be expressed as a collection of pages, which are accompanied by their corresponding weights indicating the contributions to such user group by those pages. Furthermore, analyzing the generated user profile can lead to revealing the common user access interests, such as dominant or secondary "theme" by sorting the page weights.

Algorithm for Partitioning User Sessions and Building User Profiles

Firstly, we begin with the probabilistic variable $P(s_i|z_k)$, which represents the occurrence probability in the condition of a latent class factor z_k exhibited by a given user session s_i. On the other hand, the probabilistic distribution over the factor space of a specific user session s_i can reflect the specific user access preference over the whole latent factor space, and may be utilized to uncover the dominant factors by distinguishing the top probability values. Therefore, for each user session s_i, we can further compute a set of probabilities $P(z_k|s_i)$ over the latent factor space via Bayesian formula as follows:

$$P(z_k \mid s_i) = \frac{P(s_i \mid z_k) \cdot P(z_k)}{\sum_{z_k \in Z} P(s_i \mid z_k) \cdot P(z_k)} \qquad (18)$$

Actually, the set of probabilities $P(z_k|s_i)$ is tending to be "sparse", that is, for a given s_i, typically only few entries are significant different from the predefined threshold, which is determined by different experiment setting. For example, the threshold of CTI dataset is set to be 0.01. Hence we can classify the user session into the corresponding cluster based on these probabilities greater than the given threshold. Since each user session can be expressed as a pages vector in the original n-dimensional space, we can create a mixture representation of the collection of user sessions within the same cluster that associated with the factor z_k in terms of a collection of weighted pages. The algorithm for partitioning user sessions is described as following.

Algorithm 3. Partitioning user sessions

Input: A set of calculated probability values of $P(z_k|s_i)$, a user session-page matrix $\mathbf{SP}_{ij}$, and a predefined threshold μ.

Output: A set of session clusters $SCL=(SCL_1, SCL_2, \ldots, SCL_k)$.

1. Set $SCL_1=SCL_2=\ldots=SCL_k=\mu$.
2. For each $s_i \in S$, select $P(z_k|s_i)$, if $P(z_k|s_i) \geq \mu$, then $SCL_k=SCL_k \cup s_i$.
3. If there are still users sessions to be clustered, go back to step 2.
4. Output session clusters $SCL=\{SCL_k\}$.

Algorithm 4. Generating user profiles

Input: A session cluster set $SCL=\{SCL_k\}$.
Output: A set of user profiles $UP=\{UP_k\}$ represented by the vectors $\{\mathbf{UP}_k\}$.

1. For each factor z_k, choose all candidate sessions in SCL_k.
2. Represent each session s_i as a page vector and compute their *centroids* in the form of page vector as:

$$UP_k = \frac{\sum_i \mathbf{s}_i \cdot P(z_k \mid s_i)}{|R|} \qquad (19)$$

where $|R|$ denotes the total number of sessions in the cluster,

3. If there are still user session clusters not to be processed, go back to step 1.
4. Output the centroid of session cluster in the form of page vector as the aggregated user profile corresponding to each factor z_k.

By now, we assign user sessions into the corresponding clusters which can be considered to represent user navigational patterns based on the calculated conditional probability distributions from PLSA model and characterize the representations of the user profiles in terms of weighted page vector as well. As discussed above, it can be seen that a particular user session does not only belong to just one cluster, but also to other different clusters associated with different latent factors. For example, a user session may exhibit different interests (with different probabilities) on two aspects z_1 and z_2. This can be "explained" as that a user may, indeed, perform different tasks during the same session and really reflect the nature of user access pattern in real world. It can be implied, in turn, PLSA model partitions user session-page pairs, which is different from clustering either user sessions or pages or both. In other words, the user session-page probabilities in PLSA model reflect "overlay" of latent factors, while the conventional clustering model assumes there is just one cluster-specific distribution contributed by all user sessions in the cluster (Hofmann, 1999).

Characterizing Latent Semantic Factors

As mentioned in the previous section, the core of PLSA model is the latent factor space. From this point of view, how to characterize the factor space or explain the semantic meaning of factors is a crucial issue in PLSA model. Similarly, we can also utilize another obtained conditional probability distribution $P(p_j|z_k)$ by PLSA model to identify the semantic meaning of the latent factors by partitioning Web pages into corresponding categories associated with the latent factors.

For each hidden factor z_k, we may consider that those pages, whose conditional probabilities $P(p_j|z_k)$ are greater than a predefined threshold determined by the empirical approach described above, can be viewed to provide similar functional components corresponding to the latent factor. In this way, we can select all pages with probabilities exceeding the certain threshold to form an aspect-specific page group. By analyzing the URLs of the pages and their weights derived from the conditional probabilities, which are associated with the specific factor, we may characterize and interpret the semantic meaning of each factor. In Experiments and Results, we will present two examples with respect to the discovered latent factors. The algorithm to generating the latent semantic factor space is briefly described as follows:

Algorithm 5. Characterizing latent semantic factors

Input: A set of conditional probabilities, $P(p_j|z_k)$, a predefined threshold μ.
Output: A set of latent semantic factors represented by several dominant pages.
1. Set $PCL_1=PCL_2=\ldots=PCL_k)=\phi$.
2. For each z_k, choose all Web pages such that $P(p_j|z_k)\geq\mu$ and $P(z_k|p_j)\geq\mu$, then construct $PCL_k=p_j\cup PCL_k$.
3. If there are still pages to be classified, go back to step 2.
4. Output $PCL=\{PCL_k\}$.

Experiments and Results

In this section, we present some results regarding user profiles and latent semantic factor obtained by conducting experiments on two selected Web log datasets. We first give the latent semantic factor knowledge mined from two datasets, which is titled by the interpretation of the dominant pages. Some examples of user profiles via partitioning the user sessions and calculating the centroids of the session clusters are presented as well.

Data Sets

The first dataset named KDDCUP for experiments has been described in the previous section. Here, we would not repeat the descriptions, but only outline the brief information regarding the dataset size and attribute number. Data filtering technique is used to filter out these user sessions, leaving only sessions with at least 4 pages. After data preparation, it includes 9308 user sessions and 69 pageviews, where the average session length is 11.88 pages. In this data set, the entries in session-page matrix are determined by the numbers of Web page hits since the numbers of a user coming back to a specific page is a good measure to reflect the user interest on the page.

The second data set is downloaded from msnbc.com[3], which describes the page visits by users who visited msnbc.com on September 28, 1999. Visits are recorded at the level of URL category and in time order. There are 989818 user sessions with 5.7 visits of pages in average for per user in the original data set. After filtering out the user sessions with low visit frequencies, we have constructed the data set for further analysis, which includes 373229 user sessions and 17 URL categories as well. The 17 categories are "frontpage", "news", "tech", "local", "opinion", "on-air", "misc", "weather", "health", "living", "business", "sports", "summary", "bbs" (bulletin board service), "travel", "msn-news", and "msn-sports". In addition, the visit frequency for each user is taken to calculate the weight of the corresponding usage data. We name this data set as "msnbc" dataset.

By considering the number of Web pages and the content of the Web site carefully and referring to the selection criteria of factors in (Hofmann,

2001; Jin, Zhou, & Mobasher, 2004), we choose *k*=13 (i.e. 13 factors) for KDDCUP dataset and *k*=6 for msnbs dataset as the initial parameters used in PLSA implementation.

Examples of Latent Semantic Factors

We conduct the experiments on the datasets to extract the latent factors and generate the user profiles. Firstly, we present the examples of the latent factors derived from two real data sets by using the proposed PLSA model.

(Table 2) first lists 13 extracted latent factors and their corresponding characteristic descriptions from KDDCUP dataset. And (Table 3) depicts 3 factor examples selected from whole factor space in terms of associated page information including page number, probability and description. From this table, it is seen that factor #3 indicates the concerns about vendor service message such as customer service, contact number, payment methods as well as delivery support. The factor #7 describes the specific progress which may include customer login, product order, express checkout and financial information input such steps occurred in Internet shopping scenario, whereas factors #13 actually captures another focus exhibited by Web content, which reveals the fact that some Web users may pay more attentions to the information regarding department itself.

As for msnbc dataset, it is hard to extract the exact latent factor space as the page information provided is described at a coarser granularity level, i.e. URL category level. Hence we only list two examples of discovered latent factors to illustrate the general usage knowledge hidden in the usage data (shown in Table 4). The two extracted factors indicate that factor #1 is associated with all kinds of local information that come from miscellaneous information channel such as bbs, while factor #2 reflects the interests or opinions which are often linked with health, sport as well as technical development in physical exercise.

Examples of User Profiles

Furthermore, we can generate user profiles according to the session-specified conditional probabilities $P(z_k|s_j)$ which represent the common visit interests/ access patterns of users within the session group. Generally, the aggregated user access profile is expressed as a collection of Web pages ranked by their associated weights, which can reflect the contribution to the specific profile by the corresponding pages. (Table 5) presents two examples of the generated user profiles. For each profile, the pages are listed in a page sequence ordered by their associated significances in terms of probabilistic values. It may be inferred that the greater weight a page possesses, the more significance contributed by the page exhibits. In other words, it is more likely to be visited by users compared to other pages in the user session group. For example, in (Table 5), the user profile #7 represents the detailed on-line shopping activities, especially occurring in purchasing leg-wear products or fashion clothes, whereas user profile #13 reflects one kind of customers' concern focused on the information with regard to the

Table 2. The Latent factors and their characteristic descriptions from KDDCUP

Factor #	Characteristic title
1	Department_search_results
2	ProductDetailLegwear
3	Vendor_ service
4	Freegift
5	ProductDetailLegcare
6	Shopping_cart
7	Online_shopping
8	Lifestyle_assortment
9	Assortment2
10	Boutique
11	Departmet_replenishment
12	Department_article
13	Home page

Table 3. Two factor examples and their associated page information from KDDCUP

Factor #	Page #	$P(p_j|z_k)$	Page description
#3	10	0.865	main/vendor\.jhtml
	36	0.035	main/cust_serv\.jhtml
	37	0.021	articles/dpt_contact\.jhtml
	39	0.020	articles/dpt_shipping\.jhtml
	38	0.016	articles/dpt_payment\.jhtml
	41	0.016	articles/dpt_faqs\.jhtml
	40	0.013	articles/dpt_returns\.jhtml
#7	27	0.249	main/login2\.jhtml
	44	0.18	checkout/expresCheckout.jhmt
	32	0.141	main/registration\.jhtml
	65	0.135	main/welcome\.jhtml
	45	0.135	checkout/confirm_order\.jhtml
	42	0.045	account/your_account\.jhtml
	60	0.040	checkout/thankyou\.jhtml
#13	12	0.232	articles/dpt_about\.jhtml
	22	0.127	articles/new_shipping\.jhtml
	13	0.087	articles/dpt_about_mgmtteam
	14	0.058	articles\dpt_about_boardofdirectors
	20	0.058	articles/dpt_affiliate\.jhtml
	16	0.053	articles/dpt_about_careers
	19	0.052	articles/dpt_refer\.jhtml
	23	0.051	articles/new_returns\.jhtml

Table 4. Factor examples from msnbc data set

Factor #	Category #	$P(p_j|z_k)$	URL category
Factor #1	4	0.316	local
	7	0.313	misc
	6	0.295	on-air
	15	0.047	summary
	16	0.029	bbs
Facto #2	10	0.299	health
	5	0.262	opinion
	13	0.237	msn-sport
	3	0.203	tech

department store itself. Such explanations of user profiles drawn from (Table 5) are consistent with the discovery from (Table 3).

In addition, from the discovered user profiles, we can further conclude that there are more than one kinds of access interests or exist "overlapping" of visiting tendencies involved in one user profile. But we may still distinguish the dominant or secondary "theme" from others based on the corresponding weights associated with Web contents. Furthermore, the discovered user access profiles make it feasible to benefit further Web analysis

applications, for example, Web recommendation or prediction.

APPLICATIONS OF USER PROFILING: COLLABORATIVE WEB RECOMMENDATION

Collaborative Web Recommendation

In this section, we present a collaborative Web recommendation algorithm based on the discovered user communities of interests. In Modeling User Communities of Interests Using Probabilistic Latent Semantic Analysis Model, we have derived user communities of interests (i.e. user profiles) via a probability inference algorithm. In the following parts, we aim to incorporate the discovered usage knowledge with the collaborative filtering algorithm for Web recommendation.

As discussed in the previous section, Web usage mining will result in a set of user session clusters $SCL=\{SCL_1,SCL_2,...,SCL_k\}$, where each

Table 5. Two examples of user access profiles

	Page #	Weight	Page description
Profile #7	4	1.20E-4	products/productDetailLegwear
	29	8.44E-5	main/shopping_cart
	27	6.50E-5	main/login2
	8	5.20E-5	main/home
	44	5.03E-5	checkout/expresCheckout
	65	3.86E-5	main/welcome
	2	3.77E-5	main/boutique
	7	3.75E-5	main/search_results
	6	3.75E-5	main/departments
	45	3.72E-5	checkout/confirm_order
	32	3.57E-5	main/registration
	42	1.65E-5	account/your_account
Profile #13	12	1.73E-4	articles/dpt_about
	8	9.77E-5	main/home
	13	7.17E-5	articles/dpt_about_mgmtteam
	4	5.91E-5	products/productDetailLegwear
	14	5.17E-5	articles\dpt_about_boardofdirectors
	2	4.85E-5	main/boutique
	16	4.79E-5	articles/dpt_about_careers
	22	4.55E-5	articles/new_shipping
	17	4.26E-5	articles/dpt_about_investor
	18	4.14E-5	dpt_about_pressreleases
	15	3.83E-5	dpt_about_healthwellness
	20	3.78E-5	articles/dpt_affiliate

SCL_i is a collection of user sessions with similar access preference. And from the discovered user session clusters, we can then generate their corresponding centroids of the user session clusters, which are considered as usage profiles, or user access patterns. The complete formulation of usage profiling algorithm is expressed as follows.

Given a user session cluster SCL_i, the corresponding usage profile of the cluster is represented as a sequence of page weights, which are dependent on the mean weights of all pages engaged in the cluster:

$$up_i = \left(w_1^i, w_2^i, \ldots w_n^i \right) \qquad (20)$$

where the contributed weight, w_j^i, of the page p_j within the user profile up_i is:

$$w_j^i = \frac{1}{|SCL_i|} \sum_{t \in SCL_i} a_{tj} \qquad (21)$$

And a_{tj} is the element weight of page p_j in user session $s_t, s_t \in SCL_i$. To further select the most significant pages for recommendation, we can use the filtering method to choose a set of dominant pages with weights exceeding a certain value as an expression of user profile, that is, we preset a threshold μ and filter out those pages with weights greater than the threshold for constructing the user profile. Given w_j^i, then:

$$w_j^i = \begin{cases} w_j^i, w_j^i > \mu \\ 0, otherwise \end{cases} \qquad (22)$$

This process performs repeatedly on each user session cluster and finally generates a number of user profiles, which are expressed by a weighted sequence of pages. These usage patterns are then used into collaborative recommending operation.

Generally, Web recommendation process is to predict and customize Web presentations in a user preferable style according to the interests exhibited by individual or groups of users. This goal is usually carried out in two ways. On the one hand, we can take the current active user's historic behavior or pattern into consideration, and predict the preferable information to this specific user. On the other hand, by finding the most similar access pattern to the current active user from the learned usage models of other users, we can recommend the tailored Web content. The former one is sometime called memory-based approaches, whereas the latter one is called model-based recommendations, respectively. In this study, we adopt the model-based technique in our Web recommendation framework. We consider the usage-based user profiles generated in Constructing User Communities of Interests and Identifying Latent Factors with PLSA Model as the aggregated representatives of common navigational behaviors exhibited by all individuals in the same particular user category, and utilize them as a usage knowledge base for recommending potentially visited Web pages to the current user.

Similar to the method proposed in (Mobasher, et al., 2002) for representing user access interest in the form of n-dimensional weighted page vector, we utilize the commonly used cosine function to measure the similarity between the current active user session and discovered usage pattern. We, then, choose the best suitable profile, which shares the highest similarity with the current session, as the matched pattern of the current user. Finally, we generate the top-N recommendation pages based on the historically visited probabilities of the pages by other users in the selected profile. The detailed procedure is described as follows.

Algorithm 6. Top-N collaborative Web recommendation algorithm based on PLSA

Input: An active user session s_a and a set of user profiles $up=\{up_j\}$.
Output: The top-N recommendation pages $REC_{PLSA}(s_a)=\{p_j^{mat} \mid p_j^{mat} \in P, j=1,2,\ldots,N\}$.
1. The active session s_a and the discovered user profiles up are viewed as

n-dimensional vectors over the page space within a site, i.e. $\mathbf{up}_j=[w^i_1, w^i_2, \ldots, w^i_n]$, where w^i_j is the significant weight contributed by page p_i in the up_j user profile, similarly $\mathbf{s}_a=[w^a_1, w^a_2, \ldots, w^a_n]$, where $w^a_i=1$, if page p_i is already accessed, and otherwise $w^a_i=0$.

2. Measure the similarities between the active session and all derived usage profiles, and choose the maximum one out of the calculated similarities as the most matched pattern:

$$sim(\mathbf{s}_a, \mathbf{up}_j) = (\mathbf{s}_a \cdot \mathbf{up}_j) \big/ \|\mathbf{s}_a\|_2 \|\mathbf{up}_j\|_2 \qquad (23)$$

where $\mathbf{s}_a \cdot \mathbf{up}_j = \sum_{i=1}^{n} w_i^j w_i^a$,

$\|\mathbf{s}_a\|_2 = \sqrt{\sum_{i=1}^{n} (w_i^a)^2}$, $\|\mathbf{up}_j\|_2 = \sqrt{\sum_{i=1}^{n} (w_i^j)^2}$

$$sim(\mathbf{s}_a, \mathbf{up}_{mat}) = \max_j (sim(\mathbf{s}_a, \mathbf{up}_j)) \qquad (24)$$

3. Incorporate the selected profile up_{mat} (defined by vector $\mathbf{up}_{mat}$) with the active session represented by vector $\mathbf{s}_a$, then calculate the recommendation score $rs(p_i)$ for each page p_i:

$$rs(p_i) = \sqrt{w_i^{mat} \times sim(\mathbf{s}_a, \mathbf{up}_{mat})} \qquad (25)$$

Thus, each page in the profile will be assigned a recommendation score between 0 and 1. Note that the recommendation score will be 0 if the page is already visited in the current session.

4. Sort the calculated recommendation scores in step 3 obtained in a descending order, i.e. $rs=(w^{mat}_1, w^{mat}_2, \ldots, w^{mat}_n)$, and select the N pages with the highest recommendation score to construct the top-N recommendation set:

$$REC_{PLSA}(s_a) = \{p_j^{mat} \mid rs(p_j^{mat}) > rs(p_{j+1}^{mat}), j = 1, 2, \ldots N-1\}$$

Evaluations and Comparisons

Experiment Dataset and Evaluation Metric

The data set is from a university website log files and was made available by the author of (Mobasher, 2004). The data is based on a random collection of users visiting this site for a 2-week period during April of 2002. After data pre-processing, the filtered data contains 13745 sessions and 683 pages. This data file is expressed as a session-page matrix where each column is a page and each row is a session represented as a vector. The entry in the table corresponds to the amount of time (in seconds) spent on a page during a given session. For convenience, we refer this data as "CTI data". For each dataset, we randomly choose 1000 user sessions as the evaluation set, whereas the remainder part is selected as the training set for constructing user profiles.

From the viewpoint of user, the effectiveness of the proposed approach is evaluated by the recommendation performance. Here, we exploit a metric called hit ratio (Mobasher, et al., 2002) to measure the effectiveness in the context of top-N recommendation. Given a user session in the test set, we extract the first j pages as an active session to generate a top-N recommendation set via the procedure described in Future Research Directions. We then compare the $(j+1)$th page of the testing session with the recommendation list. If the $(j+1)$th page is appeared in the recommended set, it is considered a hit. We count the total number of the hits, and calculate the hit ratio by averaging it by the total number of testing session i.e. *hit ratio*= $|hit|/|T|$, where $|hit|$ and $|T|$ represent the number of hits and testing data in the whole test set, respectively. Thus, hit ratio indicates the performance of the of Web recommendation process. Obviously, a bigger value of N (number of recommendations) results in a higher hit ratio in the test set In order to compare our approach with other existing methods, we implement a baseline method that is based on the clustering technique (Mobasher, et al., 2002).

Experimental Results

(Figure 5) depicts the comparison results of recommendation accuracy in terms of *hit ratio* parameter using PLSA-based and clustering-based recommendation algorithm respectively with CTI dataset. From the (Figure 5), it is shown that the proposed PLSA-based technique consistently overweighs standard clustering-based algorithm in terms of hit precision parameter. In this scenario, it can be concluded that our approach is capable of making Web recommendation more accurately and effectively against conventional method. In addition to the advantage of high recommendation accuracy, these approaches are also able to identify the latent semantic factors why such user sessions or Web pages are grouped together in same category.

FUTURE RESEARCH DIRECTIONS

The future work can be continued along the following directions:

- Integration of ontology knowledge of Web pages into Web recommendation. The current research is mainly based on analysis of Web usage knowledge, not taking other Web data sources into account. With the development of Semantic Web and ontology research, it is believed that ontology knowledge of Web pages can provide deeper understanding or semantic linking of Web page as a result of conveying the conceptual information. Ontology knowledge could be viewed as a high-level knowledge representation over the intuitive content knowledge. Hence, integrating the ontol-

Figure 5. Web recommendation evaluation upon hit ratio comparison for CTI dataset

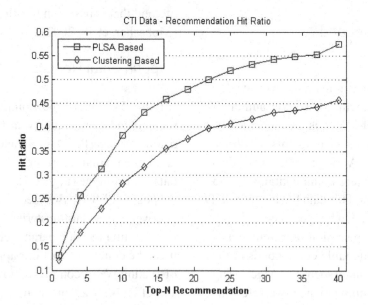

ogy knowledge with the usage knowledge will substantially improve the accuracy and efficiency of Web recommendation.

- Employing the latest progress of other related research areas into Web data management. The successes and contributions from data mining, machine learning, information retrieval domains always brings in new data models and algorithms to Web data research. It is believed these progresses will produce a big potential for Web researchers to address the open research problems not solved yet.

- Expanding the scope of current research to other related areas. Web data mining and community analysis on Web pages or users provides an interesting and promising way to discover the aggregation nature of co-occurrence based on statistical learning approaches. With the emerging of new applications over the Internet, especially Web 2.0 technology, many new types of Web data, such as email traffic, blogs, wiki pages are available. These data types have produced a large amount of new knowledge

resources, which leads to new research directions, for example, social network analysis.

CONCLUSION

With the rapid development of Web applications and great flux of Web information available on the Internet, Web has become a very massive data repository and brought us a powerful platform to disseminate information and retrieve information as well as analyze information. Although the progress of the Web-based data management research results in developments of many useful Web applications or services, like Web search engine, users are still facing the problems of information overload and drowning due to the significant and rapid growth in amount of information and the number of users. In particular, Web users usually suffer from the difficulties of finding desirable and accurate information on the Web due to two problems of low precision and low recall caused by above reasons. Thus, the emerging of Web has put forward a great deal of challenges to Web researchers for Web-based information management and retrieval.

Web mining could be partly used to solve the problems mentioned above directly or indirectly. In principle, Web mining techniques are the means of utilizing data mining methods to induce and extract useful information from Web information and service.

Web recommendation or personalization could be viewed as a process that recommends customized Web presentation or predicts tailored Web content to users according to their specific taste or preference. There are two kinds of approaches and techniques commonly used in Web recommendation, namely content-based filtering and collaborative filtering systems. Nowadays, Web usage mining has been proposed as an alternative method for not only revealing user access patterns, but also making Web recommendations.

On the other hand, *Latent Semantic Analysis* (LSA) is an approach to capture the latent or hidden semantic relationships among co-occurrence activities, which has been widely used in information indexing and retrieval applications. Despite the considerable progress of traditional LSA approach, it still has some shortcomings, such as computational difficulty with sparsity problem of co-occurrence matrix, overfitting problem, capability of capturing latent semantic space etc. To address this, some studies have extended the standard LSA techniques via introducing various statistical background principles, such as PLSA and LDA models.

In this chapter, we have addressed discovering user communities of interests by using Web usage mining. This chapter mainly focuses on discovering Web usage pattern in terms of task-oriented Web user profile and Web page groups from Web log file to support Web recommendation via various latent semantic analysis (LSA) paradigms. To achieve these goals a mathematical framework is established for Web usage mining and a series of algorithms are proposed to predict Web user navigational preference and recommend the customized Web contents to Web user. Two kinds of latent semantic analysis models, namely standard LSA and PLSA, are proposed to address Web usage mining and Web recommendation respectively. Comprehensive experiments and evaluations have been performed to demonstrate the effectiveness and applicability of the proposed approaches.

REFERENCES

Agarwal, R., Aggarwal, C., & Prasad, V. (1999). A Tree Projection Algorithm for Generation of Frequent Itemsets. *Journal of Parallel and Distributed Computing*, *61*(3), 350–371. doi:10.1006/jpdc.2000.1693

Agrawal, R., & Srikant, R. (1994, Sept. 1994). *Jorge B. Bocca and Matthias Jarke and Carlo Zaniolo.* Paper presented at the Proceedings of the 20th International Conference on Very Large Data Bases (VLDB), Santiago, Chile.

Agrawal, R., & Srikant, R. (1995, March 1995). *Mining Sequential Patterns.* Paper presented at the Proceedings of the International Conference on Data Engineering (ICDE), Taipei, Taiwan.

Baeza-Yates, R., & Ribeiro-Neto, B. (1999). *Modern Information Retrieval. Addison Wesley.* ACM Press.

Blei, D. M., Ng, A. Y., & Jordan, M. I. (2003). Latent Dirichlet Allocation. *Journal of Machine Learning Research*, (3): 993–1022. doi:10.1162/jmlr.2003.3.4-5.993

Broder, A., Glassman, S., Manasse, M., & Zweig, G. (1997, April). *Syntactic Clustering of the Web.* Paper presented at the Proceedings of the 6th International WWW Conference, Santa Clara, CA, USA.

Datta, B. N. (1995). *Numerical Linear Algebra and Application.* Brooks/Cole Publishing Company.

Dempster, A. P., Laird, N. M., & Rubin, D. B. (1977). Maximum Likelihood from Incomplete Data via the EM Algorithm. *Journal of the Royal Statistical Society. Series B. Methodological, 39*(2), 1–38.

Dunja, M. (1996). *Personal Web Watcher: design and implementation* (Technical Report No. IJS-DP_7472). Department of Intelligent Systems, J. Stefan Institute, Slovenia.

Flake, G. W., Tarjan, R. E., & Tsioutsiouliklis, K. (2004). Graph Clustering and Minimum Cut Trees. *Internet Mathematics, 1*(4).

Han, E., Karypis, G., Kumar, V., & Mobasher, B. (1998). Hypergraph Based Clustering in High-Dimensional Data Sets: A Summary of Results. *A Quarterly Bulletin of the Computer Society of the IEEE Technical Committee on Data Engineering, 21*(1), 15–22.

Han, J., & Kamber, M. (2007). *Data Mining: Concepts and Techniques*. Morgan Kaufmann.

Herlocker, J., Konstan, J., Borchers, A., & Riedl, J. (1999, August 1999). *An Algorithmic Framework for Performing Collaborative Filtering*. Paper presented at the Proceedings of the 22nd ACM Conference on Researchand Development in Information Retrieval (SIGIR'99), Berkeley, CA.

Herlocker, J. L., Konstan, J. A., Terveen, L. G., & Riedl, J. T. (2004a). Evaluating collaborative filtering recommender systems. [TOIS]. *ACM Transactions on Information Systems, 22*(1), 5–53. doi:10.1145/963770.963772

Herlocker, J. L., Konstan, J. A., Terveen, L. G., & Riedl, J. T. (2004b). Evaluating Collaborative Filtering Recommender Systems. [TOIS]. *ACM Transactions on Information Systems, 22*(1), 5–53. doi:10.1145/963770.963772

Hofmann, T. (1999, August). *Probabilistic Latent Semantic Analysis*. Paper presented at the Proceedings of the 22nd Annual ACM Conference on Research and Development in Information Retrieval, Berkeley, California, USA.

Hofmann, T. (2001). Unsupervised Learning by Probabilistic Latent Semantic Analysis. *Machine Learning Journal, 42*(1), 177–196. doi:10.1023/A:1007617005950

Hofmann, T. (2004). Latent Semantic Models for Collaborative Filtering. *ACM Transactions on Information Systems, 22*(1), 89–115. doi:10.1145/963770.963774

Hou, J., & Zhang, Y. (2002). *Constructing Good Quality Web Page Communities*. Paper presented at the Proc. of the 13th Australasian Database Conferences (ADC2002), Melbourne, Australia.

Hou, J., & Zhang, Y. (2003a). Effectively Finding Relevant Web Pages from Linkage Information. *IEEE Transactions on Knowledge and Data Engineering, 15*(4), 940–951. doi:10.1109/TKDE.2003.1209010

Hou, J., & Zhang, Y. (2003b). *Utilizing Hyperlink Transitivity to Improve Web Page Clustering*. Paper presented at the Proceedings of the 14th Australasian Database Conferences (ADC2003), Adelaide, Australia.

Jin, X., Zhou, Y., & Mobasher, B. (2004, July 2004). *A Unified Approach to Personalization Based on Probabilistic Latent Semantic Models of Web Usage and Content*. Paper presented at the Proceedings of the AAAI 2004 Workshop on Semantic Web Personalization (SWP'04), San Jose.

Konstan, J., Miller, B., Maltz, D., Herlocker, J., Gordon, L., & Riedl, J. (1997). Grouplens: Applying Collaborative Filtering to Usenet News. *Communications of the ACM, 40*(3), 77–87. doi:10.1145/245108.245126

Mobasher, B. (2004). Web Usage Mining and Personalization. In M. P. Singh (Ed.), *Practical Handbook of Internet Computing* (pp. 15.11-37). CRC Press.

Mobasher, B., Dai, H., Nakagawa, M., & Luo, T. (2002). Discovery and Evaluation of Aggregate Usage Profiles for Web Personalization. *Data Mining and Knowledge Discovery*, *6*(1), 61–82. doi:10.1023/A:1013232803866

O'Conner, M., & Herlocker, J. (1999, August 1999). *Clustering Items for Collaborative Filtering*. Paper presented at the Proceedings of the ACM SIGIR Workshop on Recommender Systems, Berkeley, CA, USA.

Otsuka, S., Toyoda, M., Hirai, J., & Kitsuregawa, M. (2004). *Extracting User Behavior by Web Communities Technology on Global Web Logs*. Paper presented at the Proc. of the 15th International Conference on Database and Expert Systems Applications (DEXA'04), Zaragoza, Spain.

Perkowitz, M., & Etzioni, O. (1998, July 1998). *Adaptive Web Sites: Automatically Synthesizing Web Pages*. Paper presented at the Proceedings of the 15th National Conference on Artificial Intelligence, Madison, WI.

Perkowitz, M., & Etzioni, O. (1999). *Adaptive Web Sites: Conceptual Cluster Mining*. Paper presented at the Proceeding of 16th International Joint Conference on Artificial Intelligence, Stockholm, Sweden.

Pierrakos, D., Paliouras, G., Papatheodorou, C., Karkaletsis, V., & Dikaiakos, M. D. (2003). *Construction of Web Community Directories by Mining Usage Data*. Paper presented at the Proceeding of the 2nd Hellenic Data Management Symposium (HDMS'03), Athens, Greece.

Sarwar, B. M., Karypis, G., Konstan, J. A., & Riedl, J. (2001, May 2001). *Item-based collaborative filtering recommendation algorithms*. Paper presented at the Proceedings of the 10th International World Wide Web Conference (WWW10), Hong Kong.

Shardanand, U., & Maes, P. (1995, May 1995). *Social Information Filtering: Algorithms for Automating 'Word of Mouth'*. Paper presented at the Proceedings of the Computer-Human Interaction Conference (CHI95), Denver, CO.

Srivastava, J., Cooley, R., Deshpande, M., & Tan, P. (2000). Web Usage Mining: Discovery and Applications of Usage Patterns from Web Data. *SIGKDD Explorations*, *1*(2), 12–23. doi:10.1145/846183.846188

Wang, Y., & Kitsuregawa, M. (2001, 3-6 December). *Use Link-based Clustering to Improve Web Search Results*. Paper presented at the Proceedings of the 2nd International Conference on Web Information Systems Engineering (WISE2001), Kyoto, Japan.

Xiao, J., Zhang, Y., Jia, X., & Li, T. (2001). *Measuring Similarity of Interests for Clustering Web-Users*. Paper presented at the Proceedings of the 12th Australasian Database conference (ADC2001), Queensland, Australia.

Xu, G., Zhang, Y., & Zhou, X. (2005). *A Latent Usage Approach for Clustering Web Transaction and Building User Profile*. Paper presented at the First International Conference on Advanced Data Mining and Applications (ADMA 2005), Wuhan, china.

Xu, G., Zhang, Y., & Zhou, X. (2005). *A Web Recommendation Technique Based on Probabilistic Latent Semantic Analysis*. Paper presented at the Proceeding of 6th International Conference of Web Information System Engineering (WISE'2005), New York City, USA.

Zhang, Y., Yu, J. X., & Hou, J. (2006). *Web Communities: Analysis and Construction*. Berlin, Heidelberg: Springer.

ENDNOTES

[1]   The centroid of a cluster is the object which is the most similar to all the other objects.

[2]   http://www.ecn.purdue.edu/kddcup

[3]   http://kdd.ics.uci.edu/databases

Chapter 5
Collaborative Recommendation Systems and Link Analysis

François Fouss
Facultés Universitaires Catholiques de Mons (FUCaM), Belgium

ABSTRACT

Link analysis is a framework usually associated with fields such as graph mining, relational learning, Web mining, text mining, hyper-text mining, visualization of link structures. It provides and analyzes relationships and associations between many objects of various types that are not apparent from isolated pieces of information. This chapter shows how to apply various link-analysis algorithms exploiting the graph structure of databases on collaborative-recommendation tasks. More precisely, two kinds of link-analysis algorithms are applied to recommend items to users: random-walk based models and kernel-based models. These link-analysis based algorithms do not use any feature of the items in order to compute the recommendations, they first compute a matrix containing the links between persons and items, and then derive recommendations from this matrix or part of it.

INTRODUCTION

Link analysis is a data-mining technique based on the analysis of various kinds of networks. Link-analysis methods can be used, for example, for classification, prediction, clustering or association-rules discovery.

A traditional link-analysis subfield that has attracted considerable interest and curiosity from the social and behavioral science community in recent decades (Carrington, et al., 2006; Lazega, 1998; White & Smyth, 2003) is the field aiming at analyzing links existing in various kinds of social networks. Much of this interest can be attributed to the appealing focus of social network analysis on relationships among social entities, and on the patterns and implications of these entities. Many researchers have realized that the network perspective allows new leverage for answering standard-social and behavioral-science research questions by giving precise formal definitions to aspects of the political, economic, or social structural

DOI: 10.4018/978-1-61520-841-8.ch005

Copyright © 2011, IGI Global. Copying or distributing in print or electronic forms without written permission of IGI Global is prohibited.

environment. From the view of social-network analysis, the social environment can be expressed as patterns or regularities in relationships among interacting units. The focus on relations and on patterns of relations, requires a set of methods and analytic concepts that are distinct from the methods of traditional statistics and data analysis. Such phrases as webs of relationships, closely knit networks of relations, social role, social position, group, clique, popularity, isolation, centrality, prestige, prominence, etc. are given mathematical definitions by social-network analysis.

More generally, *link analysis* (see (Thelwall, 2004) for an introduction on link analysis) is a framework usually associated with fields such as graph mining, relational learning, Web mining, text mining, hyper-text mining, visualization of link structures. It provides relationships and associations between many objects of various types that are not apparent from isolated pieces of information. Computer-assisted or fully automatic computer-based link analysis is increasingly used in diverse application fields such as database marketing (find typical features of customers, identify frequent patterns in purchase behavior, etc.), fraud detection (discover suspicious behaviors), Web mining (find good Web pages relatively to a specific query), telecommunication-network analysis (visualize the main communication patterns and potential network bottlenecks), criminal investigations, text mining, epidemiology and pharmacology, or search engines.

The work described in this chapter shows how to apply various link-analysis algorithms exploiting the graph structure of databases on collaborative-recommendation tasks. More precisely, two kinds of link-analysis algorithms are applied to recommend items to users.

The first type of algorithms is based on a Markov-chain model. A *random-walk model* through the database is defined by assigning a transition probability to each link. Thus, a virtual random walker can jump from element to element and each element therefore represents a state of a Markov chain. From this random-walk model, we define quantities such as the average commute time, the average first-passage time, the average first-passage cost, and the pseudoinverse of the Laplacian matrix of the graph. This chapter also introduces the Euclidean Commute-Time Distance (ECTD) (corresponding to the square root of the average commute-time distance), which is a distance between nodes.

The second type of algorithms is based on *graph kernels*. The common idea behind kernel-based algorithms is to express similarities between pairs of points in a data space in terms of a kernel function, and thereby to implicitly construct a mapping to a feature space in which the kernel appears as the inner product between pairs of points (implying that the entries of the kernel matrix can be considered as similarities between the points). Seven kernels on a graph (namely, the exponential diffusion kernel, the Laplacian exponential diffusion kernel, the von Neumann diffusion kernel, the regularized Laplacian kernel, the commute-time kernel, the Markov diffusion kernel, and the cross-entropy diffusion matrix) are reviewed.

This chapter focuses on *collaborative algorithms*. Indeed, all the suggested link-analysis based algorithms (including random-walk based algorithms and kernel-based algorithms) first compute a matrix containing the links between persons and items, and then derive recommendations from this matrix or part of it. These algorithms do not use any feature of the items in order to compute the recommendations. Actually, the link-analysis framework has been recently applied in the context of collaborative recommendation (see Some Related Work), with encouraging results.

Definition of the weighted graph. A weighted, undirected, graph G is associated with a database in the following obvious way: database elements correspond to nodes of the graph and database links correspond to edges.

The weight $w_{ij} > 0$ of the edge connecting node i and node j should be set to some meaningful value, with the following convention: the more important the relation between node i and node j, the larger the value of w_{ij}, and consequently the easier the communication through the edge. Notice that we require the weights to be both positive ($w_{ij}>0$) and symmetric ($w_{ij}=w_{ji}$). The elements a_{ij} of the adjacency matrix $\mathbf{A}$ of the graph are defined in a standard way as:

$$a_{ij} = \begin{cases} w_{ij} & \text{if node } i \text{ is connected to node } j \\ 0 & \text{otherwise} \end{cases}$$

$$(1)$$

where $\mathbf{A}$ is symmetric. We also introduce the Laplacian matrix $\mathbf{L}$ of the graph, defined in the usual manner:

$$\mathbf{L} = \mathbf{D} - \mathbf{A} \qquad (2)$$

where $\mathbf{D}=diag(a_{i.})$ with:

$$d_{ii} = \left[\mathbf{D}\right]_{ii} = a_{i.} = \sum_{j=1}^{n} a_{ij}$$

where element i,j of $\mathbf{D}$ is $[\mathbf{D}]_{ij}=d_{ij}$, if there are n nodes in total.

We also suppose that the graph is connected, that is, any node can be reached from any other node. In this case, $\mathbf{L}$ has rank n-1 [20]. If e is a column vector made of 1's (i.e. $\mathbf{e}=[1,1,...,1]^{T}$, where T denotes the matrix transpose) and $\mathbf{o}$ is a column vector made of 0's, $\mathbf{Le}=\mathbf{0}$ and $\mathbf{e}^{T}\mathbf{L}=\mathbf{0}^{T}$ hold: $\mathbf{L}$ is doubly centered. The null space of $\mathbf{L}$ is therefore the one-dimensional space spanned by $\mathbf{e}$. Moreover, one can easily show that $\mathbf{L}$ is symmetric and positive semidefinite (see for instance (Chung, 1997)). Notice that, if the graph is not connected, the graph can be decomposed into closed subsets of nodes which are independent (there is no communication between them), each closed subset being irreducible, and the analysis can be applied independently on these closed subsets.

RANDOM-WALK BASED ALGORITHMS[1]

A Markov chain describing the sequence of nodes visited by a random walker is called a random walk. We associate a state of the Markov chain to every node; we also define a random variable, $s(t)$, representing the state of the Markov model at time step t. If the random walker is in state i at time t, then $s(t)=i$.

We define a random walk with the following single-step transition probabilities:

$$*P(s(t+1) = j \mid s(t) = i) = \frac{a_{ij}}{a_{i.}} = p_{ij}, \text{where } a_{i.} = \sum_{j=1}^{n} a_{ij}$$

$$(3)$$

In other words, to any state or node $i=s(t)$, we associate a probability of jumping to an adjacent node $j=s(t+1)$, which is proportional to the weight w_{ij} of the edge connecting i and j. The transition probabilities only depend on the current state and not on the past ones (first-order Markov chain). Since the graph is totally connected, the Markov chain is irreducible, that is, every state can be reached from any other state. If this is not the case, the Markov chain can be decomposed into closed sets of states which are completely independent (there is no communication between them), each closed set being irreducible.

If we denote the probability of being in state i at time t by $x_i(t)=*P(s(t)=i)$ and define $\mathbf{P}$ as the transition-probability matrix with entries $p_{ij}=*P(s(t+1)=j|s(t)=i)$, the evolution of the Markov chain is characterized by:

$$\begin{cases} x_i(0) = x_i^0 \\ x_i(t+1) = *P(s(t+1) = i) \\ \qquad = \sum_{j=1}^{n} *P(s(t+1) = i \mid s(t) = j)x_j(t) \\ \qquad = \sum_{j=1}^{n} p_{ji}x_j(t) \end{cases}$$

Or, in matrix form:

$$\begin{cases} \mathbf{x}(0) = \mathbf{x}^0 \\ \mathbf{x}(t+1) = \mathbf{P}^T\mathbf{x}(t) \end{cases} \qquad (4)$$

where T is the matrix transpose. This provides the state probability distribution $\mathbf{x}(t)=[x_1(t), x_2(t), \dots, x_n(t)]^T$ at time t once the initial probability density $\mathbf{x}^0$ is known. It is well-known (see Ross (1996)) that such a Markov chain of random walk on a graph is time-reversible ($\pi_i p_{ij} = \pi_j p_{ji}$) with the long-run proportions of time that the process will be in state i given by:

$$\pi_i = \frac{\sum_{j=1}^{n} a_{ij}}{\sum_{i,j=1}^{n} a_{ij}} = \frac{a_{i.}}{a_{..}} \qquad (5)$$

This value is the probability of finding the Markov chain in state $s=i$ in the long-run behavior if the Markov chain is aperiodic.

For more details on Markov chains, the reader is invited to consult standard textbooks on the subject, e.g. (Kemeny & Snell, 1976; Norris, 1997).

Average First-Passage Time/Cost and Average Commute Time

In this section, we review two basic quantities that can be computed from the definition of the Markov chain, that is, from its transition-probability matrix: the average first-passage time, and the average commute time. We also introduce the average first-passage cost which generalizes the average first-passage time. Relationships allowing to compute these quantities are derived in a heuristic way, see e.g. (Kemeny & Snell, 1976; Norris, 1997).

The Average First-Passage Time and Average First-Passage Cost

The *average first-passage time $m(k|i)$* is defined as the average number of steps that a random walker, starting in state $i \neq k$, will take to enter state k for the first time (Norris, 1997). More precisely, we define the minimum time until hitting state k as:

$$T_{ik} = \min\left(t \geq 0 \mid s(t) = k \text{ and } s(0) = i\right)$$

for one realization of the stochastic process. The average first-passage time is the expectation of this quantity, when starting from state i: $m(k|i)=E[T_{ik}]$.

In a similar way, we define the *average first-passage cost, $o(k|i)$* as the average cost incurred by the random walker starting from state i to reach state k. The cost of each transition is given by $c(j|i)$ (a cost matrix) for any states i, j. Notice that $m(k|i)$ can be obtained as a special case where $c(j|i)=1$.

More precisely (see Fouss, et al. (2007a) for details about the derivation of the recurrence relation), we obtain, for $o(k|i)$:

$$\begin{cases} o(k \mid k) = 0 \\ o(k \mid i) = \sum_{j=1}^{n} p_{ij} c(j \mid i) + \sum_{j=1, j \neq k}^{n} p_{ij} o(k \mid j), \text{for } i \neq k \end{cases}$$

$$(6)$$

For $m(k|i)$, $c(j|i)=1$ and we obtain:

$$\begin{cases} m(k \mid k) = 0 \\ m(k \mid i) = 1 + \sum_{j=1, j \neq k}^{n} p_{ij} m(k \mid j), \text{for } i \neq k \end{cases}$$

$$(7)$$

These equations can be used in order to iteratively compute the first-passage times (Norris, 1997) or first-passage costs. The meaning of these formulas is quite obvious: in order to go from state i to state k, one has to go to any adjacent state j and proceed from there. Once more, these quantities can be obtained by using the pseudoinverse of the Laplacian matrix of the graph, as shown in the next section or by algorithms developed in the Markov-chain community (for instance, Kemeny & Snell (1976) proposed a general method in the appendix of their book; see also (Isaacson & Madsen, 1976; Parzen, 1962)).

The Average Commute Time

We now introduce a closely related quantity, the *average commute time $n(i,j)$*, defined as the average number of steps that a random walker, starting in state $i \neq j$, will take before entering state j for the first time, and go back to i.

That is:

$$n(i, j) = m(j \mid i) + m(i \mid j)$$

Notice that, while $n(i,j)$ is symmetric by definition, $m(i|j)$ is not. Tetali (1991) shows how to compute the average first passage time from the average commute time:

$$m(i \mid j) = \frac{1}{2} \sum_{k=1}^{n} d(k)[n(i, j) + n(j, k) - n(i, k)]$$

where $d(k)$ denotes the degree of node k.

As shown by several authors (Gobel & Jagers, 1974; Klein & Randic, 1993), the average commute time is a distance measure between states since, for any states i, j, k:

$$\begin{cases} n(i, j) \geq 0 \\ n(i, j) = 0 \text{ if and only if } i = j \\ n(i, j) = n(j, i) \\ n(i, j) \leq n(i, k) + n(k, j) \end{cases}$$

It will therefore be referred to as the *commute-time distance*. Because of a close relationship between the random-walk model and electrical-networks theory, this distance is also called *resistance distance* as shown in Relations to Electrical Networks.

As already mentioned, the commute-time distance between two points has the desirable property of decreasing when the number of paths connecting the two points increases and when the length of one of these paths decreases (see (Doyle & Snell, 1984) for a proof based on electrical-networks theory). Intuitively, this is "normal" since the commute-time distance is equivalent to the effective resistance of the equivalent electrical network (see Relations to Electrical Networks).

The most used distance on graphs, the *shortest-path distance* (also called geodesic distance), does not have this property: the shortest-path distance does not capture the fact that strongly connected nodes are at a smaller distance than weakly connected nodes.

The next section describes (providing a definition and the main properties) another quantity that can be computed from the definition of the Markov chain and that is closely related to the probability of absorption, the average first-passage time, and the average commute time: the pseudoinverse of the Laplacian matrix of the graph.

The Pseudoinverse of the Laplacian Matrix of the Graph

Let us denote by l_{ij} element i,j of the Laplacian matrix $\mathbf{L}$. In other words, $l_{ij} = [\mathbf{L}]_{ij}$. The Moore-Penrose pseudoinverse of $\mathbf{L}$ (see (Barnett, 1992)) is denoted by $\mathbf{L}^+$, with elements $l_{ij}^+ = [\mathbf{L}^+]_{ij}$. The concept of pseudoinverse generalizes the matrix inverse to matrices which are not of full rank, or even rectangular. It provides closed-form solutions to systems of linear equations for which there is no exact solution (in which case it provides a solution in the least-square sense) or when there is an infinity of solutions. A thorough treatment of matrix pseudoinverses and their applications can be found in (Ben-Israel & Greville, 2003). Moreover, some useful properties of the pseudoinverse of the Laplacian matrix of the graph can be derived ($\mathbf{L}$ is an EP-matrix, $\mathbf{L}^+$ is a positive semidefinite and symmetric matrix, and $\mathbf{L}^+$ is a kernel, see (Fouss, et al., 2007a) for details), while the last part of this section shows how formulae for computing the average first-passage time, the average first-passage cost, and the average commute time can be derived from equations (6) and (7), by using $\mathbf{L}^+$.

Indeed, in (Fouss, et al., 2007a), it is shown, starting from equation (6), that the average first-passage cost can be computed in terms of the elements of $\mathbf{L}^+$, from equation:

$$o(k \mid i) = \sum_{j=1}^{n} \left(l_{ij}^+ - l_{ik}^+ - l_{kj}^+ + l_{kk}^+ \right) b_j \tag{8}$$

where $b_i = \sum_{j=1}^{n} a_{ij} c(j \mid i)$

Notice that in the case of the average first-passage time, starting from equation (8) where $c(j|i)=1$ and:

$$b_i = \sum_{j=1}^{n} a_{ij} c(j \mid i) = a_{i.} = d_{ii}$$

is the sum of the weights reaching node i. We obtain:

$$m(k \mid i) = \sum_{j=1}^{n} \left(l_{ij}^+ - l_{ik}^+ - l_{kj}^+ + l_{kk}^+ \right) d_{jj} \tag{9}$$

Since we already have the formula for the average first-passage time (equation (9)), computing the average commute time is trivial:

$$n(i, j) = m(j \mid i) + m(i \mid j)$$

$$= \sum_{k=1}^{n} \left(l_{ik}^+ - l_{ij}^+ - l_{jk}^+ + l_{jj}^+ \right) d_{kk} \tag{10}$$

$$+ \sum_{k=1}^{n} \left(l_{jk}^+ - l_{ji}^+ - l_{ik}^+ + l_{ii}^+ \right) d_{kk} \tag{11}$$

$$= \sum_{k=1}^{n} \left(l_{ii}^+ + l_{jj}^+ - 2 l_{ij}^+ \right) d_{kk} \tag{12}$$

$$= \left(l_{ii}^+ + l_{jj}^+ - 2 l_{ij}^+ \right) \sum_{k=1}^{n} d_{kk} \tag{13}$$

$$= V_G \left(l_{ii}^+ + l_{jj}^+ - 2 l_{ij}^+ \right) \tag{14}$$

where V_G is the volume of the graph ($V_G = \sum_{k=1}^{n} d_{kk}$).

If the matrices are too large, the computation based on the pseudoinverse becomes impractical; in this case, one may use iterative techniques based on equations (6), (7) and on the sparseness of the transition-probability matrix (Fouss, et al., 2007a). Notice, however, that there exist efficient methods such as the one proposed by Ho & Van Dooren (2005) to calculate the pseudoinverse of the Laplacian of a bipartite graph.

If we define $\mathbf{e}_i$ as the ith column of $\mathbf{I}$:

$$\mathbf{e}_i = [\underset{1}{0}, \ldots, \underset{i-1}{0}, \underset{i}{1}, \underset{i+1}{0}, \ldots, \underset{n}{0}]^{\mathrm{T}}$$

Equation (14) can be put in matrix form:

$$n(i, j) = V_G (\mathbf{e}_i - \mathbf{e}_j)^{\mathrm{T}} \mathbf{L}^+ (\mathbf{e}_i - \mathbf{e}_j) \tag{15}$$

where each node i is represented by a unit vector, $\mathbf{e}_i$, in the node space (the space spanned by $\{\mathbf{e}_i\}$).

We easily observe that $[n(i,j)]^{\frac{1}{2}}$ is a distance in the Euclidean space of the nodes of the graph since $\mathbf{L}^+$ is positive semidefinite. It will therefore be called the *Euclidean Commute-Time Distance* (ECTD). This is nothing else than a Mahalanobis distance with a weighting matrix $\mathbf{L}^+$.

Relations to Electrical Networks

There is an intriguing correspondence between random walk on a graph and electrical-networks theory, as popularized by Doyle and Snell (1984). Probability of absorption and average commute time both have equivalents in terms of electrical networks.

The developments in this section are inspired by the work of Klein & Randic (1993) which proved, based on the electrical equivalence, that the effective resistance (which is also equivalent to the average commute time, as shown in this section) can be computed from the Laplacian matrix. We extend their results by showing how the formula computing the average commute time in terms of $\mathbf{L}^+$ can be directly derived from equation (7), and by providing formulae for the average first-passage time, the average first-passage cost, and the probability of absorption. Notice that, as developed by Qiu & Hancock (2007) whose approach is posed as a diffusion process on the graph, the computation of the commute-time can be generalized using the normalized Laplacian and the Green's function.

Definition of the Electrical Network

We view our weighted graph as an electrical network where the weights on edges represent *conductances*. Conductances are defined as the inverse of resistances: $c_{ij} = 1/r_{ij}$. In other words, we define an electrical network with conductances $c_{ij} = w_{ij}$.

The main quantities of interest are the *potential* v_i, defined at each node of the network, as well as the *current*, i_{ij}, defined on each edge. If we denote by $N(i)$ the set of adjacent nodes of node i, the fundamental equations relating these basic quantities are:

$$i_{ij} = c_{ij}(v_i - v_j) \qquad (16)$$

$$i_{ki} = I_k \sum_{i \in N(k)} i_{ki} = I_k \qquad (17)$$

where I_k is the source of current at node k.

Another quantity of fundamental importance is the *effective resistance*, r^e_{ij}. Suppose we impose a potential difference V between nodes i and j: a potential $v_i = V$ is established at node i while $v_j = 0$ at node j. A current I_i defined by:

$$I_i = \sum_{k \in N(i)} i_{ik}$$

will flow into the network from source i (we assume that current flows from higher potential to lower potential) to sink j. The amount of current that flows depends upon the overall resistance in the network. The effective resistance between i and j is defined by $r^e_{ij} = (v_i - v_j)/I_i = V/I_i$. The reciprocal quantity $c^e_{ij} = 1/r^e_{ij}$ is the *effective conductance*.

In (Chandra, et al., 1989), it is shown that $n(i,j) = V_G r^e_{ij}$, where V_G is the volume of the graph:

$$V_G = \sum_{i,j=1}^{n} a_{ij}$$

In other words, average commute time and effective resistance basically measure the same quantity; this quantity is therefore also called *resistance distance* - in the sequel, we indifferently use resistance distance or commute-time distance.

We now show how the general solution of the electrical network equations can be computed in function of the Laplacian matrix, for a network with a single current source at node a and a current sink at node b. The developments are largely inspired by (Klein & Randic, 1993). From Kirchoff's law, we have:

$$\begin{cases} \sum_{j \in N(i)} i_{ij} = 0, \text{ for } i \neq a, b \\ \sum_{j \in N(a)} i_{aj} = I \\ \sum_{j \in N(b)} i_{bj} = -I \end{cases}$$

where $N(k)$ is the set of nodes directly connected to node k (the neighbors), and the current $i_{ij} = -i_{ji}$. I is the current flowing from source a to sink b; in other words:

$$\sum_{j \in N(k)} i_{kj} = I\delta(k,a) - I\delta(k,b) \text{ for any node } k$$

(18)

where δ is the delta of Kronecker.

For the potential δ_i, we have:

$$i_{ij} = c_{ij}(v_i - v_j)$$

(19)

where the c_{ij} are the conductances.

By replacing equation (19) in equation (18), we easily obtain:

$$I\delta(k,a) - I\delta(k,b) = \sum_{j \in N(k)} c_{kj}(v_k - v_j)$$

$$= \sum_{j \in N(k)} c_{kj}v_k - \sum_{j \in N(k)} c_{kj}v_j$$

$$= v_k \sum_{j \in N(k)} c_{kj} - \sum_{j \in N(k)} c_{kj}v_j$$

$$= d_{kk}v_k - \sum_{j \in N(k)} a_{kj}v_j$$

(20)

since we define $a_{ij} = c_{ij}$, and $\mathbf{D} = diag(a_i)$, with $a_i = \sum_j a_{ij}$ and $[\mathbf{D}]_{ij} = d_{ij}$. If we define $\mathbf{e}_i$ as the unit column vector:

$$\mathbf{e}_i = [0, \ldots, \underset{i-1}{0}, \underset{i}{1}, \underset{i+1}{0}, \ldots, \underset{n}{0}]^T$$

We can rewrite equation (20) in matrix form:

$$I(e_a - e_b) = (\mathbf{D} - \mathbf{A})v$$

$$= \mathbf{L}v$$

where v is the vector of the potentials of the network nodes. Since the null space of $\mathbf{L}$ is spanned by $\mathbf{e}$, we immediately deduce that:

$$v = I\mathbf{L}^+(e_a - e_b) + \mu e$$

(21)

where μ is a scalar.

The second term of equation (21) indicates that the potential is defined up to a constant term. The difference of potential between any two nodes i,j is therefore:

$$v_i - v_j = \mathbf{e}_i^T v - \mathbf{e}_j^T v$$

$$= (\mathbf{e}_i - \mathbf{e}_j)^T v$$

$$= I(\mathbf{e}_i - \mathbf{e}_j)^T \mathbf{L}^+(\mathbf{e}_a - \mathbf{e}_b) + \mu(\mathbf{e}_i - \mathbf{e}_j)^T \mathbf{e}$$

$$= I(\mathbf{e}_i - \mathbf{e}_j)^T \mathbf{L}^+(\mathbf{e}_a - \mathbf{e}_b)$$

(22)

This indicates how the potential can be computed from $\mathbf{L}^+$; the currents are then easily obtained from equation (19).

Electrical Equivalent to Average Commute Time

We already know that, in the case of a single current source at a and a sink at b, the difference of potential between any two nodes i,j can be computed (see equation (22)) as:

$$v_i - v_j = I(\mathbf{e}_i - \mathbf{e}_j)^T \mathbf{L}^+(\mathbf{e}_a - \mathbf{e}_b)$$

The effective resistance is therefore the ratio of the difference of potential between nodes a and b on the current flowing from a to b:

$$\frac{v_a - v_b}{I} = (\mathbf{e}_a - \mathbf{e}_b)^T \mathbf{L}^+(\mathbf{e}_a - \mathbf{e}_b)$$

which is exactly what we found previously for the commute times (see equation (14)), up to a proportionality constant, V_G.

Some Related Work

Chebotarev & Shamis (1997; 1998b) propose a similarity measure between nodes of a graph integrating indirect paths, based on the matrix-forest theorem. Interestingly enough, this quantity is also related to the Laplacian matrix of the graph. While the authors prove some nice properties about this similarity measure, no experiment investigating the effectiveness of this quantity is performed. Notice that this matrix-forest based measure is the same as the one computed from the regularized Laplacian kernel described in Kernel Based Algorithms.

Some authors recently consider similarity measures based on random-walk models. For instance, Harel & Koren (2001) investigate the possibility of clustering data according to some random-walk related quantities, such as the probability of visiting a node before returning to the starting node. They show through clustering experiments that their algorithm is able to cluster arbitrary non-convex shapes. White & Smyth (2003), independently of our work, investigate the use of the average first-passage time as a similarity measure between nodes. Their purpose was to generalize the random-walk approach of Page, Brin, et al. (1998) by capturing a concept of "relative centrality" of a given node with respect to some other node of interest.

More recently, Newman (2005) suggested to use a random-walk model in order to compute the "betweenness centrality" of a given node in a graph. Newman counts how often a node is traversed during a random walk between two other nodes (a couple of nodes). Then, this quantity is averaged over every couple of nodes, providing a general measure of betweenness (Wasserman & Faust, 1994) associated to each node.

Still another approach is investigated by Faloutsos, et al. (2004) who extract the "most relevant" connected subgraph containing two nodes of interest, using a method based on electrical flow. Moreover, Palmer & Faloutsos (2003) define a similarity function between categorical attributes, called "refined escape probability", based on random-walks and electrical-networks concepts. They show that this quantity provides a reasonably good measure for clustering and classifying categorical attributes.

Brand (2005) proposes the use of various quantities derived from the commute time for collaborative recommendations. He shows, as we do, that angular-based quantities perform much better than the commute time because the commute time is quite sensible to the node degree.

Very recently, Qiu and Hancock (2007) suggest an approach posed as a diffusion process on the graph, generalizing the computation of the average commute time using the normalized Laplacian and the Green's function. Moreover, they show in their experiments how computer vision problems such as image segmentation and motion tracking can be cast into commute time framework and solved effectively.

Notice finally that our approach based on a random-walk model on a graph is closely related to spectral-clustering and spectral-embedding techniques (for a recent account, see (von Luxburg, 2007)), as detailed in (Saerens, et al., 2004). It can be shown that it has a number of interesting links with both spectral clustering (see for instance Shi and Malik (2000); details are provided in (Saerens, et al., 2004)) and spectral embedding (Belkin & Niyogi, 2003; Belkin & Niyogi, 2001); in particular, the ECTD PCA provides a natural interpretation for both spectral clustering and embedding. Random-walk models on a graph also proved useful in the context of learning from labeled and unlabeled data; see for instance (Zhou, et al., 2005).

Figure 1. A simple movie database with three sets of elements (People, Movie, and Movie_category) and two relationships (has_watched and belongs_to)

Application to Collaborative Recommendation

Imagine a simple movie database with three sets of elements (see Figure 1) *people*, *movie*, and *movie_category*, and two relationships *has_watched*, between *people* and *movie* (notice that this relationship could also have been symmetrically called *has_been_watched*, showing that a movie has been watched by a particular user), and *belongs_to*, between *movie* and *movie_category* (notice that this relationship could also have been symmetrically called *contains*, showing that a movie category contains a particular movie): (1) computing proximity measures between people allows to cluster them into communities of interests about watched movies, (2) computing proximity measures between people and movies allows to suggest movies to watch or not to watch, or (3) computing proximity measures between people and movie categories allows to attach a most relevant category to each person. Our work focuses on the second task: **to suggest movies to watch or not to watch**. Applying random-walk based measures for the first task (clustering task) as well as for the third task is investigated in the work of Yen, et al. (2005).

Let us take an example containing 6 persons (*P1*, *P2*, *P3*, *P4*, *P5*, and *P6*), 4 movies (*M1*, *M2*, *M3*, and *M4*), and 2 movie categories (*C1* and *C2*).

(Figure 2) shows a graph derived from the movie database described in (Figure 1), containing the links (either an *has_watched* link or a *belongs_to* link) between the 12 nodes of the graph: for example, person *P1* has watched movie *M1*

(indeed, there is a link between nodes *P1* and *M1* in the graph) while person *P4* has watched movies *M1*, *M2*, and *M3* (remember that all the links are undirected). Movie category *C1* contains movies *M2* and *M3*; movie category *C2* contains movies *M1* and *M4*. The symmetric adjacency matrix *A* associated with this graph is shown in Figure 3, where the first 6 rows (columns) correspond to persons (from *P1* to *P6*), the next 4 rows (columns) to movies (from *M1* to *M4*) and the last 2 rows (columns) to movie categories (from *C1* to *C2*). A "0" means no link (or a missing link) between the corresponding nodes while a "1" represents the existence of a link between them. For example, the fact that person *P1* has only watched movie *M1* is represented in the matrix by a "1" in the 1st row (column) and 7th column (row) and "0" in the same row (column) but the next 3 columns (rows). Notice that, by the way this block matrix is built, **A** is symmetric. In this section, we show how the average commute time, the average first-passage time and the pseudoinverse Laplacian matrix of the graph are applied in the context of collaborative recommendation.

Average Commute Time

We use the average commute time $n(i,j)$ (which can be computed, for instance, by using equation (14)) to rank the elements of the considered set, where i and j are elements of the *people* and/or *item* sets. The average commute time between *people* elements and *item* elements is computed; the lower the value is, the more similar the two elements are.

Figure 2. A graph derived from the movie database

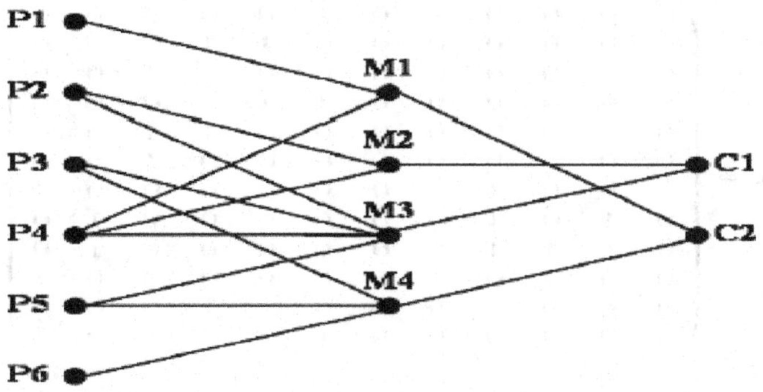

Average First-Passage Time

The *average first-passage time one-way* (FPTo) (which can be computed for instance by using equation (7)), $m(i|j)$, allows to rank element i of the *item* set with respect to element j of the *people* set. This provides a dissimilarity measure between person j and any element i of the *item* set.

The *average first-passage time return* (FPTr) (which can be computed for instance by using equation (7)), $m(j|i)$, allows to rank element i of the *item* set with respect to element j of the *people* set. More precisely, as a dissimilarity between element j of the *people* set and element i of the *item* set, $m(j|i)$ (the transpose of $m(i|j)$), that is, the average first-passage time return (FPTr) needed to reach j (from the *people* set) when starting from i (from the *item* set), is computed.

Pseudoinverse of the Laplacian Matrix of the Graph

The pseudoinverse of the Laplacian matrix of the graph can be computed by taking the pseudoinverse of the Laplacian matrix introduced in equation (2). $\mathbf{L}^+$ provides a similarity measure since it is the matrix containing the inner products of the node vectors in the Euclidean space where the nodes are exactly separated by the ECTD (see (Saerens, et al., 2004) for more details). Once

we have computed the similarity matrix, items are ranked according to their similarity with the user, and the closest item that has not been rated is proposed first.

KERNEL-BASED ALGORITHMS[2]

A function k of the form $k:\Omega\times\Omega\rightarrow R$ that, given two objects represented by $\mathbf{x}$ and $\mathbf{y}$ in some input space Ω, returns a real number $k(\mathbf{x},\mathbf{y})$ can be considered a similarity measure (i.e. enjoying natural properties of similarity, like the triangular property, among others (Chebotarev & Shamis, 1998a)) if it characterizes in a meaningful manner (i.e. intuitively adequate for applications) the similarities and differences (i.e. distance, proximity) between $\mathbf{x}$ and $\mathbf{y}$. A simple and classical similarity measure is the inner product of $\mathbf{x}$ and $\mathbf{y}$, if $\mathbf{x}$ and $\mathbf{y}$ are expressed in a vector (or inner-product) space. Positive definite functions k (or kernel functions) (Scholkopf and Smola, 2002; Scholkopf and Smola, 1998) enjoy the property that computing $k(\mathbf{x},\mathbf{y})$ is equivalent to computing the inner product of some transformation of $\mathbf{x}$ and $\mathbf{y}$ in another space.

In summary, kernel-based algorithms are characterized by at least two important properties: they allow (i) to compute inner products (i.e. similarities) in a high-dimensional space (often

Figure 3.

$$\mathbf{A} = \begin{pmatrix} 0 & 0 & 0 & 0 & 0 & 0 & 1 & 0 & 0 & 0 & 0 & 0 \\ 0 & 0 & 0 & 0 & 0 & 0 & 0 & 1 & 1 & 0 & 0 & 0 \\ 0 & 0 & 0 & 0 & 0 & 0 & 0 & 0 & 1 & 1 & 0 & 0 \\ 0 & 0 & 0 & 0 & 0 & 0 & 1 & 1 & 1 & 0 & 0 & 0 \\ 0 & 0 & 0 & 0 & 0 & 0 & 0 & 0 & 1 & 1 & 0 & 0 \\ 0 & 0 & 0 & 0 & 0 & 0 & 0 & 0 & 0 & 1 & 0 & 0 \\ 1 & 0 & 0 & 1 & 0 & 0 & 0 & 0 & 0 & 0 & 0 & 1 \\ 0 & 1 & 0 & 1 & 0 & 0 & 0 & 0 & 0 & 0 & 1 & 0 \\ 0 & 1 & 1 & 1 & 1 & 0 & 0 & 0 & 0 & 0 & 1 & 0 \\ 0 & 0 & 1 & 0 & 1 & 1 & 0 & 0 & 0 & 0 & 0 & 1 \\ 0 & 0 & 0 & 0 & 0 & 0 & 0 & 1 & 1 & 0 & 0 & 0 \\ 0 & 0 & 0 & 0 & 0 & 0 & 1 & 0 & 0 & 1 & 0 & 0 \end{pmatrix}$$

called "feature space") where the data is more likely to be well-separated while not requiring to map explicitly the input space to feature space, and (ii) to compute similarities between structured objects that cannot be naturally represented by a simple set of features. The latter property will be illustrated in this chapter, with the general objective of computing similarities between nodes of a graph.

Thus, a useful kernel is expected to capture an appropriate measure of similarity for a particular task (such as a collaborative-recommendation task or a classification task, as investigated in this chapter) and to require significantly less computation than would be needed via an explicit evaluation of the corresponding mapping from the input space into the feature space. In addition, mathematically, a kernel function must satisfy two requirements: (a) it must be symmetric (since the inner product of vectors is symmetric) and (b) it must be positive semidefinite.

An $n \times n$ symmetric kernel matrix $\mathbf{K}$ ([$\mathbf{K}$]$_{ij}$=k_{ij}=$k(\mathbf{x}_i, \mathbf{y}_j)$) computing the kernel function between $n \times n$ pairs of objects indexed by i, j satisfies the following properties (that are all alternative definitions for symmetric positive semidefinitiveness): (a) $\mathbf{x}^T\mathbf{K}\mathbf{x}=0$ for all $\mathbf{x} \in R^n$; (b) all the eigenvalues of $\mathbf{K}$ are positive; (c) $\mathbf{K}$ is the Gram (inner product) matrix of some collection of linearly independent vectors $\mathbf{x}_1, \ldots, \mathbf{x}_n \in R^n$ for some r, and (d) $\mathbf{K}$ can be viewed as a diagonal matrix Λ in another coordinate system ($\mathbf{K}=\mathbf{U}\Lambda\mathbf{U}^T$).

Various types of kernels were described in (Shawe-Taylor & Cristianini, 2004), such as polynomial kernels, Gaussian kernels, anova kernels, kernels on a graph, kernels on sets, kernels on real numbers, randomized kernels, etc. This chapter focuses on graph kernels: it gives an overview of the field, and it reports on applying various graph kernels to a collaborative-recommendation task and to a semi-supervised classification task.

Mining structured data, like graphs and relational databases, has been the focus of growing interest (see for instance (ACM SIGKDD, 2003; Wilson, et al., 2005). Graph kernels allow to address certain issues about graph structure. Indeed, a number of interesting measures, like a distance measure between graph nodes, are easily derived from a kernel. Distances between pairs of nodes allow, for example, to determine the items that are most similar to a given item, which facilitates labeling and clustering items.

A comprehensive description of graph kernels can be found in (Fouss, et al., 2007b; Fouss, et al., 2006b); this section is based on these references. The kernel-based similarity measures studied in this work take into account all paths (direct and indirect) between graph nodes. They have the nice property of increasing when the number of paths connecting two nodes increases and when the "length" of any path decreases. In short, the more short paths connect two nodes, the more similar those nodes are. On the contrary, the usual "shortest path" (also called "geodesic" or "Dijkstra" distance) between nodes of a graph does not necessarily decrease when connections between nodes are added and thus it does not capture the fact that strongly connected nodes are at a smaller distance than weakly connected ones.

The distance measure naturally derived from a kernel can easily be shown to be Euclidean, that is, the nodes of the graph can be embedded in a Euclidean space preserving distances between nodes. This property can be used to visualize the graph in a lower-dimensional space or, more generally, via a principal-component analysis (Saerens, et al., 2004; Scholkopf, et al., 1998; Shawe-Taylor & Cristianini, 2004) or a discriminant analysis, to define a subspace projection that enjoys some optimality property.

Kernels on a Graph

This section reviews the basic theory behind graph kernels. In a very general setting, once some proximity measure between the nodes of a graph has been shown to be a kernel, then a number of derived quantities and interesting results automatically follow almost for free. More precisely, from a kernel matrix, it is possible to define a data matrix where each row represents a node of the graph (a node vector), as an r-dimensional vector in a Euclidean space. These node vectors are such that their inner products are the elements of the kernel matrix. Through those node vectors, the graph can be viewed as a cloud of points in this r-dimensional space and standard multivariate statistical-analysis techniques become applicable.

In this work, we are interested in intuitively meaningful similarity measures defined on every pair of nodes in a graph. Mathematically, most of these similarity matrices are graph kernels, i.e. positive semidefinite matrices.

A real symmetric matrix that is not positive semidefinite can be changed to a positive semidefinite one by adding the identity matrix $\mathbf{I}$ multiplied by a suitably positive value to the original matrix (see, for example, (Roth, et al., 2002)). Indeed,

if $\mathbf{M}$ is a symmetric matrix, the matrix $(\mathbf{M}+\alpha\mathbf{I})$, with $\alpha \geq |\lambda_{\min}|$ (the smallest eigenvalue of $\mathbf{M}$) is positive semidefinite. This is because $\mathbf{M}$ and $(\mathbf{M}+\alpha\mathbf{I})$ have the same eigenvectors u_i associated with eigenvalues λ_i for $\mathbf{M}$ and $(\lambda_i+\alpha)$ for $(\mathbf{M}+\alpha\mathbf{I})$. Thus, by choosing $\alpha \geq |\lambda_{\min}|$, all the eigenvalues are non-negative and $(\mathbf{M}+\alpha\mathbf{I})$ is positive semidefinite.

Nine similarity matrices, defined from the adjacency matrix A and whose elements are the values of the kernel function on all pairs of nodes, are defined in Section 3.3 (results on collaborative-recommendation tasks are provided in (Fouss, et al., 2007b)). We review the main concepts behind this idea in the next sections. These concepts basically come from the fields of multidimensional scaling (Borg & Groenen, 1997; Cox & Cox, 2001; Mardia, et al., 1979) and kernel methods (Scholkopf & Smola, 2002; Shawe-Taylor & Cristianini, 2004).

The Data Matrix Associated to a Kernel Matrix

Let us first recall the fundamental spectral-decomposition theorem from standard linear algebra, underlying kernel-based work (see, e.g. (Mardia, et al., 1979; Noble & J. Daniels, 1998)):

"Any $n \times n$ real positive semidefinite matrix $\mathbf{K}$ of rank r can be expressed as $\mathbf{K}=\mathbf{U}\Lambda\mathbf{U}^{\mathrm{T}}=\mathbf{U}\Lambda^{\frac{1}{2}}(\mathbf{U}\Lambda^{\frac{1}{2}})^T=XX^T$, where Λ is a diagonal matrix containing the eigenvalues of $\mathbf{K}$, $\mathbf{U}$ is a $n \times r$ orthonormal matrix whose columns are the normalized eigenvectors $\mathbf{u}_i$ of $\mathbf{K}$, and $X=\mathbf{U}\Lambda^{\frac{1}{2}}$ is a $n \times r$ matrix of rank r. Thus, the columns $\mathbf{c}_i = \sqrt{\lambda_i}\mathbf{u}_i$ of X correspond to the orthonormal eigenvectors $\mathbf{u}_i$ of $\mathbf{K}$ multiplied by the square root of their corresponding eigenvalue."

Thus, if $\mathbf{x}_i$ is the column vector corresponding to column i of X^{T}, then the entries of $\mathbf{K}$ are inner products $[\mathbf{K}]_{ij}=k_{ij}=\mathbf{x}_i^{\mathrm{T}}\mathbf{x}_j$, in accordance with the fact that $\mathbf{K}$ is a kernel. The nodes of the graph are thus represented as vectors x_i in a r-dimensional Euclidean space and they form a cloud of n points in R^r. The $\mathbf{x}_i$'s are called *node vectors*, while matrix $\mathbf{X}=[\mathbf{x}_1,\mathbf{x}_2,\ldots,\mathbf{x}_n]^T$ containing the transposed node vectors as rows is the *data matrix* associated to the graph kernel.

The Euclidean space in which the node vectors are defined is the so-called feature space. A whole bundle of different algorithms can be used to visualize the nodes in a low-dimensional space (Lee & Verleysen, 2007) but this question is not investigated in this chapter.

Centering the Data Matrix

Usually, there is a preference for working with centered vectors, so that the center of gravity of the node vectors x_i is 0. For instance, most multivariate statistical techniques assume that the data has been centered on the center of gravity of the data cloud (Jolliffe, 2002; Mardia, et al., 1979). A data matrix is centered if $\mathbf{X}^T\mathbf{e}=\mathbf{0}$, that is, the sum of the elements of each column of $\mathbf{X}$ is 0. Now, it can easily be shown that a symmetric kernel matrix $\mathbf{K}$ is centered (that is, it corresponds to inner products of centered node vectors) if and only if $\mathbf{Ke}=\mathbf{0}$.

A centered kernel matrix $\overline{\mathbf{K}}$ is therefore defined by centering the node vectors, that is, by applying the symmetric centering matrix $\mathbf{H}=1-n^{-1}\mathbf{e}\mathbf{e}^T$ (Mardia, et al., 1979) to the data matrix $\mathbf{X}$. Indeed, pre-multiplying a data matrix by $\mathbf{H}$ re-expresses each element of the matrix as a deviation from its column mean, i.e. $\overline{\mathbf{X}} = \mathbf{HX}$ has its $(i,j)^{\text{th}}$ element $x_{ij} - \overline{x}_j$, where $\overline{x}_j$ is the mean of the jth column of I. Thus, the *centered kernel matrix* $\overline{\mathbf{K}}$ is defined as:

$$\overline{\mathbf{K}} = (\mathbf{HX})(\mathbf{HX})^T = \mathbf{HXX}^T\mathbf{H} = \mathbf{HKH}$$

The Cosine or Normalized Kernel Matrix

Inner product scores are not always an appropriate similarity measure. In some fields, such as information retrieval (Baeza-Yates & Ribeiro-Neto, 1999), the cosine similarity measure is preferred:

$$\cos_{ij} = \frac{\mathbf{x}_i^T\mathbf{x}_j}{\|\mathbf{x}_i\|\|\mathbf{x}_j\|} = \frac{k_{ij}}{\sqrt{k_{ii}k_{jj}}} \tag{23}$$

It is a kernel matrix since its elements are the inner products of the normalized node vectors $\mathbf{x}_i/\|\mathbf{x}_i\|$ (Shawe-Taylor & Cristianini, 2004).

In matrix form, $\mathbf{Cos}=\mathbf{Diag(K)}^{-\frac{1}{2}}\mathbf{K}\,\mathbf{Diag(K)}^{-\frac{1}{2}}$, where $\mathbf{Diag(K)}$ is a diagonal matrix containing the diagonal of $\mathbf{K}$.

Natural Distance Measure Associated to a Kernel Matrix

A *distance measure* between any pair of nodes in the feature space (therefore also corresponding to a Euclidean distance between the node vectors of the data matrix) can be derived from the kernel matrix:

$$\delta_{ij}^2 = \|\mathbf{x}_i - \mathbf{x}_j\|^2 = (\mathbf{x}_i - \mathbf{x}_j)^T(\mathbf{x}_i - \mathbf{x}_j)$$

$$= \mathbf{x}_i^T\mathbf{x}_i + \mathbf{x}_j^T\mathbf{x}_j - 2\mathbf{x}_i^T\mathbf{x}_j = k_{ii} + k_{jj} - 2k_{ij}$$

$$= (\mathbf{e}_i - \mathbf{e}_j)^T\mathbf{K}(\mathbf{e}_i - \mathbf{e}_j) \tag{24}$$

Since δ_{ij} corresponds to a Euclidean distance in R^r, it satisfies all the properties of a distance (positiveness, triangular inequality, etc.). Distances between pairs of elements allow, for instance, to use a clustering algorithm to group the nodes that are most similar (Yen, et al., 2007; Yen, et al., 2005).

In matrix form, $\Delta=\mathbf{diag}(\mathbf{K})\mathbf{e}^T+\mathbf{e}(\mathbf{diag}(\mathbf{K}))^T-2\mathbf{K}$, where $\mathbf{diag}(\mathbf{K})$ is a column vector containing the diagonal elements of $\mathbf{K}$, and $[\Delta]_{ij}=\delta_{ij}^2$ contains the squared distances (Borg & Groenen, 1997; Cox & Cox, 2001; Mardia, et al., 1979). As for notations, the name of column vectors is in bold lowercase while that of matrices is in bold uppercase.

With the cosine similarity measure, the distance reduces to $\delta_{ij}=sqrt(2(1-cos_{ij}))$. The other way around, given a square Euclidean distance matrix Δ, the natural centered kernel matrix associated to Δ is $\mathbf{K}=-\frac{1}{2}\mathbf{H}\Delta\mathbf{H}$ (Borg & Groenen, 1997; Cox & Cox, 2001; Mardia, et al., 1979).

The Principal-Component Analysis of the Kernel Matrix

Once a data matrix $\mathbf{X}$ has been derived from $\mathbf{K}$, standard multivariate statistical-analysis methods can be applied to investigate the structure of the data cloud. For instance, principal-component analysis can provide a low-dimension view of the data, keeping as much variance as possible in terms of the distance induced by the kernel. It is well-known that the principal-component analysis of a centered data matrix $\overline{\mathbf{X}}$ yields, as k^{th} principal axis, the eigenvector $\mathbf{v}_k$ of $\overline{\mathbf{X}}^T\overline{\mathbf{X}}$ (which is the variance-covariance matrix since the $\overline{x}_i$'s are centered). In (Fouss, et al., 2007a; Saerens, et al., 2004), it is shown that the node vectors $\overline{x}_i$ are expressed in the principal-component coordinate system. Although this is not investigated in this chapter, these node vectors can thus be used as such in order to visualize the graph. This is a consequence of classical multidimensional scaling (Borg & Groenen, 1997; Cox & Cox, 2001; Mardia, et al., 1979). Kernel-based algorithms, such as kernel principal-component analysis, are applied directly to the kernel matrix without computing the data matrix in the feature space (Scholkopf, et al., 1998; Shawe-Taylor & Cristianini, 2004).

Related Work

This section provides an overview of the various similarity measures between nodes of a graph that were proposed in the literature, to the best of our knowledge, and that are investigated later on.

Similarity between nodes is also called relatedness (White & P. Smyth, 2003) in the literature and the most well-known quantities measuring relatedness are co-citation (Small, 1973) and bibliographic coupling (Kessler, 1963). These are the two baseline measures that are adopted in our collaborative-recommendation experiments.

More sophisticated measures were suggested as well. For instance, a similarity measure between nodes of a graph integrating indirect paths, based on the matrix-forest theorem, was proposed in (Chebotarev & Shamis, 1997, Chebotarev & Shamis, 1998b). While some nice properties were proven about this similarity measure, no experiment investigating its effectiveness was reported. We therefore investigated this matrix-forest based measure (which actually is the same measure as the regularized Laplacian kernel described in Application to Collaborative Recommendation).

A modified regularized Laplacian kernel was proposed in (Ito, et al., 2005) as an extension of the regularized Laplacian kernel, by introducing a new parameter controling importance and relatedness. Moreover, in (Ito, et al., 2005; Shimbo & Ito, 2006), it was shown that the regularized Laplacian kernel overcomes some limitations of the von Neumann kernel (Kandola, et al., 2002), when ranking linked documents. This modified regularized Laplacian kernel is also closely related to a graph-regularization framework introduced by Zhou & Schölkopf (2004) and extended to directed graphs in (Zhou, et al., 2005). The resulting graph kernel is a normalized version of the "regularized Laplacian kernel" involving the extension of the Laplacian matrix for directed graphs (Chung, 2005). Chen, et al. (2007) studied graph embedding and semi-supervised classification by using this directed version of the "regularized Laplacian kernel".

The exponential and the von Neumann diffusion kernels, based on the adjacency matrix, were introduced in (Kandola, et al., 2002; Shawe-Taylor & Cristianini, 2004). They are computed through a power series of the adjacency matrix of the graph; they are therefore closely related to graph regularization models (Kondor & Lafferty, 2002). Indeed, Kondor & Lafferty (2002), as well as Smola & Kondor (2003), introduced a general method for constructing natural families of kernels over discrete structures, based on the matrix-exponentiation idea. The focus of that work is on generating kernels on graphs, with the proposal of a special class of exponential kernels called diffusion kernels (see Application to Collaborative Recommendation).

The "commute-time" kernel was introduced in (Fouss, et al., 2007a; Saerens, et al., 2004); it was inspired by the work of (Chandra, et al., 1989; Klein & Randic, 1993). It takes its name from the average commute time, which is the average number of steps that a random walker, starting from a given node, takes for entering another node for the first time and then going back to the starting node. The commute-time kernel is defined as the inner product in a Euclidean space where the nodes are exactly separated by the commute-time distance. This kernel performs well in collaborative recommendation, as shown in (Fouss, et al., 2007a). At the same time, Qiu & Hancock (2005; 2007), Ham, et al. (2004), Yen, et al. (2001) as well as Brand (2005) defined the same commute-time embedding, preserving the commute-time distance, and applied it to image segmentation and multi-body motion tracking (Qiu & Hancock, Qiu & Hancock, 2007), to dimensionality reduction of manifolds (Ham, et al., 2004), to clustering Yen, et al. (2001), and to collaborative filtering (Brand 2005; Fouss, et al., 2007a), with interesting results. The commute-time kernel is also closely related to the "Fiedler vector" (Fiedler, 1975; Mohar, 1992), widely used

for graph partitioning (Carrington, et al., 2006; Pothen, et al., 1990) and clustering (Donetti & Munoz, 2004), as detailed in (Fouss, et al., 2007a), but also to discrete Green functions (Ding, et al., 2007). Finally, a family of dissimilarity measure reducing to the shortest-path distance at one end and to the commute-time (or resistance) distance at the other end was proposed in (Yen, et al., 2008).

Recent papers (Latapy & Pons, 2005; Nadler, et al., 2005; Nadler, et al., 2006; Pons & Latapy, 2006) proposed an intuitively appealing distance measure between nodes of a graph based on a continuous-time diffusion process, called the "diffusion distance". We defined a discrete-time counterpart of their distance and used it to define the "Markov diffusion kernel" (Fouss, et al., 2006b). An application of the diffusion distance to dimensionality reduction and graph visualization was described in (Lafon & Lee, 2006). The natural embedding induced by the diffusion distance was called the "diffusion map" by Nadler, et al. (2005; 2006).

Other recent papers attempted to adapt the well-known PageRank procedure (Brin & Page, 1998; Page, Brin, et al., 1998) to define meaningful similarities between nodes. A random-walk with a restart procedure was proposed in (Pan, et al., 2006; Tong, et al., 2008). A random-walk process starting from a node of interest, controlled by some precomputed correlation matrix between nodes, was described in (Gori & Pucci, 2006a) and is presented in the next section.

Recently, Yajima & Kuo (2006) proposed a kernel approach for recommendation tasks based on one-class support-vector machines with graph kernels generated from a Laplacian matrix. Preliminary experiments on the MovieLens dataset produced interesting results with the commute-time kernel, the regularized commute-time kernel, and the regularized Laplacian kernel.

Several attempts to define similarity measures for regular directed graphs were proposed as well. For instance Chung (2005) proposed to start from the transition-probability matrix $P=D^{-1}A$ where

D is, as before, a diagonal matrix containing the outdegrees of the graph nodes. Then, they compute the left eigenvector of $\mathbf{P}$, $\boldsymbol{\pi}^T\mathbf{P}=\lambda\boldsymbol{\pi}^T$, which corresponds to the stationary distribution of the Markov chain. If the diagonal matrix containing the elements of $\boldsymbol{\pi}$ is denoted by $\mathbf{\Pi}=\mathbf{Diag}(\boldsymbol{\pi})$, the Laplacian matrix of the directed graph is then defined by:

$$\mathbf{L} = \mathbf{\Pi} - \frac{\mathbf{\Pi P} + \mathbf{P}^T\mathbf{\Pi}}{2} \tag{25}$$

It has a number of interesting properties generalizing those of the usual Laplacian matrix for undirected graphs. In particular, it is positive semidefinite and therefore defines a kernel matrix.

The normalized Laplacian matrix can be defined as:

$$\tilde{\mathbf{L}} = \mathbf{\Pi}^{-\frac{1}{2}}\mathbf{L}\mathbf{\Pi}^{-\frac{1}{2}}$$

Zhou, et al. (2005) used the regularized normalized Laplacian kernel matrix:

$$(\mathbf{I} - \alpha\tilde{\mathbf{L}})^{-1}$$

in the context of semisupervised classification of labeled nodes of a graph while Chen, et al. (2007) used the regularized Laplacian kernel matrix for directed graph embedding. Based on the same idea, Zhao, et al. (2007) proposed a directed contextual distance and defined a directed graph from which the Laplacian matrix is computed. It was then used for ranking and clustering images. For undirected graphs, it can be shown that these kernel matrices reduce to variants of the regularized Laplacian kernel. Since all the graphs investigated in our experiments are undirected, we do not provide comparisons with those kernels.

Yet another attempt to define similarities between nodes on a directed graph based on the matrix-forest theorem was described in (Agaev & Chebotarev, 2000; Agaev & Chebotarev, 2001).

Application to Collaborative Recommendation

This section describes in more detail the nine kernel-based algorithms, introduced in Related Work (i.e. the exponential diffusion kernel, the Laplacian exponential diffusion kernel, the von Neumann diffusion kernel, the regularized Laplacian kernel, the commute-time kernel, the Markov diffusion kernel, the cross-entropy diffusion matrix, the random-walk-with-restart similarity matrix, and the regularized commute-time kernel).

The Exponential Diffusion Kernel

The so-called *exponential diffusion kernel* ($\mathbf{K}_{ED}$), introduced by Kondor & Lafferty (2002), is defined as:

$$\mathbf{K}_{ED} = \sum_{k=0}^{\infty} \frac{\alpha^k\mathbf{A}^k}{k!} = \exp(\alpha\mathbf{A}) \tag{26}$$

where $\mathbf{A}$ is the adjacency matrix of the graph and exp is the matrix exponential. Element $a^k_{ij}=[\mathbf{A}^k]_{ij}$ of matrix $\mathbf{A}^k$ ($\mathbf{A}$ to the power k) is the number of paths (assuming that direct weights a_{ij} are interpreted as the number of direct links between the two nodes i and j) between node i and node j with exactly k transitions or steps. Thus the kernel integrates a contribution from all paths connecting node i and node j, discounting paths according to their number of steps. It favors shorter (in terms of number of steps) paths between two nodes by giving them a heavier weight. The discounting factor is $\alpha^k/k!$. Other choices for that factor lead to other kernels, like the von Neumann diffusion kernel, described later on.

The $\mathbf{K}_{ED}$ matrix is clearly positive semidefinite since the exponential of $\mathbf{A}$ amounts to replacing

Λ (a diagonal matrix containing the eigenvalues of $\mathbf{A}$) by $\exp(\Lambda)$ in the spectral decomposition of $\mathbf{A}$ (the matrix exponential of a diagonal matrix is a diagonal matrix whose (i,j) element is the exponential of the corresponding element in the original matrix, therefore always positive).

The Laplacian Exponential Diffusion Kernel

A meaningful alternative to $\mathbf{K}_{ED}$ is a diffusion model (Kelly, 1979; Smola & Kondor, 2003) that substitutes the adjacency matrix with minus the Laplacian matrix in equation (26). As an intuitive insight into the model, suppose that a quantity x_i is defined on each node i of the graph and that it diffuses to neighboring nodes with a symmetric diffusion rate a_{ij}. Thus, during a small time interval δt, an amount $a_{ij}x_i\delta t$ is transferred from node i to node j, proportional to both the time interval δt, the weight a_{ij}, and to the quantity $x_i(t)$ present at node i at time t. The balance equation is given by:

$$x_i(t + \delta t) = x_i(t) + \sum_{j=1}^{n}a_{ji}x_j\delta t - \sum_{j=1}^{n}a_{ij}x_i\delta t$$

(27)

Since $\mathbf{A}$ is symmetric, this last equation leads to, for $\delta t \to 0$:

$$\frac{dx_i(t)}{dt} = \sum_{j=1}^{n}a_{ji}x_j - a_{i\bullet}x_i$$

$$= \sum_{j=1}^{n}(a_{ji}x_j - a_{i\bullet}\delta_{ij}x_j)$$

$$= -\sum_{j=1}^{n}(a_{i\bullet}\delta_{ij} - a_{ij})x_j$$

(28)

where δ_{ij} is the Kronecker delta. The elements $l_{ij} = (a_{i.}\delta_{ij} - a_{ij})$ are the entries of the Laplacian matrix.

In matrix form:

$$\frac{d\mathbf{x}(t)}{dt} = -\mathbf{L}\mathbf{x}(t)$$

(29)

This system of differential equations leads to the following solution

$$\mathbf{x}(t) = \exp(-\mathbf{L}t)\mathbf{x}_0$$

(30)

where $\mathbf{x}_0$ is the initial vector $\mathbf{x}$ at time $t=0$ and exp is the matrix exponential. This leads to the *Laplacian exponential diffusion kernel*, introduced in (Kondor & Lafferty, 2002; Smola & Kondor, 2003), and defined as:

$$\mathbf{K}_{LED} = \exp(-\alpha\mathbf{L})$$

(31)

which is similar to equation (26), except that it involves the Laplacian matrix as basis matrix instead of the adjacency matrix. Equation (30) shows that column i of $\mathbf{K}_{LED}$ corresponds to the quantity $\mathbf{x}$ observed at time $t=\alpha$ when the initial vector is:

$$\mathbf{x}_0 = \mathbf{e}_i = [\underset{1}{0},\dots,\underset{i-1}{0},\underset{i}{1},\underset{i+1}{0},\dots,\underset{n}{0}]^{\mathrm{T}}$$

3.3.3. The von Neumann Diffusion Kernel

The *von Neumann diffusion kernel* ($\mathbf{K}_{VND}$) (Kandola, et al., 2002; Shawe-Taylor & Cristianini, 2004) differs from the exponential diffusion kernel by the discounting scheme. The von Neumann diffusion kernel has an exponential discounting rate α^k:

$$\mathbf{K}_{VND} = \sum_{k=0}^{\infty}\alpha^k\mathbf{A}^k = (\mathbf{I} - \alpha\mathbf{A})^{-1}$$

(32)

$\mathbf{K}_{\text{VND}}$ is well-defined only if $0<\alpha<\|\mathbf{A}\|_2^{-1}$ where $\|\mathbf{A}\|_2$ is the spectral radius of the symmetric matrix $\mathbf{A}$. In this case, $\mathbf{K}_{\text{VND}}$ is positive definite. It was shown in (Ito, et al., 2005) that this kernel applied to document ranking defines a link-analysis measure intermediate between co-citation/bibliographic coupling (Kessler, 1963; Small, 1973) and HITS (Kleinberg, 1999).

The Regularized Laplacian Kernel

The *regularized Laplacian kernel* (Ito, et al., 2005; Smola & Kondor, 2003) differs from the von Neumann diffusion kernel only by substituting the negated Laplacian matrix -$\mathbf{L}$ for the adjacency matrix $\mathbf{A}$:

$$\mathbf{K}_{\text{L}} = \sum_{k=0}^{\infty} \alpha^k (-\mathbf{L})^k = (\mathbf{I} + \alpha\mathbf{L})^{-1} \qquad (33)$$

where $0<\alpha<\|\mathbf{L}\|_2^{-1}$ where $\|\mathbf{L}\|_2$ is the spectral radius of $\mathbf{L}$. $\mathbf{K}_{\text{L}}$ is positive semidefinite. The regularized Laplacian kernel has been shown to provide better performance than the von Neumann kernel in a bibliographic citation task (Ito, et al., 2005).

This similarity measure has an interesting interpretation in terms of the matrix-forest theorem (Chebotarev & Shamis, 1997; Chebotarev & Shamis, 1998b). Let F^i be the set of all spanning forests rooted at node i of graph G and F^{ij} be the set of those spanning rooted forests for which nodes i and j belong to the same tree rooted at i. A spanning rooted forest is an acyclic subgraph of G that has the same nodes as G and one marked node (a root) in each component. It is shown in (Chebotarev & Shamis, 1997; Chebotarev & Shamis, 1998b) that the matrix $(\mathbf{I}+\mathbf{L})^{-1}$ exists and that $[(\mathbf{I}+\mathbf{L})^{-1}]_{ij} = \varepsilon(F^{ij})/\varepsilon(F^i)$ where $\varepsilon(F^{ij})$ and $\varepsilon(F^i)$ are the total weights of forests that belong to F^{ij} and F^i respectively. The elements of this matrix are therefore called "relative forest accessibilities" between nodes. This interpretation can be gener-

alized to the matrix $(\mathbf{I}+\alpha\mathbf{L})^{-1}$ with a parameter α weighting the number of edges belonging to the forests as well as limiting the size of forests (in terms of number of edges; see (Chebotarev & Shamis, 1997; Chebotarev & Shamis, 1998b) for more details); it can be shown that this matrix is a similarity measure.

A modified regularized Laplacian kernel was proposed in (Ito, et al., 2005), by introducing a new parameter controlling importance and relatedness. A modified Laplacian matrix is defined as $\mathbf{L}_\gamma = \gamma\mathbf{D}-\mathbf{A}$ with $0<\gamma\leq1$. The modified regularized Laplacian kernel $\mathbf{K}_{\text{RL}}$ is computed as:

$$\mathbf{K}_{\text{RL}} = \sum_{k=0}^{\infty} \alpha^k (-\mathbf{L}_\gamma)^k = (\mathbf{I} + \alpha\mathbf{L}_\gamma)^{-1} \qquad (34)$$

It was shown that, for $\alpha>0$ and $0<\gamma\leq1$, if the series (34) converges, $\mathbf{K}_{\text{RL}}$ is positive semidefinite and that it also yields a measure intermediate between relatedness and importance (Ito, et al., 2005).

The Commute-Time Kernel

Consider a discrete Markov chain and let $s(t)$ be a random variable representing the state of the Markov chain at time step t. Thus, if the process is in state $i\in\{1,...,n\}$ at time t, then $s(t)=i$. Let us denote the probability of being in state i at time t by $x_i(t)=*P(s(t)=i)$ and define $\mathbf{P}$ as the transition-probability matrix with entries $p_{ij}=[\mathbf{P}]_{ij}=*P(s(t+1)=j \mid s(t)=i)$, where $[\mathbf{P}]_{ij}$ is the i,j element of matrix $\mathbf{P}$. We consider a Markov model for which the transition probabilities are provided by $p_{ij}=a_{ij}/a_i$ with $a_i=\sum_j a_{ij}$. In other words, to any state or node $s(t)=i$, we associate a probability of jumping to an adjacent node $s(t+1)=j$ that is proportional to the weight $a_{ij}\geq0$ of the edge connecting i and j (this corresponds to a standard random-walk model on a graph). The transition probabilities depend only on the current state and not on the past ones (first-order Markov chain).

Since the graph is undirected and connected, the Markov chain is irreducible, that is, every state can be reached from any other state.

In matrix form, the evolution of the Markov chain is characterized by $\mathbf{x}(t+1)=\mathbf{P}^T\mathbf{x}(t)$, which provides the state probability distribution $\mathbf{x}(t)=[x_1(t),x_2(t),\ldots,x_n(t)]^T$ at time t once the initial probability density $\mathbf{x}(0)=\mathbf{x}^0$ at $t=0$ is known. It is clear that after t steps, the probability distribution will be given by $\mathbf{x}(t)=(\mathbf{P}^T)^t\mathbf{x}^0$.

The commute-time kernel (Fouss, et al., 2007a; Saerens, et al., 2004) takes its name from the *average commute time $n(i,j)$*, which is the average number of steps that a random walker, starting in node $i\neq j$, takes before entering node j for the first time and then going back to i. The average commute time can be computed as [29, 73]:

$$n(i,j) = V_G(\mathbf{e}_i - \mathbf{e}_j)^T \mathbf{L}^+(\mathbf{e}_i - \mathbf{e}_j) \qquad (35)$$

where every node i of the graph is represented by a basis vector $\mathbf{e}_i$ in the Euclidean space $\mathbb{R}^n$ and V_G is the volume of the graph. $\mathbf{L}^+$ is the Moore-Penrose pseudoinverse of the Laplacian matrix of the graph and it is positive semidefinite. Thus, equation (35) is a Mahalanobis distance between the nodes of the graph and is referred to as the "commute-time distance" or the "resistance distance" because of a close analogy with the effective resistance in electrical networks (Fouss, et al., 2007a).

It can be shown that the elements of $\mathbf{L}^+$ are inner products of the node vectors in the Euclidean space where these node vectors are exactly separated by commute-time distances. In other words, the elements of $\mathbf{L}^+$ can be viewed as similarity measures between nodes. Hence the *commute-time kernel* ($\mathbf{K}_{CT}$) is defined as:

$$\mathbf{K}_{CT} = \mathbf{L}^+ \qquad (36)$$

with no parameter tuning necessary. The commute-time kernel is simply the pseudoinverse of the Laplacian matrix of the original graph, as described in The Pseduoinverse of the Laplacian Matrix of the Graph.

There is of course a close relationship between the commute-time kernel and the regularized Laplacian kernel. Indeed, if $\mathbf{L}$ has eigenvalues λ_i (in decreasing order), $(\mathbf{L}+\alpha^{-1}\mathbf{I})$ has corresponding eigenvalues $(\lambda_i+\alpha^{-1})$ and both matrices share the same eigenvectors $\mathbf{u}_i$. Remember that $\mathbf{L}$ and its Moore-Penrose pseudoinverse $\mathbf{L}^+$ have the same set of eigenvectors, but inverse eigenvalues, except the zero eigenvalues which remain equal to zero. Moreover, the Laplacian matrix of a connected graph has rank $n-1$ and therefore has only one eigenvalue equal to 0 (Chung, 1997). Thus a spectral decomposition of the corresponding kernels yields:

$$\mathbf{L}^+ = \sum_{i=1}^{n-1}\lambda_i^{-1}\mathbf{u}_i\mathbf{u}_i^T$$

(by definition of the Moore-Penrose pseudoinverse) and:

$$(\mathbf{I} + \alpha\mathbf{L})^{-1} = \alpha^{-1}\sum_{i=1}^{n}(\lambda_i + \alpha^{-1})^{-1}\mathbf{u}_i\mathbf{u}_i^T$$

Since the normalized eigenvector of $\mathbf{L}$ corresponding to the last eigenvalue $\lambda_n=0$ is $\mathbf{u}_n = \mathbf{e}/\sqrt{n}$, the nth term for the commute-time kernel is simply 0, while it is $\mathbf{e}\mathbf{e}^T/n$ for the regularized Laplacian kernel. Therefore, this last term simply adds a constant value $(1/n)$ to all the elements of the matrix and, if α is large, $\lambda_i+\alpha^{-1}$ will be close to λ_i, so that the two kernels essentially differ by a multiplication factor and a constant value added to all the elements of the matrix.

The Markov Diffusion Kernel

This graph kernel, introduced in (Fouss, et al., 2006b), is based on a diffusion distance defined in (Latapy & Pons, 2005; Nadler, et al., 2005; Nadler, et al., 2006; Pons & Latapy, 2006) between nodes of a graph in a continuous-time diffusion model.

We adapted their definition of diffusion distance to discrete-time processes and to periodic Markov chains (as nonperiodic Markov chains are unrealistic for collaborative recommendation) to define a valid kernel on a graph (Fouss, et al., 2006b). It was shown in (Nadler, et al., 2005; Nadler, et al., 2006) that the low-dimension representation of the data by the first few eigenvectors of the corresponding Markov matrix is optimal under a given mean-square error criterion involving the diffusion distance. An application of the diffusion distance to dimensionality reduction and graph visualization was described in (Lafon & Lee, 2006).

The average visiting rate $\bar{x}_{ik}(t)$ in state k after t steps for a process that started in state i at time t=0 is computed as follows:

$$\bar{x}_{ik}(t) = \frac{1}{t}\sum_{\tau=1}^{t} {}^{*}P(s(\tau) = k \mid s(0) = i) \qquad (37)$$

From this quantity, we define the diffusion distance at time t between node i and node j as:

$$d_{ij}(t) = \sum_{k=1}^{n}\left[\bar{x}_{ik}(t) - \bar{x}_{jk}(t)\right]^2 \qquad (38)$$

which corresponds to the sum of the squared differences between the average visiting rates at node k after t transitions, when starting from node i and node j at time t=0. This is a natural definition which quantifies the dissimilarity between two nodes based on the evolution of the probability distribution. Thus, if two nodes influence the graph in the same way, the distance is zero. Of course, when i=j, $d_{ij}(t)$=0.

This diffusion distance was proposed by Nadler, et al. (2005) and by Latapy & Pons (2005) in the context of diffusion processes. Actually, their definition, namely:

$$d_{ij}(t) = \sum_{k=1}^{n}\left(x_{ik}(t) - x_{jk}(t)\right)^2$$

involves $x_{ik}(t)$, the probability of finding the random walker in state k at time t, when starting in node i at time 0 (i.e. $\mathbf{x}(0)$=$\mathbf{e}_i$) instead of $\bar{x}_{ik}(t)$ as in equation (38). Their definition does not work with periodic Markov chains that are relevant to collaborative recommendation (with a bipartite graph). The definition of (Latapy & Pons, 2005; Nadler, et al., 2005; Nadler, et al., 2006; Pons & Latapy, 2006) also adds a weighting factor proportional to the inverse of the stationary distribution of the Markov chain, therefore putting more weight on low-density nodes. We do not include that factor because experiments (see (Fouss, et al., 2006b)) showed that it does not improve the performance.

We first compute $\bar{x}_{ik}(t)$ from equation (37):

$$\bar{x}_{ik}(t) = \frac{1}{t}\sum_{\tau=1}^{t} {}^{*}P(s(\tau) = k \mid s(0) = i) \qquad (39)$$

$$= \frac{1}{t}\sum_{\tau=1}^{t}\mathbf{e}_k^{\mathrm{T}}(\mathbf{P}^{\mathrm{T}})^{\tau}\mathbf{e}_i = \mathbf{e}_k^{\mathrm{T}}\left[\frac{1}{t}\sum_{\tau=1}^{t}\mathbf{P}^{\tau}\right]^{\mathrm{T}}\mathbf{e}_i \qquad (40)$$

since ${}^{*}P(s(t)$=$k \mid s(0)$=$i)$=$\mathbf{e}_k^{\mathrm{T}}\mathbf{x}(t)$=$\mathbf{e}_k^{\mathrm{T}}(\mathbf{P}^{\mathrm{T}})^t\mathbf{e}_i$ since $\mathbf{x}^0$=$\mathbf{e}_i$.

By defining $\mathbf{Z}(t) = \frac{1}{t}\sum_{\tau=1}^{t}\mathbf{P}^{\tau}$, we obtain:

$$\bar{x}_{ik}(t) = \mathbf{e}_k^{\mathrm{T}}\mathbf{Z}^{\mathrm{T}}(t)\mathbf{e}_i \qquad (41)$$

We now turn to the evaluation of the Markov diffusion distance equation (38):

$$d_{ij}(t) = \sum_{k=1}^{n}\left(\bar{x}_{ik}(t) - \bar{x}_{jk}(t)\right)^2 \qquad (42)$$

$$= \sum_{k=1}^{n} \left(\mathbf{e}_k^{\mathrm{T}} \mathbf{Z}^{\mathrm{T}}(t) \mathbf{e}_i - \mathbf{e}_k^{\mathrm{T}} \mathbf{Z}^{\mathrm{T}}(t) \mathbf{e}_j \right)^2 \qquad (43)$$

$$= \| \mathbf{Z}^{\mathrm{T}}(t)(\mathbf{e}_i - \mathbf{e}_j) \|^2 \qquad (44)$$

$$= (\mathbf{e}_i - \mathbf{e}_j)^{\mathrm{T}} \mathbf{Z}(t) \mathbf{Z}^{\mathrm{T}}(t)(\mathbf{e}_i - \mathbf{e}_j) \qquad (45)$$

which has exactly the same form as equation (24). We immediately deduce the form of the *Markov diffusion kernel* ($\mathbf{K}_{\mathrm{MD}}$):

$$\mathbf{K}_{\mathrm{MD}}(t) = \mathbf{Z}(t) \mathbf{Z}^{\mathrm{T}}(t) \mathrm{with} \mathbf{Z}(t) = \frac{1}{t} \sum_{\tau=1}^{t} \mathbf{P}^{\tau} \qquad (46)$$

Notice that in order to evaluate $\mathbf{Z}(t)$, we use a trick similar to the one used in PageRank (Langville & Meyer, 2005): a dummy absorbing state linked to all the states of the Markov chain is created with a very small probability of jumping to this state. This aims to subtract some small quantity from every element of $\mathbf{P}$, with the result that the matrix $\mathbf{P}$ is now substochastic and that $\mathbf{Z}(t)$ admits the following analytical form:

$$\mathbf{Z}(t) = \frac{1}{t}(\mathbf{I} - \mathbf{P})^{-1}(\mathbf{I} - \mathbf{P}^t)\mathbf{P} \qquad (47)$$

The Cross-Entropy Diffusion Matrix

Instead of using a least-square distance for comparing two probability distributions as in equation (38), it is more appropriate to use the symmetric cross-entropy divergence (Cover & Thomas, 2006; Kapur & Kesavan, 1992), as computed by:

$$d_{ij}(t) = \sum_{k=1}^{n} \left[\overline{x}_{ik}(t) \log \frac{\overline{x}_{ik}(t)}{\overline{x}_{jk}(t)} + \overline{x}_{jk}(t) \log \frac{\overline{x}_{jk}(t)}{\overline{x}_{ik}(t)} \right] \qquad (48)$$

This leads to the *cross-entropy diffusion matrix* ($\mathbf{K}_{\mathrm{CED}}$) (since the distance cancels out the asymmetric part of the matrix, the kernel matrix can be symmetrized without change):

$$\mathbf{K}_{\mathrm{CED}}(t) = \mathbf{Z}(t) \log(\mathbf{Z}^{\mathrm{T}}(t)) + \log(\mathbf{Z}(t)) \mathbf{Z}^{\mathrm{T}}(t) \mathrm{with} \mathbf{Z}(t) = \frac{1}{t} \sum_{\tau=1}^{t} \mathbf{P}^{\tau} \qquad (49)$$

where the element-wise logarithm is taken on each element of the matrix. We did not prove the positive semi-definitiveness of this similarity matrix; it therefore cannot be considered as a kernel.

The Random-Walk-with-Restart Similarity Matrix

Pan, et al. (2006) (see also (Tong, et al., 2006; Tong, et al., 2008)) recently introduced a similarity matrix between nodes inspired by the well-known PageRank algorithm (Brin & Page, 1998; Page, Brin, et al., 1998). This model has been applied to various interesting applications, including center-piece subgraph discovery and content-based image retrieval (Pan, et al., 2006; Tong, et al., 2006; Tong, et al., 2008). The same idea was introduced also in (Gori & Pucci, 2006a; Gori & Pucci, 2006b) in the context of collaborative recommendation.

Like the diffusion kernel, the model considers a random walker jumping from some node i and to some neighbor node j with a probability proportional (apart from normalization) to the edge weight:

$$p_{ij} = \mathrm{P}(s(t+1) = j \mid s(t) = i) = a_{ij} / a_{i\bullet}$$

In addition, at each step of the random walk, the random walker has some probability $(1-\alpha)$ to return to node i instead of continuing to neighbor nodes. In other words, the probability distribution of finding the random walker on each node at time t is provided by:

$$\begin{cases} \mathbf{x}(0) = \mathbf{e}_i \\ \mathbf{x}(t+1) = \alpha \mathbf{P}^{\mathrm{T}} \mathbf{x}(t) + (1-\alpha)\mathbf{e}_i \end{cases} \quad (50)$$

where $\mathbf{e}_i$ is a column vector with "0" entries, except in position i whose entry is "1".

Considering the steady-state solution $\mathbf{x}(t+1) = \mathbf{x}(t) = \mathbf{x}$ and extracting the probability distribution $\mathbf{X}$ of finding the random walker on each node when starting from node i yields:

$$\mathbf{x} = (1-\alpha)(\mathbf{I} - \alpha \mathbf{P}^{\mathrm{T}})^{-1}\mathbf{e}_i \quad (51)$$

which corresponds, up to a scaling factor, to column i of the matrix $(\mathbf{I}-\alpha\mathbf{P}^{\mathrm{T}})^{-1}$. Notice that since the matrix $\alpha\mathbf{P}$ is substochastic, the inverse of $(\mathbf{I}-\alpha\mathbf{P})$ exists if the Markov chain is regular. Vector $\mathbf{x}$ can be viewed as containing a similarity between node i and the other nodes of the graph.

Now, since $\mathbf{x}$ is column i of matrix $(\mathbf{I}-\alpha\mathbf{P}^{\mathrm{T}})^{-1}$, the *random-walk-with-restart matrix* ($\mathbf{K}_{\mathrm{RWR}}$) is defined as the matrix whose i^{th} row contains the similarities to node i (the matrix is transposed):

$$\mathbf{K}_{\mathrm{RWR}} = (\mathbf{I} - \alpha \mathbf{P})^{-1} \quad (52)$$

with the same form as the fundamental matrix $(\mathit{I}-\mathit{P})^{-1}$ of the Markov chain. $\mathbf{K}_{\mathrm{RWR}}$ can be rewritten as:

$$\mathbf{K}_{\mathrm{RWR}} = (\mathbf{D}^{-1}(\mathbf{D} - \alpha\mathbf{A}))^{-1} = (\mathbf{D} - \alpha\mathbf{A})^{-1}\mathbf{D} \quad (53)$$

since $\mathbf{P} = \mathbf{D}^{-1}\mathbf{A}$.

The Regularized Commute-Time Kernel

Remember that the Laplacian matrix, whose pseudoinverse is called the commute-time kernel in our work, is not invertible. Instead of taking the pseudoinverse of the matrix, a simple regularization framework could be applied as for the regularized Laplacian kernel. One such regularization leads to what we call the *regularized commute-time kernel* ($\mathbf{K}_{\mathrm{RCT}}$):

$$\mathbf{K}_{\mathrm{RCT}} = (\mathbf{D} - \alpha\mathbf{A})^{-1} \quad (54)$$

with $\alpha \in]0,1[$. Since $\mathbf{K}_{\mathrm{RCT}}$ is the matrix inverse of the sum $((1-\alpha)\mathbf{D}+\alpha\mathbf{L})$ of a positive definite matrix and a positive semidefinite matrix, it is positive definite and it is a valid kernel.

Another justification of the interest of this graph kernel is as follows. Consider the following random-walk model starting at node i:

$$\begin{cases} \mathbf{x}(0) = \mathbf{e}_i \\ \mathbf{x}(t+1) = \mathbf{P}^{\mathrm{T}}\mathbf{x}(t) \end{cases} \quad (55)$$

The column vector $\mathbf{x}(t)$ contains the probability distribution of finding the random walker in each state of the finite Markov chain. Thus, the random walker starts at node i and diffuses through the network. Let us define the similarity vector between node i and other nodes of the network by:

$$\mathbf{sim}_i = \sum_{\tau=0}^{\infty} \alpha^\tau \mathbf{D}^{-1}\mathbf{x}(\tau) \quad (56)$$

with $\alpha \in]0,1[$. The weighting factor $\mathbf{D}^{-1}$ compensates for the fact that $\mathbf{x}(t)$ converges to the stationary distribution, which is proportional to the diagonal elements of $\mathbf{D}$ with undirected graphs (Ross, 1996). A similarity measure based on $\mathbf{x}(t)$ only (without weighting factor) would therefore favor the nodes with a high outdegree $[\mathbf{D}]_{ij}$. equation (56) thus accumulates, with a damping factor α (late visits are less important than early visits), the probability of visiting each node when starting from node i.

We easily find:

$$\mathbf{sim}_i = \sum_{\tau=0}^{\infty} \alpha^\tau \mathbf{D}^{-1}\mathbf{x}(\tau) \quad (57)$$

$$= \mathbf{D}^{-1} \sum_{\tau=0}^{\infty} \alpha^{\tau} \left(\mathbf{P}^{\mathrm{T}} \right)^{\tau} \mathbf{e}_i \qquad (58)$$

$$= \mathbf{D}^{-1} (\mathbf{I} - \alpha \mathbf{P}^{\mathrm{T}})^{-1} \mathbf{e}_i \qquad (59)$$

$$= \mathbf{D}^{-1} \left((\mathbf{D} - \alpha \mathbf{A}) \mathbf{D}^{-1} \right)^{-1} \mathbf{e}_i \qquad (60)$$

$$= (\mathbf{D} - \alpha \mathbf{A})^{-1} \mathbf{e}_i \qquad (61)$$

$$= \mathrm{col}_i (\mathbf{K}_{\mathrm{RCT}}) \qquad (62)$$

where we used $\mathbf{P} = \mathbf{D}^{-1}\mathbf{A}$ and the fact that $\mathbf{D}$ is diagonal and $\mathbf{A}$ is symmetric.

Thus, the i,j element of $\mathbf{K}_{\mathrm{RCT}}$ can be interpreted as the discounted cumulated probability of visiting node j when starting from node i. The regularized commute-time kernel (equation (54)) differs from the random-walk-with-restart similarity matrix (equation (53)) only in the fact that the latter post-multiplies the former by $\mathbf{D}$: $\mathbf{K}_{\mathrm{RCT}}$ is not a kernel since it is not symmetric and therefore not positive semidefinite.

CONCLUSION

This chapter is devoted to promising link-based approaches applied recently and successfully to collaborative-recommendation systems. First, a general procedure for computing similarities between elements of a database is defined. It is based on a Markov-chain model of random walk through a graph representation of the database. More precisely, we compute quantities (the average first-passage time, the average commute time, and the pseudoinverse of the Laplacian matrix) that provide similarity measures between any pair of elements of a connected graph. These similarity measures can be used in order to compare items belonging to database tables that are not necessarily directly connected. They rely on the degree of connectivity between these elements. Second, intuitively meaningful similarity measures defined on every pair of nodes in a graph are suggested in a common kernel-based (these similarity matrices are graph kernels, i.e. positive semidefinite matrices) framework. Nine of such matrices (as well as derived measures - a distance measure, the centered kernel, the cosine kernel, the principal components) are investigated in this work. Another interesting property of the kernel-based algorithms is that they induce a data matrix on which standard multivariate statistical analysis methods can be applied for mining graphs or databases. This allows to generalize useful techniques, like clustering, principal-component analysis, discriminant analysis, or canonical correlation analysis to the study of graphs or databases.

Further work will investigate the use of user or item features as well as the incorporation of ratings on the edges of the adjacency matrix. Other kernel-based multivariate statistical techniques, such as the already mentioned discriminant analysis or canonical correlation analysis will also be studied in the context of graph mining. Finally, we are working on generalizations to directed weighted graphs for which the weights are not necessarily positive.

REFERENCES

ACM SIGKDD (2003). Special issue on Multi-Relational Data Mining: The Current Frontiers. *ACM SIGKDD Explorations Newsletter, 5*(1).

Agaev, R., & Chebotarev, P. (2000). The matrix of maximum out forests of a digraph and its applications. *Automation and Remote Control, 61*(9), 1424–1450.

Agaev, R., & Chebotarev, P. (2001). Spanning forests of a digraph and their applications. *Automation and Remote Control, 62*(3), 443–466. doi:10.1023/A:1002862312617

Baeza-Yates, R., & Ribeiro-Neto, B. (1999). *Modern information retrieval*. Addison-Wesley.

Barnett, S. (1992). *Matrices: Methods and Applications*. Oxford University Press.

Belkin, M., & Niyogi, P. (2001). Laplacian eigenmaps and spectral techniques for embedding and clustering. []. MIT Press.]. *Advances in Neural Information Processing Systems, 14*, 585–591.

Belkin, M., & Niyogi, P. (2003). Laplacian eigenmaps for dimensionality reduction and data representation. *Neural Computation, 15*, 1373–1396. doi:10.1162/089976603321780317

Ben-Israel, A., & Greville, T. (2003). *Generalized Inverses: Theory and Applications* (2nd ed.). Springer-Verlag.

Borg, I., & Groenen, P. (1997). *Modern multidimensional scaling: Theory and applications*. Springer.

Brand, M. (2005). A random walks perspective on maximizing satisfaction and profit. In *Proceedings of the 2005 SIAM International Conference on Data Mining*.

Brin, S. & Page, L. (1998). The anatomy of a large-scale hypertextual Web search engine. *Computer Networks and ISDN Systems, 30*(1–7), 107–117.

Carrington, P., Scott, J., & Wasserman, S. (2006). *Models and Methods in Social Network Analysis*. Cambridge University Press.

Chan, T., Ciarlet, P., & Szeto, W. (1997). On the optimality of the median cut spectral bisection graph partitioning method. *SIAM Journal on Scientific Computing, 18*(3), 943–948. doi:10.1137/S1064827594262649

Chandra, A. K., Raghavan, P., Ruzzo, W. L., Smolensky, R., & Tiwari, P. (1989). The electrical resistance of a graph captures its commute and cover times. *Annual ACM Symposium on Theory of Computing*, (pp. 574–586).

Chebotarev, P., & Shamis, E. (1997). The matrix-forest theorem and measuring relations in small social groups. *Automation and Remote Control, 58*(9), 1505–1514.

Chebotarev, P., & Shamis, E. (1998a). On a duality between metrics and s-proximities. *Automation and Remote Control, 59*(4), 608–612.

Chebotarev, P., & Shamis, E. (1998b). On proximity measures for graph vertices. *Automation and Remote Control, 59*(10), 1443–1459.

Chen, T., Yang, Q., & Tang, X. (2007). Directed graph embedding. In *Proceedings of the International Joint Conference on Artificial Intelligence (IJCAI)* (pp. 2707–2712).

Chung, F. R. (1997). *Spectral graph theory*. American Mathematical Society.

Chung, F. R. (2005). Laplacians and the Cheeger inequality for directed graphs. *Annals of Combinatorics, 9*, 1–19. doi:10.1007/s00026-005-0237-z

Cover, T. M., & Thomas, J. A. (2006). *Elements of Information Theory* (2nd ed.). John Wiley & Sons.

Cox, T., & Cox, M. (2001). *Multidimensional scaling* (2nd ed.). Chapman and Hall.

Ding, C., Jin, R., Li, T., & Simon, H. (2007). A learning framework using Green's function and kernel regularization with application to recommender system. In *Proceedings of the International Conference on Knowledge Discovery in Databases (KDD2007)* (pp. 260–269).

Donetti, L., & Munoz, M. (2004). Detecting network communities: A new systematic and efficient algorithm. *Journal of Statistical Mechanics*, (2004, Oct), P10012. doi:10.1088/1742-5468/2004/10/P10012

Doyle, P. G., & Snell, J. L. (1984). *Random Walks and Electric Networks*. The Mathematical Association of America.

Faloutsos, C., McCurley, K. S., & Tomkins, A. (2004). Fast discovery of connection subgraphs. In *Proceedings of the tenth ACM SIGKDD International Conference on Knowledge Discovery and Data Mining* (pp. 118–127).

Fiedler, M. (1975). A property of eigenvectors of nonnegative symmetric matrices and its applications to graph theory. *Czechoslovak Mathematical Journal, 25*(100), 619–633.

Fouss, F., Pirotte, A., Renders, J.-M., & Saerens, M. (2005). A novel way of computing similarities between nodes of a graph, with application to collaborative recommendation. In *Proceedings of the 2005 IEEE/WIC/ACM International Joint Conference on Web Intelligence* (pp. 550–556).

Fouss, F., Pirotte, A., Renders, J.-M., & Saerens, M. (2007a). Random walk computation of similarities between nodes of a graph, with application to collaborative recommendation. *IEEE Transactions on Knowledge and Data Engineering, 19*(3), 355–369. doi:10.1109/TKDE.2007.46

Fouss, F., Pirotte, A., & Saerens, M. (2006a). A novel way of computing similarities between nodes of a graph, with application to collaborative filtering. In *Proceedings of the Workshop on Statistical Approaches for Web Mining (ECML 2004 - SAWM)*.

Fouss, F., Yen, L., Pirotte, A., & Saerens, M. (2006b). An experimental investigation of graph kernels on a collaborative recommendation task. In *Proceedings of the 6th International Conference on Data Mining (ICDM 2006)* (pp. 863–868).

Fouss, F., Yen, L., Pirotte, A., & Saerens, M. (2007b). An experimental investigation of seven kernels on two collaborative recommendation tasks.

Gobel, F., & Jagers, A. A. (1974). Random walks on graphs. *Stochastic Processes and their Applications, 2*, 311–336. doi:10.1016/0304-4149(74)90001-5

Gori, M., & Pucci, A. (2006a). A random-walk based scoring algorithm with application to recommender systems for large-scale e-commerce. In *Proceedings of the 12th ACM SIGKDD International Conference on Knowledge Discovery and Data Mining*.

Gori, M., & Pucci, A. (2006b). Research paper recommender systems: A random-walk based approach. In *Proceedings of the 2006 IEEE/WIC/ACM International Conference on Web Intelligence*.

Ham, J., Lee, D., Mika, S., & Scholkopf, B. (2004). A kernel view of the dimensionality reduction of manifolds. In *Proceedings of the 21st International Conference on Machine Learning (ICML2004)*.

Harel, D., & Koren, Y. (2001). On clustering using random walks. *Proceedings of the conference on the Foundations of Software Technology and Theoretical Computer Science* (LNCS 2245, pp. 18–41).

Ho, N.-D., & Dooren, P. V. (2005). On the pseudo-inverse of the laplacian of a bipartite graph. *Applied Mathematics Letters, 18*(8), 917–922. doi:10.1016/j.aml.2004.07.034

Isaacson, D., & Madsen, R. (1976). *Markov chains theory and applications*. John Wiley & Sons.

Ito, T., Shimbo, M., Kudo, T., & Matsumoto, Y. (2005). Application of kernels to link analysis. In *Proceedings of the eleventh ACM SIGKDD International Conference on Knowledge Discovery and Data Mining* (pp. 586–592).

Jolliffe, I. (2002). *Principal components analysis* (2nd ed.). Springer-Verlag.

Kandola, J., Cristianini, N., & Shawe-Taylor, J. (2002). Learning semantic similarity. *Advances in Neural Information Processing Systems*, 657–664.

Kapur, J. N., & Kesavan, H. K. (1992). *Entropy optimization principles with applications*. Academic Press.

Kelly, F. P. (1979). *Reversibility and stochastic networks*. John Wiley.

Kemeny, J. G., & Snell, J. L. (1976). *Finite Markov Chains*. Springer-Verlag.

Kessler, M. M. (1963). Bibliographic coupling between scientific papers. *American Documentation, 14*(1), 10–25. doi:10.1002/asi.5090140103

Klein, D. J., & Randic, M. (1993). Resistance distance. *Journal of Mathematical Chemistry, 12*, 81–95. doi:10.1007/BF01164627

Kleinberg, J. M. (1999). Authoritative sources in a hyperlinked environment. *Journal of the ACM, 46*(5), 604–632. doi:10.1145/324133.324140

Kondor, R. I., & Lafferty, J. (2002). Diffusion kernels on graphs and other discrete structures. In *Proceedings of the 19th International Conference on Machine Learning* (pp. 315–322).

Lafon, S., & Lee, A. B. (2006). Diffusion maps and coarse-graining: A unified framework for dimensionality reduction, graph partitioning, and data set parameterization. *IEEE Transactions on Pattern Analysis and Machine Intelligence, 28*(9), 1393–1403. doi:10.1109/TPAMI.2006.184

Langville, A., & Meyer, C. D. (2005). A survey of eigenvector methods for web information retrieval. *SIAM Review, 47*, 135–161. doi:10.1137/S0036144503424786

Latapy, M., & Pons, P. (2005). Computing communities in large networks using random walks. In *Proceedings of the 20th International Symposium on Computer and Information Sciences* (pp. 284–293).

Lazega, E. (1998). *Réseaux sociaux et structures relationnelles*. Presses Universitaires de France.

Lee, J., & Verleysen, M. (2007). *Nonlinear dimensionality reduction*. Springer. doi:10.1007/978-0-387-39351-3

Mardia, K. V., Kent, J. T., & Bibby, J. M. (1979). *Multivariate Analysis*. Academic Press.

Mohar, B. (1992). Laplace eigenvalues of graphs – a survey. *Discrete Mathematics, 109*, 171–183. doi:10.1016/0012-365X(92)90288-Q

Nadler, B., Lafon, S., Coifman, R., & Kevrekidis, I. (2005). Diffusion maps, spectral clustering and eigenfunctions of Fokker-Planck operators. *Advances in Neural Information Processing Systems, 18*, 955–962.

Nadler, B., Lafon, S., Coifman, R., & Kevrekidis, I. (2006). Diffusion maps, spectral clustering and reaction coordinate of dynamical systems. *Applied and Computational Harmonic Analysis, 21*, 113–127. doi:10.1016/j.acha.2005.07.004

Newman, M. (2005). A measure of betweenness centrality based on random walks. *Social Networks, 27*(1), 39–54. doi:10.1016/j.socnet.2004.11.009

Noble, B., & Daniels, J. (1988). *Applied linear algebra* (3rd ed.). Prentice-Hall.

Norris, J. R. (1997). *Markov Chains*. Cambridge University Press.

Page, L., Brin, S., Motwani, R., & Winograd, T. (1998). *The PageRank citation ranking: Bringing order to the web (Tech. Rep.)*. Computer System Laboratory, Stanford University.

Palmer, C., & Faloutsos, C. (2003). Electricity based external similarity of categorical attributes. In *Proceedings of the 7th Pacific-Asia Conference on Knowledge Discovery and Data Mining (PAKDD'03)*, (pp. 486–500).

Pan, J.-Y., Yang, H.-J., Faloutsos, C., & Duygulu, P. (2006). Automatic multimedia cross-modal correlation discovery. *Proceedings of the 10th ACM SIGKDD International Conference on Knowledge Discovery and Data Mining, 82*(4), 331–338.

Parzen, E. (1962). *Stochastic Processes*. Holden-Day.

Pons, P., & Latapy, M. (2006). Computing communities in large networks using random walks. *Journal of Graph Algorithms and Applications*, *10*(2), 191–218.

Pothen, A., Simon, H. D., & Liou, K.-P. (1990). Partitioning sparse matrices with eigenvectors of graphs. *SIAM Journal on Matrix Analysis and Applications*, *11*(3), 430–452. doi:10.1137/0611030

Qiu, H., & Hancock, E. R. (2005). Image segmentation using commute times. *Proceedings of the 16th British Machine Vision Conference (BMVC 2005)* (pp. 929–938).

Qiu, H., & Hancock, E. R. (2007). Clustering and embedding using commute times. *IEEE Transactions on Pattern Analysis and Machine Intelligence*, *29*(11), 1873–1890. doi:10.1109/TPAMI.2007.1103

Ross, S. (1996). *Stochastic Processes* (2nd ed.). Wiley.

Roth, V., Laub, J., Buhmann, J., & Muller, K.-R. (2002). Going metric: Denoising pairwise data. In *Proceedings of the 15th Neural Information Processing Systems conference*.

Saerens, M., Fouss, F., Yen, L., & Dupont, P. (2004). The principal components analysis of a graph, and its relationships to spectral clustering. In *Proceedings of the 15th European Conference on Machine Learning (ECML 2004)* (LNCS 3201, pp. 371-383).

Scholkopf, B., & Smola, A. (2002). *Learning with kernels*. The MIT Press.

Scholkopf, B., Smola, A., & Muller, K.-R. (1998). Nonlinear component analysis as a kernel eigenvalue problem. *Neural Computation*, *5*(10), 1299–1319. doi:10.1162/089976698300017467

Shawe-Taylor, J., & Cristianini, N. (2004). *Kernel Methods for Pattern Analysis*. Cambridge University Press.

Shi, J., & Malik, J. (2000). Normalised cuts and image segmentation. *IEEE Transactions on Pattern Matching and Machine Intelligence*, *22*, 888–905. doi:10.1109/34.868688

Shimbo, M., & Ito, T. (2006). *Kernels as link analysis measures* (pp. 283–310). John Wiley & Sons.

Small, H. (1973). Co-citation in the scientific literature: a new measure of the relationship between two documents. *Journal of the American Society for Information Science American Society for Information Science*, *24*(4), 265–269. doi:10.1002/asi.4630240406

Smola, A. J., & Kondor, R. (2003). Kernels and regularization on graphs. In *Proceedings of the Conference on Learning Theory (COLT)*.

Tetali, P. (1991). Random walks and the effective resistance of networks. *Journal of Theoretical Probability*, *4*, 101–109. doi:10.1007/BF01046996

Thelwall, M. (2004). *Link Analysis: An Information Science Approach*. Elsevier.

Tong, H., Faloutsos, C., & Pan, J.-Y. (2006). Fast random walk with restart and its applications. In *Proceedings of sixth IEEE International Conference on Data Mining (ICDM 2006)* (pp. 613–622).

Tong, H., Faloutsos, C., & Pan, J.-Y. (2008). Random walk with restart: fast solutions and applications. *Knowledge and Information Systems*, *14*(3), 327–346. doi:10.1007/s10115-007-0094-2

von Luxburg, U. (2007). *A tutorial on spectral clustering*. Statistics and Computing.

Wasserman, S., & Faust, K. (1994). *Social Network Analysis: Methods and Applications*. Cambridge University Press.

White, S., & Smyth, P. (2003). Algorithms for estimating relative importance in networks. In *Proceedings of the ninth ACM SIGKDD International Conference on Knowledge Discovery and Data mining* (pp. 266–275).

Wilson, R. C., Hancock, E. R., & Luo, B. (2005). Pattern vectors from algebraic graph theory. *IEEE Transactions on Pattern Analysis and Machine Intelligence, 27*, 1112–1124. doi:10.1109/TPAMI.2005.145

Yajima, Y., & Kuo, T.-F. (2006). Efficient formulations for 1-SVM and their application to recommendation tasks. *Journal of Computers, 1*(3), 27–34. doi:10.4304/jcp.1.3.27-34

Yen, L., Fouss, F., Decaestecker, C., Francq, P., & Saerens, M. (2007). Graph nodes clustering based on the commute-time kernel. In *Proceedings of the 11th Pacific- Asia Conference on Knowledge Discovery and Data Mining (PAKDD 2007)* (LNAI 4426, pp. 1037–1045).

Yen, L., Mantrach, A., Shimbo, M., & Saerens, M. (2008). A family of dissimilarity measures between nodes generalizing both the shortest-path and the commute-time distances. In *Proceedings of the 14th SIGKDD International Conference on Knowledge Discovery and Data Mining* (pp. 785–793).

Yen, L., Vanvyve, D., Wouters, F., Fouss, F., Verleysen, M., & Saerens, M. (2005). Clustering using a random walk-based distance measure. In *Proceedings of the 13ᵗʰ European Symposium on Artificial Neural Networks (ESANN2005)* (pp. 317–324).

Zhao, D., & Tang, Z. L. X. (2007). Contextual distance for data perception. In *Proceedings of the eleventh IEEE International Conference on Computer Vision (ICCV)*, 57, 1–8.

Zhou, D., Huang, J., & Scholkopf, B. (2005). Learning from labeled and unlabeled data on a directed graph. *Proceedings of the 22nd International Conference on Machine Learning*, pages 1041–1048.

Zhou, D., & Scholkopf, B. (2004). Learning from labeled and unlabeled data using random walks. In *Proceedings of the 26th DAGM Symposium, (Eds.) Rasmussen* (pp. 237–244).

ENDNOTES

[1] This work, done in collaboration with M. Saerens, P. Dupont, A. Pirotte, J.-M. Renders, and L. Yen, has been motivated by (Saerens, et al., 2004), and some of the results have been published in (Fouss, et al., 2005a; Fouss, et al., 2006a; Fouss, et al., 2007a).

[2] This work has been done in collaboration with M. Saerens, L. Yen, A. Pirotte, and J.-M. Renders. The introduction of the Markov-diffusion kernel, the cross-entropy diffusion matrix, and the regularized commute-time kernel, as well as the measures derived from kernels on graph already in (Fouss, et al., 2007b; Fouss, et al., 2006b).

Chapter 6
A Semi–Supervised Algorithm to Manage Communities of Interests

Pascal Francq
Paul Otlet Institute, Belgium & Université Catholique de Louvain, Belgium

ABSTRACT

This chapter presents a genetic algorithm, called the Similarity-based Clustering Genetic Algorithm (SCGA), used to group users' profiles. This algorithm is integrated in an approach which allows to share documents among users browsing a collection of documents. The users are described in terms of profiles, with each profile corresponding to one area of interest. While browsing through the collection of documents, users' profiles are computed. These profiles are then grouped into communities of interests using the SCGA which is based on the Grouping Genetic Algorithm (GGA). In fact, the SCGA can solve other similar problems under certain circumstances. The approach is part of a more generic model to manage information called the GALILEI Framework. This framework, which provides promising results, has been developed in a software platform available under the GNU GPL license.

INTRODUCTION

With the wide spread of document-oriented systems, such as the Internet, the amount of information available through electronic documents has exploded (Lawrence & Giles, 1999). Because of this expansion, information retrieval systems that facilitate the information extraction process by structuring and retrieving it are most welcome, since finding all the relevant information is still

a crucial problem (Fogarty & Bahls, 2002). As this book claims, communities of interests are one of the solutions to share interesting knowledge between users. As explained in the first chapter, managing communities of interests is a difficult task, in particular detecting which users belongs to which community.

Several approaches exist to build communities of interests. One of them is to "profile" the users interests based on the content of the documents they read, and then grouping them regarding these profiles. I call this approach "*social brows-*

DOI: 10.4018/978-1-61520-841-8.ch006

Copyright © 2011, IGI Global. Copying or distributing in print or electronic forms without written permission of IGI Global is prohibited.

ing" (Francq, 2007) since the idea is to gather information to regroup similar users while they are browsing documents on the Internet or in intranets. The GALILEI platform implements this approach (Mathhys, et al., 1998; Francq, 2003). It is an open source platform that proposes a complete implementation of a framework to manage numeric information (called the *GALILEI Framework*) which allows the building and the maintaining of communities of interests[1]. One of the main issues of the framework is to group users into such communities, in particular because the number of communities (*clusters*) is unknown and the method has to be run frequently (typically communities are weekly updated).

This chapter presents the Similarity-based Clustering Genetic Algorithm (SCGA) that tackles this latest problem. Section 2 presents the general approach used to build communities of interests in the GALILEI Framework, and section 3 provides a technical overview on how users' interests are computed. Section 4 studies the grouping problems in general, while section 5 describes the SCGA in particular. Section 6 proposes a validation methodology for the proposed approach which is then used to provide the results discussed in section 7. Finally, section 8 proposes some future research directions, section 9 presents a case study where communities of researchers are detected, and section 10 draws the conclusions of this chapter.

THE GALILEI FRAMEWORK

The main purpose of the GALILEI Framework[2] is to propose an integrated model to manage digital information (mostly electronic documents). A complete description of the framework is outside the scope of this chapter, but an important feature is to identify users' interests as precisely as possible and consequently grouping them. The approach integrated in the GALILEI Framework, and called social browsing, proposes (a) to model the multiple interests of a given user as separate *profiles* (each

profile corresponds to a particular interest), (b) to automatically compute the descriptions of these profiles based on documents assessments done by the corresponding users and (c) to group these profiles into communities of interests (one user belonging to as many communities as the number of his or her profiles).

In order to compute the profiles descriptions, the GALILEI framework uses the relevance assessments of documents read by the users for a particular profile[3] and the analysis of their content (Technical Overview describes the document analysis process). Currently, three different assessments have been adopted:

1. The document is *relevant*. A Web page about the Beatles is, for example, a relevant document for a "Beatles profile" representing a fan of this group.
2. The document is partially relevant (*fuzzy relevant*), but does not fall exactly within the scope of the domain. A Web page about the Wings may be considered by a "Beatles profile" as fuzzy relevant since there are connections between the two groups (Paul McCartney plays in both).
3. The document is outside the scope of the interest (*irrelevant*). The home page of Steve Jobs is (probably) completely irrelevant for a "Beatles profile" (Apple, the name of the company he founded, is not related with the record label of the Beatles while having the same name).

Of course, other types of assessments are possible such as rating the documents on a scale (for example between 0 and 5). But, it is always difficult for users to determine the "right rating" corresponding to their perception of the relevance of a given document. Limiting the choice to three well-defined categories of relevance makes the approach more intuitive for the users.

The users' profiles are then clustered based on their descriptions: similar profiles are grouped

Figure 1. The Social browsing approach

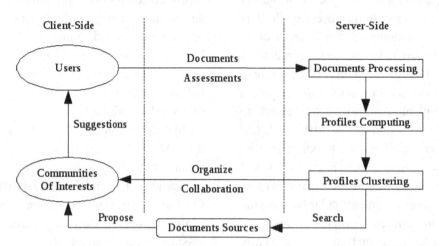

together in order to define a number of communities of interests. Each user may specify if a given profile is a "social" one or not: a *social profile* must always be grouped (the user prefers to be grouped with less similar profiles rather than to remain alone). Once these communities have been defined, relevant information can be exchanged between the different users of the same community. For instance, some documents relevant to most of the users in a given community could be shared across the whole community. Moreover, document sources can be scanned to search for new relevant documents which are then proposed to the communities.

(Figure 1) illustrates the complete flow of the social browsing approach. There is a client-side part that interacts with the users (assessing documents, retrieving suggested documents, etc.), and a server-side performing the computations (for example the GALILEI platform). The process is dynamic: the different elements can be updated regularly (for example every week). Social browsing has several advantages:

- the users must not define explicitly their interests (such as providing keywords or choosing in a list of predefined categories), a profile is just a label identifying a particular interest;

- while some approaches (such as collaborative filtering) need that different users rate the *same* documents, the proposed approach only needs that different users assess *similar* documents;

- the communities are not fixed: new communities may appear and others may disappear.

An important effort was made to provide an effective and open source implementation of the GALILEI Framework. The development of the GALILEI platform was driven by the concept of software modularity to allow new elements to be easily integrated. In practice, it is composed of a set of basic libraries and several plug-ins, each plug-in implementing a specific method to solve a particular task (analyse a document, compute a profile, etc.). This architecture makes it very easy to replace an existing method by another one: it is enough to develop a new plug-in. Moreover, the GALILEI platform provides several validation methodologies (such as the one described in Validation Methodology) in order to evaluate a particular method and compare its performances with others solving the same task. The GALILEI platform is therefore not only a solution for industrial applications (for example helping a world-wide organization to identify employees sharing similar information needs), but it is also designed as a research platform. At the time of writing, the whole GALILEI platform (including the different official plug-ins) represents more than 150,000 lines of C++ source code (estimated to 40 person-years for the development effort only).

TECHNICAL OVERVIEW

It is far beyond the scope of this chapter to present in details all the models and the algorithms used in the GALILEI Framework; the interested reader is invited to consult (Francq, 2003; Francq, 2004;Francq, 2007) and the Web site for more recent information. Nevertheless, the main ideas will be described in this section.

Once documents are assessed by users, the first step is to extract knowledge from these documents ("documents processing" on Figure 1). Since an increasing number of documents are XML ones, the framework supposes that all electronic documents are structured with XML. In practice, non-XML documents (such as earlier MS-Word documents) are converted through *filters* into a XML representation which can be further analyzed. This choice has two advantages: the documents analysis method is independent of particular formats, and structured semantic-oriented information (if available) can be exploited (since this is the motivation behind XML). The GALILEI framework supposes that different semantic levels can be extracted from a XML document. Currently, three types of information are extracted by the analyzer implemented:

1. The *content* of the documents, i.e. the different terms appearing in the documents. In practice, the analyzer extracts the stems contained in the documents after removing the stopwords (Luhn, 1957; Francis & Kucera, 1982; Frakes, 1992).

2. The *structure* of the documents, i.e. the different XML schemata used. This makes sense since the choice of a given XML schema (or a part of it) to structure a XML document has a semantic meaning[4].

3. The *metadata* contained in the documents. In the case of XML documents, most tags (*informative tags*) contain information with less or no description value for the document, while a few of them (*metadata tags*) provide, combined with their content, useful information to describe the document. A practical example of metadata tags are those proposed by the Dublic Metacore Initiative (DMCI, 1999) such as the tag "*author*". Ideally, these tags should be previously identified (by an analysis of the XML schemata), but it is possible to develop an heuristic that tries to automatically detect such tags[5].

Once the knowledge is extracted, it is necessary to adopt a *knowledge model* which can take the different types of information into account. A classical model to represent documents is the classical *vector model* (sometimes called "bag of words"): documents are represented as a set of features (the terms extracted) and a weight is associated with each feature to quantify its importance. Several methods exist to compute these weights, but the mostly used is based on the *tf* and *idf* factors (Salton, 1968; Salton, 1971). A formal adaptation of this model using structure information was proposed by Fox (1983), and the GALILEI Framework introduces an adaptation of this model. The proposition is to represent any object (documents, profiles and communities) by different types of *semantic representation units* (SRU) represented by *subvectors* in different types of spaces (each space corresponds to a particular SRU type). Based on the information extracted, it is possible to define different spaces: the content spaces (one space per language), the language-independent meaningful entities space (Chinchor, 1998), the structure space and the metadata space. The description of an object may thus be seen as a global *vector* composed of these subvectors.

An adaptation of the model suggested by Fox has already been proposed for the well-known INEX 2005 XML collection (Crouch, Apte & Bapat, 2002), where each SRU type corresponds to a particular metadata available in the collection. In comparison, the model deployed in the GALILEI Framework is not specifically adapted for a particular collection but can be used for any XML document.

Previously, the choice was made to compute a separate profile description for each language (Francq, 2007), i.e. a single profile was made up of different subprofiles (each subprofile was represented by a vector in the corresponding content space). The communities of interests were therefore also language-based. The actual knowledge model used by the GALILEI Framework makes this separation lapsed. The different languages are integrated in a common model that simplifies the framework.

Since the profiles are described in the same way than documents, the computation of their descriptions is directly based on the vectors representing the documents assessed ("profiles computing" on Figure 1). The idea behind the method is intuitive: the vector of a profile should be similar to the vectors of documents assessed as relevant and dissimilar to those of the irrelevant documents (for that particular profile). This idea is inspired by the query expansion approaches proposed for the classical vector model (Rocchio, 1971; Ide, 1971). In practice, a description is computed as a linear combination of the vectors corresponding to the documents assessed by the corresponding profile (a positive coefficient is associated with the relevant and fuzzy relevant documents, and a negative coefficient with the irrelevant documents). Initially, the vector space model supposes that the weights of the vectors are positive or null. But, with the introduction of negative coefficients in the profiles computing, some vectors may have some negative values. Currently, the method implemented in the GALILEI platform limits the vectors representing the profiles to the 60 most

relevant features extracted from the documents (it is a parameter of the corresponding plug-in).

To group the profiles ("profiles clustering" on Figure 1), it is necessary to have at least one measure to determine if two profiles are similar or not. In the traditional vector space model, the similarity between two objects is computed as the cosine between their vectors (Salton & McGill, 1983). I have already proposed a little adaptation of this measure when vectors may have negative values (as for the profiles)[6]. In the GALILEI Framework, the vector of an object is composed of subvectors representing different SRU types forming three classes of SRU types: the content (terms in different languages), the structure and the metadata. Therefore, I propose to first compute a *local similarity* for each class of SRU types and then to combine them to obtain the final similarity. To compute the local similarities, different methods are proposed:

1. For the content spaces (including the language-independent space), the local similarity is computed as a linear combination of the cosines between each subvectors weighted by the number of common terms of the objects in the different languages. If the documents are in one language only, this local similarity is just the cosine of the subvectors of the corresponding space.

2. For the structure spaces, the local similarity is simply the cosines between the corresponding subvectors.

3. For the metadata space, another measure is proposed based on a raw comparison between the metadata defined by the same tag. This method is driven by two hypothesis. On the one hand, it makes no sense to compare metadata related to different tags (for example a "title" and an "author"). On the other hand, if two tags ("author" for example), share some terms (for example a common name), they are somewhat related. In practice, the local similarity tries to mea-

sure the ratio of the number of common terms appearing in the content associated with the same metadata tags.

To combine the different local similarities, several possibilities are provided by the platform, from taking only the content into account to a more complex aggregating method based on the integral of Choquet (Grabisch & Roubens, 2000). Different tests have shown that for rich structured XML documents using the integral of Choquet provides better results (the similarity between related documents increases). This suggests that it takes in a better way the semantic of XML documents into account.

As explained in the previous section, one of the advantages of the GALILEI approach is that the profiles do not need to read the same documents to be grouped together. However, if two profiles assess the same documents, it would be a shame to not use this information. In particular, since the social browsing approach suggests to the user documents assessed as relevant by profiles grouped in the same community, it includes a feedback process. In practice, if two profiles assess several documents as relevant, there is a probability that they are similar. Moreover, if two profiles assess several documents differently (one of them finding them relevant and the other one irrelevant), there is a probability that the two profiles are not similar. Two measures catch these situations: the agreement and the disagreement ratios. The agreement ratio is the one between the number of documents assessed as relevant by both profiles and the total number of documents assessed by both profiles. The disagreement ratio is the one between the number of documents assessed differently by both profiles and the total number of documents assessed by both profiles. Of course, it makes no sense to compute these ratios if there is not a minimum number of common documents (it is impossible to conclude that two people have identical musical taste because they bought one identical album). Therefore, in

the GALILEI Framework, it is supposed that if there are not at least 10 common documents, these ratios are null. As we will see in The Similarity Based Clustering Genetic Algorithm (SCGA), the algorithm proposed in this chapter uses also these measures for the profiles clustering (it is its "supervised" aspect).

Once the communities are built (knowing which profiles constitute them), it is possible to describe them. Because the community and the profiles composing it use the same model, an operation on the vectors of the profiles can be used to describe the corresponding community. The most intuitive idea is to define the centre of gravity of the profile vectors as this operator (the community is designed as an "average profile"). Once the communities are described, these descriptions may be used to automatically generate queries to search engines in order to find new interesting documents. It was shown that it is more appropriate to build such search queries on a profile basis using both the community and the profile descriptions terms (Abbaci-Gaultier, Francq & Delchambre, 2005).

THE GROUPING PROBLEMS

Algorithms, Heuristics and Meta-Heuristics

The area of interest of applied computer science is to solve *problems*. There are different kinds of problems, but the ones related to the profiles clustering are the optimization problems where the aim is to find the best solution among all possible ones. For example, in the bin packing problem the aim is to find the right number of bins of a given size to store a set of objects of given sizes; optimization involves, for example, to find the smallest number of bins. It is important to make the distinction between a problem which refers to a general class (such as the bin packing), and an *instance* representing a special type of the problem (for example when the bins have a size of 5 and there are 25 objects of size 3 to cluster). Furthermore, distinct problems may share a same "structure" in which case they form a *class of problems*. For example, the bin packing problem and the profiles clustering belong to the same class of problem where "a set of objects must be grouped in an unknown number of clusters with regards to some constraints in order to achieve a given goal" (the next section proposes a more formal definition of the grouping problems).

An *optimization problem* can be defined as a finite set of variables, where the correct values for the variables specify the optimal solution. If the variables range over real numbers, the problem is called continuous, and if they can only take a finite set of distinct values, the problem is called combinatorial. In the case of the profiles clustering, we are dealing with combinatorial optimization problems because the number of communities of interests is finite. A combinatorial optimization problem is defined (Papadimitriou & Steiglitz, 1982) as the set of all the instances of the problem, with each instance being defined by a pair (F,c), where F is called the search space (the set of all possible solutions for a particular instance), and c is a cost function calculated for each solution of F and used to determine the performances of each solution (most of the time it is a mathematical expression directly computable from the solutions). The goal is to find the solution of F that maximize or minimize the cost function.

To solve problems it is necessary to develop methods, often called *algorithms* in computer science, that describe the set of actions to be performed under given circumstances. In one of the definitions found in the literature (Garey & Johnson, 1979), an algorithm is stated as the list of precise rules that specify "what to do" under all possible conditions. This definition includes the one of the Turing Machine (Turing, 1936), which is an abstract representation of any computing device. Another definition is to describe an algorithm as a finite set of instruc-

tions (evaluations and assignations), which leads to a solution.

The complexity, O, of an algorithm defines a relationship between the size of an instance (such as the number of objects in the bin packing problem) and the necessary resources to solve it (the amount of memory and number of CPU cycles required). A complexity of $O(n^2)$ for example signifies that the resources required evolutes as the square of the size of the instance, i.e. an instance two times larger than another one needs four times more resources. An important category of problems consists of the NP-hard ones, for which no polynomial time algorithm has been found so far. With these problems, the CPU time increases exponentially with the size of an instance. In other words, when the size of the problem increases, it becomes impossible to compute all the valid solutions. For example, in a bin packing problem involving 5 objects it is possible to compute all the different solutions to determine the best one. Whereas for 500 objects, it may become no longer possible. NP-hard problems can only be solved by *approximation algorithms* which try to reach a near-optimal solution (a solution as close as possible to the optimal one) in a "reasonable time".

Several classes of approximation algorithms exist when dealing with NP-hard problems. One class of algorithms is known as *heuristics*. A heuristic is an "intuitive" way to find a valid and often reasonably good solution for a given problem in a "reasonable" lapse of time, i.e. a heuristic is based on rules of practices, ideas that seem to be helpful in some typical instances, though without providing any guarantee of the quality of the solution. For most heuristics, the initial conditions limit the search space scanned, and the results are highly dependent of these initial conditions (which are generally randomly chosen). For example, in the bin packing problem, the "first-fit descending heuristic" which consists in treating objects in descending order of size and putting one into the first group that can take it, is a well-known heuristic giving good results in such cases (depending on the sizes of the bins), though not necessarily the optimal one. The biggest problem about heuristics is that it is strongly instance- and problem-dependent, and that the results may be very poor. When the essential factor is the time of execution, heuristics is the best solution. For example, a first-fit heuristic is used in an operating system to find a memory zone when a program allocates a given amount of data. In this case, the fact that the solution proposed is not the best one is less important than the time needed. But, because of their drawbacks, heuristics rarely reach the status of being able to provide a solution when the quality of the solution is important, and cannot be considered as a general approach.

So, the two disadvantages of heuristics are that the solutions proposed can often be of very low-quality and are strongly instance- and problem-dependent. Computer science has developed another class of approximation algorithms to work-around these disadvantages. All these methods use heuristics in some way or another, but enable the entire search space to be searched in (or at least the most interesting part of it); this is the reason why the term *meta-heuristics* is employed. Meta-heuristics are specific to a given class of problem[7], and it is sometimes necessary to adapt them to obtain the best solutions for a particular problem (as it will be shown in The Similarity Based Clustering Genetic Algorithm (SCGA)). Most of them generate different solutions in the search space (using integrated heuristics), evaluate them using cost functions, determine which parts of the search space (solutions) seem the most interesting and then focus the scanning on these parts.

Over the time, several meta-heuristics were proposed by researchers, the most known probably being simulated annealing (Kirkpatrick, Gelatt & Vecchi, 1983; van Laarhoven & Aarts, 1987), tabu search (Glover, Laguna, Werra & Taillard, 1992; Glover & Laguna, 1997) and genetic algorithms; the latest being the ones used in the work presented in this chapter. Like in other domains of science, the different meta-heuristics

have given rise to "schools of thoughts", each school claiming its meta-heuristic approach is the most effective. I think that every meta-heuristic is able to solve most optimization problems if it is intelligently applied. So, the problem is not to choose which meta-heuristic to use, but how to use it. Too many people forget to adapt their meta-heuristic to the particular class of problem they are facing. I believe that, if some meta-heuristic approaches obtain very good results for a given class of problems, it is more related to the skills of the researchers rather than an intrinsic capability of a particular meta-heuristic.

What are Grouping Problems?

Grouping problem are defined as problems where a set of objects must be clustered with respect to certain constraints in order to optimize a given cost function. As shown previously, the bin packing problem is a particular class of grouping problems where the aim is to find the minimum number of bins to hold a set of objects of a given size, where each bin has a maximum capacity.

Many of the grouping problems are NP-Hard (Garey & Johnson, 1979), which means that there are no known algorithms that find the exact solutions in a reasonable amount of computing time. Several clustering methods have been developed to solve grouping problems (Jain, Murty & Flynn, 1999), but they become unusable when the size of the data is growing. Most of the time, these methods are used by meta-heuristics.

There are two different categories of grouping problems:

- **Hard.** Each object is assigned to a single cluster.
- **Fuzzy.** Each object has a degree of membership for each cluster (Zadeh, 1965).

In the approach described in this chapter, we are faced with hard grouping problems (each profile belongs to only one community of interests).

One of the central questions with grouping problems is the cost function, i.e. how to determine the quality of a given solution. It is impossible to define a unique measure that would work for all grouping problems. Therefore, to be effective, the cost function must be adapted to the particular problem. In fact, the more information available on a problem, the greater the possibility will be of understanding the underlying characteristics of the clusters and of determining the quality of a solution (Jain & Dubes, 1988). Moreover, this kind of information helps to improve the quality of main parameters like similarity computation or the representation of the clusters (Murty & Jain, 1995).

To express that two objects are similar, most clustering algorithms use the concept of distance between these objects (that must be minimized) or the concept of their similarity (that must be maximized). Moreover, most of the time, the values of the distance and the similarity are between 0 and 1. In this case, it is possible to use a simple relation between distance and similarity: the square of the similarity between two objects is equal to 1 minus the square of their distance. In this chapter, I use the similarities but the reader can replace "similarity" by "distance" if he or she replaces "maximize" by "minimize" and "greater" by "smaller".

Partitional algorithms

Partitional algorithms involve the one step partitioning of objects into clusters. One of the main problems with most of these algorithms is that the number of clusters to be formed must be specified. Despite the fact that a lot of work has been done in this field (Dubes, 1987), it is still a crucial problem.

k-Means Clustering Algorithm

The k-means clustering algorithm introduced by MacQueen (1967) is one of the most known clustering algorithm. Starting from an initial partitioning and based on a similarity measure, the algorithm tries to change the assignments of the objects until a stop condition is met. The main steps of this method involve:

1. Determining the number of clusters, k, to form.
2. Choosing a center for each cluster, this can be carried out by randomly choosing k objects in a set.
3. Assigning each object to the cluster with the closest center[8] (the greatest similarity).
4. Recomputing the centers of the clusters.
5. If a given condition is met, stop the method; if not go to step 3. For the stop condition, most k-Means stop when the centers have not changed between two iterations.

The k-Means algorithm optimizes the intra-cluster similarities, i.e. the sum of the similarities between the profiles and their centers is reduced during the steps 2 and 3 of the algorithm. Many variants of the k-Means algorithm have been developed (Anderberg, 1973).

One possible adaptation was proposed by Marco Saerens and David Wartel during the development of the GALILEI platform (Francq, Wartel, Kumps & Vandaele, 2003). Called the k-Means with prototypes, their idea is to define a cluster not only by its center but also by a given number of prototypes. To assign a given object to a cluster, rather than using only the similarity with the centers, the algorithm uses a linear combination of this similarity and the highest similarity of the object with one of the prototypes. The use of prototypes ensure that the clusters are not too large since all the objects must not only be similar to the center but also to other objects (the prototypes). Once the number of prototypes are fixed, they must be chosen. They propose the following method:

1.   A normal k-Means is carried out in order to divide the cluster into as many sub-clusters as prototypes needed.
2.   The prototypes of the clusters are chosen as the centers of each sub-cluster.

Other possible adaptations are based on the idea that a method can be used to optimally choose the initial centers rather than taking them randomly. One method to define the centers is proposed by Bradley and Fayyad (1998). It is decomposed in several steps:

1.   Several sub-sets of objects are randomly created from the complete set of objects to group. This is the subsampling step.
2.   A modified k-Means is carried out on each sub-set to construct an initial set of centers that will be used to group the whole set.
3.   A k-Means is run on the complete set using the initial set of centers of each sub-set. At the end, each k-Means defines a new set of centers.
4.   The best set of centers is determined using the sum of square errors.

More recently, another approach called k-means++ was proposed to choose the initial center with interesting primarily results (Arthur & Vassilvitskii, 2007).

As already explained, a main problem is to choose the correct number of clusters. Some adaptations enable clusters to be split or merged during the k-Means by using conditions relative to the similarities between the centers of the clusters and between the centers and the objects in the same cluster, such as the ISODATA algorithm (Ball & Hall, 1965). When additional constraints exist for the clustering, another way to evaluate the number of clusters is to use a simple heuristic, such as the first-fit, to quickly build a clustering and then suppose that the number of clusters obtained is the correct one (Francq, Wartel, Kumps & Vandaele, 2003).

Graph-Related Theoretical Clustering

As suggested in their names, graph-related theoretical clustering methods are based on the graph theory (Gibbons, 1985; McHugh, 1990). A graph is a mathematical structure that describes a set of elements that are connected together. A graph is defined by two sets: a set of vertices, V, which represent the elements, and a set of edges, E, which represent the connections. The whole is expressed as G(V,E). When the edges and/or vertices are removed from a graph G, a subgraph of G is obtained. It is also possible to associate a weight to an edge to express the strength of the relationship between the corresponding vertices.

If we suppose that each object represents a vertex and that the weigh associated with an edge between two vertices is the similarity between the corresponding objects, the clustering problem can be seen as how to identify the subgraphs representing the clusters to maximize the weights of the edges in each subgraph. A very simple application of this approach was proposed by Zhan (1971). His idea is to construct a maximum spanning tree for the vertices, and then remove the edges with the smallest weights so that each set of connected vertices forms a cluster[9]. In the chapter about collaborative-recommendation systems and link analysis (in this book), Fuss presents several graph-related techniques that could be also used to cluster objects.

It is necessary to pilot these methods since they do not define how to ideally "cut" the graph. A simple way is to fix the number of clusters, k, to create which implies that the method cuts the k-1 shortest paths. But, as for partitional methods, this is a tricky problem. Another approach is to add some constraints (such as defining a minimum similarity that two objects must have to be grouped together) to help the methods to choose the right edges to cut, but it is still a difficult task.

Hierarchical Clustering

Hierarchical clustering methods do not compute a single partition of the objects, but a series of partitions starting from one object per cluster to end with a single cluster containing all the objects. It is then possible to choose the partition that fit the best the particular problem (for example the one defining a given number of clusters). Hierarchical clustering methods are *agglomerative* if they begin with one object per cluster and merge then two clusters at each step, or *divisive* if they start with one cluster containing all the objects and divide then one cluster into two at each step.

CURE (Guha, Rastogi & Shim, 1998) is a simple agglomerative algorithm. Its main steps are:

1. Each object is put alone into a cluster.
2. Each cluster is characterized by a given number of prototypes in a similar way as in the k-Means algorithm with prototypes (Algorithms, Heuristics, and Meta-Heuristics).
3. The method determines the two most similar clusters and merges them. The two most similar clusters are chosen as the ones having the greatest similarity between their prototypes.
4. While a given condition is not reached (such as a given number of clusters), the method goes to step 2.

Again, the problem is to know which partition to choose (or when to stop the agglomerative or divisive method). The best method is to fix the number of clusters, but, as already explained, this not a simple task.

Nearest Neighbor Clustering

Because the aim of forming clusters is to bring similar objects together, the concept of the proximity of objects is important when dealing with the underlying structure of clusters. Some clustering methods are therefore based on nearest neighbors (Jain & Dubes, 1988). Most of these methods are based on the idea that two objects are nearest neighbors if their similarity is greater than a given threshold.

An interactive and simple clustering method has been proposed by Lu and Fu (1978). Each unassigned object is inserted into the cluster of its nearest neighbor if the corresponding similarity is greater than a given threshold.

THE SIMILARITY-BASED CLUSTERING GENETIC ALGORITHM (SCGA)

This section presents the Similarity-based Clustering Genetic Algorithm (SCGA) used to group the profiles based on three profiles-profiles matrices, each matrix storing one of the measures described in the previous section (similarities, agreement and disagreement ratios). First, the Grouping Generic Algorithms (GGA), on which the SCGA is based, are introduced. Then, the different elements of the SCGA are presented: the parameters, the heuristic used, the initialization of the population, the evaluation of the chromosomes and the local optimization operator developed.

Grouping Genetic Algorithms (GGA)

Genetic Algorithms (GA) are a particular type of meta-heuristics introduced first by Holland (1975). Before studying the different elements of GA, it may be interesting first of all to define what are GA. GA can be defined as an exploration algorithm based on the mechanisms of natural selection and the genetic science (Goldberg, 1991). GA use the survival of the best adapted structure and an exchange of pseudo-random information to search the solution space. At each generation, a new set of artificial artifacts is constructed by using parts of the best elements of the previous generation and, sometimes, by adding new characteristics.

GA are not only based on random exploration but also use information obtained from the past to evaluate the best positions to explore in the future. The population is evaluated at each generation against a cost function to determine its adaptation.

GA are based on the natural evolution of species as described by Darwin (1859): in any population, the best adapted (fitted) individuals have a greater chance of reproducing than less adapted ones; this is called natural selection. In nature, new characteristics are transmitted to offsprings by crossing two individual genes. This process is not deterministic, and some uncertainty in these characteristics is introduced. Furthermore, mutations may occur as genes are passed from parents to children implying that a small modification occurs in the copy, i.e. the child will have a characteristic not present in the parents. If this mutation has a positive influence on the child, the child will be better adapted than its fellows without this mutation; this newly introduced characteristic may thus be present in the next generations as the result of natural selection. Natural selection is thus based on the fact that some characteristics in a population reflect the specifications of the strongest (best adapted) individuals and thus should lead generally speaking to a better adapted population. As in nature, where individuals may be represented by their chromosomes alone, GA work with a population of abstract representations of solutions called *chromosomes*, the structure of these chromosomes is called the *coding* of the GA. The coding uses a set of values called the *chromosome genes*. At each iteration, called a *generation*, the chromosomes representing the best solutions[10] are selected and used for a crossover to produce new solutions. Their children replace the less adapted ones. By exchanging "good information" between chromosomes, GA try to create new chromosomes with a better value with respect to the cost function (sometimes called the *fitness function*). Note that the "bad" genes are not taken into account by GA.

The generic structure of a genetic algorithm is shown in (Figure 2). The different steps are:

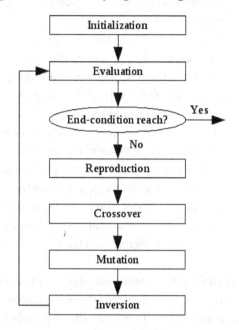

Figure 2. Structure of a genetic algorithm

1. A population is constructed which is made up of a fixed number of solutions, known as chromosomes. To do so, a heuristic specific to the problem should be developed.

2. Each chromosome is evaluated through a cost function describing the optimum targeted.

3. The genetic algorithm stops when a final condition is reached that indicates that an acceptable solution exists; otherwise it makes a new generation by processing further.

4. The genetic algorithm reproduces some of the statistically best chromosomes. These chromosomes replace others, statistically the worst since the size of the population remains static.

5. The genetic algorithm constructs new chromosomes by making a crossover between existing ones.

6. There is a level of given probability that some of the chromosomes will be affected by a mutation. As in nature, the role of the mutation is to add new characteristics to the population. If these characteristics have a positive benefit regarding the cost func-

tion, they would be reproduced in the next generations (steps 4).

7. There is a level of given probability that some of the chromosomes will be affected by an inversion. The role of this operator is highly dependent of the particular coding. In fact, sometimes a same solution may be coded differently. Moreover, some operators may be sensible to a particular representation of a solution, i.e. the same solution represented differently will be treated differently. The inversion operator allows then to modify the representation so that a solution may be represented differently in the population.

All modern GA hold a separate copy of the best chromosome ever computed to avoid its accidental destruction when it forms part of the population. Moreover, the stop condition is generally either the convergence of the cost function or a fixed number of generations to run.

The central concept in the GA theory is schemata. Schemata are the parts of a chromosome defined by the constant values of some of the chromosome genes. Typically, the operators work on the genes (for example the crossover combines genes from the parents to construct the children). Schemata with little usable length and good performances enjoy such an importance in the GA theory, that they are called *building blocks*. GA use a juxtaposition of these building blocks to find a quasi-optimal solution. There are many empirical results that have confirmed the importance of these building blocks (Bagley, 1967; Rosenberg, 1967; Grefenstette, 1985).

They are four major differences between GA and traditional approaches to solving optimization problems. First, GA use a parameter coding rather than the parameters themselves, i.e. GA do not have to know the meaning of the parameters. This makes it easier to adapt them to a given class of problems (different problems with the same structure). Then, GA work on a population of solutions and not on a single one, and so explore different portions of the search space in parallel. Next, GA use a value of the function to be optimized and not another form of this function. In particular, the cost function does not need to have any special analytical properties. Finally, GA use probabilistic transitions and not deterministic ones. For the same instance of a problem (same initial conditions and inputs), the results may be different after two different runs[11].

The Grouping Genetic Algorithms (GGA) developed by Falkenauer (1998) are a genetic framework to solve grouping problems. This framework proposes a new encoding scheme and specific genetic operators adapted to the grouping problems that do not suppose the existence of a specific metric. Moreover, this framework does not need to know the number of clusters. A complete description of the GGA is outside the scope of this chapter and the reader can find more information in (Falkenauer, 1998). Nerveless, the main characteristics are outlined next:

1. GGA adopt an encoding scheme where the chromosomes are defined by two elements: an *object part* representing the assignation of the objects and a *group part* containing the cluster composition. All the operators work on the group part of the chromosomes.

2. GGA suppose that a heuristic is defined to build a chromosome and one (possibly the same) to complete it (if some objects are unassigned). For example, in the adaptation of the GGA to the bin packing problem, Falkenauer (1998) uses a first-fit heuristic (for the building) and a first-fit descending heuristic (for the completion).

3. To select the chromosomes to use as parents and children in the population, Falkenauer (1998) suggests the tournament strategy (Goldberg, Korb & Deb, 1989). The idea is to create an ordered list of the chromosomes with the best solution always at the top, and the others ordered according to a specific method. This method selects randomly two

chromosomes in the population that are not in the list, compares their cost functions and puts the best one in the list. This process is repeated until all the chromosomes are in the list. Then, the upper part of the list will further be used when parents chromosomes are needed, while the lower part will be used for the children chromosomes.

4. The crossover operator creates a child chromosome by combining different groups from the corresponding parents. If the groups copied from the parents are "good", the resulting child will survive in the population and enhance its quality. If, during the crossover, an object is contained in two groups (one of each parent), one of these groups is destroyed. Therefore, some objects may be unassigned after the crossover operation, and GGA complete the chromosome with the corresponding heuristic.

5. The mutation operator destructs randomly some groups of a given chromosome and GGA complete this chromosome with the corresponding heuristic.

6. The inversion operator modifies the order of the groups in a chromosome.

Several implementations of GA (including the GGA) are part of the open source libraries included in the GALILEI platform.

Parameters of the SCGA

The SCGA has several parameters specific to genetic algorithms that have to be fixed manually (size of the population, number of generations, etc.). Moreover, the SCGA includes three *hard constraints*:

- a *minimum similarity threshold* between two profiles to be grouped together;
- a *minimum agreement threshold* which is the minimum agreement ratio to force grouping two profiles together (if two

profiles have assessed as relevant a given number of documents, they must be grouped together independently of other criteria such as the similarity);

- a *minimum disagreement threshold* which is the minimum disagreement ratio to avoid grouping two profiles together (if two profiles don't agree on the relevance of a given number of documents, they should not be grouped together independently of other criteria such as the similarity).

The role of the minimum similarity threshold is to limit the search space. In fact, it makes no sense to put two profiles in the same communities of interests if their descriptions do not share any common features. Or to say it differently, if the contents of documents read by two profiles are too dissimilar, the SCGA should not group them together. The minimum agreement and minimum disagreement thresholds integrate supervised information in the algorithm. In practice, if enough feedback information is provided from the profiles, it should be used to control the clustering. As in supervised classification algorithms where the training set is used to "learn" the classes, in the SCGA, the feedback information (considered as a sort of training set) is used to "learn" the communities of interests.

Since the mutation and inversion operators must not be used at each generation and on each chromosome, it is therefore necessary to choose when and where to apply these operators. A first strategy widely used in GA is to assign to each operator a probability, each chromosome having these probabilities of being chosen for a mutation or an inversion at each generation. I choose to implement another method where two situations trigger one of these operators:

1. A number of generations has been run through without the best chromosome computed ever changing. When a given threshold is reached, the best chromosome ever com-

puted is chosen, a mutation is effected on it and the result replaces the chromosome with the lowest fitness value in the population.

2. A given number of generations has been run through without the best chromosome in the population changing. When a given threshold is reached, the best chromosome in the population is chosen, a mutation is effected on it and the result replaces the chromosome with the lowest fitness value in the population.

Actually, the threshold for the first case is set to 10 generations for the mutation and the inversion operators. For the second case, the threshold is set to 10 generations for the inversion operator and 5 generations for the mutation operators.

Heuristic for Grouping Profiles

One of the main elements in a GGA is the heuristic used (in particular to initialize the population). A specific heuristic was developed for the profile clustering. Firstly, the heuristic inserts each profile not already assigned to a community into one. Then, all the social profiles alone in a community are assigned to another existing community. The community selected is the one containing the most similar profile.

The philosophy of the heuristic proposed for the SCGA to assign profiles to communities of interests is very intuitive and is based on the nearest neighbor clustering methods (Nearest Neighbor Clustering). The idea is to insert a profile into the "best" community of interests able to accept it. The heuristic treats the profiles in a random order to ensure the diversity of the population. When a community has to be found for a profile, p_k, three steps are followed:

1. If an already assigned profile has an agreement ratio with p_k greater than the minimum agreement threshold, its community is chosen.

2. If not, the heuristic parses all the existing communities to find all the "valid" ones, i.e. the communities that can accept p_k.

3. If no community of interests can be found, the heuristic creates a new one and assigns p_k to it; otherwise the heuristic assigns p_k to the best valid community.

To determine whether a community of interests is valid for p_k or not, two assumptions are made. Firstly, all pairs of grouped profiles must have a level of similarity greater than the minimum similarity threshold. Thus, if two profiles are too dissimilar, they cannot be grouped together. Secondly, all pairs of grouped profiles must have a disagreement ratio smaller than the minimum disagreement threshold, i.e. two profiles which have assessed differently too many common documents cannot be grouped together. If p_k doesn't respect these two constraints for a given community, this community is not a valid one.

Once all the valid communities of interests for p_k have been determined, the heuristic chooses the best one. The best valid community of interests is assumed to be the one that is most similar to p_k in terms of similarity and agreement ratio. In practice, the heuristic looks which valid community contains the profile sharing the highest agreement ratio with p_k:

1. If several valid communities are identified, the one containing the most similar profile is chosen.

2. If no community is found, the heuristic chooses the community with the most similar profile to p_k.

The heuristic favors more the agreement ratio than the similarity measure. This is normal since the agreement ratio is based on a direct feedback of the users.

Population Initialization

One of the aspects of the social browsing approach is that it is a continuous process (Introduction), in particular the profiles clustering should evolute with the changes of the profiles. In practice, this means that, except for the initialization of the system, the problem is to adapt a previous clustering to the new situation rather than creating each time a new clustering from scratch. The SCGA must therefore be incremental.

The initialization operator constructs an initial population using the current situation as a basis. The operator tries to copy each existing community of interests in the current situation into a new one in the chromosome. During this step, the operator verifies that the communities of interests are still valid as defined in the previous subsection for the different profiles previously attached to this community of interests. At this stage some profiles are not assigned to any community of interests either because they are new, or because their old communities of interests are no longer valid for them. A second step is thus required, and the heuristic integrated in the SCGA is used to insert these profiles. The population constructed by this process has interesting characteristics:

- these chromosomes are as close as possible to the current situation;
- they contain only valid communities of interests.
- each profile is assigned to a community of interests.

At this stage, the chromosomes offer initial solutions that will be refined by the SCGA.

It must be taken care of the fact that, after the initial construction of the population, all its chromosomes could be identical. A third step of the initialization becomes necessary to ensure the diversity of the population. The idea is to use the mutation operator on all the chromosomes that are identical while leaving one unchanged

(Falkenauer, 1998). Since the mutation randomly removes some communities of interests and reinserts the profiles attached in the clustering, all the previously identical chromosomes will become different. The population diversification is therefore ensured.

Evaluation of the Solutions

As already explained, the cost function should represent as closely as possible the quality of the solution and use as much information as possible. For the profile clustering, it is not possible to find a function or a set of functions which exactly reflects the quality of a solution, because the concept of "two profiles that are sufficiently similar to be grouped together" is difficult to evaluate. Moreover, each user has different expectations concerning the result of the clustering: some of them prefer to be grouped together with a maximum of other users and to accept a certain latitude in quality, while others want to be grouped with highly similar users, even if the corresponding community of interests only contains a few profiles.

In practice, when dealing with the profiles clustering, the three types of information are available: the similarities between the profiles descriptions, and the agreement and the disagreement ratios. It is possible to define for each of these types of information a corresponding criteria that should be optimized:

1. A *similarity criterion* expresses the fact that profiles being grouped into the same community of interests should be as similar as possible while the profiles grouped in different communities should be as dissimilar as possible. It is measured as a ratio between the compactness of the clustering and the maximum similarity separating two communities of interests (Ray & Turi, 1999), and has to be maximized. In practice, for each community, the center is computed. The

compactness of the clustering is the average similarity of each center to the other profiles of its community. The maximum similarity separating two communities of interests is simply the maximum similarity between the centers.

2. An *agreement criterion* expresses that the agreement ratio between two profiles indicates if *a priori* they must be grouped together. It is computed as the average agreement ratio between the profiles grouped together and has to be maximized.

3. A *disagreement criterion* expresses that the disagreement ratio between two profiles indicates if *a priori* they must not be grouped together. It is computed as the average disagreement ratio between the profiles grouped together and has to be minimized.

So, with the evaluation of the profile clustering, the SCGA is dealing with an *approximate multi-criteria problem*:

- there are three criteria to optimize (the similarity criterion, the agreement criterion and the disagreement criterion);
- each criterion represents a characteristic of a solution without guaranteeing an exact match between this criterion and the ideal solution.

For the evaluation, the SCGA uses the multi-criteria decision aid method called PROMETHEE (Brans & Mareschal, 2002). Without going into details, the PROMETHEE method allows to outrank between different solutions with regard to several criteria that are not comparable (such as the price, the fuel consumption and the power in a comparison between different cars). Moreover, it permits to attribute different weights to quantify the importance of the different criteria. The idea of using the PROMETHEE method to enhance the classical GGA was already proposed by Rekiek (2000).

At each generation, the SCGA compares the chromosomes of the population and the best solution ever computed. If one of the chromosomes is better than the best ever computed solution, the latest is replaced by the former. Moreover, this ranking is used by the tournament strategy (Grouping Genetic Algorithms (GCA)).

Local Optimization Operator

Falkenauer (1998) has pointed out the importance of a local optimization operator for a GGA. The basic idea is that, since the crossover operator is not specific to a particular problem, the chromosomes it creates may be optimized with some minor changes. For example, in the case of profiles grouping, an exchange of a profile between two communities of interests may increase the quality of the solution.

It is the role of the local optimization operator to try to locally optimize a chromosome. In practice, it is called after the crossover and before the heuristic is used to find a group for all unassigned objects. It is important to understand that this operator should only do "minor changes" to the solution in order to optimize it. In fact, since the grouping problems are NP-hard, it makes no sense to search the global optimization. Moreover, this operator should be fast (because it is called very often), which limits the search in the neighborhood of the chromosome to optimize.

For the SCGA, an optimization operator based on the k-Means algorithm is implemented (k_Means Clustering Algorithm). Whereas the idea of mixing a GA with a k-Means-based algorithm has previously been successfully applied, for example to the image segmentation problem (Ramos & Muge, 1999), the way I use this approach is quite different. The idea is to see if a set of minor disturbances in the structure, by merging two communities of interests or by dividing one of them, can produce a better solution than the one represented by the optimized chromosome. The optimization operator is divided into three steps:

1. The first step performs a number of small disturbances in the structure. In practice, it does a maximum of n merges or divisions (2 in the current configuration). This step constructs therefore 2n+1 new temporary solutions:
    - an exact copy of the chromosome to optimize;
    - n solutions obtained by recursively dividing communities from the chromosome to optimize;
    - n solutions obtained by recursively merging communities from the chromosome to optimize.
2. The k-Means algorithm is performed on all these temporary solutions. In practice, the number of interactions is limited to a few ones (typically 10).
3. The 2n+1 temporary solutions and the original chromosome are evaluated and ranked using the PROMETHEE method described previously. If one of the solution is better than the original chromosome, it will replace it.

Let us assume that a community of interests should be divided. Two problems must be solved: selecting the community of interests to divide and choosing how to divide the selected one. It can be assumed that if dissimilar profiles are grouped together, the corresponding community of interests will not be correct at all. This means that the "worst" community of interests is the one containing the two most dissimilar profiles, p_1 and p_2. Once, this community is selected, it is divided into two new communities. Because p_1 and p_2 correspond to the minimum similarity value and are the most dissimilar, it can be assumed that each profile will go into one of the two new communities of interests. The other profiles are then inserted into the newly created community of interests corresponding to the most similar profile, either p_1 or p_2.

If two communities of interests should be merged, it is necessary to select them. It can be assumed that if very similar profiles are grouped into different communities of interests, the clustering method will lead to too many communities of interests. One method for choosing which are the communities of interests to merge is therefore to select those that contain the two most similar profiles.

As already explained, the k-Means algorithm optimizes the intra-cluster similarities, i.e. it optimizes only the similarity criterion. On the other hand, since the PROMETHEE method is used to determine if one of the modified solutions is better than the current chromosome, if the optimization of the intra-clusters similarities deteriorates the global quality of the chromosome (regarding all the criteria), it will not be replaced. It is important to understand the articulation of the local optimization operator in comparison with the hard constraints, in particular the minimum agreement and minimum disagreement thresholds. If enough supervised information is provided to the SCGA (there are many non null agreement and disagreement ratios between the profiles), it should definitively be used to group the profiles. In this case, the corresponding agreement and disagreement criteria will always prefer the solutions taking this information into account rather than solutions optimizing mainly the similarities. On the other hand, when this feedback information is not existing, the only reliable information that can be used for the grouping is the similarities. This is the reason why the local optimization operator works on this aspect. This means that it can be supposed that the importance of the local optimization operator increases with the sparseness of the matrices storing the agreement and disagreement ratios between the profiles.

VALIDATION METHODOLOGY

The validation methodology defines test cycles simulating how users proceed. The basic material used by the methodology is a collection of pre-categorized documents (Methodology). A large amount of experimental simulations has been performed (Francq, 2003); only two of these will be detailed here:

- a test procedure that studies the influence of different parameters of the SCGA (Sketch of the Test Procedure);
- a procedure that simulates a real system during a period defined by 500 "time units" (Simulation of A Real System).

Each procedure implements two features:

- new users are added during the creation processes where initial assessments are generated (Initial Assessments);
- existing users share relevant documents and provide a relevance feedback on these documents (Relevance Feedback Process).

A performance measurement is then used to evaluate the quality of the resulting profile clustering (Measure of Quality of a Solution).

Methodology

For validation purposes, the methodology uses document collections that are pre-categorized into topics. Moreover, it is supposed that the topics may be organized hierarchically: different topics of documents may share a same "main topic". The assumption is made that each topic can be seen as an ideal community of interests, i.e. all the profiles that are interested by the same topic should be grouped into the same community.

In practice, each object of the system (documents, profiles and communities) is therefore assigned to one topic. Knowing the topic assigned to a profile and a document, it is possible to simulate an assessment (for example if the profile and the document are from the same topic, the profile assesses the document as relevant). Without knowing the topics, the system computes the profiles

descriptions and groups them into communities of interests. Once the communities are built, it is possible to compare how the profiles are grouped with their original assignment. Ideally, to each topic should correspond one and only one computed community of interests regrouping all the profiles assigned to it.

Sketch of the Test Procedure

The test procedure is divided into the following steps:

1. **Initialization (at $t=t_0$).** A given number of profiles is generated for each topic (between 5 and 10 in the tests presented here) as well as a set of initial assessments on documents, eventually with some noise. That is, I simulate the initial assessments of the profiles. In other words, I generate profiles interested by a topic of the collection. These topics are hidden to the system.
2. **Update.** The corresponding profiles and communities of interests are computed by the system. I compare this computed clustering with the ideal one based on our knowledge of the topics.
3. **Feedback.** Some relevant documents are shared between users of the same community. I simulate a relevance feedback process on these shared documents.
4. **Cycle.** Repeat the steps 2 and 3 several times (4 for the tests presented in this chapter).

Of course, the final clustering computed by the system should exactly match the topics. I performed 10 runs of this test procedure with different initializations and computed the average results.

Simulation of a Real System

The objective here is to simulate a system in "real life". During the life time of the system, new profiles use it. Sometimes these new profiles are related to existing interests of other users, and sometimes these profiles are related to a completely new topic. To simulate this, the process performs the following steps:

1. **Initialization (at $t=t_0$ and $t=t_0+1$).** Two profiles are created and each one is assigned to a topic. I generate a set of initial assessments on documents. The corresponding profiles and communities of interests are computed by the system. I compare this computed clustering with the ideal one based on our knowledge of the topics.

2. **Feedback (until $t_1=t+\text{randunif}(0,t_{feedback})$).** During a number of steps randomly chosen (between 0 and 3 in the test presented here), some relevant documents are shared between users of the same community. I therefore simulate a relevance feedback process on these shared documents. The corresponding profiles and communities of interests are computed by the system. I compare this computed clustering with the ideal one based on our knowledge of the topics.

3. **Creation (at $t=t_1$).** A new profile is created related to a randomly selected topic among the set of available topics. In practice, there is a given probability (60% in the tests presented here) that the chosen topic has already at least one existing profile assigned to it rather than to be a "new" one (the profile created is the first assigned to it)[12]. This simulates the fact that a new user connects to the system, with eventually a new interest (he or she belongs to a new topic). I generate for this profile a set of initial assessments on documents. The corresponding profiles and communities of interests are computed by the system. I compare this computed clustering with the ideal one based on our knowledge of the topics.

4. **Cycle (until $t=t_{stop}$).** Repeat steps 2 and 3 until a given number of steps is reached.

In the experiments presented in this chapter, the simulation process is repeated until $t_{stop}=500$. Moreover, since the system creates some profiles that are, for a given number of steps, assigned alone to a topic, all the created profiles in this process are supposed to be "non social" (the algorithm is not forced to put them in a community with other profiles).

Initial Assessments

The creation processes responsible for the simulation of initial assessments for newly created profiles generate three types of assessments for each profile:

- **Relevant.** A given percentage (10% in the tests) of the documents within the profile's topic are chosen randomly.
- **Fuzzy Relevant.** A given percentage (10% in the tests) of the documents within topics having the same main topic as the profile are chosen randomly.
- **Irrelevant.** Some documents within topics having another main topic than the profile are chosen randomly. The number of such documents is set up to a percentage (50% in the tests) of the number of relevant documents.

Relevance Feedback Process

Once the communities of interests have been computed, relevant information is exchanged between the different profiles having their corresponding profiles in the same community. For instance, some documents relevant to most of the profiles in a community could be shared across the whole community. This way, it is possible to propose a list of potentially interesting documents for each profile that he or she has not already assessed. Because the documents and the profiles are both described in the knowledge model of the GALILEI Framework, the similarity measure presented in

Technical Overview can be used to sort the list of proposed documents in a descending order of similarities.

The following method is proposed to simulate a feedback process. A given number of the highest ranked documents (10 in the tests) is chosen for each profile and an assessment is simulated for the corresponding profile. The assessment for a given document is:

- **Relevant.** The document is on the same topic than the profile's.
- **Fuzzy Relevant.** The document is from a topic of the same main topic as the profile's.
- **Irrelevant.** The document is from a main topic other than the profile's.

This process constructs a list of assessments for each profile.

Measure of Quality of a Solution

Many different clustering measures were studied in (Milligan & Cooper, 1986), and the recommendation is to use the adjusted Rand index for an overall comparison. In (Francq, 2003), two other measures adapted from information retrieval problems were used: the recall and the precision (Baeza-Yates & Ribeiro-Neto, 1999). Since these measures do not propose an overall comparison, they are not detailed here. Nevertheless, the reader should know that these measures are useful to study if the algorithm generates too many communities (typically a good precision and a poor recall) or too few communities (typically a poor precision and a good recall).

The aim of the adjusted Rand index is to establish an overall comparison between the computed and the ideal clusterings. It is based on the Rand index (Rand, 1971), where a comparison is made between the assignments of each pair of profiles in the ideal and the computed clusterings. Roughly speaking, the Rand index computes the percentage of pairs of profiles for which both classification methods, the computed and the ideal one, agree. A problem with the Rand index is that two randomly computed clusterings have not a constant index, for example zero. Hubert and Arabie therefore introduce the adjusted Rand index (Hubert & Arabie, 1985), which is based on the assumption that the process is the generalized hypergeometric distribution, i.e. the ideal and computed clusterings are selected at random so that the number of profiles in both clusterings is fixed. Notice that a random clustering corresponds to an adjusted Rand index of 0.

RESULTS

This section presents some results based on the procedures of the validation methodology described in the previous section. The reader should remember that a complete SCGA is run at each step of the test procedures (10 times for each test) and of the simulations (500 times for each simulation). The complete set of tests cannot be described here, but can be found in (Francq, 2003).

Document Collections

Three different documents collections of pre-categorized documents were used for the different tests.

The *20 newsgroups* data set is an English-language collection which consists of 20 topics (newsgroups) and 19,778 documents. The documents are e-mails extracted from newsgroups. Since the GALILEI Framework manages only XML documents, the e-mails are automatically converted into XML documents. For each e-mail, an XML document is generated with a root tag "<email>" having two child tags:

1. A "<header>" part corresponding to the header of the e-mail. Child tags are cre-

ated for each field appearing in the header ("<From>", "<Subject>", "<Newsgroups>", etc.).
2. A "<body>" part corresponding to the content of the e-mail, i.e. the raw text.

Notice that some topics can be regrouped further into "main topics". For example, the topics "Windows", "Windows/X" and "Graphics" are regrouped into a main topic "Computer".

The *Ziff-Davis* data set is an English-language collection which consists of 26 topics and 31,619 documents. The documents are articles from the *San Jose Mercury News* newspaper formated using SGML-like tags easily transformed into XML documents.

The *Le Soir* data set is a French-language collection which consists of 9 topics and 13,552 documents. The documents are on-line articles gathered from different subjects of the Web site of the Belgian *Le Soir* newspaper in HTML. The documents were preprocessed in order to transform them into XHTML.

The *20 newsgroups* and *Ziff-Davis* data sets contain powerful metadata such as the e-mail addresses of the senders or the name of the author of the articles. Since this metadata provides information that identifies clearly a given topic (for example a given newsgroup contains the same sub-set of e-mail addresses), it is probably possible to correctly group the profiles using only this metadata (for example all the profiles assigned to a given newsgroup will have its name in its attributes). Therefore, to test the real performances of the SCGA, I decide not to take any metadata into account while computing the similarities between the profiles. These similarities are thus computed as the modified cosine between the English or French subvectors (Technical Overview).

Parameters of the SCGA

The different SCGA parameters used are:

- a population size of 16;
- the SCGA exit condition is fixed to 30 generations;
- the maximal number of k-Means iterations used for the local optimization is set to 10;
- the minimum similarity threshold is computed as the addition of the average value of the similarities between all the profiles with the three-quarters of the standard deviation of these similarities[13];
- the minimum agreement threshold is set to 0.6 (when 60% of the same documents were assessed by two profiles as relevant, the profiles are grouped together);
- the minimum disagreement threshold is set to 0.6 (when 60% of the same documents were assessed differently by two profiles, the profiles are never grouped together).

These parameters were fixed regarding two elements:

1. The algorithm should be fast since it has to work on large data sets and to be run very often. This is the reason why we have chosen small values for the population size, the number of generations and the number of iterations.
2. Choosing a minimum agreement and disagreement thresholds just above 0.5 seems intuitive at first glance.

Variations of most of these parameters were tested in (Francq, 2003), and have shown that other values do not significantly change the results. The population size is the only parameter for which no variations were observed. But, finding the "right size" for the population is not an easy task. Actually, the choice of a small population size was driven by performance purposes and by the low number of profiles (between 150 and 350). If the number of profiles grows, and expands the search space, it may be interesting to increase the population size to 32 or even 64.

Robustness

The test procedure described in Sketch of the Test Procedure was used on the *20 newsgroups* collection to study the robustness with respect to some parameters of the test methodology. First, since many clustering methods are dependent of the number of clusters, it is interesting to study if the SCGA is able to find the correct number of topics. To do so, the test procedure was run with 100%, 75% and 50% of the topics. The average values of the adjusted Rand index are shown in (Table 1), and demonstrate that the quality of the solutions is quite good. In particular, the SCGA is not optimized for a particular number of clusters (communities of interests) to reach.

Moreover, the results of (Table 1) show that the computed clustering is already good after the first step of this test procedure, and becomes better with the feedback processes (which is the expected behavior).

Secondly, because users are subject to "error"[14], it is not realistic to consider that each assessment submitted to the system is correct. It is therefore necessary to simulate user "errors", which can be done by defining an error percentage, i.e. the probability that a user makes a "wrong" assessment during the relevance feedback and creation processes. Four series of tests were made with error percentages of 0%, 5%, 10% and 30%. The average values of the adjusted Rand index are shown in (Table 2[15]).

As expected, the quality of the results seems to decrease when the error percentage increases, but these results show that the performances of the SCGA are still good with an error rate of 30%. For reasonable levels of wrong assessments, this influence is not very important. The main reason is that, in the heuristic, the agreement ratio is the most influential measure. With the succession of feedback processes, this ratio increases also if the users disagree on a given number of individual documents.

Role of the Operators

The test procedure described earlier was used on the *20 newsgroups* data set to study the influence of different operators of the SCGA. Firstly, (Table 3) shows the minimum, maximum, and average values and the standard deviation of the adjusted Rand index in "normal conditions".

In Local Optimization Operator, a local optimization operator based on the k-Means algorithm was described. To test the importance of this operator, the test procedure was carried out without using the local optimization operator.

The minimum, maximum, and average values and the standard deviation of the adjusted Rand index (Table 4) show that the quality of the clustering has decreased. It can be therefore concluded that the local optimization operator is an important operator in the SCGA as already pointed out by Falkenauer (1998). Again, as already explained in Local Optimization Operator, the local optimiza-

Table 1. Results using part of the topics, based on 10 runs

Step	100%	75%	50%
Initial Assessment	0.921	0.971	0.962
Feedback Process 1	0.968	0.998	0.999
Feedback Process 2	0.999	0.999	0.999
Feedback Process 3	0.991	0.999	0.999
Feedback Process 4	0.996	0.999	0.999

Table 2. Results with erroneous assessments, based on 10 runs

Step	0%	5%	10%	30%
Initial Assessment	0.979	0.976	0.972	0.906
Feedback Process 1	0.998	0.990	0.964	0.944
Feedback Process 2	0.995	0.977	0.982	0.950
Feedback Process 3	0.999	0.998	0.989	0.955
Feedback Process 4	0.999	0.998	0.990	0.956

Table 3. Results in "normal conditions" based on 10 runs

Step	Minimum	Maximum	Average	Deviation
Initial Assessment	0.872	0.975	0.921	0.031
Feedback Process 1	0.936	0.998	0.968	0.024
Feedback Process 2	0.991	0.998	0.999	0.002
Feedback Process 3	0.917	1.000	0.991	0.026
Feedback Process 4	0.962	1.000	0.996	0.012

Table 4. Results without local optimization based on 10 runs

Step	Minimum	Maximum	Average	Deviation
Initial Assessment	0.705	0.842	0.785	0.050
Feedback Process 1	0.778	0.946	0.852	0.056
Feedback Process 2	0.779	0.914	0.849	0.049
Feedback Process 3	0.794	0.930	0.865	0.036
Feedback Process 4	0.787	0.894	0.850	0.034

tion operator is particularly important when there is no supervised information available (first steps of the test procedure).

As explained in Parameters of the SCGA, a small value for the minimum similarity threshold enhances the search space (because the constraint to group two profiles decreases). Therefore, I chose to carry out two test procedures using a threshold of 0 (any profiles can be grouped together regarding their similarity):

1. One procedure using only the initialization operator of the SCGA (Population Initialization).
2. One procedure using the whole SCGA.

The results of the minimum, maximum, and average values and the standard deviation of the adjusted Rand index using the initialization operator only (Table 5) and the complete SCGA (Table 6) show that, in average, the complete SCGA gives better and more stable results than a simple local-based method. Moreover, it shows that a "good" choice of the minimum similarity plays an important role in large search spaces.

Simulation of a Real System

In this subsection, the results of the procedure simulating a real system are shown. At each step, the method computes the adjusted Rand index. (Figure 3) shows the results of one simulation for the different data sets.

The results of the simulations of a real system show that the system seems to converge to a near-optimal clustering for all the document collections analyzed (the reader should remember that the same values for the parameters were used for all the collections). The main problems that have been identified during a complete simulation analysis (Francq, 2003) are local ones, i.e. they do not disturb the system for a long period:

1. Since the adjusted Rand Index is based on a comparison, two solutions presenting the same characteristics may have different values for it. For example, let us assume that only one profile is not correctly grouped. Depending on the community of interests in which it is contained, the adjusted Rand index may have different values. So, from

Table 5. Results with the only use of the initialization operator of the SCGA based on 10 runs and a null minimum similarity threshold

Step	Minimum	Maximum	Average	Deviation
Initial Assessment	0.307	0.451	0.344	0.081
Feedback Process 1	0.380	0.851	0.485	0.136
Feedback Process 2	0.385	0.779	0.610	0.141
Feedback Process 3	0.394	0.784	0.649	0.123
Feedback Process 4	0.395	0.698	0.614	0.094

Table 6. Results in "normal conditions" based on 10 runs and a null minimum similarity threshold

Step	Minimum	Maximum	Average	Deviation
Initial Assessment	0.617	0.755	0.694	0.044
Feedback Process 1	0.824	0.940	0.889	0.032
Feedback Process 2	0.860	1.000	0.932	0.052
Feedback Process 3	0.734	0.962	0.863	0.052
Feedback Process 4	0.762	1.000	0.880	0.072

one step to another, the quality of the solutions may remain constant because they have the same characteristics, while the adjusted Rand index changes. This explains some small fluctuations between consecutive steps and cannot be seen as a problem.

2. Since the profile clustering is an approximate multi-criteria problem, it may happen that a slightly worse solution is preferred according to the multi-criteria decision-aid method used. In such cases, after the evaluation of the population, the SCGA control strategy may suppose that one of the solutions in the population could be better in reality than the best ever computed solution. This is called the sub-evaluation problem which is always implicitly present in every approximate multi-criteria problem. The consequence of this problem is that the quality of the solution identified as the best one by the SCGA may locally decrease, i.e. the best solution at a given step may be worse than the one at the next step.

3. A small number of profiles that are not related to the same topic can be grouped together because their similarities are greater than the minimum similarity threshold. This explains why profiles related to a topic in which they are alone, are mostly grouped with other profiles (also if they are not social ones). When the number of profiles of a given topic increases, they are generally grouped together. At the end of the simulation several profiles have been created for each existing topic, the system can identify these topics in an easier way which explains why the system seems to converge.

On the basis of these remarks, it can be concluded that the algorithm proposed in this chapter seems sufficiently robust to be used in a real life situation.

Figure 3. Simulation of a real system

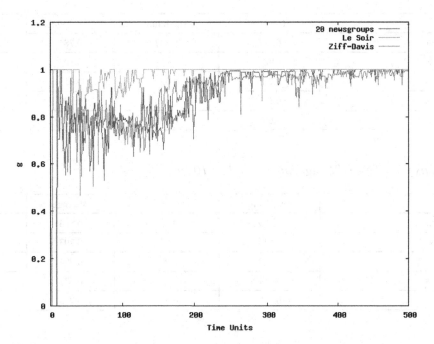

Other Clustering Methods

Since the GALILEI platform allows different methods to be implemented as plug-ins, three other clustering methods to group the profiles were implemented (Francq, Wartel, Kumps & Vandaele, 2003). The test procedure used to test the SCGA was also run with these methods:

- the k-Means algorithm with prototypes (k_Means Clustering Algorithm);
- the CURE algorithm (Hierarchical Clustering);
- a k-Means algorithm including the refining of the centers (k_Means Clustering Algorithm) and a method to detect the correct number of clusters.

The different clustering methods were optimized for the *20 newsgroups* data set used for the comparisons. The same tests (documents assessed, profiles and feedback processes) as for the SCGA were performed. All computations run on the same computer: a two-processors Intel Xeon with 1 Gb of RAM running GNU/Linux.

(Table 7) shows the minimum, maximum, and average values and the standard deviation of the adjusted Rand index computed at each step using the k-Means algorithm with two prototypes. Several tests have shown that the best results were achieved with two prototypes and a similarity to a community computed as the average of the similarity of the profile with the center and its maximum similarity with the prototypes. The correct number of communities was manually specified to the algorithm. The results obtained are worse than the reference ones (Table 3, third column).

(Table 8) shows the minimum, maximum, and average values and the standard deviation of the adjusted Rand index computed at each step using the CURE algorithm (each group is also defined by two prototypes). Again, the correct number of communities was manually specified to the algorithm. Here also, the results obtained are worse than the reference ones (Table 3, third column).

Table 7. Results with the k-Means algorithm with prototypes based on 10 runs

Step	Minimum	Maximum	Average	Deviation
Initial Assessment	0.731	0.837	0.783	0.034
Feedback Process 1	0.986	0.918	0.808	0.063
Feedback Process 2	0.736	0.929	0.913	0.064
Feedback Process 3	0.757	0.906	0.830	0.053
Feedback Process 4	0.669	0.889	0.821	0.064

Table 8. Results with the CURE algorithm based on 10 runs

Step	Minimum	Maximum	Average	Deviation
Initial Assessment	0.729	0.920	0.804	0.060
Feedback Process 1	0.548	0.878	0.793	0.106
Feedback Process 2	0.603	0.903	0.794	0.092
Feedback Process 3	0.581	0.907	0.774	0.121
Feedback Process 4	0.608	0.920	0.778	0.110

The last clustering method tested is a k-Means using the refining method proposed by Bradley and Fayyad (1998) and explained in k_Means Clustering Algorithm, combined with a heuristic detecting the correct number of clusters. Wartel who has developed it, call it the SUP k-Means algorithm (Francq, Wartel, Kumps & Vandaele, 2003). The heuristic used is the one developed for the SCGA (Heuristic for Grouping Profiles). The test procedure was carried out using this profile clustering method. The minimum, maximum, and average values and the standard deviation of the adjusted Rand index were computed at each step (Table 9). The results obtained with the SUP k-Means algorithm are slightly worse than those obtained with the SCGA (Table 3, third column). The reader should notice that for different runs, the SUP k-Means detects different number of communities of interests (depending of the initial conditions), which explains that the results of the minimum adjusted Rand Index are worse than those obtained with the SCGA (Table 3, first column).

When the results of the different clustering algorithms are compared, it seems that the SCGA proposed in this chapter obtains the best results. The k-Means algorithm refining the centers and detecting the number of groups is the algorithm producing the results which are the most similar to those of the SCGA.

The execution times of the test procedure with the different clustering methods are shown in (Table 10). These execution times show that the k-Means algorithm with the prototypes seems to be the fastest clustering method, that the SCGA and the CURE algorithms have similar execution times, and that the SUP k-Means seems to be the slowest clustering method. Meanwhile, the SCGA and the SUP k-Means seem to be the clustering methods obtaining the best results. It can be therefore concluded that the SCGA seems to be the best compromise between quality and rapidity.

FUTURE RESEARCH DIRECTIONS

The SCGA uses three profiles-profiles matrices of measures to build the communities of the interests: the similarities, the agreement ratios and the disagreement ratios. In practice, the similari-

Table 9. Results with the SUP k-Means algorithm based on 10 runs

Step	Minimum	Maximum	Average	Deviation
Initial Assessment	0.832	0.962	0.895	0.042
Feedback Process 1	0.827	0.990	0.930	0.051
Feedback Process 2	0.918	1.000	0.970	0.026
Feedback Process 3	0.918	1.000	0.962	0.028
Feedback Process 4	0.893	1.000	0.972	0.036

Table 10. Execution times of the different algorithms

Method	Execution Time
SCGA	1h 5min 33s
CURE	59 min 7s
k-Means with prototypes	35 min 17s
SUP k-Means	1h 44min 44s

ties matrix is the only one needed by the SCGA for the clustering, the two other ones are used as constraints to "learn" the communities if some supervised information is available. Since the documents similarities are computed with the same measure as the profiles, it is possible to build a documents-documents matrix of similarities and the SCGA can also cluster documents. In fact, it is also possible to define the agreement and disagreement ratios between documents:

- the agreement ratio between two documents is the one between the number of same profiles assessing both documents as relevant and the total number of profiles assessing both documents;
- the disagreement ratio between two documents is the one between the number of same profiles assessing differently both documents and the total number of profiles assessing both documents.

Applied to the SCGA, these two ratios have comparable interpretations as for the profiles. If

a same profile (same interest) assesses as relevant two documents, there is a probability that these two documents are related to the same topic. If a same profile assesses differently two documents, there is a probability that these two documents are not related to the same topic. If these ratios are greater than given thresholds, two documents can be forced to be grouped together (minimum agreement threshold) or forced not to be grouped together (minimum disagreement threshold). As for the profiles, these ratios make sense only if there are suffice assessments (for example at least five profiles have assessed two documents). Some preliminary results show that the SCGA is able to cluster documents with fairly good results. In fact, the SCGA can be applied to any grouping problems where a similarity measure (or a distance measure) is defined between the objects to group. Moreover, any available supervised information can be represented as matrices of agreement and disagreement ratios[16] and being used to "learn" the clusters that the SCGA must obtain. Therefore, the scope of the SCGA is beyond the profiles clustering in particular and the GALILEI Framework in general. This is the reason why it is implemented in an open source C++ library integrated in the GALILEI platform, but that can be used independently of it.

The preliminary tests on documents clustering (using the same number of generations and population size as for the profiles clustering) have shown that the minimum similarity threshold has to be changed: the formula given in Parameters of the SCGA does not provide good results and different thresholds must be fixed for different collections. Of course, the results have shown that the SCGA converges also with a null threshold for the minimum similarity. In fact, by increasing the number of generations run and the population size, we can scan a bigger search space (characterized by very low values of this minimum similarity threshold). But, in the case of documents collections, we are dealing with larger instances (a little collection such as *Le Soir* represents more than ten thousands objects to group and some documents collections have millions of documents). It is therefore impossible to scan a big part of the corresponding search space. Moreover, the actual formula is based on the average and standard deviation of the similarities, suggesting that the whole documents-documents matrix of similarities should be computed, which is also impossible for big documents collections. Two solutions can be used for this problem:

1. Changing the way the minimum similarity threshold is computed. One possible method actually tested is to use a method of approximate nearest neighbours in order to determine this threshold (for example the minimum similarity between an object and its approximate nearest neighbours). But, limiting the similarity matrix to the nearest neighbours implies to change some operators of the SCGA, in particular the local optimization.

2. Restricting the search space with another hard constraint that can be more easily controlled. Such constraints may include a minimum number of objects to form a cluster, a maximum number of objects in a cluster, pre-defined clusters of objects, etc.

In fact, the best approach is probably to work on the two solutions: (a) approximating the minimum similarity threshold for large similarities matrices and (b) integrating new hard constraints than can be modified for a particular problem (for example

defining different minimum number of objects to form a cluster).

The results have shown the importance of the local optimization operator for the SCGA. Even if the k-Means algorithm is limited to a few iterations, the computation time of this operator increases when the size of the problem increases. In particular, if the SCGA is applied on large documents collections, the execution time of the local optimization operator can become a drawback. In the future, it will therefore be necessary to develop another operator. A first solution is to modify the current operator in order not to run the k-Means, but simply to look if the division or the merging of communities increases the quality of the solution without having to reassign the whole profiles. Falkenauer (1998) propoes, in his adaptation of the GGA for the bin packing problem, a local optimization operator based on a method used to evaluate the number of bins for this problem (Martello & Toth, 1990). As explained, the local optimization operator is called after the crossover (where some objects may remain unassigned) and before the heuristic completes the clustering. The operator proposed by Falkenauer looks if it is possible to replace up to three objects in a bin by one or two unassigned objects while optimizing the cost function (the bins are better filled). If this is the case, the unassigned objects are put in the bin and the previously assigned objects become unassigned. It is possible to adapt this local optimization operator for the SCGA. One possible adaptation is to compute for each cluster not only the center but also a given number of prototypes defined as the most dissimilar objects of the cluster. A new local optimization operator could then, as done by the one developed for the bin packing problem, look if it is possible to replace some of these prototypes with unassigned profiles while optimizing the criteria, and consequently replace them.

Currently, the SCGA supposes that each profile and each document have equal importance. But, in practice, it is not the case: the users have different levels of authority and some documents are considered as more important than others. In fact, several existing methods can be adapted to assign a "rating" to documents and profiles in a given community, to cite a few: (Kleinberg, 1998; Jureta, Faulkner, Achbany & Saerens, 2007; Koren, 2008). It is then possible to use this information to influence how the SCGA clusters the profiles in at least two ways:

1. The agreement and disagreement ratios can be weighed by the ratings on the documents. The most rated is a document, the most important is its contribution to these ratios.
2. When computing the center of a community (its most representative profile), the ratings on the profiles influence it. A highly rated profile may become the center of its community also if it is not the profile being the most similar to all other profiles of its community, while the most similar profile to all other profiles of the community may not be the center because it is poorly rated.

Of course, these modifications work identically for the documents clustering: the ratings on the profiles are used to weigh the agreement and the disagreement ratios, and the ratings on the documents influence the computing of the centers of a documents topic.

CASE STUDY: DETECTING COMMUNITIES OF RESEARCHERS

As explained, the social browsing approach is based on interactions with users (assessments on documents, suggestions, etc.). It should therefore be integrated in the information system of organizations. In practice, it means an integration project of the GALILEI platform in an organization and some developments to gather the needed information from the users and to store the results.

But it is also possible to use the GALILEI platform, in particular the SCGA, in a "one shot" project. A Belgian university was interested to know which researchers could collaborate together. They were convinced that several teams were working on similar research topics without knowing it, because they are located on different campuses and integrated in different faculties. Within a few days of work, I developed a program that was able to detect such *communities of researchers*. Concretely, I performed the following steps:

1. Using different bibliographical databases, I extracted all the publications references where the university appeared for the five last years. For each reference, a XML document was created containing the title and the abstract (the authors were hidden to the system to avoid that clusters were being made only of researchers having published together).
2. For each author, I looked if he or she was a staff member of the university. If so, a unique "research" profile was created, and a relevance assessment was associated with all the XML documents representing his or her publications.
3. The profiles were computed and then grouped into communities of researchers.

The academical authorities were very interested by the results. In fact, the current vice-rector at that time recognized herself and confirmed that her research community inside the institution corresponded to the one computed by the system.

One problem with the prototype developed was that the bibliographical databases used did not referenced all the publications of the researchers of the university (in particular in human sciences). To overcome this problem, a solution could be to extract the information not from bibliographical databases, but from the institutional repository where all the publications of an university are self-archiving (an increasing number of universities build such repositories). Since several standards emerge to access these repositories, such as the Open Archives Initiative Protocol for Metadata Harvesting (OAI-PMH) (Lagoze & Van de Sompel 2001), it should be possible in the future to generalize this approach and to develop a program that performs it automatically and proposes to the universities a tool to analyze the research topics of their members.

CONCLUSION

In this chapter, I present a genetic algorithm suited for the users' profile clustering called the Similarity-based Clustering Genetic Algorithm (SCGA). This algorithm is part of an integrated method to share documents among users, and a validation methodology was described. Different tests made on several document collections showed that the system converges to a near-optimal clustering. This is mainly due to the relevance feedback process based on shared documents, and a clustering strategy exploiting both the agreement between the users of the system and their profiles.

A discussion has shown that some local problems may appear during the profile clustering. These problems do not disturb the overall stability of the system, and solving these problems constitutes the future work. Some preliminary results show that the same algorithm can be successfully applied to the documents clustering problem. Moreover, several possible modifications were proposed to enhance the SCGA in order to increase both the quality of the clustering and the execution speed (this last element being crucial to treat large documents collections). A practical example has shown that the algorithm could be used to detect communities of researchers.

The complete GALILEI platform is available under the GNU LGPL license. Its libraries integrate the genetic algorithms presented in this chapter (GGA and SCGA). Since these algorithms are part of libraries that can be used outside the GALILEI platform, they can easily be applied by other researchers to solve their own problems.

ACKNOWLEDGMENT

Many persons have directly or indirectly contributed to the work reported in this chapter, in particular the members of the GALILEI research project. I want to especially thank Prof. Marco Saerens from the Université Catholique de Louvain (UCL) who developed the idea of the k-Means combined with prototypes and David Wartel who implemented the other clustering methods which results were presented in Other Clustering Methods.

I would also like to thank the Région wallonne who has funded the GALILEI research project during which the first versions of the GALILEI Framework and platform were developed (contract 01/1/4675).

REFERENCES

Abbaci, F., Francq, P., & Delchambre, A. (2005). Query Generation for Personalized Tracking of Information. In *Proceedings of the 2005 Internation Conference on Internet Computing* (Vol. 348). Las Vegas, USA: Hamid R. Arabnia and Rose Joshua.

Anderberg, M. R. (1973). *Cluster Analysis for Applications*. New York: Academic Press, Inc.

Arthur, D., & Vassilvitskii, S. (2007). k-means++: the advantages of careful seeding. In *Proceedings of the eighteenth annual ACM-SIAM symposium on Discrete algorithms* (pp. 1027-1035). Society for Industrial and Applied Mathematics Philadelphia, PA, USA.

Baeza-Yates, R., & Ribeiro-Neto, B. (1999). *Modern Information Retrieval*. Addison-Wesley.

Bagley, J. D. (1967). *The behavior of adaptive systems which employ genetic and correlation algorithms*. PhD thesis, University of Michigan.

Ball, G. H., & Hall, D. J. (1965). ISODATA, a novel method of data analysis and classification. Stanford, CA.

Bradley, P. S., & Fayyad, U. M. (1998). Refining initial points for k-means clustering. In *Proc. 15th International Conf. on Machine Learning* (Vol. 727).

Brans, J., & Mareschal, B. (2002). *PROMETHEE-GAIA. Une méthodologie d'aide à la décision en présence de critères multiples*. Editions de l'Université de Bruxelles.

Chinchor, N. A. (1998). Overview of MUC-7/MET-2. In *Proceedings of the Seventh Message Understanding Conference (MUC-7)* (Vol. 1).

Crouch, C., Apte, S., & Bapat, H. (2002). Using the extended vector model for XML retrieval. In *Proceedings of the 1st Workshop of the Initiative for the Evaluation of XML Retrieval (INEX). Dagstuhl, Germany*.

Darwin, C. (1859). *On the Origin of Species*. John Murray.

DCMI. (1999). *Dublin Core Metadata Element Set, Version 1.1: Reference Description*. (White Paper). Dublin Core Metadata Initiative.

Dubes, R. C. (1987). How many clusters are best? -- an experiment. *Pattern Recognition, 20*(6), 645–663. doi:10.1016/0031-3203(87)90034-3

Falkenauer, E. (1998). *Genetic Algorithms and Grouping Problems*. John Wiley & Sons.

Fogarty, M., & Bahls, C. (2002). Information Overload: Feel the pressure? *Scientist (Philadelphia, Pa.), 16*(16).

Fox, E. A. (1983). *Extending the Boolean and Vector Space Models of Information Retrieval with P-norm Queries and Multiple Concept Types*. PhD thesis, Cornell University.

Frakes, W. B. (1992). Stemming Algorithms. In Frakes, W. B., & Baeza-Yates, R. (Eds.), *Information Retrieval: Data Structures & Algorithms* (pp. 131–160). Prentice-Hall.

Francis, W., & Kucera, H. (1982). *Frequency Analysis of English Usage*. New York: Houghton.

Francq, P. (2003). *Collaborative and structured search: an integrated approach for sharing documents among users*. PhD thesis, Université Libre de Bruxelles.

Francq, P. (2007). The GALILEI Platform: Social Browsing to Build Communities of Interests and Share Relevant Information and Expertise. In Lytras, M. D., & Naeve, A. (Eds.), *Open source for knowledge and learning management: strategies beyond tools* (pp. 319–342). Idea Group Publishing.

Francq, P., & Delchambre, A. (2005). Using documents assessments to build communities of interests. In *Proceedings of the The 2005 Symposium on Applications and the Internet (SAINT'05)* (Vol. 327). Trento, Italy.

Francq, P., Wartel, D., Kumps, N., & Vandaele, V. (2003). *GALILEI -- Troisième Rapport Semestriel (Technical Report)*. Belgium: Université Libre de Bruxelles.

Garey, M., & Johnson, D. (1979). *Computers and Intractability - A Guide to the Theory of NP-completeness*. San Francisco: W.H. Freeman Co.

Gibbons, A. (1985). *Algorithmic Graph Theory*. Cambridge: Cambridge University Press.

Glover, F., & Laguna, M. (1997). *Tabu Search*. Kluwer Academic Publishers.

Glover, F., Laguna, M., Werra, D. D., & Taillard, E. (1992). Tabu Search. In *Annals of Operations Research* (*Vol. 41*). Basel, Switzerland: J.C. Baltser Pub.

Goldberg, D., Kork, B., & Deb, K. (1989). Messy genetic algorithms: motivation, analysis, and first results. *Complex Systems, 3*(5), 493–530.

Goldberg, D. E. (1991). *Genetic Algorithms in Search*. Addison-Wesley.

Grabisch, M., & Roubens, M. (2000). Application of the Choquet integral in multicriteria decision making. *Fuzzy measures and integrals, 40*, 348–374.

Grefenstette, J. J. (Ed.). (1987). *Genetic Algorithms and Their Applications: Proceedings of the 2nd International Conference on Genetic Algorithms*.

Guha, S., Rastogi, R., & Shim, K. (1998). *CURE: An Efficient Clustering Algorithm for Large Database* (pp. 73–84). New York: ACM Press.

Holland, J. H. (1975). *Adaptation in Natural and Artificial Systems*. University of Michigan Press.

Hubert, L., & Arabie, P. (1985). Comparing partitions. *Journal of Classification, 2*(1), 193–218. doi:10.1007/BF01908075

Ide, E. (1971). New experiments in relevance feedback. In Salton, G. (Ed.), *The SMART Retrieval System -- Experiments in Automatic Document Processing* (pp. 337–354). Englewood Cliffs, NJ: Prentice Hall Inc.

Jain, A. K., & Dubes, R. (1988). *Algorithms for Clustering Data. Prentice-Hall advanced reference series*. Upper Saddle River, NJ: Prentice-Hall, Inc.

Jain, A. K., Murty, M. N., & Flynn, P. J. (1999). Data Clustering: A Review. *ACM Computing Surveys, 31*(3), 264–323. doi:10.1145/331499.331504

Jureta, I., Faulkner, S., Achbany, Y., & Saerens, M. (2007). Dynamic Web Service Composition within a Service-Oriented Architecture. In *IEEE International Conference on Web Services, 2007* (pp. 304-311).

Kirkpatrick, S., Gelatt, C., & Vecchi, M. (1983). Optimization by simulated annealing. *Science, 220*(4598), 671–680. doi:10.1126/science.220.4598.671

Kleinberg, J. (1998). Authoritative sources in a hyperlinked environment. *Journal of the ACM, 46*(5), 604–632. doi:10.1145/324133.324140

Lagoze, C., & Van de Sompel, H. (2001). The Open Archives Initiative: Building a Low-Barrier Interoperability Framework. In *Proceedings of the first ACM/IEEE-CS Joint Conference on Digital Libraries (JCDL'01)* (pp. 54-62). New York: ACM Press.

Lawrence, S., & Giles, C. L. (1999). Accessibility of Information on the Web. *Nature, 400*, 107–109. doi:10.1038/21987

Lu, S. Y., & Fu, K. S. (1978). A sentence-to-sentence clustering procedure for pattern analysis. *IEEE Transactions on Systems, Man, and Cybernetics, 8*(5), 381–389. doi:10.1109/TSMC.1978.4309979

Luhn, H. P. (1957). A Statistical Approach to Mechanized Encoding and Searching of Literary Information. *IBM Journal of Research and Development, 1*(4), 309–317. doi:10.1147/rd.14.0309

MacQueen, J. (1967). Some methods for classification and analysis of multivariate observations. In *Proceedings of Berkeley Symposium on mathematical statistics and probability* (Vol. 1, pp. 281-297).

Martello, S., & Toth, P. (1990). Lower bounds and reduction procedures for the bin packing problem. *Discrete Applied Mathematics, 28*(1), 59–70. doi:10.1016/0166-218X(90)90094-S

Matthys, B., Falkenauer, E., Francq, P., & Delchambre, A. Robert & F., Gilson, H. (2000). An integrated system for navigation help, informational retrieval and suggestions in a hypertext structure. In Proceedings of Recherche d'Information Assistée par Ordinateur 2000 (p. 10). Paris, France.

McHugh, J. (1990). *Algorithmic Graph Theory*. London: Prentice Hall International.

Milligan, G. W., & Cooper, M. C. (1986). A study of the comparability of external criteria for hierarchical cluster analysis. *Multivariate Behavioral Research, 21*(4), 441–458. doi:10.1207/s15327906mbr2104_5

Murty, M. N., & Jain, A. K. (1995). Knowledge-based clustering scheme for collection management and retrieval of library books. *Pattern Recognition, 28*(7), 949–963. doi:10.1016/0031-3203(94)00173-J

Newell, A., & Simon, H. (1972). *Human problem solving*. NJ: Prentice-Hall Englewood Cliffs.

Papadimitriou, C., & Steiglitz, K. (1982). *Combinatorial Optimization, Algorithms and Complexity*. Englewood Cliffs, New Jersey: Prentice-Hall.

Ramos, V., & Muge, F. (1999). Image Segmentation by Colour Cube Genetic K-Mean Clustering. In *3rd Workshop on Genetic Algorithms and Artificial Life GAAL* (pp. 319-323). Lisbon, Portugal.

Rand, W. M. (1971). Objective criteria for the evaluation of clustering methods. *Journal of the American Statistical Association, 66*, 846–850. doi:10.2307/2284239

Ray, S., & Turi, R. H. (1999). Determination of Number of Clusters in K-Means Clustering and Application in Colour Image Segmentation. In *4th International Conference on Advances in Pattern Recognition and Digital Techniques (ICAPRDT'99)* (pp. 137-143).

Rekiek, B. (2000). *Assembly Line Design: multiple objective grouping genetic algorithm and the balancing of mixed-model hybrid assembly line*. PhD thesis, Université libre de Bruxelles.

Rocchio, J. J. (1971). Relevance feedback in information retrieval. In Salton, G. (Ed.), *The SMART Retrieval System -- Experiments in Automatic Document Processing*. Englewood Cliffs, NJ: Prentice Hall Inc.

Rosenberg, R. (1967). *Simulation of genetic populations with biochemical properties*. PhD thesis, University of Michigan.

Salton, G. (1968). *Automatic Information Organization and Retrieval*. New York: McGraw-Hill.

Salton, G. (1971). *The SMART Retrieval System -- Experiments in Automatic Document processing*. Englewood Cliffs, NJ: Prentice Hall Inc.

Salton, G., & McGill, M. (1983). *Modern Information Retrieval*. New York: McGraw-Hill Book Co.

Turing, A. (1936). On computable Numbers, With an Application to the Entscheidungsproblem. *Proceedings of the London Mathematical Society, 2*(42), 230–265.

van Laarhoven, P. J. M., & Aarts, E. H. L. (1987). *Simulated Annealing: Theory and Applications*. Springer.

Zadeh, L. A. (1965). Fuzzy sets. *Information and Control, 8*, 338–353. doi:10.1016/S0019-9958(65)90241-X

Zahn, C. T. (1971). Graph-theoretical methods for detecting and describing gestalt clusters. *IEEE Transactions on Computers, 100*(20), 68–86. doi:10.1109/T-C.1971.223083

ENDNOTES

[1] It is important not to confuse the GALILEI framework and the GALILEI platform. The

first is a conceptual and mathematical model built to manage numeric information (knowledge modeling, algorithms, etc.) while the second is an open source implementation of it.

[2] http://www.otlet-institute.org/galilei

[3] In practice, it means that a real system implementing the social browsing approach should allow the users to interact with it to specify which documents are relevant or not for which profile. Some prototypes were developed where a toolbar was inserted in the user's applications (file manager, browser, etc.). A combobox allows the users to choose his or her active profile and different buttons are used to associate an assessment on the current document with the active profile.

[4] Concretely, the complete names of the tags and attributes are indexed including their namespace (the URI pointing to the corresponding DTD or XML schema).

[5] A basic idea is to suppose that, most of the time, metadata tags have small content (typically a few terms) in one language only. Moreover, it can be also considered that generic information are "on top" of the documents, which means that metadata tags are probably high in the hierarchy of an XML document. Concerning the informative tags, it is probable that they constitute the major part of the tags of an XML document, and that most of them contain child tags. Based on these assumptions, it is possible for a heuristic to detect which tags are metadata ones and which are not.

[6] In fact, if two vectors have negative values corresponding to a specific feature (meaning the corresponding objects are not related to it), the product used in the cosine will add a positive contribution and the corresponding similarity will increase. But, knowing that two objects are not related to a feature does not mean that they are related to a same subject. Therefore, two negative values should

not increase the similarity. The modification suggested is that, when two values are negative, the corresponding product is not added when computing the cosine.

[7] In fact, there were some attempts to develop "universal algorithms" able to solve any kind of problems such as the General Problem Solver (GPS) from Newell and Simon (1972). Despite the hopes in the progress of artificial intelligence, it is still necessary to develop algorithms specifically for a class of problems.

[8] The center of a cluster is defined as the object which is the most similar to all other objects of that cluster.

[9] In his publication, Zhan works with distances and builds a minimum spanning tree.

[10] The solutions with the best values for a given cost function.

[11] In fact, this can make debugging more difficult because it is impossible to reproduce the bugs from one run to another. Because of this, there is generally a debug mode in GA, where under same initial conditions two different runs will produce the same results. This can be done by implementing a pseudo-random generator which reproduces the same sequence of numbers if asked.

[12] Of course, after a given number of steps, all available topics have at least one profile assigned to it.

[13] This relation was empirically determined with one particular sub-set of 2000 documents of the *20 newsgroups* data set. Since the same relation was then used for all the tests and with all collections, the risk of overfitting is greatly reduced.

[14] The concept of "error" must not be understand strictly. It does not mean that a user cannot evaluate the relevance of a document, but that two users finding the same topic relevant (having the same interest) may disagree on the relevance of a particular document in this topic.

[15] Since the simulation of "errors" is using the same random number generator as the simulation and the SCGA, the results for 0% are not equal to those obtained for 100% in Table 1. In fact, due to the simulation of "errors", it is not the same set of documents that is used to compute the profiles and do the clustering.

[16] Of course, the way these two ratios are computed will certainly differ from one problem to another.

Chapter 7
P2P Semantic Coordination for Collective Knowledge Organization

Silvana Castano
Università degli Studi di Milano, Italy

Alfio Ferrara
Università degli Studi di Milano, Italy

Stefano Montanelli
Università degli Studi di Milano, Italy

ABSTRACT

In this chapter, we present a P2P coordination approach for setting up and exploiting collective peer knowledge provided by autonomously emerging semantic communities. This approach aims at providing a practical means for allowing a peer to move from a restricted peer knowledge space, where it is considered as a single agent with its personal knowledge, towards an intermediate collective knowledge space, where it is considered as a member of a community storing a part of the overall collective knowledge, up to a final collective peer-knowledge space, where the peer builds its personal and coordinated view of the collective knowledge of interest harvested from the underlying communities. In this respect, ontologies and Semantic matching techniques are exploited to set up collective knowledge and to effectively enforce distributed resource sharing.

INTRODUCTION

In open and networked infrastructures, each single agent needs to evolve its ontology knowledge over time not only by adding new concepts on its own, but also by (re)using external *knowledge chunks* provided by other partners as a result of collaborative activities (Arenas, et al., 2003; Castano, Ferrara, & Montanelli, 2006b). In this sense, there is the need of shifting from rigid data integration architectures to more flexible *knowledge coordination platforms* where agents are organized in *semantic communities of interest* defined to explicitly *give shape* to the collective knowledge of groups of peers with similar expertise/resources.

DOI: 10.4018/978-1-61520-841-8.ch007

Copyright © 2011, IGI Global. Copying or distributing in print or electronic forms without written permission of IGI Global is prohibited.

In this chapter, we present a P2P coordination approach for setting up and exploiting collective peer knowledge provided by autonomously emerging semantic communities. This approach aims at providing a practical means for allowing a peer to move from a restricted *peer knowledge space*, where it is considered as a single agent with its personal knowledge, towards an intermediate *collective knowledge space*, where it is considered as a member of a community storing a part of the overall collective knowledge, up to a final *collective peer-knowledge space*, where the peer builds its personal and coordinated view of the collective knowledge of interest harvested from the underlying communities. In particular, the following challenging issues will be discussed in the chapter.

- **Semantic community formation and management**. This is related to the capability of recognizing group of peers with similar interests and maintaining semantic links with selected peers storing relevant knowledge. In the chapter, we present *handshake techniques* to enforce semantic community formation. In contrast with most existing solutions, our notion of semantic community is *lightweight*, in the sense that community membership is open and approval/rejection of a peer is not determined by the decision of a supervisor. This way, community maintenance is efficient due do the fact that peers can autonomously join/leave communities at any moment, without requiring community reorganization or structural adjustment.
- **Community-based knowledge harvesting**. This is related to the capability of discovering peers that can provide prominent knowledge on-demand for satisfying a given need. In the chapter, we present a *routing-by-community* mechanism based on ontology matching techniques for the automatic selection of the most appropriate communities to query. This allows peers to harvest the relevant collective knowledge of existing communities which is acquired in the form of *knowledge chunks*, each one representing a pertinent unit of knowledge (i.e., a concept) provided by an external peer source.
- **P2P knowledge coordination**. This is related to the capability of supporting a peer in building its own view of a specific concept of interest by coordinating the collective knowledge harvested from the underlying communities. In the chapter, we present clustering-based techniques to abstract a *collective concept* out of a set of underlying matching knowledge chunks. Semantic links are maintained by the peer to keep track of the source node from which the various knowledge chunks composing a collective concept have been acquired during harvesting. Collective concepts constitute the user-level interface for querying and accessing information resources spread over the network and to mediate between their possibly heterogeneous representations. For gradual improvement of the system effectiveness, coordination is cyclically performed to refine the collective concepts by including new knowledge chunks acquired from recently added members of communities.

BACKGROUND

Work related to the issues addressed in this chapter is mainly concerned with *semantics-based P2P systems*, with particular focus on those systems where the notion of peer community is supported for enforcing formation and maintenance of groups of nodes with similar interests (Khambatti, Ryu, & Dasgupta, 2002; Crespo & Garcia-Molina, 2004; Wang & Vassileva, 2004; Liu, Bhaduri, Das, Nguyen, & Kargupta, 2006). In this context, peer communities (when supported) are conceived as

Figure 1. A reference schema of community-based P2P systems

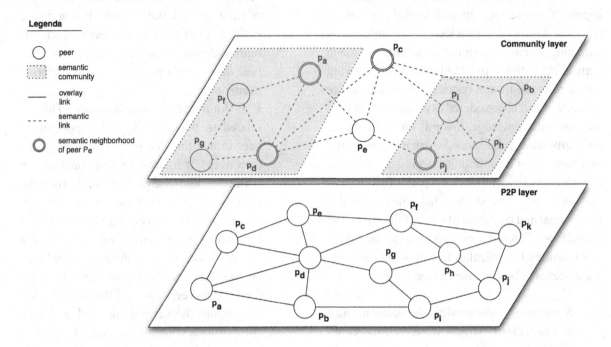

thematic overlays (see Figure 1) where different degrees of dynamism and flexibility are allowed. In this respect, the notion of collective knowledge refers to the overall bulk of knowledge that peers belonging to a given community are willing to share with other intra- and inter-community partners.

For this chapter, we are interested in analyzing what are the specific contributions of peer communities for semantics-based P2P systems. On one hand, we will discuss how peer communities are supported during their overall life-cycle, starting from aspects related to community formation, right to community maintenance and final disbandment. On the other hand, we will discuss how the collective knowledge of peer communities is exploited and how it impacts on the standard functionalities of the P2P system. In the literature, aspects related to community formation and maintenance and collective-knowledge exploitation greatly vary from one approach to another. In the following, we critically compare the main existing proposals and solutions.

Community Formation and Maintenance

Literature on peer communities is characterized by the use of unstructured P2P infrastructures where communication links between peers are adaptively modified during time according to changing traffic and load conditions. This is due to the need to efficiently manage peer insertions/ deletions frequently occurring in typical P2P networks. In such a dynamic scenario, the capability to support the construction of a structured grid of connections based on semantic similarities among peers contents is challenging and solutions in such a direction have not been investigated yet. On the opposite, approaches and techniques for enabling the formation of semantic peer communities on top of an unstructured P2P infrastructure have being widely emerging in the recent years. As shown in (Figure 1), these approaches are characterized by a basic *network layer* where peer communication links are established without any specific semantics-based criterion. Over this communication layer, the *community layer* is built and it is characterized by *semantic links* between pairs of peers, each one representing a semantic binding (i.e., a relationship) between the knowledge of the involved nodes. The community overlay gives shape to the notion of *semantic neighborhood* where i) each peer is directly connected with those nodes that are most similar according to a certain semantic-based matching function, and ii) semantic affinity decreases as long as the distance in terms of hops (i.e., the number of nodes to traverse) between two considered peers increases. In this schema, the notion of peer community depends on the kind of matching function that is adopted to evaluate peer similarity and on the kind of peer knowledge on which matching is performed.

In some approaches, the notion of peer community is implicitly defined. This means that a community is determined by a pair (p,r) where p is the founder/initiator peer of the community and r is the community radius, namely the maximum number of semantic links to follow from p for identifying the community members. As a consequence, peer groups with similar knowledge are not supported as explicit system entities and only the semantic neighborhood is considered by a peer for selecting the partners to interact with. This is the case of many popular knowledge sharing systems (e.g., Loser, Staab, & Tempich, 2007; Haase, Siebes, & Van Harmelen, 2008; Hidayanto & Bressan, 2007; Montanelli & Castano, 2008).

In other approaches, the notion of community is explicitly supported and it is determined through escalation/advertisement techniques. This is the case of Khambatti, et al. (2002) where peer interests expressed through attributes (i.e., keywords) are propagated to neighbors in order to allow the receiving nodes to detect the existence of common interest and thus communities. A similar approach is proposed in Das, Nandi, & Ganguly (2009) where the advertisement phase of peer interests is used by the network nodes to build routing indexes that are subsequently exploited in the search phase

to improve the efficiency of query propagation. In Liu, et al. (2006), a statistical mechanism based on the quantile measure is used to evaluate the similarity among the advertised peer interests. In the proposed approach, a peer can decide to promote the formation of a new community according to the level of similarity between its own interests and the received advertisements. An invitation procedure is then enforced by the community creator to initiate and supervise the concrete formation of the group. Peer interests can be inferred through mining techniques as proposed in Gu & Wei (2006). In that work, each community is defined as a vector of topics and it is assigned to a community manager which has the role of periodically advertising the community topics.

The main limit of this kind of approaches is the traffic overhead due to community advertisement. To overcome such a restriction, the use of a shared and centralized taxonomy of community topics is enforced. The list of communities is thus prefixed and a peer can choose one or more preferred communities to join by simply matching its interests with the centralized topics taxonomy. In Crespo & Garcia-Molina (2004), communities are clusters of similar peers whose contents are classified according to a predefined classification hierarchy (i.e., a tree of concepts). Keyword-based matching techniques are used by peers to determine the clusters to join. A more semantically rich approach is proposed in Bloehdorn, Haase, Hefke, Sure, & Tempich (2005) where ontologies are used for representing both the shared conceptualization of the allowed community topics and the expertise of each system node. The use of a shared ontology is enforced also in Wang & Vassileva (2004) where the notions of team, coalition, and congregation are proposed to distinguish among three different levels of cohesion when creating a peer community. In that work, the notion of peer reputation is defined to allow the selection of more reliable partners when multiple alternatives are available. However, trust and privacy issues in community-based P2P systems are only marginally considered in the current literature (Xiong & Liu, 2004; Rana & Hinze, 2004).

In most of the considered examples, both peer interests and community topics are expressed as keywords and basic string matching techniques are exploited in the community formation process to enable peers to choose the most interesting communities to join. The use of Semantic Web technologies (i.e., ontologies and ontology-based matching techniques) have being recently exploited to provide a semantically rich representation of peer interests and/or community descriptions and to support similarity-based query/answer mechanisms (Wang & Vassileva, 2004; Castano & Montanelli, 2005; Bloehdorn, et al., 2005).

As a final remark, we observe that supervising authorities are frequently employed to coordinate the overall community behavior and to perform access control for the selection of the community participants according to a centralized policy. For instance, in Asvanund & Krishnan (2004), the notion of ultrapeer is introduced as a super-node with community management responsibilities. Ultrapeers are dynamically created in the system as long as the need of a new community on a given topic emerges. Any peer in the system can decide to promote a new community and it becomes ultrapeer by advertising its proposal to a set of randomly-selected invited peers. The participation of a peer in a community depends on the result of a valuation function which measures the degree of overlapping between the proposed community topics and the interests of the invited peers. Candidate peers use the valuation function to measure their interest in the community topics, while the community ultrapeer uses this function to decide whether to accept those interested peers that reply to the invitation.

Collective Knowledge Exploitation

In most of the existing community-based P2P systems, the collective knowledge of peer groups is mainly exploited as a sort of structured infrastruc-

ture for knowledge discovery aimed at improving the effectiveness of sharing mechanisms (Aleman-Meza, Halaschek-Wiener, & Arpinar, 2005). As argued in Khambatti, et al. (2002), communities of peers can be used to realize an efficient query propagation strategy in a populated P2P space. This means that communities are used as query recipients and the community structure allows to efficiently propagate the request to all the community members. In the same direction, Aiello & Alessi (2007) propose a P2P system based on Web services to support sharing of XML documents. In that work, node pairs are interconnected according to similarities between their contents and the notion of collective knowledge is introduced to denote the knowledge fragments about a certain concept of interest that are interlinked across nodes. In other approaches like Sigurbjörnsson & van Zwol (2008), collective knowledge is defined to support recommendation systems for multimedia resource annotation. The idea is that the system suggests the tags to use for annotation by analyzing statistics on tag co-occurrence derived from the experience of other users. As a general remark, we observe that all the considered systems deal (at different levels) with the notion of *collective semantics*, and they propose their own idea of "Social Network Analysis" aimed at enforcing effective knowledge retrieval (Avrithis, Kompatsiaris, Staab, & Vakali, 2008).

In a more recent vision, P2P systems are seen as modern collaboration platforms where knowledge and data belonging to a possibly large set of peers (i.e., a collectivity of active agents) have to be managed in an effective way. As proposed in Jung & Euzenat (2007), social relationships among individuals and similarity relations among ontology concepts are the basis of an integrated system for knowledge sharing capable of handling different layers of knowledge in a coordinated way. In this respect, the problem shifts from a mere discovery issue to a more comprehensive semantic coordination need. In P2P environments, *semantic coordination* is defined as the capability to discover and maintain content mappings between pairs of independent peers in a "harmonized" way (Bouquet, Serafini, & Zanobini, 2004). For example, Scarlet (Sabou, d'Aquin, & Motta, 2008) provides techniques for discovering relations (i.e., mappings) between two concepts by making use of harvested Semantic Web ontologies as background knowledge. In open distributed systems, this kind of mappings can be exploited for lightweight integration purposes with the goal of establishing and maintaining a network of P2P semantic relations instead of a shared centralized schema (McBrien & Poulovassilis, 2003; Calvanese, De Giacomo, Lenzerini, & Rosati, 2004; Castano, Ferrara, & Montanelli, 2006a). In other words, knowledge coordination in P2P systems requires to a peer both the capability to discover other nodes storing similar knowledge and the capability to advertise its own expertise. Due to the dynamism and to the (possible) large size of this kind of systems, the idea to globally advertise the knowledge of each single peer to all the other network nodes is not a feasible solution. Similarly, classical integration-oriented approaches based on the construction of a global and unified knowledge representation of the overall network contents is not convincing as well. Conventional mediator-based architectures leave the floor to emergent peer-oriented architectures, where each peer is equipped with flexible matching techniques to coordinate its dynamically discovered relationships with the other peer schemas. An emerging point of view emphasizes the idea of the "pay-as-you-go" data management where an incremental approach is pursued. In this approach, a basic integrated schema and related services are immediately provided without any setup time to wait, while progressive service improvements are made available as soon as refined mappings are defined (Halevy, Rajaraman, & Ordille, 2006; Madhavan, et al., 2007). However, we note that while techniques for P2P mapping discovery and refinement are becoming more and more reliable,

techniques for exploiting mappings and subsequently building a distributed data integration space are still at an initial stage of development.

Original Contribution

Goal of our approach is to go beyond the existing state-of-the-art solutions for P2P community formation and management by adopting an *unsupervised handshaking approach* where the choice of joining/leaving a community is autonomously taken by each interested peer according to its own preferences. Moreover, the use of Semantic Web technologies like ontologies and ontology-based matching techniques allows to enforce a semantically rich approach to community and peer content description thus overcoming the need of a centralized/shared taxonomy. In this sense, our approach can be considered as a concrete attempt to combine the benefits of recently emerging social-based approaches with more consolidated Semantic Web technologies (Gruber, 2008).

With respect to P2P knowledge coordination, our approach is characterized by the notion of collective concept which enables a peer to focus the integration process on a single concept of interest (target concept), thus allowing to build a unified peer-view of the matching knowledge chunks harvested from the network about the considered target. Collective concepts represent a suitable solution for P2P knowledge coordination since it is based on a periodic and incremental approach to refresh/update of the unified peer-views.

COLLECTIVE KNOWLEDGE COORDINATION IN P2P SYSTEMS

Our approach to collective knowledge coordination is realized through a community-based P2P system composed of a set of independent peers, without prior reciprocal knowledge and without predefined relationships. In the following, we

Figure 2. Architecture of a P2P system for collective knowledge coordination

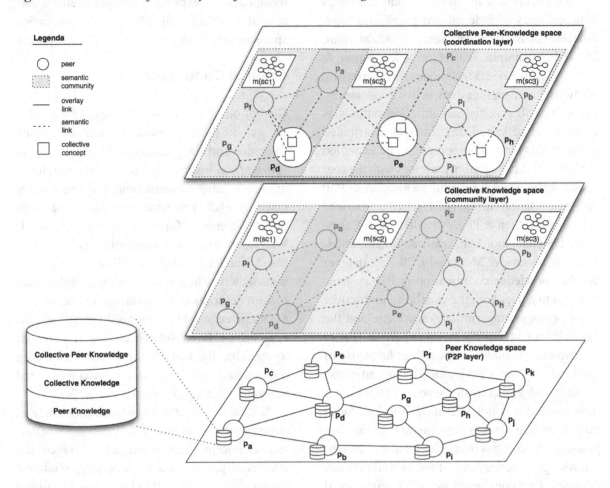

Architectural Overview

Our community-based P2P system is characterized by a three-layer architecture (see Figure 2). At the bottom, peers are inserted in a basic P2P layer, called *Peer Knowledge space*, responsible of maintaining the peer connectivity by means of a shuffling-based mechanism based on overlay links. Shuffling is a robust gossip-based mechanism which exploits randomness to disseminate information across the P2P network (Voulgaris, Gavidia, & Van Steen, 2005). The basic idea of

present the architectural overview of our approach and we discuss the knowledge equipment of a network peer.

shuffling is to keep a node connected to a small set of other nodes that are continuously changed through random exchange of neighborhood. This way, message propagation in the P2P layer is epidemic and inexpensive in terms of traffic overhead since piggybacked on shuffling. Moreover, experiments show that shuffling-based system like Cyclon (Voulgaris, et al., 2005) is robust and self-healing to multiple peer failures.

In the P2P layer, each peer is considered as a single agent having view only of its personal knowledge, namely its *peer ontology*. By joining semantic communities of interest, a peer is inserted in a community layer, called *Collective Knowledge space*. This space is organized in a set of semantic communities which are autonomously emerging from the P2P layer by handshaking those nodes that spontaneously agree on a proposed topic of interest expressed through an ontology-based *manifesto*. Within the Collective Knowledge space, peers are interconnected by semantic links, denoting the existence of semantic relations between the knowledge contained in their respective peer ontologies. Semantic links are progressively discovered and thus established through harvesting. When a peer P starts harvesting on a concept c' of interest, a probe query pq with target c' is defined and submitted to the network. A routing-by-community mechanism is adopted to select as query recipients those semantic communities whose members can provide relevant (i.e., similar, semantically related) answers to pq. Receiving the probe query, a peer replies with a set of matching concepts, namely *knowledge chunks*, extracted from its peer ontology. Collecting replies to probe queries, the requesting peer P identifies similar peers in the network and it can decide to establish a direct semantic link with such nodes.

On top of the community layer, a coordination layer, called *Collective Peer-Knowledge space*, is defined. In this layer, the harvested knowledge and the semantic links are used to move from a network of peers to a network of *collective concepts*. A collective concept cc' represents the view of the peer P about c' based on the knowledge harvested on c' from the network. In other words, a collective concept provides a coordinated representation of the various knowledge chunks collected during harvesting, by relying on semantic links (i.e., mappings) to keep track of the source peers from which the chunks have been acquired. This way, all collective concepts provide a reference interface for querying the network and for transparently accessing distributed resources about a given collective concept.

Knowledge Equipment of a Peer

A peer is equipped with a multi-layer *knowledge repository* where we distinguish the *peer knowl-*edge layer, the *collective knowledge layer*, and the *collective peer knowledge layer*, respectively (see Figure 1).

Before describing the knowledge equipment of a peer, we introduce the notion of *knowledge chunk* to give explicit formalization to the unit of knowledge that will be considered in our approach for knowledge coordination purposes.

Knowledge chunk. Given an ontology O, let NC be the set of concept names in the signature of O, NR the set of relation names in O, D the set of datatypes in O, and NP the set of peer identifiers of the considered P2P network. A knowledge chunk kc is a structured representation of an ontology concept $c \in O$ in terms of its constituent axioms, both explicitly and implicitly defined. To this end, kc is defined as a set of axioms $kc = <a_1(kc), a_2(kc), ..., a_n(kc)>$ constituting the specification of the corresponding ontology concept c. An axiom $a_i(kc)$ with $i \in [1,n]$ has the form $a_i(kc) = <n(kc), r(a_i), v(a_i), p(kc)>$ where:

- $n(kc) \in NC$ is the name of the knowledge chunk kc, which coincides with the name of c.
- $r(a_i) \in R$ is a semantic relation contained in the specification of c, with $R = NR \cup \{equivalentClass, subClassOf\}$.
- $v(a_i) \in V$ is the value of the corresponding relation $r(a_i)$, with $V = NC \cup D$.
- $p(kc) \in NP$ is the provenance of kc, namely the identifier of the peer from which the knowledge chunk originates (e.g., the peer MAC address).

Peer knowledge. This layer stores the personal knowledge of a peer P in the form of a *peer ontology $PO(P)$* and a set of *knowledge chunks $KC(P)$*. A peer ontology is a Semantic-Web compatible description (i.e., RDF(S), OWL) of the peer contents/resources that are made available for sharing. Besides existing methodologies and editing tools for manual ontology engineering, tool-supported approaches can be adopted for creating a peer ontology. A viable approach is based on (semi-) automated derivation of OWL axioms from ER/UML schemas and from relational database schemas of the peer resources (e.g., see Sattler, Calvanese, & Molitor, 2003; Motik, Horrocks, & Sattler, 2009). This way, domain knowledge already encoded in data schemas can be reused in form of peer ontologies, thus sensibly reducing the manual effort required. In more recent work, approaches suitable for non-specialist users are being proposed to generate the peer ontology by relying on the results of semantic annotation of the peer resources (e.g., see Specia & Motta, 2007; Mukherjee & Ramakrishnan, 2008). For the peer ontology *PO(P)*, the set of corresponding knowledge chunks *KC(P)* is stored in the peer knowledge layer by specifying the identifier of the peer *P* as the value of the provenance *p(kc)* for each knowledge chunk $kc \in KC(P)$.

Collective knowledge. This layer stores the knowledge harvested from communities during interactions with other system nodes. In particular, the collective knowledge contains a) the manifestos of the joined communities, and b) the harvested knowledge chunks.

- *Manifestos of the joined communities*. The set *M(P)* contains the manifestos related to the communities joined by the peer *P*. Given a semantic community *sc*, the community manifesto *m(sc)* is an ontological description of the community topics and it is represented as a set of knowledge chunks where the provenance attributes denote the identifier of the community founder (i.e., the peer proposing the community formation).

- *Harvested knowledge chunks*. The set *HKC(P)* contains the knowledge chunks harvested from the network by the peer *P* in response to a probe query. For this reason, the provenance *p(kc)* contains the identifier of the peer from which $kc \in HKC(P)$ has been harvested.

Collective peer knowledge. This layer stores the collective concepts built by the peer on the basis of the harvested knowledge chunks. Through collective knowledge coordination, a peer generates a collective concept in the form of a *collective knowledge chunk*. Compared with knowledge chunks, a distinguishing feature of collective knowledge chunks is that provenance is expressed in terms of a mapping set *MAP* storing the harvested knowledge chunks from which the collective concept has been derived and the respective peer provenances. In particular, a collective knowledge chunk *ckc* is defined as a set of representative axioms $ckc = \{a_1(ckc), a_2(ckc), ..., a_m(ckc)\}$ constituting the specification of *ckc*. A representative axiom $a_j(ckc)$ with $j \in [1,m]$ has the form $a_j(ckc) = <n(ckc), r(a_j), v(a_j), MAP(a_j)>$ where $n(ckc)$, $r(a_j)$, and $v(a_j)$ are defined like in knowledge chunks, while $MAP(a_j) = \{a_k(kc) \mid kc \in HKC(P)\}$ is a set of axioms in the underlying harvested knowledge chunks H*KC(P)* from which a_j has been built. We denote as *CKC(P)* the set of collective knowledge chunks of the peer *P*.

Example. As an example of peer knowledge, we consider a portion of an OWL-DL peer ontology $PO(P_d)$ in the Health-Care domain and we show the corresponding set of knowledge chunks $KC(P_d)$. In particular, the ontology concepts Health-Care_Organization, Medical_Laboratory, and Professional_Group are considered according to their OWL-DL specification shown in Table 1, where the symbols $\sqsubseteq$, $\exists$, and $\cap$ denote concept subsumption, existential role quantification, and concept intersection, respectively (Baader, Calvanese, McGuinness, Nardi, & Patel-Schneider, 2003).

The concept Health-Care_Organization is characterized in $PO(P_d)$ by the DL axioms Health-Care_Organization $\sqsubseteq \exists$employs.Professional_Group and Health-Care_Organization $\sqsubseteq \exists$mission.Health-Care. Through standard DL-reasoning techniques, we calculate the set S(Health-Care_Organization)={owl:Thing, $\exists$employs.Professional_Group, $\exists$mission.Health-Care} which

Table 1. Example of peer ontology PO(P_d) and corresponding set of knowledge chunks KC(P_d)

Ontology concept	OWL-DL concept specification	Knowledge chunk
Health-Care Organization	Health-Care_Org. $\subseteq$ $\exists$employs.Professional_Group Health-Care_Org. $\subseteq$ $\exists$mission.Health-Care	a_1(Health-Care_Org.) = < Health-Care_Org., rdf:subClassOf, owl:Thing, peer P_d > a_2(Health-Care_Org.) = < Health-Care_Org., employs, Professional_Group, peer P_d > a_3(Health-Care_Org.) = < Health-Care_Org., mission, Health-Care, peer P_d >
Medical_Laboratory	Medical_Lab. $\subseteq$ Health-Care_Org. Medical_Lab. $\subseteq$ $\exists$produces.Test_Result	a_1(Medical_Lab.) = < Medical_Lab., rdf:subClassOf, Health-Care_Org., peer P_d > a_2(Medical_Lab.) = < Medical_Lab., employs, Professional_Group, peer P_d > a_3(Medical_Lab.) = < Medical_Lab., mission, Health-Care, peer P_d > a_4(Medical_Lab.) = < Medical_Lab., produces, Test_Result, peer P_d >
Professional_Group	Professional_Group $\subseteq$ Team $\cap$ $\exists$exploits.Testing_Tool Professional_Group $\subseteq$ Team $\cap$ $\exists$exploits.Analysis_Tool	a_1(Professional_Group) = < Professional_Group, rdf:subClassOf, owl:Thing, peer P_d > a_2(Professional_Group) = < Professional_Group, rdf:subClassOf, Team, peer P_d > a_3(Professional_Group) = < Professional_Group, exploits, Testing_Tool, peer P_d > a_4(Professional_Group) = < Professional_Group, exploits, Analysis_Tool, peer P_d >

represents the complete set of super concepts of Health-Care_Organization. Each element in this set produces an axiom a_i of the knowledge chunk Health-Care_Organization (see right side of Table 1). In particular, the concept owl:Thing generates the axiom a_1(Health-Care_Organization) = < Health-Care_Organization, rdf:subClassOf, owl:Thing, peer P_d >, while the axioms a_2(Health-Care_Organization) = < Health-Care_Organization, employs, Professional_Group, peer P_d > and a_3(Health-Care_Organization) = < Health-Care_Organization, mission, Health-Care, peer P_d > are generated by the restrictions $\exists$employs. Professional_Group and $\exists$mission.Health-Care, respectively. In this example, the string peer P_d is used to represent the identifier of P_d, then the provenance of the knowledge chunk Health-Care_Organization is set to p(Health-Care_Organization) = peer P_d.

For the concept Medical Laboratory, through DL-reasoning, we find the set S(Medical Laboratory) = S(Health-Care Organization) $\cup$ {Health-Care Organization, $\exists$ produces Test Results}.

This is due to the fact that the concept Medical Laboratory is defined as a subclass of the concept Health-Care Organization (Medical Laboratory $\subseteq$ Health-Care Organization). In the same way, we find the set S(Professional Group) = {owl: Thing, Team, $\exists$ exploits Testing Tool, $\exists$ exploits Analysis Tool}. The axioms of the knowledge chunks Medical Laboratory and Professional Group are defined according to the sets S(Medical Laboratory) and S(Professional Group), respectively.

The Role of Ontology Matching for Collective Knowledge Coordination

Ontology matching has the role of measuring the level of match between concept descriptions of different peers through a process of semantic affinity evaluation with the goal of enabling effective comparison of independent peer ontologies with heterogeneous vocabularies.

Ontology matching is invoked in different moments of our knowledge coordination approach. First, it is invoked during community handshaking to measure the level of semantic affinity between the proposed manifesto of a new semantic community and the peer ontology of a receiving peer. Moreover, during knowledge harvesting, ontology matching is invoked to compare a probe query against the manifestos of semantic communities to select the more adequate query recipients. At the same time, ontology matching is also invoked upon reception of a probe query to evaluate whether a peer can provide matching knowledge chunks in reply to it.

A number of ontology matching systems are currently available in the literature which can be successfully exploited for performing ontology matching in the presented coordination scenario, like HMatch 2.0 (Castano, Ferrara, & Montanelli, 2006c), Falcon-AO (Jian, Hu, Cheng, & Qu, 2005), and COMA++ (Aumueller, Do, Massmann, & Rahm, 2005). In our approach, we use our HMatch 2.0 ontology matching engine which has been specifically conceived to work in open distributed systems, like P2P systems. HMatch 2.0 has been extensively and successfully tested and evaluated over the 2006 and 2007 benchmarks of the Ontology Alignment Evaluation Initiative (OAEI) (Castano, Ferrara, & Messa, 2006), and over real datasets in the framework of the BOEMIE research project (EU FP6 BOEMIE Project, 2006).

Matching in HMatch 2.0 is defined as a process at the ontology level which takes as input two ontologies and that returns as output the mappings between pairs of concepts in the two ontologies with the same or the closest intended meaning. In addition, matching at the concept level is supported in HMatch 2.0 to measure the semantic affinity of two concepts by exploiting information in their corresponding knowledge chunk representations. Given two knowledge chunks kc' and kc'', the function $SA(kc', kc'') \to [0,1]$ calculates a semantic affinity value as the linear combination of a linguistic affinity value $LA(kc', kc'')$ and a contextual affinity value $CA(kc', kc'')$. The linguistic affinity function of HMatch 2.0 provides a measure of similarity between two knowledge

chunks computed on the basis of their linguistic features, namely the names $n(kc')$ and $n(kc'')$. For the linguistic affinity evaluation, HMatch 2.0 relies on a thesaurus of terms and terminological relationships automatically extracted from the WordNet lexical system. The contextual affinity function of HMatch 2.0 provides a measure of similarity between two knowledge chunks by taking into account their contextual features, namely the semantic relations $r(a_i)$ and $r(a_j)$, and the corresponding values $v(a_i)$ and $v(a_j)$ of the axioms $a_i \in kc'$ and $a_j \in kc''$. In this respect, the matching models of HMatch 2.0 customize the behavior of the contextual affinity function by allowing to choose the different kinds of axioms to consider in the context of kc' and kc'' (e.g., equivalentClass and subClassOf relations). The comprehensive semantic affinity value computed by $SA(kc', kc'')$ is defined as follows:

$$SA(kc',kc'') = W_{LA} \cdot LA(kc', kc'') + (1 - W_{LA}) \cdot CA(kc', kc'')$$

where W_{LA} is a weight expressing the relevance assigned to the linguistic affinity in the semantic affinity evaluation process. A threshold-based mechanism is enforced to set the minimum level of semantic affinity required to consider two concepts as matching concepts on the basis of the SA value of their corresponding knowledge chunks. A detailed description of HMatch 2.0 and related ontology matching models and techniques is provided in Castano, et al. (2006c).

HANDSHAKING LIGHTWEIGHT SEMANTIC COMMUNITIES

Semantic communities in P2P systems are typically characterized by the adoption of supervised handshake techniques for allowing the peer which promotes the community (i.e., the *community founder*) to manage the formation process by leading the phases of participant identification and community commitment. In other words, the supervised handshake techniques are characterized by an explicit negotiation phase where the approval/rejection of a peer is determined by the choice of a supervisor (i.e., the community founder) and the list of community participants (i.e., community members) is "network-aware". With supervised handshake, high computation/traffic overhead is generated due to explicit negotiation operations and to membership advertisement. In this chapter, we propose lightweight communities which are characterized by *unsupervised handshake techniques*, thus exhibiting the following key features:

- *Implicit negotiation.* The choice of joining the community is autonomously taken by each peer according to its level of interest in the topic(s) addressed in the community. No peer with coordination authority is defined to manage approval/rejection of potential participants.
- *Soft membership.* The complete list of community participants is not shared within the community. This means that, at a given moment, the community participants are "hidden" and each community member is not aware of the other peers currently joining the community

Formally, a lightweight semantic community *sc* is defined as a pair of the form $sc = < UCI(sc), m(sc) >$ where *UCI(sc)* is the *Universal Community Identifier* that characterizes the community *sc*, and *m(sc)* is the *community manifesto*.

Handshaking of a lightweight semantic community *sc* consists in the dissemination of an *advertisement message* containing both the identifier *UCI(sc)* and the manifesto *m(sc)*. Entering the network, a peer becomes part of the P2P layer where the manifestos of existing communities are periodically advertised through shuffling.

Evaluation of an Incoming Manifesto

When a peer *P* receives the advertisement of a community *sc*, it invokes its HMatch 2.0 engine to compare the incoming manifesto *m(sc)* against its peer ontology *PO(P)* with the aim to identify possible semantic affinities between them (Figure 3(a)). In particular, matching is performed at the concept level by calculating $SA(kc', kc'')$ for each knowledge chunk $kc' \in m(sc)$ and $kc'' \in KC(P)$.

Results of matching are used to evaluate the level of interest of the peer *P* in *sc* and to decide whether to join the community or not. To this end, each peer defines its own set of *join constraints* which are used to configure HMatch 2.0 and to specify the minimal matching conditions that are required in order to join a community (e.g., at least one concept in the peer ontology must match the manifesto). If the join constraints are satisfied, the peer enters the community, otherwise the advertisement message is discarded. The list of joined communities is maintained by each peer in its collective knowledge layer by storing corresponding manifestos in *M(P)*. At the same time, the received community advertisement message is exploited by the shuffling mechanism for continuing to forward it throughout the P2P layer.

We stress that, for each peer *P*, *M(P)* has a pre-fixed size, which means that, at a given moment, a peer *P* has a maximum number of communities to join. For this reason, a peer *P* defines its own policy for autonomously managing the set *M(P)* through a sort of LRU mechanism in order to drop less interesting communities. This policy can enforce a completely automatic approach, where *M(P)* is progressively populated with the most interesting community manifestos and where a manifesto $m(sc_i) \in M(P)$ is replaced by a manifesto $m(sc_j)$ when concepts belonging to $m(sc_j)$ better satisfy the join constraints of the peer *P* than concepts in $m(sc_i)$. Moreover, the policy for *M(P)* management can enforce a semi-automatic approach, where the peer *P* specifies one or more topics of interest with higher priority than others.

Figure 3. Schema of (a) community handshaking, and (b) knowledge harvesting

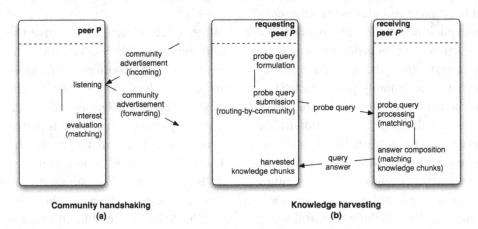

In this case, a community manifesto $m(sc_i) \in M(P)$ can be replaced only by a more interesting (i.e., matching) manifesto $m(sc_j)$ on the same topic.

Creation of a New Semantic Community

Each peer can act as community founder by promoting a new community sc. This requires to the founder to generate a community identifier $UCI(sc)$ and a manifesto $m(sc)$. In general, a community manifesto $m(sc)$ consists of a focused ontology and it is extracted from the peer ontology of the community founder, although the level of detail used for specifying $m(sc)$ depends on the community goal and can be decided by the founder. As in the previous case, the shuffling-based mechanism is used to perform community advertisement.

To enable new network nodes to be informed of existing semantic communities, each member of a given community sc (i.e., a peer P storing $m(sc)$ in its set $M(P)$) periodically executes community advertisement through shuffling with neighboring peers in the P2P layer.

A peer can assess the popularity of a semantic community sc by observing the traffic it generates. In particular, the number of answer messages produced by community members in response to

a probe query is a valid parameter to estimate the number of participants in a community and their reactivity. When replies to a probe query from a community sc_i are poor (i.e. the number of replies is persistently lower than a prefixed threshold), the peer issuing the probe query can start the formation of a new semantic community sc_j by proposing a better focused manifesto on the same topic. The advertisement of the new community sc_j can imply the replacement of the manifesto $m(sc_i)$ with $m(sc_j)$ in the set $M(P)$ of the receiving peers, thus producing the progressive obsolescence of sc_i. This way, no explicit procedure for disbandment of lightweight semantic communities is required. A community sc is active in the system as long as the corresponding manifesto $m(sc)$ is maintained in the set $M(P)$ of at least one peer P. Furthermore, a lightweight semantic community is considered as disbanded when the associated identifier is dropped by all the peers in the network.

Finally, we stress that, in the lightweight community approach, peers are not responsible for member deletion and failure events. Due to the absence of a supervising authority and to the unstructured peer organization, a leaving member is not required to notify changes to its status.

Example. We consider the peer P_d which is inserted in the peer knowledge space (i.e., P2P layer) of the system. Through shuffling, the fol-

Table 2.

Community Identifier UCI(sc)	Community Manifesto m(sc)			
	Concept name	Semantic relation	Relation value	Provenance
sc1	Health-Care_Organization	rdf:subClassOf	owl:Thing	Peer P_g
	Health-Care_Organization	employs	Medical_Staff	Peer P_g
	Medical_Staff	provides	Health-Care_Treatment	Peer P_g
	Hospital	rdf:subClassOf	Health-Care_Organization	Peer P_g
sc2	Professional_Group	rdf:subClassOf	owl:Thing	Peer P_c
	Professional_Group	owl:equivalentClass	Medical_Staff	Peer P_c
	Medical_Staff	makes	Diagnosis	Peer P_c
	Medical_Staff	examines	Patient	Peer P_c
	Doctor	rdf:subClassOf	Medical_Staff	Peer P_c
sc3	Therapeutic_Procedure	rdf:subClassOf	owl:Thing	Peer P_b
	Therapeutic_Procedure	treats	Disease	Peer P_b
	Therapeutic_Procedure	uses	Drug	Peer P_b
	Drug	rdf:subClassOf	Pharmaceutical_Preparation	Peer P_b
	Drug	has_Ingredient	Active_Ingredient	Peer P_b

lowing community advertisements are received by this peer (see Table 2).

For the sake of clarity, we show the manifesto of a community in terms of knowledge chunks and related axioms where the provenance attributes denote the identifier of the community founder. Receiving the advertisements of sc_1, sc_2, and sc_3, the peer P_d invokes the HMatch 2.0 engine to detect possible semantic affinities between the incoming community manifestos and its own knowledge chunks in $KC(P_d)$. In particular, for each semantic community sc_k, HMatch 2.0 matches each knowledge chunk $kc_i \in m(sc_k)$ against each knowledge chunk $kc_j \in KC(P_d)$. The following matching results are returned by HMatch 2.0 (see Table 3).

Table 3.

HMatch(m(sc₁), KC(P_d))
SA(Health-Care_Organization, Health-Care_Organization) = 0.67

HMatch(m(sc₂), KC(P_d))
SA(Professional_Group, Professional_Group) = 0.53

Since at least one matching knowledge chunk is required to join a community, the peer P_d becomes member of both sc_1 and sc_2 by storing the corresponding manifestos $m(sc_1)$ and $m(sc_2)$ in $M(P_d)$. On the opposite, the advertisement of sc_3 is discarded since no matching knowledge chunks are detected by HMatch 2.0.

HARVESTING COLLECTIVE KNOWLEDGE

Knowledge Harvesting

Knowledge harvesting has the goal to support a peer in effectively exploiting the knowledge of the joined semantic communities with the aim to retrieve from the network the available matching knowledge chunks about a certain concept of its own interest.

For knowledge harvesting, a requesting peer *P* formulates a probe query *pq* containing an ontological specification of a target concept of interest expressed in the form of a knowledge chunk. The probe query *pq* can represent a generic, poorly structured request with only basic axioms (e.g. a concept without semantic relations). This can be useful when the peer *P* intends to have an estimation about the availability of knowledge on the target concept of interest, both from the qualitative and quantitative point of view. On the opposite, a more articulated probe query *pq* can be specified by enriching the chunk with more axioms (e.g. subClassOf and objectProperty relations with other concepts). This leads to a more precise probe query, aimed at obtaining a focused and possibly restricted list of matching knowledge chunks.

The probe query *pq* is submitted to the network and the routing-by-community mechanism is invoked to select query recipients by choosing communities whose members are most likely capable of providing knowledge chunks matching the target (Figure 3(b)). Through routing-by-communities, the query *pq* is marked with a list of communities as query recipient, thus allowing the peer members of these communities to receive the query for processing (see below for details).

Receiving *pq*, a peer *P'* invokes its HMatch 2.0 engine to compare the incoming probe query against its knowledge chunks *KC(P')* and to identify possible semantic affinities. In particular, *SA(pq, kc)* is calculated by the peer *P'* for each knowledge chunk *kc* ∈ *KC(P')*. A (possibly empty) list of matching knowledge chunks (i.e., concepts semantically related to the target query *pq*) is returned by HMatch 2.0. If a non-empty result is produced, these matching knowledge chunks are used to compose an answer to *pq* that is returned to the requesting peer *P*.

The peer *P* stores the answers to the query *pq* in *HKC(P)* as harvested knowledge chunks. We observe that also knowledge chunks *KC(P)* in the peer knowledge layer of *P* can be relevant for the query *pq*. In this case, matching knowledge

chunks of *KC(P)* can be stored also in *HKC(P)* as harvested knowledge chunks.

As we will discuss in the next section, the set of harvested knowledge chunks *HKC(P)* both received as a reply to the probe query *pq* and coming from the set of local knowledge chunks in *KC(P)* constitutes the starting point for constructing the peer *P* view of the considered concept of interest in terms of a set of collective concepts. The collective concepts of the peer *P* require to be periodically updated with the aim at refreshing the harvested knowledge chunks which can be changed due to creation of new communities and/ or membership updates of existing ones. Periodic knowledge harvesting on the probe query *pq* is then executed by the peer *P* to this end.

The Routing By Community Mechanism

Routing-by-community is exploited by a requesting peer *P* for choosing the communities to select as recipient of a probe query *pq*. Semantic communities are used as "*virtual query recipients*" on the basis of their associated community manifesto. This way, queries are propagated throughout the network according to shuffling and peer members of a community *sc* can filter the incoming queries by considering (i.e. processing) only requests having *sc* (and the other joined communities) as recipient.

The following steps constitute the routing-by-community mechanism:

1. *Selection of candidate communities*. It is performed by matching *pq* against the community manifestos in *M(P)* using HMatch 2.0. A community *sc* is considered as a candidate recipient for the query *pq* when at least one matching knowledge chunk *kc* ∈ *m(sc)* is found for *pq* by HMatch 2.0.

2. *Selection of recipient communities*. Candidate communities are ranked accord-

ing to the semantic affinity values produced by HMatch 2.0. Candidate communities with the highest ranking are then selected as query *pq* recipients. In this respect, different strategies can be adopted by the peer to govern the scale of recipients. For example, top-k communities in the ranking can be selected. This way, by setting the parameter k, the peer can specify the exact number of query recipients to contact. Alternatively, a threshold-based mechanism can be enforced. In this case, through the threshold, the peer specifies the minimum level of semantic affinity of a recipient community, thus obtaining a (potentially) larger set of recipients than in the previous case.

3. *Distribution of credits* (optional). The routing-by-community mechanism can be extended with an optional step for enabling a peer *P'* receiving *pq* to in turn forward the query to its joined communities, thus enlarging the scope of *pq*. In particular, a *credit-based strategy* can be adopted to associate with a probe query a certain amount of credits. Credits are progressively consumed by the answers of the receiving peers. Remaining credits are forwarded by receiving peers to their joined communities according to routing-by community[1]. The credit-based strategy has been implemented with positive results in the HLink mechanism for semantic query routing in P2P systems. The interested reader can refer to Montanelli & Castano (2008) for technical descriptions and simulation results.

Example. We consider the peer P_a belonging to both the communities sc_1 and sc_2. This peer is interested in constructing its own view of the existing knowledge about health-care organizations. To this end, a probe query $pq_1 = \{$<Organization, has_goal, Health-Care, peer P_a>$\}$ is formulated for knowledge harvesting. The routing-by-community mechanism is then invoked to select the recipients

of query pq_1. The manifestos of both sc_1 and sc_2 are matched against the probe query pq_1 and the community sc_1 is eventually selected as recipient (SA(Organization, Health-Care_Organization)= 0.18). Receiving the query, sc_1 members evaluates pq_1 in order to assess whether they can reply with matching knowledge chunks. In this respect, we consider the peer P_d and the corresponding set $KC(P_d)$ shown in (Table 1). The following matching knowledge chunks are detected with HMatch 2.0 by matching the probe query pq_1 against the knowledge chunks in $KC(P_d)$ (see Table 4).

As a result, both the knowledge chunks Health-Care_Organization and Medical_Laboratory are returned to the requesting peer P_a in reply to pq_1 which are then stored in the set $HKC(P_a)$. At the same time, the probe query pq_1 is locally processed by the requesting peer P_a for discovering possible matching knowledge chunks in its set $KC(P_a)$. The following knowledge chunk Organization (Table 5) matches with the probe query pq_1 (SA(Organization, Organization)= 0.2).

This knowledge chunk Organization $\in KC(P_a)$ is also stored in $HKC(P_a)$ together with externally harvested knowledge chunks.

COORDINATING PEER VIEWED COLLECTIVE KNOWLEDGE

When a peer receives answers to a probe query *pq*, it is interested in creating its own view of the collected knowledge chunks, called *collective concept*, in order to exploit it for finding resources of interest. The process that leads to the creation of collective concepts is called coordination. More in detail, the input of the coordination process is the set *HKC(P)* of harvested knowl-

Table 4.

HMatch(pq_1, KC(P_d))
SA(Organization, Health-Care_Organization) = 0.47 SA(Organization, Medical_Laboratory) = 0.37

edge chunks received by the peer P as answers to a probe query pq. We recall that $HKC(P)$ may contain also knowledge chunks coming from the ontology of the peer P, since P processes probe queries also against its own ontology when sending it to a community. Since collective concepts are represented as collective knowledge chunks, the output of coordination is a set $CKC = \{ckc_1, ckc_2, ..., ckc_n\}$ of collective knowledge chunks, each one providing the peer-view of a concept of interest described in a probe query pq.

The coordination process is articulated in two main phases: i) *classification of knowledge chunks*, where collected knowledge chunks are matched and clustered, and ii) *construction of collective knowledge*, where the clustering results are used in order to create the final set of collective knowledge chunks CKC. In this section, we first describe the coordination process and then we present an example of how the results of coordination are exploited in order to retrieve resources of interest distributed over the network.

Classification of Knowledge Chunks

Goal of the classification phase is to group together those concept axioms of the harvested knowledge chunks that denote the same or similar knowledge. In order to reach this goal, we use a hierarchical clustering procedure based on the affinity between concept axioms. The first step of the classification phase is the evaluation of affinity among the concept axioms of the harvested knowledge chunks. Given two knowledge chunks $kc_i, kc_j \in HKC(P)$, we exploit the contextual affinity func-

tion of HMatch 2.0 in order to calculate the level of affinity between the concept axioms of kc_i and the concept axioms of kc_j, respectively. The contextual affinity function $CA(kc_i, kc_j)$ finds, for each axiom $a_i(kc_i)$, the best-matching axiom $a_j(kc_j)$, by evaluating the similarity between names, semantic relations, and relation values of $a_i(kc_i)$ and $a_j(kc_j)$, respectively. A comprehensive semantic affinity value $SA(a_i(kc_i), a_j(kc_j)) \rightarrow [0,1]$ is returned by HMatch 2.0. The matching step is repeated for each pair of knowledge chunks in $HKC(P) \times HKC(P)$. This procedure creates an affinity matrix $A(HKC(P))$ of dimension k, where k is the number of axioms of the knowledge chunks in $HKC(P)$. $A(HKC(P))$ stores the mappings retrieved among concept axioms in the collected knowledge chunks together with their affinity value.

Given the affinity matrix produced by the matching step, we group all concept axioms that have affinities by exploiting a *hierarchical* and *agglomerative* clustering algorithm (Castano, De Antonellis, & De Capitani di Vimercati, 2001). The algorithm used is agglomerative in that it proceeds by a series of successive merging of axioms into groups; hierarchical refers to the property of the algorithm to classify axioms into groups at different levels of affinity to form a tree, called *affinity tree*. The clustering procedure is executed as follows: given the affinity matrix $A(HKC(P))$, the clustering algorithm places each axiom a_i in a cluster Cl_i by itself. Then, the algorithm iteratively selects the two clusters Cl_i and Cl_j having the greatest semantic affinity in $A(HKC(P))$ and merges them. The merge operation is performed by taking the union of Cl_i and Cl_j. The affinity

Table 5.

Concept name	Semantic relation	Relation value	Provenance
Organization	rdf:subClassOf	owl:Thing	Peer P_a
Organization	Involve	Professional_Society	Peer P_a
Organization	Function	owl:Thing	Peer P_a
Organization	Member	Person	Peer P_a

values among the newly created cluster $Cl_i \cup Cl_j$ and each remaining cluster Cl_k in $A(HKC(P))$, with $Cl_k \neq Cl_j$, are determined as the maximum between the semantic affinity values that Cl_i and Cl_j have with each remaining cluster Cl_k. After that, $A(HKC(P))$ is updated by deleting the row and the column corresponding to the cluster Cl_j in $A(HKC(P))$. The procedure terminates when the dimension of $A(HKC(P))$ is 1. The resulting affinity tree is a tree where leaves correspond to axioms, and intermediate nodes correspond to virtual elements, which are represented by an affinity value SA_i. On the affinity tree, we select the clusters candidate to be used for the construction of collective knowledge by exploiting a threshold t. In particular, all the axiom clusters in the affinity tree that are rooted by a node $SA_i \geq t$ are selected as candidate clusters. Each candidate cluster Cl is characterized by its *size* and its *level of homogeneity*. The size is the number of concept axioms in Cl, while the level of homogeneity is the value of semantic affinity SA_{Cl} associated with Cl. We note that, by adopting a high threshold t, we will obtain a high number of homogenous, small-size candidate clusters. On the opposite, using a lower threshold t, we will obtain less homogeneous but larger candidate clusters. Thus, the threshold should be chosen by taking into account the kind of queries that the peer expects to support at the collective knowledge layer.

Example. As an example of knowledge chunk classification, we consider the peer P_a and the knowledge chunks in its set $HKC(P_a)$ (Table 6) collected during knowledge harvesting (see the example of the previous section).

As a first step of the classification phase, we execute HMatch 2.0 on the axioms of (Table 6) and we obtain the affinity matrix shown in (Table 7).

Starting from the affinity matrix, we execute the clustering procedure and we build the affinity tree shown in (Figure 4).

As shown in the figure, by setting a threshold $t = 0.6$, we obtain five candidate clusters:

```
1.   Cl01 = { 01: <Health-Care_Orga-
nization, rdf:subClassOf, owl:Thing>,
08: <Organization, rdf:subClassOf,
owl:Thing>, 05: <Medical_Laboratory,
rdf:subClassOf, Health-Care_Organiza-
tion> }
2.   Cl02 = { 02: <Health-Care_ Or-
ganization, employs, Professional_
Group>, 09: <Organization, involve,
Professional_Society>, 04: <Medi-
cal_Laboratory, employs, Profession-
al_Group > }
```

Table 6. Example of harvested knowledge chunks in HKC(P$_a$)

Axiom ID	Concept name	Semantic relation	Relation value	Provenance
01	Health-Care_Org.	rdf:subClassOf	owl:Thing	Peer P$_d$
02	Health-Care_Org.	employs	Professional_Group	Peer P$_d$
03	Health-Care_Org.	mission	Health-Care	Peer P$_d$
04	Medical_Lab.	employs	Professional_Group	Peer P$_d$
05	Medical_Lab.	rdf:subClassOf	Health-Care_Org.	Peer P$_d$
06	Medical_Lab.	produces	Test_Result	Peer P$_d$
07	Medical_Lab.	mission	Health-Care	Peer P$_d$
08	Organization	rdf:subClassOf	owl:Thing	Peer P$_a$
09	Organization	involve	Professional_Society	Peer P$_a$
10	Organization	function	owl:Thing	Peer P$_a$
11	Organization	member	Person	Peer P$_a$

3.   Cl03 = { 03: <Health-Care_ Organization, mission, Health-Care>,
07: <Medical_Laboratory, mission,
Health-Care>, 10: <Organization,
function, owl:Thing> }
4.   Cl04 = { 06: <Medical_Labora-
tory, produces, Test_Result> }
5.   Cl05 = { 11: <Organization,
member, Person> }

Clusters Cl04 and Cl05 have the highest level of homogeneity (1.0) but are singleton. All Cl01, Cl02, and Cl03 have size 3, but the level of homo-

geneity of Cl01 and Cl02 is higher (0.67) than the one of Cl03 (0.61). The semantics behind these three clusters is that Cl01 groups information about the types of organizations retrieved, Cl02 groups information about the people working in these organizations, while Cl03 groups information about the goal of the organizations.

Construction of Collective Knowledge

The construction of collective knowledge is the activity of creating a set of collective knowledge

Table 7. Example of affinity matrix

	01	02	03	04	05	06	07	08	09	10	11
01	1.0	0.0	0.0	0.0	0.67	0.0	0.0	0.95	0.0	0.0	0.0
02	0.0	1.0	0.0	0.67	0.0	0.0	0.0	0.0	0.89	0.0	0.0
03	0.0	0.0	1.0	0.0	0.0	0.0	0.67	0.0	0.0	0.61	0.0
04	0.0	0.67	0.0	1.0	0.0	0.0	0.0	0.0	0.61	0.0	0.0
05	0.67	0.0	0.0	0.0	1.0	0.0	0.0	0.61	0.0	0.0	0.0
06	0.0	0.0	0.0	0.0	0.0	1.0	0.0	0.0	0.0	0.0	0.0
07	0.0	0.0	0.67	0.0	0.0	0.0	1.0	0.0	0.0	0.0	0.0
08	0.95	0.0	0.0	0.0	0.61	0.0	0.0	1.0	0.0	0.0	0.0
09	0.0	0.89	0.0	0.61	0.0	0.0	0.0	0.0	1.0	0.0	0.0
10	0.0	0.0	0.61	0.0	0.0	0.0	0.0	0.0	0.0	1.0	0.0
11	0.0	0.0	0.0	0.0	0.0	0.0	0.0	0.0	0.0	0.0	1.0

Figure 4. Affinity tree after the clustering procedure

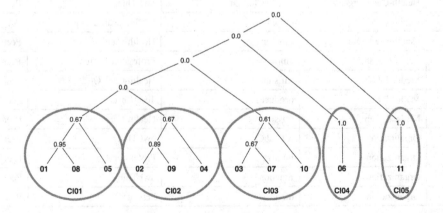

chunks that represent the peer view of the network knowledge of interest. A collective knowledge chunk is created by a peer P out of the clustered axioms. The construction phase is performed in two steps. In the first step we order the knowledge chunks in *HKC(P)* according to a ranking value $R(kc_i)$. The idea behind this step is that the higher $R(kc_i)$ is, the higher is the relevance of kc_i for the subsequent merging step. Merging has the goal of creating the final collective knowledge chunk by selecting a representative axiom for each candidate cluster. In this step, we choose as representative the axiom coming from the knowledge chunk having the highest ranking value. Given a knowledge chunk kc_i, its ranking value $R(kc_i)$ is calculated as follows:

$$R(kc_i) = c + H(kc_i) + S(kc_i)$$

where:

- c is a constant value which is equal to the sum of the degrees of homogeneity and size of all the candidate clusters if kc_i belongs to the peer ontology of P and it is equal to 0 otherwise;
- $H(kc_i)$ is the average degree of homogeneity of the clusters containing axioms of kc_i;
- $S(kc_i)$ is the average size of the clusters containing axioms of kc_i normalized in the range [0,1].

According to this approach, axioms of knowledge chunks in the local peer ontology are always taken as representative. In case of two or more knowledge chunks with the same ranking, the choice is left to the user. Given the ordered list of knowledge chunks to be coordinated, we start the second step. In particular, given a set of candidate clusters $CL = \{Cl_1, Cl_2, ..., Cl_n\}$, for each candidate cluster $Cl_i \in CL$ we choose a representative axiom $u_i \in Cl_i$. The representative axiom u_i is the axiom associated with the knowledge chunk with the highest ranking value $R(kc_i)^2$. Moreover,

we add to u_i the set *MAP(u_i)* containing all the axioms in the candidate cluster Cl_i. Given the representative axiom for each candidate cluster, a collective knowledge chunk ckc_i is defined as the set of representative axioms referring to the same concept name $n(kc)$.

Example. As an example of construction of collective knowledge chunks, we take into account the candidate clusters of Figure 4 and the corresponding knowledge chunks of Table 2. As a first step, we calculate the ranking value of each involved knowledge chunk. Considering the knowledge chunk Health-Care_Organization, its ranking value R(Health-Care_Organization) is calculated as follows: we have $c = 0$, since the provenance of Health-Care_Organization is P_d, while collective knowledge is created by P_a. The clusters containing Health-Care_Organization are Cl01, Cl02, and Cl03. Thus, the average degree of homogeneity H(Health-Care_Organization) is equal to 0.65 and the normalized average size S(Health-Care_Organization) is equal to 1.0. According to these measures, the final ranking is calculated as shown in Table 8.

Thus, merging will be performed according to the following order: Organization, Health-Care_Organization, Medical_Laboratory. Then, we proceed by defining a representative axiom for each candidate cluster. Given the cluster Cl01, we define <Organization, rdf:subClassOf, owl:Thing> as the representative axiom being the one referred to the knowledge chunk with the highest ranking value (i.e., Organization). Then, we create a mapping between <Organization, rdf:subClassOf, owl:Thing> and all the axioms contained in Cl01 (Table 9). By iterating this pro-

Table 8.

R(Health-Care_Organization)	0 + 0.65 + 1	1.65
R(Medical_Laboratory)	0 + 0.74 + 0.83	1.57
R(Organization)	7.55 + 0.74 + 0.83	9.12

cedure for all the candidate clusters, we obtain the collective knowledge chunks and the associated mapping table shown in (Table 10).

Exploiting Collective Knowledge

A peer can exploit its collective knowledge in order to search data/resources of interest in the network by posing only one query that we call *collective query*[3]. The collective query is rewritten into a set of *peer queries* using the peer axioms in the mapping set *MAP* associated with the collective knowledge chunk involved in the query. Peer queries are processed against the knowledge chunks of each involved peer and specify the type and the semantic relations that feature data/resources of interest. Each peer then, will transform the peer query according to the original format of its own data/resources. The results are then sent back to

the requesting peer, which collects them. This process is shown in (Figure 5).

In this section, we give an example of how a class of simple collective queries over the collective knowledge can be transformed into specific peer queries over the local peer knowledge.

A collective query *cq* is a SQL-like query of the form:

```
RETRIEVE FROM Collective Knowledge
[WHERE <condition>]
[HAVING <constraint>]
```

The *WHERE* clause is a predicate of the form:

```
concept name = <name> | semantic re-
lation = <relation> | relation value
= <value type>
```

Table 9.

Axiom ID	Concept name	Semantic relation	Relation value	Mapping
U01	Organization	rdf:subClassOf	owl:Thing	<M01,M02,M03>
U02	Organization	involve	Professional_Society	<M04,M05,M06>
U03	Organization	function	owl:Thing	<M07,M08,M09>
U04	Organization	member	Person	<M11>
U05	Medical_Lab.	produces	Test_Result	<M10>

Table 10. Example of collective knowledge chunks and related mappings

Mapping ID	Peer axiom
M01	<Organization, rdf:subClassOf, owl:Thing, P_a>
M02	<Health-Care_Organization, rdf:subClassOf, owl:Thing, peer P_d>
M03	<Medical_Lab., rdf:subClassOf, Health-Care_ Org., peer P_d>
M04	<Health-Care_Org., employs, Professional_Group, peer P_d>
M05	<Medical_Lab., employs, Professional_Group, peer P_d>
M06	<Organization, involve, Professional_Society, peer P_a>
M07	<Health-Care_Org., mission, Health-Care, peer P_d>
M08	<Medical_Lab., mission, Health-Care, peer P_d>
M09	<Organization, function, owl:Thing, peer P_a>
M10	< Medical_Lab., produces, Test_Result, peer P_d>
M11	<Organization, member, Person, peer P_a>

Figure 5. Example of collective query processing

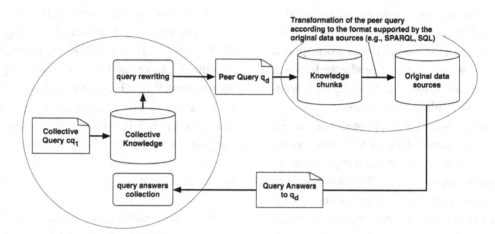

Properly combined through AND or OR operators to express composite conditions. The HAVING clause is a predicate of the form:

```
<value type> = <value>
```

or a combination of them through AND or OR operators. Goal of the WHERE clause is to denote which collective axioms are involved in the query, while goal of the HAVING clause is to denote the value constraints that have to be satisfied by the data that we are searching for.

Given a collective query *cq*, it is transformed into a set of peer queries $\{q_1, q_2, ..., q_n\}$ by applying the following rules. As a first step, we take into account the representative axioms *U* that satisfy the *WHERE* clause of *cq*. Each representative axiom u_i is also associated with the set of name, relations and/or values requested in the query. Then, we exploit the *MAP* set of each representative axiom u_i in order to replace every representative axiom u_i with the corresponding axiom $a_i \in MAP$. The resulting axioms are then grouped with respect to the provenance of the axioms. The idea here is that we will define a new query for each peer, rewritten according to its peer knowledge chunks. For each peer, we create the corresponding peer query *q* by applying the following rules:

- **R1 RETRIEVE FROM:** the FROM clause of *q* contains the provenance of the axioms used for query rewriting.
- **R2 WHERE:** for each predicate in the *WHERE* clause of *cq*:
  - If the predicate has the form *concept name = <name>*: For each representative axiom u_i satisfying the *WHERE* clause of *cq*, we replace *<name>* with the concept name of the corresponding axiom a_i. When more than one axiom a_i corresponds to u_i, we create a predicate for each axiom a_i, by concatenating each predicate with the OR operator.
  - If the predicate has the form *semantic relation = <relation>*: For each representative axiom u_i satisfying the *WHERE* clause of *cq*, we replace *<relation>* with the semantic relation of the corresponding axiom a_i. When more than one axiom a_i corresponds to u_i, we create a predicate for each axiom a_i, by concatenating each predicate with the OR operator.
  - If the predicate has the form *relation value = <value type>*: For each representative axiom u_i satisfying

the *WHERE* clause of *cq*, we replace *<value type>* with the relation value of the corresponding axiom a_i. When more than one axiom a_i corresponds to u_i, we create a predicate for each axiom a_i, by concatenating each predicate with the OR operator.

- **R3 HAVING:** for each predicate in the *HAVING* clause of *cq* of the form *<value type> = <value>*: For each representative axiom u_i satisfying the *WHERE* clause of *cq*, we replace *<value type>* with the relation value of the corresponding axiom a_i. When more than one axiom a_i corresponds to u_i, we create a predicate for each axiom a_i, by concatenating each predicate with the OR operator.

The final set of peer queries is obtained by iteratively applying the rules R1-R3 for each peer query. Queries are then sent to their corresponding peers, which process the query according to the query format supported by their data sources (e.g., SPARQL, SQL). Finally, the answer of each peer query is sent back to the requesting peer as an XML document containing information about the data/resources of interest and an additional *contentURI* element that specifies the location where related files can be downloaded if needed. The requesting peer collects the query results according to their provenance for presentation to the user.

Example. As an example of how collective knowledge can be exploited in order to answer queries, we suppose that P_a, which has created the collective knowledge shown in Table 4, is interested in finding organizations that have a first-aid function. To this end, P_a composes the following collective query cq_1:

```
RETRIEVE FROM Collective Knowledge
WHERE Concept Name = 'Organization'
AND Semantic Relation = 'function'
HAVING function = 'first-aid'
```

The WHERE clause of the collective query cq_1 is satisfied by the representative axiom U03 (i.e., <Organization, function, owl:Thing, <M07, M08, M09>>). By exploiting the mapping table of Table 4, we create two peer queries q_a and q_d for the peers P_a and P_d, respectively. The query q_a for P_a is trivial. The query q_d for P_d is created by rewriting cq_1 as follows. By applying the rule R1 we first obtain the RETRIEVE clause:

```
RETRIEVE FROM Pd
```

Then, we consider the predicate Concept Name = 'Organization' in the WHERE clause of cq_1. Since the representative axiom <Organization, function, owl:Thing> has a mapping with two axioms of P_d, namely <Health-Care_Organization, mission, Health-Care, peer P_d> and <Medical_Laboratory, mission, Health-Care, peer P_d>, we apply the rule R2 obtaining the predicates:

```
Concept Name = 'Health-Care_Organiza-
tion' OR Concept Name = 'Medical_Lab-
oratory'
Considering the second predicate Se-
mantic Relation = 'function' of cq1,
we apply again the rule R2 to obtain
the predicate Semantic Relation =
'mission', originating the following
WHERE clause:
(Concept Name = 'Health-Care_Organi-
zation' OR Concept Name = 'Medical_
Laboratory') AND
Semantic Relation = 'mission'
```

Then, we consider the HAVING clause of cq_1. By applying the rule R3, the predicate function = 'first-aid' is rewritten as mission = 'first-aid'. Finally, the whole query q_d is defined as follows:

```
RETRIEVE FROM Pd
WHERE
(Concept Name = 'Health-Care_Organi-
zation' OR Concept Name = 'Medical_
```

```
Laboratory') AND
Semantic Relation = 'mission'
HAVING
mission = 'first-aid'
```

We suppose that P_d has only two hospitals (i.e., "Hospital 1" and "Hospital 2") that are health-care organizations and provide also first-aid facilities, but no medical laboratories. Consequently, an example of query results that are sent back to P_a is the following:

```
<Result provenance = "P_d">
<Health-Care_Organization contentURI
= "http://domain.com/hospital1.html">
Hospital 1
</Health-Care_Organization>
<Health-Care_Organization contentURI
= "http://domain.com/hospital2.html">
Hospital 2
</Health-Care_Organization>
</Result>
```

In this section, we have discussed only an example of how queries over collective knowledge can be transformed into peer queries. Query rewriting has been widely studied in literature and a general survey on the problem of answering queries in data integration systems is given in Halevy (2001). Interesting examples of how queries can be rewritten from aggregated data schemas to local schemas are also available (Beneventano, et al., 2002; Cohen, Nutt, & Sagiv, 2006).

FUTURE RESEARCH DIRECTIONS

With respect to P2P semantic coordination, we believe that next-future research work will be devoted to investigate aspects related to integration with social network systems, participated community formation, and collaborative knowledge design and evolution.

Integration with social network systems. The growing success of social-network systems (e.g. facebook, wikipedia, flickr, del.icio.us) is producing a huge bulk of data with heterogeneous and (usually) poor annotations. In this kind of systems, social relations among users are exploited to improve the effectiveness of data sharing and collaboration activities. For instance, in many folksonomy-based systems like flickr and del.icio. us, user annotations and bookmarks are submitted to a statistical analysis aimed at classifying terms according to their co-occurrence frequency. As a result, it is possible to support a recommendation mechanism where terms already employed by other users are proposed as possible suggestions, thus eliciting the creation of a common vocabulary. Usually, in this kind of recommendation systems, user suggestions are calculated by marking with a higher priority the preferences of other users with a similar (i.e. matching) profile. As far as we know, all these systems are independent and they do not support any kind of interoperability mechanism.

An interesting research direction is to investigate the opportunity to use our approach to P2P semantic coordination for considering social network systems as data sources to be exploited for constructing collective concepts and vocabularies. One possible idea is to consider each social network as a community where probe queries are propagated for knowledge harvesting by relying on social relations among users to efficiently forward requests within the social network members. Another possible research direction is to include social network members as single peers in the P2P layer and to acquire resource annotation and bookmarks as knowledge chunks. This way, it is possible to build a collective concept by putting together knowledge chunks of resources belonging to different social networks, thus enforcing their interoperation.

Participated community formation. The handshake approach described in the chapter for lightweight semantic communities is characterized by a proposal of a single founder which authoritatively defines the community manifesto according to its own preferences. This choice has the benefit to dramatically simplify the community formation mechanism, although the active participation of a peer is limited to a mere join/non-join choice.

In this context, an interesting research direction is represented by the definition of a *participated* approach to semantic community formation. The idea is that each peer interested in a community, could contribute to modify/enrich the associated manifesto with the aim to better focus it on its own interests. Two different approaches to participated community formation could be envisaged. One possible approach is characterized by a *voting procedure*, where the community formation process initially requires to identify the set of peers that are interested in a really generic concept of interest, by subsequently allowing potential members to choose the community manifesto through election among a set of alternative proposals. By relying on a sort of leader election protocol, the favorite (i.e., the most voted) manifest is assigned to the community and propagated to the members. Another possible approach is based on an *amendment procedure*, where the initial community manifesto proposed by the founder is submitted to a collaborative design phase. Peers interested in the community can propose amendments to the initial manifesto by changing an existing chunk or by adding new axioms. Collaborative design of the community manifesto is based on a scheduling algorithm, which allows to transfer the manifesto from one peer to another for progressive approval/rejection of each proposed amendment. Both the presented approaches to participated community formation go in the direction to reduce the number of existing communities by fostering the creation of a small number of really focused peer coalitions. However, participated community formation is more suitable for focused networks, like federations/consortiums of collaborative peers due to

the need to clearly detect the set of members involved in voting/amendment procedures.

Collaborative knowledge design and evolution. In recent years, the interest around Semantic Web technologies has produced the development of many ontologies regarding a number of different domains of interest. For this reason, in modern approaches, the opportunity to support knowledge design and evolution through reuse of existing ontology artifacts is becoming an appealing and advocated solution. This means that the traditional "from scratch" approach, where the ontology is completely generated from data according to the design choices of the involved team of ontology engineers, is being replaced by a "by-reuse" strategy, where the ontology is produced as the result of both manual design activities and reuse of already existing pieces of knowledge extracted from other ontologies.

In this context, open challenging issues concerns i) how to support on-the-fly selection of relevant knowledge chunks to suggest for reuse, and ii) how to perform reuse in a consistent and safe mode when a certain knowledge chunk coming from an external ontology is actually selected for being included in the local one. To this end, our approach to P2P coordination of collective knowledge represents an interesting research direction. In particular, through periodic harvesting of semantic communities based on appropriate probe queries, it is possible to collect the available knowledge chunks about a given concept of interest. This enables a peer to build a thematic library of externally harvested knowledge chunks which can be exploited during knowledge design and/or evolution for providing suggestions of similar knowledge chunks that can be considered for reuse. In particular, ontology matching techniques can be employed to extract from the library the most relevant knowledge chunks that will be proposed as suggestions for reuse. For knowledge design, the idea is that a harvested knowledge chunk can be selected for merging with a given concept draft under design, thus simplifying the specification of a new ontology concept. Merging of a harvested knowledge chunk with a concept draft under design can be performed in a sort of lightweight integration approach, as the one described in the previous section for collective concept construction. Similarly, for knowledge evolution, harvested knowledge chunks can be used as suggestions for enriching/enhancing the specification of an existing ontology concept by reusing the axioms of another one. Moreover, collective concepts can be exploited for knowledge design. Since a collective concept provides a unified representation of a set of harvested knowledge chunks, it can be exploited as a template for the design of a new concept. In other words, a collective concept can be used as a starting point for the specification of a new concept, thus avoiding a completely manual approach.

Knowledge design and evolution based on harvesting of external knowledge sources are the core aspects of the iCoord platform for semantic knowledge coordination (http://islab.dico.unimi. it/icoord/). Key contribution of iCoord concerns i) the specification/visualization of OWL ontologies through natural language-like facilities, to enable also non OWL-experts to define correct OWL assertions; and ii) support to knowledge sharing and (re)use in a given domain and across the Semantic Web, through matching-based knowledge harvesting and through merge/alignment of external knowledge chunks. Technical details about iCoord are available in Castano, Ferrara, Lorusso, & Montanelli (2008).

CONCLUSION

In this chapter, we have presented our approach to P2P semantic coordination based on collective knowledge organization. Distinguishing features of our approach are:

- the specification of a three-layer knowledge repository based on the notion of knowledge chunk for the efficient representation of both personal and collective peer knowledge;
- the definition of handshaking techniques for semantic community formation, to enable peers to become aware of their common expertise and to recognize the existence of a collective knowledge about a certain topic of interest;
- the definition of knowledge harvesting techniques for effective retrieval of knowledge of interest in the form of matching knowledge chunks provided by community members;
- the definition of P2P coordination techniques for construction of collective concepts based on harvested knowledge chunks, to enable user-level collective queries and seamless access to distributed peer resources.

A prototype version of the overall approach is currently under development in the framework of the iCoord knowledge coordination platform. Ad-hoc modules for harvesting and coordination as described in this chapter are already available as components of iCoord. Evaluation and experimental tests are planned to assess the effectiveness of the proposed approach on real scenarios of P2P knowledge coordination.

REFERENCES

Aiello, G., & Alessi, M. (2007). DNK-WSD: a Distributed Approach for Knowledge Discovery in Peer to Peer Networks. In *Proceedings of the 15th EUROMICRO International Conference on Parallel, Distributed and Network-Based Processing, PDP'07* (pp. 325-332). Naples, Italy.

Aleman-Meza, B., Halaschek-Wiener, C., & Arpinar, I. B. (2005). Collective Knowledge Composition in a P2P Network. In Rivero, L. C., Doorn, J. H., & Ferraggine, V. E. (Eds.), Encyclopedia of Database Technologies and Applications (pp. 74-77). Hershey, PA: Idea Group Inc.

Arenas, M., Kantere, V., Kementsietsidis, A., Kiringa, I., Miller, R. J., & Mylopoulos, J. (2003). The Hyperion Project: From Data Integration to Data Coordination. *SIGMOD Record. Special Issue on Peer-to-Peer Data Management, 32*(3), 53–58.

Asvanund, A., & Krishnan, R. (2004). Content-Based Community Formation in Hybrid Peer-to-Peer Networks. In *Proceedings of the of the SIGIR Workshop on Peer-to-Peer Information Retrieval*. Sheffield, UK.

Aumueller, D., Do, H., Massmann, S., & Rahm, E. (2005). Schema and Ontology Matching with COMA++. In *Proceedings of SIGMOD 2005 - Software Demonstration*, Baltimore, USA.

Avrithis, Y., Kompatsiaris, Y., Staab, S., & Vakali, A. (Eds.). (2008). *Proceedings of the CISWeb (Collective Semantics: Collective Intelligence and the Semantic Web) Workshop, located at the 5th European Semantic Web Conference ESWC 2008*. Tenerife, Spain.

Baader, F., Calvanese, D., McGuinness, D. L., Nardi, D., & Patel-Schneider, P. F. (Eds.). (2003). *The Description Logic Handbook: Theory, Implementation, and Applications*. Cambridge University Press.

Beneventano, D., Bergamaschi, S., Castano, S., De Antonellis, V., Ferrara, A., Guerra, F., et al. (2002). Semantic Integration and Query Optimization of Heterogeneous Data Sources. In *Proceedings of the Workshop on Advances in Object-Oriented Information Systems, OOIS 2002* (pp. 154-165). Montpellier, France.

Bloehdorn, S., Haase, P., Hefke, M., Sure, Y., & Tempich, C. Intelligent Community Lifecycle Support. In *Proceedings of the 5th International Conference on Knowledge Management, I-KNOW 05*. Graz, Austria.

Bouquet, P., Serafini, L., & Zanobini, S. (2004). Peer-to-Peer Semantic Coordination. *Journal of Web Semantics, 2*(1), 81–97. doi:10.1016/j.websem.2004.07.004

Calvanese, D., De Giacomo, G., Lenzerini, M., & Rosati, R. (2004). Logical Foundations of Peer-to-Peer Data Integration. In *Proceedings of the 23th ACM SIGMOD-SIGACT-SIGART symposium on Principles of Database Systems, PODS 2004* (pp. 241-251). Paris, France.

Castano, S., De Antonellis, V., & De Capitani Di Vimercati, S. (2001). Global Viewing of Heterogeneous Data Sources. *IEEE Transactions on Knowledge and Data Engineering, 13*(2), 277–297. doi:10.1109/69.917566

Castano, S., Ferrara, A., Lorusso, D., & Montanelli, S. (2008).Ontology Coordination: The iCoord Project Demonstration. In *Proceedings of the 27th International Conference on Conceptual Modeling, ER 2008* (pp. 512–513). Barcelona, Spain.

Castano, S., Ferrara, A., & Messa, G. (2006). Results of the HMatch Ontology Matchmaker in OAEI 2006. In *Proceedings of the 1st International Workshop on Ontology Matching, OM 2006, Collocated with the 5th International Semantic Web Conference, ISWC 2006*, Athens, Georgia, USA.

Castano, S., Ferrara, A., & Montanelli, S. (2006a). Dynamic Knowledge Discovery in Open, Distributed and Multi-Ontology Systems: Techniques and Applications. In Taniar, D., & Rahayu, J. W. (Eds.), *Web Semantics and Ontology* (pp. 226–258). Hershey, PA: Idea Group Inc.

Castano, S., Ferrara, A., & Montanelli, S. (2006b). Evolving Open and Independent Ontologies. *International Journal of Metadata. Semantics and Ontologies*, *1*(4), 235–249. doi:10.1504/IJMSO.2006.012949

Castano, S., Ferrara, A., & Montanelli, S. (2006c). Matching Ontologies in Open Networked Systems: Techniques and Applications. *Journal on Data Semantics*, *V*, 25–63. doi:10.1007/11617808_2

Castano, S., & Montanelli, S. (2005). Semantic Self-Formation of Communities of Peers. In *Proceedings of the ESWC Workshop on Ontologies in Peer-to-Peer Communities*, Heraklion, Greece.

Cohen, S., Nutt, W., & Sagiv, Y. (2006). Rewriting Queries with Arbitrary Aggregation Functions using Views. *ACM Transactions on Database Systems*, *31*(2), 672–715. doi:10.1145/1138394.1138400

Crespo, A., & Garcia-Molina, H. (2004). Semantic Overlay Networks for P2P Systems. In *Proceedings of the 3rd International Workshop on Agents and Peer-to-Peer Computing, P2PC 2004* (pp. 1-13). New York, NY, USA.

Das, T., Nandi, S., & Ganguly, N. (2009). Community Formation and Search in P2P: A Robust and Self-Adjusting Algorithm. In *Proceedings of the 3rd Workshop on Intelligent Networks: Adaptation, Communication & Reconfiguration, IAMCOM 2009*, Bangalore, India.

EU FP6 BOEMIE Project. (2006). *Bootstrapping Ontology Evolution with Multimedia Information Extraction*. Retrieved from http://www.boemie.org/

Gruber, T. (2008). Collective Knowledge Systems: where the Social Web meets the Semantic Web. *Journal of Web Semantics*, *6*(1), 4–13.

Gu, W., & Wei, W. (2006). Automatic Community Discovery in Peer-to-Peer Systems. In *Proceedings of the 5th International Conference on Grid and Cooperative Computing Workshops, GCC 2006* (pp. 110-116). Changsha, Hunan, China.

Haase, P., Siebes, R., & Van Harmelen, F. (2008). Expertise-based Peer Selection in Peer-to-Peer Networks. *Knowledge and Information Systems*, *15*(1), 75–107. doi:10.1007/s10115-006-0055-1

Halevy, A. (2001). Answering Queries using Views: A Survey. *The VLDB Journal*, *10*(4), 270–294. doi:10.1007/s007780100054

Halevy, A., Rajaraman, A., & Ordille, J. (2006). Data Integration: The Teenage Years. In *Proceedings of the 32nd International Conference on Very Large Data Bases, VLDB 2006* (pp. 9-16). Seoul, Korea.

Hidayanto, A. N., & Bressan, S. (2007). Towards a Society of Peers: Expert and Interest Groups in Peer-to-Peer Systems. In *Proceedings of the OTM International IFIP Workshop On Semantic Web & Web Semantics, SWWS 2007* (pp. 487-496), Vilamoura, Portugal.

Jian, N., Hu, W., Cheng, G., & Qu, Y. (2005). Falcon-AO: Aligning Ontologies with Falcon. In *Proceedings of the K-CAP Workshop on Integrating Ontologies*, Banff, Canada.

Jung, J. J., & Euzenat, J. (2007). Towards Semantic Social Networks. In *Proceedings of the 4th European Semantic Web Conference, ESWC 2007* (pp. 267-280). Innsbruck, Austria.

Khambatti, M., Ryu, K. D., & Dasgupta, P. (2002). Efficient Discovery of Implicitly Formed Peer-to-Peer Communities. *International Journal of Parallel and Distributed Systems and Networks*, *5*(4), 155–164.

Liu, K., Bhaduri, K., Das, K., Nguyen, P., & Kargupta, H. (2006). Client-side Web Mining for Community Formation in Peer-to-Peer Environments. *SIGKDD Explorations*, *8*(2), 11–20. doi:10.1145/1233321.1233323

Löser, A., Staab, S., & Tempich, C. (2007). Semantic Social Overlay Networks. *IEEE Journal on Selected Areas in Communications*, *25*(1), 5–14. doi:10.1109/JSAC.2007.070102

Madhavan, J., Cohen, S., Dong, X. L., Halevy, A., Jeffery, S. R., Ko, D., & Yu, C. (2007). Web-Scale Data Integration: You can afford to Pay as You Go. In *Proceedings of the 3rd Biennial Conf. on Innovative Data Systems Research, CIDR 2007* (pp. 342-350). Asilomar, CA, USA.

McBrien, P., & Poulovassilis, A. (2003). Defining Peer-to-Peer Data Integration Using Both as View Rules. In *Proceedings of the 1st International Workshop on Databases, Information Systems, and Peer-to-Peer Computing, DBISP2P 2003* (pp. 91-107). Berlin, Germany.

Montanelli, S., & Castano, S. (2008). Semantically Routing Queries in Peer-based Systems: the H-Link Approach. *The Knowledge Engineering Review*, *23*(1), 51–72. doi:10.1017/S0269888907001257

Motik, B., Horrocks, I., & Sattler, U. (2009). Bridging the Gap between OWL and Relational Databases. *Journal of Web Semantics*, *7*(2), 74–89. doi:10.1016/j.websem.2009.02.001

Mukherjee, C. S., & Ramakrishnan, I. V. (2008). Automated Semantic Analysis of Schematic Data. *World Wide Web Journal*, *11*(4), 427–464. doi:10.1007/s11280-008-0046-0

Rana, O. F., & Hinze, A. (2004). Trust and Reputation in Dynamic Scientific Communities. *IEEE Distributed Systems Online, 5*(1).

Sabou, M., D'Aquin, M., & Motta, E. (2008). Exploring the Semantic Web as Background Knowledge for Ontology Matching. *Journal on Data Semantics*, *XI*, 156–190. doi:10.1007/978-3-540-92148-6_6

Sattler, U., Calvanese, D., & Molitor, R. (2003). Relationships with other Formalisms. In *Description Logic Handbook* (pp. 137-177).

Sigurbjörnsson, B., & Van Zwol, R. (2008). Flickr Tag Recommendation based on Collective Knowledge. In *Proceedings of the 17th International Conference on World Wide Web, WWW 2008* (pp. 327-336). Beijing, China.

Specia, L., & Motta, E. (2007). Integrating Folksonomies with the Semantic Web. In *Proceedings of the 4th European Semantic Web Conference, ESWC 2007* (pp. 624-639). Innsbruck, Austria.

Voulgaris, S., Gavidia, D., & Van Steen, M. (2005). CYCLON: Inexpensive Membership Management for Unstructured P2P Overlays. *Journal of Network and Systems Management*, *13*(2), 197–217. doi:10.1007/s10922-005-4441-x

Wang, Y., & Vassileva, J. Trust-Based Community Formation in Peer-to-Peer File Sharing Networks. In *Proceedings of the IEEE/WIC/ACM International Conference on Web Intelligence, WI'04* (pp. 341-348). Beijing, China.

Xiong, L., & Liu, L. (2004). PeerTrust: Supporting Reputation-based Trust for Peer-to-Peer Electronic Communities. *IEEE Transactions on Knowledge and Data Engineering*, *16*(7), 843–857. doi:10.1109/TKDE.2004.1318566

ENDNOTES

[1]   Credit-based forwarding can entail that recently-created communities are poorly considered for message propagation. For this reason, a share of the available credits are assigned by each peer to a randomly-selected set of communities, as described in Montanelli & Castano (2008).

[2]   We note that, since concept axioms of the same knowledge chunk are not matched in the classification phase, candidate clusters contain at most one axiom for each knowledge chunk.

[3] A *query-by-example* approach can be enforced to support a user in specifying a collective query by providing predefined/default query templates based on the structure of the collective knowledge chunks.

Chapter 8
Collective Information Filtering for Web Observatories

Nikolaos Nanas
Center for Research and Technology, Greece & University of Thessaly, Greece

Manolis Vavalis
Center for Research and Technology, Greece & University of Thessaly, Greece

Lefteris Kellis
Center for Research and Technology, Greece & University of Thessaly, Greece

Dimitris Koutsaftikis
Center for Research and Technology, Greece & University of Thessaly, Greece

Elias Houstis
Center for Research and Technology, Greece & University of Thessaly, Greece

ABSTRACT

Web observatories are becoming a common on-line practice. Their role is to compile, organize and convey information that serves the needs of a thematically focused Web community. So far they are typically following a centralized approach, with an editorial team being responsible for finding, collecting, editing and presenting the observatory's information content. We propose a new approach for the development of Web observatories based on Collective Information Filtering. Community profiles are used to capture the collective interests of community members and evaluate the relevance of information content accordingly. We can thus build Web observatories that can be dynamically enriched and can continuously adapt their content to the interests/needs of the observatory's community. This new approach not only reduces significantly the cost of developing and maintaining a Web observatory, but also, following the current Web trends, it is community driven. In this chapter, we discuss Collective Information Filtering and we describe the architecture for applying it to a Web Observatory. We also present a series of prototype Web Observatories that adopt the proposed approach.

DOI: 10.4018/978-1-61520-841-8.ch008

Copyright © 2011, IGI Global. Copying or distributing in print or electronic forms without written permission of IGI Global is prohibited.

INTRODUCTION

Although nothing replaces the feel of a real book in your hand, nowadays for more and more people the Web is replacing regular books. The Web also replaces other commonly used artifacts, and often provides new meaning to notions and concepts. Several meanings of the word "observatory" used to exist well before the arrival of the Web. An observatory might be (1) a place for making observations on the heavenly bodies, (2) a building fitted with instruments for making systematic observations of any particular class or series of natural phenomena, (3) a place from which a view may be observed or commanded, (4) a lookout on a flank of a battery whence an officer can note the range and effect of the fire, (5) an organization dedicated in continually collecting information on critical issues, etc. As it will become apparent below, the Web added one more meaning to the word observatory.

The most common observatories are the ones concerning astronomy which share many common characteristics and practices with a plethora of other types of observatories associated with nature and natural phenomena (e.g. meteorology observatories, ocean observatories, volcano observatories, etc.). Most of these observatories are nowadays organized around a Web portal which often is one of their most important components. New type of observatories, not directly related to natural phenomena, emerged in the past few decades (e.g. health observatories (Hemmings & Wilkinson, 2003), language observatories (Mikami, et al., 2005) standards observatory (Anido, RodrÃguez, Caeiro, & Santos, 2004), etc.). These observatories are commonly built with information technology tools and several of their activities heavily involve the World Wide Web. The success of most of these observatories not only led us to a natural context switch but essentially defined the term Web Observatory.

Web Observatories (WOs) are systems which allow for the inclusion of Information Technolo-

gies (IT) and the Web in order to monitor and synthesize information within the context of a focused organization. Their main challenges remains very similar to the ones associated with conventional observatories: they have to provide an elevated chamber and a collection of facilities and tools to comfort systematic and exhaustive information collection, effective processing and proper dissemination. The only difference is that this chamber and the related facilities and tools are mostly Web entities. The reader is referred to (Nanas, Vavalis, Koutsaftikis, Kelis, & Houstis, 2009) for help on elucidating the concept "Web observatory" and identifying its characteristics and practices and to bibshonomy.org[1] for a large collection of WOs. Their main areas of interest are e-government, Information Society and the IT, the e-health, e-business, e-learning and education and e-inclusion. The general objective of these WOs is to develop an apparatus for monitoring and evaluating the effectiveness of certain activities, the implications associated with various phenomena and trends, and the reactiveness of the individual persons or groups of individuals on such activities/phenomena (Manouselis & Sampson, 2004).

There is an astonishing diversity on many of their characteristics. For example: Some of them focus only on a small geographic region or a particular narrow thematic area while others concern the whole planet and/or broad subjects. Most of them are owned and operated by non-profit organizations but privately owned WOs do exist. Many operate with less than 5 employees while some involve a large team of full time workers. As expected, these WOs also share several common properties. Unfortunately some of them are undesirable and others need to be improved. The objective of this chapter is to investigate the possibility to utilize emerging Web and Information Technology advances in order to effectively and properly reconsider these properties paving the way to next generation WOs.

The rest of this chapter is organized as follows. In the next section we provide the necessary background on profiling and information filtering, focusing on adaptive information filtering and collective information filtering. Section 3 briefly presents Nootropia, a new profiling model that exhibits significant and novel properties which allow its effective application for Collaborative Information Filtering. Next, we focus on the design and the implementation of a new generation of Web Observatories. Specifically, in Section 4 we propose a generic architecture of such WOs that offers desired properties of high importance. In Section 5, we present the design and the implementation of a platform for advanced WO which uses Nootropia's profiling model as its core component. The use of this platform for the development of a set of prototype WOs, which are publicly available on the Web, is presented through two specific examples in Section 6. Our concluding remarks can be found in Section 7.

COLLECTIVE INFORMATION FILTERING

Adaptive Information Filtering (AIF) seeks to provide a user with relevant information based on a tailored representation of the user's interests, called profile. The process is depicted in (Figure 1). Typically, a stream of documents is evaluated by the user profile and only documents assessed as relevant to the user's interests are presented. Relevance evaluation of documents is performed on the actual content of documents and in particular, on features, such as keywords, which are extracted from these documents. Feature extraction is straightforward in the case of text, but not as easy for audiovisual information and thereby, user profiling for AIF has focused on textual information. The user expresses his satisfaction or dissatisfaction of the filtering results and it is this user feedback that allows the profile to learn and continuously improve a representation of the user's interests over time. User feedback can be either explicit or implicit. In the first case the

user marks a document as relevant or not, or rates it according to some predefined scale. Implicit feedback is inferred from the user's behavior. For instance, if the user chooses to read a document then this provides some indication of relevance. Other actions like forwarding the document to another user, saving it or deleting it, can also be taken into account as implicit feedback. User feedback is vital to an AIF system. It is only through user feedback that a user profile can maintain an accurate representation of the user's interests over time. There are temporal shifts, both in the user's interests and the content of incoming documents, so inevitably a user profile has to continuously adapt to maintain a satisfactory level of performance. If the accuracy of the user profile drops bellow a certain level then the user may loose interest in the system and stop using it. AIF is a challenging, dynamic and user-dependent task.

Here we expand the scope of profiling for AIF from a single individual to a whole community of users. We will refer to this variation of AIF as Collective Information Filtering (CIF). (Figure 2) depicts the CIF process. The main steps are similar to those in traditional AIF, but dealing with many rather than a single user changes the specifications of the problem. First it implies that the collective profile should be able to represent the wide variety of topics that can be of interest to community members. Furthermore, since the collective profile can receive feedback from any community member it can become biased towards those members who provide feedback more frequently. Feedback should be collected in such a way that these biases are smoothed. Nevertheless, in communities with a large number of members the effect that each individual has on the user profile is only a small portion of the collective community feedback. As the number of community members increases the collective profile tends to represent what is of interest to the community as a whole. The documents presented to community members are those that reflect the current community interests and thus provide an

Figure 1. Adaptive Information Filtering

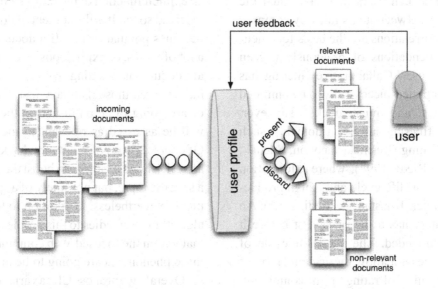

Figure 2. Collective Information Filtering

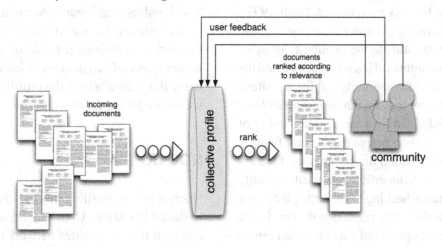

overview of popular trends within the domain of interest. Note also that unlike AIF (Figure 1), in CIF (Figure 2) it is impractical to make a distinction between relevant and non-relevant documents. Even documents that are not relevant to the community's interests may be of interest to some of its members. It is better instead to just rank documents according to relevance and let each individual user decide when to stop looking for interesting documents.

CIF should not be confused with Collaborative Filtering (Shardanand & Maes, 1995). The latter is used to provide personalized recommendations (Mooney, 2000) to each individual member of a community based on the common interests of community members (Herlocker, Konstan, Borchers, & Riedl, 1999). In particular, a user-item matrix stores the ratings that each user has assigned to the items (e.g. books, movies, music tracks) in a collection and is used to calculate correlations between users that have rated the same items, or between items rated by common users. These correlations are the basis for calculating recommendations of previously unseen items to each user. Collaborative filtering has already been applied successfully to recommend books[2], movies[3] and music tracks[4]. However, collaborative filtering suffers in domains, such as news publishing (Resnick, Iacovou, Suchak, Bergstrom, & Riedl, 1994), where information items have a short life-cycle and a high production rate (Schafer, Konstan, & Riedi, 1999). An information item has to be rated first before it can be recommended. The short life-cycle of news stories does not allow the accumulation of a sufficient number of ratings from community members and hence personal recommendations cannot be calculated with confidence (Konstan, Miller, Maltz, Herlocker, Gordon, & Riedl, 1997). Nevertheless, ratings, or votes for that matter, can be exploited to estimate the popularity of news stories in a community. This is the idea behind the voting systems of community publishing sites[5]. The problem here is again that news stories have to be read and voted by a substantial number of community members before they can confidently arise as popular within the community. Furthermore, voting systems suffer from what is usually called "reputation hacking". It refers to trust issues arising when there are votes that do not derive from the honest opinion of users but their aim is to publicize and consequently advertise a specific news story or product.

Unlike collaborative filtering, CIF does not provide personalized recommendations. It generates collective recommendations based on the actual content of documents and not their ratings. This means that recommendations can be calculated even for documents that have not yet been viewed by any user. No ratings are required. Documents can be recommended immediately, upon publication and hence, CIF can easily deal with dynamic domains, such as news publishing. In addition, the popularity of a document is not an explicit function of the ratings/votes that it has received so far. It is the content of documents that becomes popular or not. If a document receives a lot of views, or explicit positive feedback, then all documents dealing with a similar subject matter, even those that have just been published or are going to be published in the near future, will be assessed as relevant to the community. Of course, issues of reputation hacking may still arise. Dishonest views can boost the popularity of a specific topic, but not solely of a specific document. Nevertheless, in addition to technical and algorithmic remedies to this problem, we believe that within the focused Web community of a WO these phenomena are going to be more rear.

Overall, we propose CIF, a variation of personalized AIF, as an alternative to collaborative filtering and voting systems for dynamic, community-based, publishing systems. We will demonstrate this new approach in the context of WOs that serve the current information needs of a community within a specialized domain of interest. But first we will describe briefly the profiling model that we have adopted for this purpose.

NOOTROPIA

Nootropia is a profiling model for AIF, first introduced in (Nanas, Uren, Roeck, & Domingue, 2003). It uses a weighted network of features to represent user's or community's interests (Figure 3). Nodes in this network can be any descriptive feature or metadata, which is extracted from the content of relevant information items, or describes their usage or context. In the case of textual information, nodes in the network are simply words extracted from the content of relevant documents. Term weighting is deployed to statistically assess the importance of words and only the most informative[6] are selected to become nodes in the profile's network (Nanas & Vavalis, 2008). Theoretically, nodes can also correspond to features extracted from the content

Figure 3. User Profile a weighted network of features

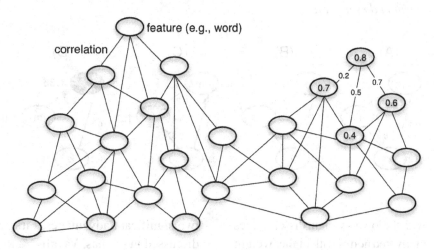

of audiovisual information. Furthermore, nodes can also correspond to metadata, such as tags, or even the IDs of the users that have already viewed an information item. Building profiles that incorporate features extracted from the content of audiovisual information and any available metadata is work in progress, which will expand the scope of Nootropia beyond text. It will also lead to the evaluation of information items (of any media) not only based on their content, but also based on additional social clues. For now we will concentrate on textual information and nodes in the profile's network will correspond to single words.

Links between nodes represent correlations between features that co-occur in the same context. For textual information, we use a sliding window to define the context of words in text. A sliding window is a span of contiguous words that slides through a document's text. Words are considered correlated and are linked whenever they appear together within the sliding window. The weight of links measures the statistical dependencies that exist between correlated terms. Words that frequently occur together within the sliding window and not individually acquire a larger link weight. How exactly term dependencies are measured is described in detail in (Nanas

& Vavalis, 2008). Capturing and measuring term dependencies is a novelty of Nootropia, since they have been generally ignored in AIF. Typically, documents have been treated as bag of words, with each word contributing independently to a document's relevance.

The profile evaluates the relevance of incoming documents, through a spreading activation process. (Figure 4) depicts a numerical example of the document evaluation process. In the figure, numbers on the left of nodes and of links correspond to indicative weights and each of the bold numbers on the right of nodes corresponds to a term's current activation. Words (nodes) in the profile that also appear in the document become activated. For binary indexing of documents, the initial activation of profile nodes is equal to one (Figure 4B). If words in the document are weighted, then the initial activation of a word in the profile's network is equal to the word's weight in the document. After activation the dissemination process takes place. The activated nodes are ordered according to increasing weight and then, in succession, each contributes part of its activation to those activated nodes with higher weights that it is linked to. The amount of activation that is disseminated between two nodes is proportional to the weight of the link between them. First the

Figure 4. Document evaluation through spreading activation (A) idle, (B) stimulated, (C) term k disseminates, (D) term m disseminates

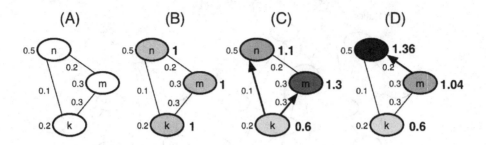

activated node with the lowest weight disseminates its activation to activated nodes with higher weight (Figure 4C). Subsequently, the next node in the weight order disseminates part of its updated activation (Figure 4D) and so on, until the activated node with the highest weight is reached. Finally, a single relevance score Rs is calculated as the weighted sum of the final activation of profile nodes. In (Figure 4) we have:

$$Rs=0.6\times0.2+1.04\times0.3+1.36\times0.5=1.112.$$

In practice, this process is applied for each position of a sliding window and so the distribution of relevance through a document's text is actually assessed. An overall relevance score is calculated as the sum of the individual relevance scores of each window position. The size of this sliding window is the same as the size of the sliding window used to identify correlations between words.

The importance of the above process is that it takes into account correlations between words. A document's relevance score increases when it activates strongly and densely interconnected nodes rather than scattered ones. For instance, in the numerical example of Figure 4, if there were no links between the three nodes, then no dissemination of activation would take place and thereafter, Rs would be equal to $1\times0.2+1\times0.3+1\times0.5=1$, which is less than the value calculated above (1.112). Taking into account correlations between words has

two significant advantages. First, as it is further discussed in (Nanas, Vavalis, & Roeck, 2009), it allows the profile to store more information and so the profile becomes more specific and accurate. Furthermore, it renders the profile more resistant to the "curse of dimensionality". When correlations between words are ignored then a profile represents equally every possible combination of words, including those combinations that are not relevant to the user's interests. As the number of words (dimensions) increases, the number of possible word combinations increases exponentially and the profile becomes more and more ambiguous. This is one of the reasons justifying the tendency of traditional approaches to AIF to break up the problem into separate profiles, one for each topic of interest to the user (Nanas, Uren, Roeck, & Domingue, 2004). In contrast, Nootropia's network profile distinguishes those word correlations which are relevant to a user's or a community's interests. Even when the profile includes a large number of words, only the explicitly represented word correlations and not every possible correlation between words are taken into account during document evaluation. This is a significant property, especially in the context of CIF, because it allows the profile to incorporate the large number of words required to represent a variety of topics. We have performed a series of comparative experiments and their results show that, as the number of interesting topics increases, taking term dependencies into account becomes increasingly important for the profile's accuracy (Nanas, Uren, Roeck, & Domingue, 2004; Nanas & Vavalis, 2008; Nanas, Vavalis, & Roeck, 2009). So, with high accuracy, Nootropia can represent the large range of potential topics that a community of users can be interested in.

The most fascinating and challenging aspect of AIF and CIF is their dynamic nature. Both the interests/needs of the community and the information space being monitored, inevitably change over time. We cannot predefine and fix the topics of interest to the community and so text classification techniques, which train a priori a separate classifier for each topic category, are not applicable. The topics of interest are fluid, multi-faceted, interwoven and never clearly defined in terms of concrete subject areas. The level of interest in each topic varies over time and in the long-term, new topics of interest emerge and others wane. We expect that in contrast to traditional AIF, which deals with a single user, the dynamic nature of the problem is further exaggerated in the case of a group of users. Interactions between community members cause positive feedback loops, which accelerate interest trends. A CIF system intensifies these positive feedback loops. Documents about an emerging topic that has received enough views (or explicit positive feedback) emerge at the top of the ranked list and attract further attention. By using a CIF an on-line community can become more responsive.

Nootropia tackles the problem of profile adaptation to a variety of interest shifts, through a biologically inspired process of self-organization. The theoretical background and the algorithmic details of Nootropia's adaptation process are described and discussed comprehensively in (Nanas & Vavalis, 2008). (Figure 5) depicts its three main steps. Given a relevant document (i.e. a document that has received positive feedback), we first use term weighting to extract the most informative words from the document's text.

Some of the extracted terms are already found in the profile (Figure 5, nodes with bold border) and some are new (Figure 5, nodes filled with diagonal lines). The first step of the adaptation process (Figure 5A) involves a redistribution of weights from profile nodes not found in the document towards those found. So profile words found in the document's content get reinforced at the expense of those that were not. As a result of this redistribution of weight some profile nodes run eventually out of weight. In the second step of the process these nodes are purged from the profile (Figure 5B, shadowed nodes). Finally, words extracted from the document that are not already in the profile become nodes and new links are generated[7]. The overall effect is the network's structural adjustment in response to user feedback. Variations in the weights of nodes can quickly reflect short-term variations in the level of interest in various topics. Furthermore, an additional network structure is generated whenever a new topic

Figure 5. Profile Adaptation (A) redistribution of weight, (B) purging of nodes, (C) recruitment of new nodes and generation of links

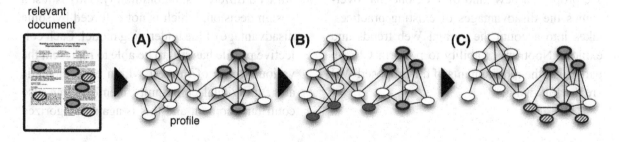

of interest emerges and parts of the network that represent no longer interesting topics disintegrate and are eventually removed from the profile. In this way, the profile can both learn and forget. In (Nanas & Vavalis, 2008; Nanas, Vavalis, & Kellis, 2009; Nanas, Vavalis, & Roeck, 2009), we have experimentally demonstrated Nootropia's adaptive capabilities in a pure AIF problem. Nootropia's comparison with the popular Rocchio's learning algorithm (Rocchio, 1971) shows an increase in performance of up to 22% (Nanas, Vavalis, & Kellis, 2009), (Nanas, Vavalis, & Roeck, 2009).

In summary, Nootropia exhibits two significant and novel properties, which allow its effective application for CIF. It is dimensionality resistant, or in other words, it can incorporate a large number of features without becoming ambiguous due to the exponential number of possible feature combinations. Therefore, it can incorporate the large number of words necessary for representing the whole range of a community's interests. In addition, Nootropia can effectively adapt to the variety of interest changes that may occur over time. So far Nootropia has been successfully applied for personalized aggregation of news and scientific publications (Nanas, Vavalis, & Houstis, 2009). Here we describe its application for building dynamic and adaptive WOs for online communities, starting with its requirements and the basic architecture.

REQUIREMENTS AND ARCHITECTURE FOR A COLLECTIVE WEB OBSERVATORY

We propose a new kind of WO, one that overcomes the disadvantages of existing practices, takes into account the current Web trends and exploits Nootropia's ability to perform CIF. In particular, the requirements of the proposed WO are the following:

- Instead of a costly editorial team collecting, editing and organizing the content of the WO, the latter should be dynamically updated and its content adapted and organized according to the interests of the observatory's community.

- The WO should trigger and exploit the participation of the community in producing additional content and in organizing it. Turning a community into content is a distinguishing characteristic of what many call Web 2.0.

- The WO must continuously adapt to temporal shifts in community interests. Only then can it become an on-line reference point for community members and will attract their active involvement.

- The direct communication and exchange of information between community members should be facilitated. The community itself will function as an additional filter, choosing from the WO the information to be further disseminated between community members.

(Figure 6) depicts the architecture of the proposed WO. Given a domain of interest, information is dynamically collected from relevant on-line sources, which the community members specify and can modify. The information is gathered periodically and is categorized according to community specified thematic areas. Although a single collective profile could be deployed for evaluating all incoming information, we decided instead to use a separate collective profile for each thematic area, because we expect that it will attract a different sub-community. This is just a design decision, which is not enforced by some disadvantage of the underlying model. Each collective profile has still to be able to represent the various topics of interest within each thematic area. Individual community members can also contribute content and this is again categorized

Figure 6. Architecture for a Collective Web Observatory

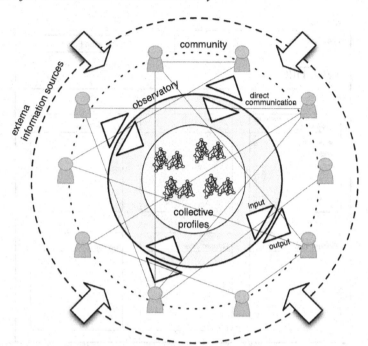

and evaluated by the community profiles. Direct communication between community members is enabled either through existing communication channels (e.g. email) or through the WO itself, with services such as instant messaging tools.

The proposed architecture is flexible and easy to implement. It does not have strict technological requirements and does not involve ontological engineering by domain experts. It is essentially domain independent and can be applied easily to a variety of thematic areas. It is part of our ongoing effort to build community-based Web sites that facilitate and enhance all aspects of information aggregation, organization and dissemination between community members. In the next section we present a series of prototype WO implementations based on the proposed architecture.

DESIGN AND IMPLEMENTATION

The Web design of the proposed collective WO has been inspired by "personalized home pages",

such as iGoogle[8] and Netvibes[9]. Personalized home pages allow a user to compile and organize according to his or her preferences a collection of "Web widgets" (also called "Web gadgets"). According to Wikipedia: "a Web widget is a portable chunk of code that can be installed and executed within any separate HTML-based Web page by an end user without requiring additional compilation". Typically, a Web widget defines a rectangular portion of a Web page and provides some service. There is a large variety of Web widgets, but here we will concentrate only on those playing the role of RSS[10] aggregators. An RSS Aggregator monitors, certain predefined and others user specified, manage RSS feeds and maintain an up to date list of all the articles that have been published by each feed's source. For instance, BBC's home page[11] allows each user to select from a series of widgets, each aggregating BBC's recently published news stories for one of BBC's subject areas (e.g. world news, economy, politics, etc.), those that will appear on the user's personalized home page. As in every

Figure 7. Web Design for a Collective Web Observatory

personalized home page, the user can position each widget within the page and even organize them in tabs. So, personalized home pages enable users to build personalized "mashups", i.e. Web sites that aggregate information from various on-line sources and organize it in space according to the user's preferences.

We have extended this practice, to design a WO that adapts to the preferences of an on-line community. (Figure 7) depicts the design of the WO's main page. Like a typical personalized home page, it consists of a series of widgets. We have developed a prototype Web platform that allows authorized community members to build the WO from scratch by creating and managing its widgets. At the moment, there are only three types of available widgets, but our future intentions are to extend the platform with additional widgets and if possible, make it open to external developers. For now the simplest type of widget allows registered users to post articles relevant to a thematic area. There are however two more widget types implementing the WO's CIF functionality.

The "RSS widget" aggregates articles from RSS feeds, which are relevant to a specific thematic area and ranks them according to the community's interests. (Figure 8) presents this process. Registered members can specify and modify at any point the list of RSS feeds to be monitored for a specific thematic area. There is no constraining on the number of RSS feeds, which can be assigned to an RSS widget. On the server side, collected articles are indexed for future search. For this purpose we adopted the open source search engine Lucene[12]. Each RSS gadget is assigned a collective profile. The profile evaluates the incoming articles according to the community's preferences. The result of the evaluation is a single relevance score for each individual article. On the client side, the RSS widget presents to the community the list of incoming articles, ordered according to decreasing relevance score. Articles relevant to the collective community interests receive a higher score and appear at the top of the ordered list. As already mentioned the whole list of items is presented so even articles with a lower score can still attract the community's attention and become popular. Every time a user chooses to view an article, it is passed as feedback for the profile's adaptation. The article's Web page is complemented with the WO's toolbar with buttons for explicit positive or negative feedback on the article and for sharing this article via email with other community members. This latter functionality is our first attempt to establish direct communication between community members through the WO and allow further dissemination of interesting articles. Future plans include extending the WO with social networking functionality that will provide additional communications channels between community members.

The "query widget" uses a somewhat different approach for aggregating articles relevant to a thematic area. As (Figure 9) depicts, each query widget is assigned one or more queries that express broadly the thematic area of the information to be retrieved. Registered members can modify these queries at will. The queries are used to retrieve indexed articles that currently appear in any of the RSS feeds that the WO is monitoring. These include the feeds assigned to RSS widgets, but also, additional user specified feeds. The queries

do not have to be specific. On the contrary, it is preferable if they exhibit high recall so that all recently published articles relevant to the thematic area of interest are retrieved. Like before, the query gadget is assigned a collective profile, which evaluates the retrieved articles according to the community's interests and then, they are presented to the community in decreasing relevance order. The CIF of the search results increases the specificity of the presented list. Out of an exhaustive set of hits only those that are relevant to the community's collective interests appear at the top of the ordered list. On the client side, a user's interaction with the query widget is exactly the same as with the RSS widget. Viewed items provide the feedback for the profile's adaptation.

We are currently developing further types of widgets to support a variety of services, such as targeted publishing, social networking, expert finding and more. We are also working on improving the underlying Web platform in terms of usability, aesthetics, flexibility, reliability and other aspects. So far, we have used the current platform to build a series of WO and their cases we discuss bellow.

Figure 8. RSS widget

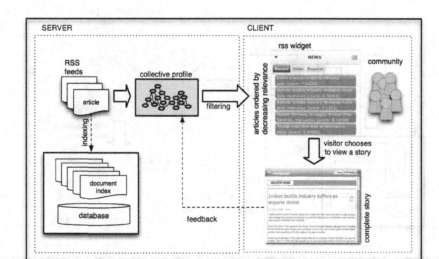

CASE STUDIES

The platform described above has been used to develop a series of prototype WOs, which are publicly available on the Web. Here we present two characteristic examples.

Innovation Observatory of Thessaly

The Innovation Observatory of Thessaly[13] has been developed in the context of the Regional Innovation Pole of Thessaly[14]. The observatory's Web site includes a series of Web pages, but of interest to the current work are three of them, each one dedicated to one of the domains of interest (textiles, biofuel and food-drinks). (Figure 10) depicts the Web page dedicated to the domain of textiles. According to the Web design described in the previous section, it comprises eleven widgets, each one dedicated to a category. These are news on the textile industry, related events and project calls, statistics, procurements, software, textile companies in the province of Thessaly (Greece),

publications, books, materials and prices[15]. Similar categories exist for the other two domains, biofuels and food-drinks. The widgets categories were specified after discussions with the members of the Innovation Pole of Thessaly. For this particular implementation the widgets are hard coded. There is no interface for adding, or removing a widget. As already discussed, a search engine indexes all articles in the RSS feeds associated with the textiles domain. Registered members can manage (add or remove) these feeds by clicking on the "Manage Feeds" link at the top of the Web page. Visitors of the Web site can search within the domain of textiles using the provided text field.

We have exploited all three types of widgets described in the design section above. For instance, the "COMPANIES" widget is a static widget displaying information about textile companies, posted by registered members. The "PRICES" widget is a Query widget, using search terms, such as "price" and "cost" to retrieve relevant, recently posted articles, from the underlying search engine. An example of an RSS widget is

Figure 9. Query widget

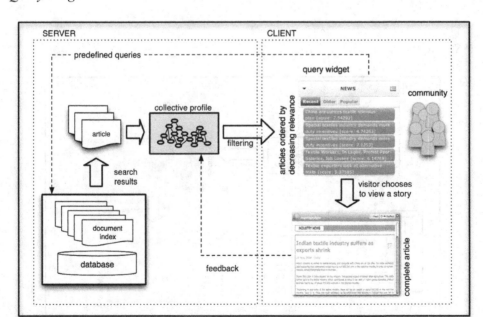

Figure 10. Innovation Observatory of Thessaly Textiles

the "STATS" widget, which aggregates articles from RSS feeds that publish statistical studies on the textile industry.

(Figure 11) depicts the "STATS" widget in detail. Both RSS and Query widgets use tabs to distinguish between "Recent" articles, i.e. those published in the last 24 hours, "Older" articles and the most "Popular" articles. A popularity score is calculated based on the views and the feedback that each article has received. Each tab presents a list of titles, ordered according to relevance score, or popularity score in the case of the "Popular" tab (Figure 11A). When a user clicks on a title, the article's short description appears accompanied by the hyperlink "More" that leads to the full article (Figure 11B). When a registered member clicks on the configuration button, at the top right corner of the widget, a configuration panel appears, which can be used to add an additional feed to the widget, or remove one of the existing feeds (Figure 11C). A similar interface is used for managing the queries in a Query gadget and for adding posts to a static gadget.

Other Web Observatories

The platform developed for the Innovation Observatory of Thessaly has been extended and deployed for building a series of prototype WOs for various domains. These are publicly available at http://observatories.cereteth.gr and cover the domains of industry in the province of Thessaly (Greece), smart energy, agricultural IT, IT security, traceability and innovation. They are all based on the proposed Web platform and use the same Web design but different aesthetics. (Figure 12) depicts, as an example, the WO dedicated to the industry sector. It comprises three widgets in English and three in Greek. At the top right of the figure appears the interface for adding a new widget. The registered member can specify the gadget's name, its title, description, type (RSS or Query), language (English or Greek) and the queries of a Query widget. With the "X" button at the top right corner of each widget, a registered member can delete the widget and with the configuration button next to it, the user can manage a widget's

Figure 11. A typical widget (A) ranked list of articles, (B) article view (C) configuration panel

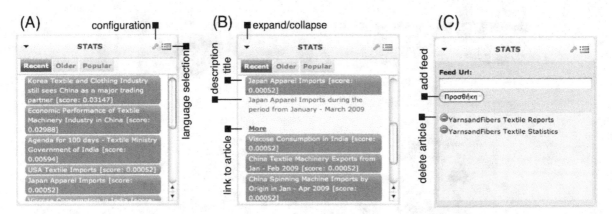

RSS feeds or widgets. Like before, registered members can use the "Feed Management" link, to manage (add or remove) the RSS feeds that the WO is monitoring and indexing.

In the case of IT security*, the WO follows a somewhat different approach. Each registered member, after signing in, is presented with a personalized view of the articles in each widget. Instead of a collective profile, each widget is associated with a personalized user profile, which performs traditional AIF, i.e. it evaluates the relevance of incoming articles according to the interests of the individual community member. Future implementations will include a combination of both a collective and a personalized view. All visitors will be able to view a common collective WO, but registered members will be able to compile and organize a personalized WO.

CONCLUSION AND FUTURE WEB OBSERVATORIES

WOs are becoming a common on-line practice and their goal is to inform a community on subjects related to a specific domain. They typically involve an editorial team, which is responsible for finding, editing, organizing and presenting relevant information from various sources. This approach has two main disadvantages.

It significantly increases the cost of building and managing a WO, while ignoring the real needs and interests of the community and the significant participatory role that it can play in the content of the WO. Following current Web trends, we proposed an alternative approach to the development of WOs, based on CIF. We use Nootropia, a profiling model that has been successfully applied to AIF, to build collective profiles which represent the collective interests of a community and adapts to changes in them. Inspired by personalized home pages, we developed a Web platform for easily developing WOs that comprise a collection of widgets. So far, widgets are article aggregators that use a collective profile to rank the articles according to their relevance to the community. In this way, the WO is dynamically updated with content from a variety of sources, which the community can specify, and also, the WO adapts to the community interests. It is the community, rather than the editorial team, that defines the content of the WO and its organization. We used the Web platform to develop a series of prototype Web observatories, which have been made publicly available on-line.

Deploying these WOs in a real situation is part of ongoing work. We are currently extending the Web platform to include further types of widgets providing a series of services. Our

Figure 12. Web Observatories Industry Sector

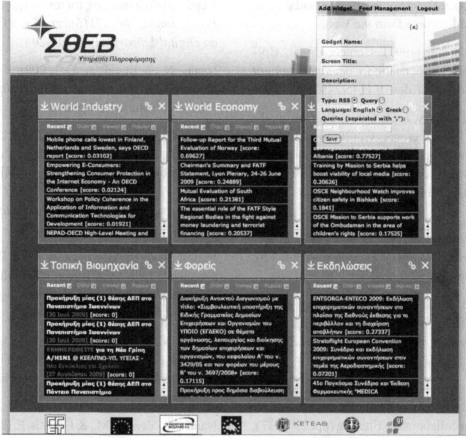

overall goal is a flexible and open Web platform that will allow collective and personalized views, it will be easily configurable and will provide to community members additional tools for direct communication and information dissemination. This platform will move beyond the scope of WOs and will provide the means for building dynamic, community publishing Web sites. The experience gained and the lessons learned from the work presented here have been significant and demonstrate the feasibility of our future plans.

ACKNOWLEDGMENT

Work supported in part by the Operational Program "Competitiveness" of the Third Community Frame of Support of the Hellenic Ministry of Development under the grand "Regional Innovation Pole of Thessaly".

Special thanks to Dimitris Koutsaftikis, for his contribution to the development of some of the Web observatories considered in this study.

REFERENCES

Adomavicius, G. (2005). Toward the next generation of recommender systems: A survey of the state-of-the-art and possible extensions. *IEEE Transactions on Knowledge and Data Engineering, 17*, 734–749. doi:10.1109/TKDE.2005.99

Anido, L. (2004). *RodrÃguez, J., Caeiro, M., & Santos, J* (pp. 922–931). Observing Standards for Web-Based Learning from the Web.

Balabanovic, M. (1997). Content-Based, Collaborative Recommendation. *Communications of the ACM, 40,* 66–72. doi:10.1145/245108.245124

Chabert, G., Marty, J. C., Caron, B., Carron, T., Vignollet, L., & Ferraris, C. (2006). The Electronic Schoolbag, a CSCW workspace: presentation and evaluation. *AI & Society, 20,* 403–419. doi:10.1007/s00146-005-0026-1

Hemmings, J., & Wilkinson, J. (2003). What is a public health observatory? *Journal of Epidemiology and Community Health, 57,* 324–326. doi:10.1136/jech.57.5.324

Herlocker, J. L. (2004). Evaluating collaborative filtering recommender systems. *ACM Transactions on Information Systems, 22,* 5–53. doi:10.1145/963770.963772

Herlocker, J. L., Konstan, J. A., Borchers, A., & Riedl, J. (1999). An algorithmic framework for performing collaborative filtering (pp. 230-237).

Konstan, J. A. (1997). Applying Collaborative Filtering to Usenet News. *Communications of the ACM, 40,* 77–87. doi:10.1145/245108.245126

Konstan, J. A., Miller, B. N., Maltz, D., Herlocker, J. L., Gordon, L. R., & Riedl, J. (1997). GroupLens: applying collaborative filtering to Usenet news. *Communications of the ACM, 40,* 77–87. doi:10.1145/245108.245126

Manouselis, N., & Sampson, D. (2004). *Recommendation of Quality Approaches for the European Quality Observatory* (pp. 1082–1083). IEEE Computer Society.

Mikami, Y., Zavarsky, P., Rozan, M. Z., Suzuki, I., Takahashi, M., & Maki, T. (2005). *The language observatory project (LOP)* (pp. 990–991). ACM.

Mooney, R. J. (2000). Content-based book recommending using learning for text categorization. In *Proceedings of the ACM International Conference on Digital Libraries* (pp. 195-204).

Nanas, N., & Roeck, A. D. (2008). *Autopoiesis, the Immune System and Adaptive Information Filtering.* Natural Computing.

Nanas, N., Uren, V., Roeck, A. D., & Domingue, J. (2003). Building and Applying a Concept Hierarchy Representation of a User Profile. In *26th Annual International ACM SIGIR Conference on Research and Development in Information Retrieval* (pp. 198-204). ACM Press.

Nanas, N., Uren, V., Roeck, A. D., & Domingue, J. (2004). Multi-Topic Information Filtering with a Single User Profile. *3rd Hellenic Conference on Artificial Intelligence* (pp. 400-409).

Nanas, N., & Vavalis, M. (2008). A Bag or a Window of Words for Information Filtering. In Arnellos, J. D. (Ed.), *Lecture Notes in Artificial Intelligence* (pp. 182–193). Springer.

Nanas, N., Vavalis, M., & Houstis, E. (2009). *Personalised News and Scientific Literature Aggregation.* Information Processing and Management.

Nanas, N., Vavalis, M., & Kellis, L. (2009). Immune Learning in a Dynamic Information Environment. *8th International Conference on Artificial Immune Systems* (pp. 192-205).

Nanas, N., Vavalis, M., Koutsaftikis, J., Kellis, L., & Houstis, E. (2009). Web Observatories: Concepts, State of the Art and Beyond. *4th Mediterranean Conference on Information Systems.*

Nanas, N., Vavalis, M., & Roeck, A. D. (2009). *Words, Antibodies and their Interactions.* Swarm Intelligence.

Observing Standards for Web-Based Learning from the Web. (2004). *Computational Science and Its Applications ICCSA 2004.*

Resnick, P., Iacovou, N., Suchak, M., Bergstrom, P., & Riedl, J. (1994). *GroupLens: an open architecture for collaborative filtering of netnews* (pp. 175–186). ACM.

Rocchio, J. (1971). *Relevance Feedback in Information Retrieval*.

Schafer, B. J., Konstan, J. A., & Riedi, J. (1999). Recommender systems in e-commerce (pp. 158-166).

Shardanand, U., & Maes, P. (1995). Social Information Filtering: Algorithms for Automating Word of Mouth. *Conference on Human Factors in Computing Systems, 1* (pp. 210-217).

ENDNOTES

1   http://www.bibsonomy.org/search/ Web+observatories

2   http://www.amazon.com

3   http://www.netflix.com

4   http://www.lastfm.com

5   See for instance reddit.com and digg.com.

6   Those with a weight over a certain threshold.

7   Negative feedbacks can also be taken into account with a somewhat reverse process.

8   http://www.google.com/ig

9   http://www.netvibes.com

10   Really Simple Syndication (RSS): For more information see http://en.wikipedia.org/wiki/Rss.

11   http://www.bbc.co.uk

12   http://lucene.apache.org

13   http://observatory.cereteth.gr

14   http://www.rip-thessaly.gr

15   Note that some of the widgets are collapsed to fit in a single screenshot.

Chapter 9
Managing Brief Data from Users to Professionals:
Collaborative Trends around Microblogging for Journalism

José Manuel Noguera
UCAM, Spain

ABSTRACT

Microblogging's explosion has provoked changes in the Blogosphere (now bloggers prefer to publish brief content in microblogs), and it has changed some roles in journalism too. Twitter is the most important tool in this phenomenon and it has served to keep connected sources, journalists and audiences. In recent years, media and news agencies are being characterized by an intensive use of microblogs. Journalists start to be collaborate within communities of interests trough microblogging, in particular Twitter. Facts like California fires are a clear example of Twitter coverages, which were started by users and gathered by journalists. This is more than a brief and fast tool for journalism, it is related with making connections with audiences, witnesses and sources of breaking news. In this sense, this chapter will show several examples in order to explain how Twitter is a new way to design collaborative coverages. Hence, it is not just a platform on fashion.

INTRODUCTION

The relation between Twitter and media is not new, in fact, we are talking about a service which "has gone mainstream in a way not anticipated by its founders" (Ruffini, 2008). However, there are not many studies explaining how microblogging could be used by journalists. For maintaining a clear methodology, this chapter will show cases of microblogging which redefine the relations among journalists, sources and audiences. In this way, the regularities among cases are a sort of argumentation by example (Perelman & Olbrechts-Tyteca, 1994). Every collaborative coverage, new trend in storytelling or special connection with audiences is a key that microblogging gives us to redefine cyberjournalism.

The main goal of this chapter is to draw the actual setting between microblogging and journalists, giving at the same time the mechanisms that

DOI: 10.4018/978-1-61520-841-8.ch009

Copyright © 2011, IGI Global. Copying or distributing in print or electronic forms without written permission of IGI Global is prohibited.

come into play in that process in order to obtain general rules to improve cyberjournalism and to explain media ecosystem. Sharing status messages is easier than ever thanks to platforms like Twitter, and the success of this tool has caused that nowadays most of digital communication includes references about how to integrate microblogging services. Cyberjournalism is not out of this process. As Luckie (2008) underlines, "Twitter has quickly become the essential tool in every newsroom's and journalist's arsenal". There are projects like ReportingOn, funded by the Knight News Challenge, with the hope that journalists would use it sharing sources, topics and ideas. ReportingOn didn't work, and the platform was rebuilt in July 2009 "from the ground up, framed around the act of asking and answering questions" (Sholin, 2009). The source code is available under a GNU General Public License and news organizations can use it to create their own backchannels. It is a clear sign of how microblogging is changing some journalistic processes, specially those related to sources, conversations and audiences.

Journalistic microblogging can be considered as a young process and there are some journalistic brief reviews (Luckie, 2008; Strupp, 2009), but there is a lack in solid academic references (Comm, et al., 2009; Java, et al., 2009; O'Reilly & Milstein, 2009) and because of this, the methodologies based on case studies can be a solution to outline microblogging's influences. In this sense, the methodology of this chapter is also to gather all the available information or at least the most relevant, about the case studies, to analyze them and establish their most significant characteristics. The chapter describes eight main cases to show how microblogging is changing journalistic coverages: Earthquake in China, California fires, plane crash lands in Hudson river, trial in Spain against P2P developer, Rick Sánchez and CNN, Ecuadorian newspaper HOY, cases of Telegraph and The Guardian, and live coverages at Homepage with microblogging, like Soitu.es.

In this work we focus on Twitter because it has been the platform chosen by the people in the same way as YouTube was for video or Flickr for images. Services such as Jaiku are considered by some authors (Franco, 2008, p. 161) as more developed than Twitter (due to the possibility to manage channels, for instance), but the social criteria of the Web has moved to give the first competitive advantage to the platform founded by Biz Stone and Evan Williams. In spite of possible technical disadvantages, the point is that the audience is in Twitter, and people (like media) want to have an audience. No matter that there exists other good microblogging services (Jaiku, Identi.ca, Plurk, etc.), the audience has already chosen. Twitter is the *killer-app* for microblogging.

Microblogging is not just a faster mode of communication. Requirements involving terms of time are lower than other platforms like blogs, but they are different in terms of format: 140 characters, shorter URLs, personal but public replies (and private messages), etc., all these elements are drawing a new scene of relations on the Internet. If people blog according to different motivations such as sharing daily experiences and publishing opinions (Nardi, et al., 2007), other authors have found that in microblogs there are four profiles in content published: daily routines, conversations, sharing URLs and publishing news (Java, et al., 2007, p. 2). The common element that connects these four actions can be "the ability to follow people outside your social network and with whom you normally do not come into contact" (Giustini & Wright, 2009, p. 11).

This chapter describes how Twitterverse is changing some relations in the Web and therefore, how digital journalists could improve their routines under these new rules. We don't have studies focused on how this new form of communication affects the field of journalism. However we start to believe that platforms or networks like Twitter are "reshaping journalism as we know it" (O'Connor, 2009) and we have several case studies, but not yet a general overview on journalistic changes due to microblogging. The chapter will try to show this process in terms of communities, conversation, sources or collaborative storytelling.

As the Blogger's co-creator, Dave Winer, underlined "Twitter is blogging. It lowers the barrier to entry to personal publishing […] That's the common denominator" (@davewiner, May 19, 2009). In any case, it is not less true that microblogging is more than a new revolution of personal publishing in the Web. It is a process (microblogging) which cannot be forgotten by media. First, Twitterverse is changing the habits of consumption of information in many people; second, some media rules must be reframed too. As Welch (2009) recalls, "we stumbled into a conversation that seems to just be getting started. We think we'll stick around".

TWITTER AS CREATOR OF COMMUNITIES OF INTERESTS

Journalists are working every day with different communities, and not always communication among them is in the best way. The last decade has had trends towards a sort of journalism more collaborative, and a big number of processes to make new connections between readers and journalists, and between media and readers in general. Tools like Twitter or Facebook, have become in the last years new challenges for media, because they do not just need to adapt their interactions, but even their narratives and news production processes.

A clear example of these changes are the attempts to socialize information through tools like Facebook Connect. Social networks have caused several movements of media towards places on the Web where people freely talk. In a similar way, what Twitter is doing for journalism is to create a new space of interaction. During The Future of Journalism Conference, held at Cardiff University School of Journalism, Media and Cultural Studies (9-10 September 2009), Twitter and Journalism

was a central issue. Alfred Hermida, professor of integrated journalism at the university of British Columbia, presented a paper where emphasized that Twitter could be described like a sort of "ambient journalism, defined as an awareness system that offers diverse means to collect, communicate, share and display news and information" (Hermida, 2009).

In one hand, this "awareness system" is the key to kept in touch with a mix of official and unofficial sources, and in consequence, to collaborate with different communities which, thanks to Twitter, have "a mental model of news and events around them" (Hermida, 2009). In other words, this new space for dissemination of short fragments of information is becoming a new paradigm in the news consumption for citizens on the Web.

In the other hand, if journalists want to be inside this space, they can not forget that in Twitter is about being more personal, accessible and, in last term, it is about building community. This tool could be a very useful resource to maintain media in touch with several communities during the different processes of news making: finding sources, comparing data, designing storytelling, etc. Nevertheless, journalist will not get any of these aims with Twitter users if he or she does not have their trust. And there is no trust without building community.

The community building process can be got thanks to the collaboration in several phases of news gathering. In fact, it is all about the concept of connectivity. The ubiquity of Twitter (the earthquake in China), its huge capacity to connect local communities (the fires in California) or its possibilities to mix sources (the plane crash at Schiphol Airport), are some of the main reasons why journalists should improve their roles to participate in Twitter. If they don't do, audiences (Twitter members) will do it for them, but if journalists do, Twitter will become one of the most powerful tools to build communities among journalists and their audiences. The point is that, when the audience is a cooperator (in so different levels), the final product is better because it is being reviewed by many individuals.

BACKGROUND

Since Twitter was launched in October 2006, it has become the most popular microblogging tool, even among most of social media sites. Therefore, Twitter "forced the social media giants to look over their shoulders and copy it" (Comm, Robbins & Burge, 2009, p. 22). Nowadays, talking about daily activities, seeking advice and sharing information are three main uses which let people obtain multiple benefits. Due to its so simple and easy mechanism, this service is becoming the *next big thing* to get breaking news. Around the easiest question to share the status (*What are you doing?*), users can update their Twitter homepage from the Web, mobile phone, instant messaging or email. Several authors (Java, et al., 2007) have worked on intentions of Twitter users and how they connect with each other and, according to the growth of this platform, these intentions (sharing opinions and news) may be the same reasons why people use Internet.

Following McFedries (2007), the big microblogging's explosion is related with the death of millions of blogs: to maintain microblogs is not as hard as to publish posts weekly or daily in a blog. It involves less effort and more possibilities to distribute messages among friends: via email, SMS, the Web or an RSS feed. Because of this reason, this kind of media are called CCM, "constant-contact media" (2007, p. 84), and also CPP: an instrument for "Continuous Partial Presence" (Mayfield, 2007).

At the same time, "it's that blend of the professional and the personal that makes Twitter such a cool tool on so many levels" (Richardson, 2008, p. 86) and as it happens with every *killer-app* like Twitter, this kind of applications not just supplants its rivals (Jones, 2003, p. 273), it

also makes a clear development of geographical communities. In this sense, several studies of geographical distribution in Twitter users (Java et. al., 2007; Orihuela, 2009b) show a lot of national communities around this platform: Argentina (@tuitiar), Bolivia (@TwittBO), Brazil (@tBrasil), Costa Rica (@CostaRica), Ecuador (@EcuaTwitt), Spain (@twitEspana), Honduras (@TwittHond), Mexico (@TwittMX), Nicaragua (@TwittNic), Portugal (@TwitPortugal), Dominican Republic (@dominicanos), Ukraine (@UAcommunity), Venezuela (TwittVen), etc.

Another way to search Twitter users is to use tools like Twitter Groups (Twittgroups.com) which tracks communities of users according to different criteria, such as: by city, by zip code, by kind of business (photographers, insurance companies, web developers, health, hotels, pets, etc.) or even, by university (Iowa, Michigan, Salford, Warwick, Panamericana, etc.). Common interests seem a much better way to group Twitter users, because possibly geography is not the best feature to describe a tool that breaks barriers.

Twitter has reached a level of maturity makes that the question around this platform (*What are you doing?*) becomes one of the biggest filters on the Web. The main issue in this perspective (important point of view for journalism) is how to filter the Buzz, and for this aim there are a lot of mechanisms similar to the rules used in the Blogosphere. In this sense, Alberto Marques (2009) remembers that we have tools like Twitter Search (search.twitter.com), and also variables of reputation and visibility, like quality and frequency of posting, number of followers, standards for quotation (RT like "ReTweeting") or tagging (words with #), which can be solutions to filter conversations (Buzz).

The sphere related to Twitter is increasingly big. In this sense, several authors have tried to draw a map of the most interesting possibilities. From the perspective of a new Twitter user, the rules and tools can be classified under five sections: start tweeting, find people, explore a bit, learn more and enhance your Twitter (Stefanov & Florea, 2009).

Inside the first point, start tweeting, it can be useful to know some practices like how to cut URLs (with TinyURL, Is.gd or Cort.as) and what the meaning of several characters and abbreviations are: # for tags, RT for Re-Tweet a message, @ for Replies or H/T for "hat tip" (to give credit to another). All these rules are conventions that enhance the language of microblogging. When the Twitter account has its first messages, it is the moment to find people, to get contacts (*Following*). In this sense, the Twitter members also have tools like JustTweetIt (a directory of Twitter users) or Twubble, a place where you can find new contacts according to a good criteria: "it searches your friend graph and picks out people who you may like to follow" (Crazybob.org/twubble, May 27, 2009). As the Home of the service showed in May 2009, the five most *twubbled* persons were the CEO of Twitter, Evan Williams (@ev); the founder of Laughing Squid, Scott Beale (@laughingsquid); the co-founder of Twitter, Biz Stone (@biz); the founder of Weblogs Inc., Jason Calacanis (@JasonCalacanis); the blogger of Silicon Valley, Robert Scoble (@scobleizer).

Finding people related to my profile is one of the most important steps to get a list of useful sources of information. For getting people, Stefanov and Florea (2009) emphasize tools like Mr. Tweet (MrTweet.net), an instrument related to engineering of credibility and reputation on Twitter. This place retrieves the old problem of the importance of the economy of attention in an environment characterized by information overload: *Millions of people on Twitter. Who should I pay attention to?* The first thing every user has to do is to follow the Mr. Tweet account (@MrTweet) and after that, the platform will send a Direct Message (DM) with relevant information according to each profile. In this DM, it appears information related to two criteria: a) Relevant people you might be interested in; b) Some fol-

lowers you are not following. In addition, Mr. Tweet invites you to make recommendations of *great* Twitter users (that makes them more visible to others Mr. Tweet users) and to check the profile and statistics (which shows information on tweets per day, amount of replies and links, and ratio of followers per friends). Moreover, it is worth remembering that Twitter has the basic function of *Find People* so as to get contacts through common labels.

The most popular searcher for the Twitter members is Twitter Search, which has its own grammar to find better information or in a more defined way. This tool includes an advanced search with up to nineteen different operators (hashtag, the exact phrase, from a person, to a person, making reference to a person, since a date, asking a question, containing links, ect.). And of course, another way to look at it is exclusively from labels, an approach that has served to develop other tools which are also very useful and very common in Web 2.0. Monitter.com and Tweetag.com also operate with tags.

The authority is another common approach to classify results on the Web. Twitority.com is an example of this related to the users of Twitter. In this case, the authority is obtained from criteria like amount of followers, and the results can be ordered (like Technorati and other searchers) by three levels of authority and a descending or ascending ordered list. From another perspective of authority, Twitter has also democratizing the influence (McCann, 2008) and routines to get information: "In fact in these days Twitter is starting to replace Google for me. If I want to know something I'll quite often ask my followers before I ask Google" (Rowse, 2008). The media should not neglect this trend, so they could adapt their production routines to the new routines of consumption.

To verify the assertion of Rowse, the author of this chapter asked his followers on Twitter: "Nowadays you ask Twitter or Google?" (@jmnoguera, June 3, 2009, 11.26 AM), and some people responded in just a few minutes as follows: "question would be: Who would you trust? Twitter is faster, but 'the answer lies in the forums' and that is Google!" (@albaladejo, June 3, 11.31 AM); "the selected questions for the community; in polls, I prefer Forms, Google, [Yahoo] Answers [...]" (@daniel3, June 3, 11.35 AM); "First to your followers, and until someone responds to miss one eye to Google, and then you mix all the knowledge acquired [...]" (@gordilloegea, June 3, 11.51 AM), among other responses obtained.

The last example, in the same line as Ruffini (2008) points out, shows us how powerful a well designed collaborative coverage it could be: "when it comes to instantly assembling raw data from several sources that then go into fully baked news stories, nothing beats it". And it is not just a new and fast version of the famous Gillmor's (2004) paradigm (my readers know more than me), it is even a renovated process of storytelling: if in the old and traditional phase for gathering sources this process was private, nowadays not just the contact with sources is public, even it is the first part of the journalist's report.

In any case, it seems clear that Twitter has a strong "learning curve" because "finding people isn't as easy as it should be" (Catone, 2008). In fact, when we ask people in the street *What is Twitter?* most of them don't know what we are talking about (Planas, 2008). Despite that this microblogging platform is one of the most powerful *killer-apps*, it does not mean that is as present in our collective imagination as we think. Thus, in order to get a progressive journalistic approach to tool we recommend: a) Start to use it. *"I have tried to explain to people why I tweet, but the best I can come up with is: Start tweeting yourself & you'll figure it out"* (Welch, 2009); b) Explore many of the lists about the Twitter resources, such as the application databases Twtbase.com and Twitdom.com, the Twitter Fan Wiki (twitter.pbworks.com), the great map of Brian Solis and Jesse Thomas - Jess3 -, "Twitterverse" (Solis, 2009), the marvellous graphic map published by

Percival (2009) or a lot of posts, specially those made by Middlebrook (2007), Smith (2008) and Snell (2008). For each person the best use of Twitter can be different, and this is also its strength.

MICROBLOGGING AS A JOURNALISTIC PARADIGM

As we have seen in the last five years, the Blogosphere as the *big thing* in the Web has finished. Now, this role is for social platforms like Facebook and others, places where people can publish, be in touch with friends, get new contacts, share content or know the latest breaking news in their environment. To sum up, places where multitasking is more a paradigm of movement in new generations than a trouble. Inside this routine of multitasking, publishing *the last* (actions) and knowing *the last* (news) have its own personality through the microblogging. In addition, this new storytelling has moved brief contents in the Web from a digital place (Blogosphere) to another one (Micro-blogosphere).

Blogs were the best tool to publish personal content in Internet since the 2000, nowadays the Web has multiple kinds of sites for self-publishing. Because of this fact, authors choose websites according to the characteristics of each platform, and in this way these platforms improve its digital identity. In this sense, microblogging lets people have a platform not just to disseminate brief messages in less than 140 characters and get breaking news of contacts, it also keeps the Blogosphere as a space for deeper contents (Encinar, 2009).

In this way, microblogs are not killing the Blogosphere, the point is more related with two complementary spaces, each one appropriate for certain tasks. For instance, Twitter seems very appropriate to design the back channel for an event. The 2007 NECC conference "had a vibrant Twitter back channel" (Stevens, 2008), and blogs seem more suitable as a space for reflection and analysis. In any case, this doesn't mean that there aren't tweets much deeper and interesting than a dozen posts in a blog (Gonzalo, 2009).

In terms of journalistic field, the digital media landscape (and the mainstream media landscape too) is recontextualised by the visibility of breaking news in microblogs, storytelling of witnesses and experts in Blogosphere. Both of them have a common element: citizens getting relations, making connections, sharing stories and, at the same time, showing coverages in a lot of cases even deeper than media's coverages. From this perspective, audiences, sources and media are exchanging their roles in Twitter. Besides, only those media with a correct behaviour in this community will be able to reach a useful feedback from microblogging users. For example, a sign of this gradual normalization inside the journalistic field is the inclusion of the concept of "Twitter" in the Associated Press Stylebook (AP, 2009).

However it is not just an issue related to breaking news. It is a matter of interacting with people in a new space of conversation. Twitter "is being used as a first alert mechanism for the dissemination of news and for immediate discussion surrounding that news" (Catone, 2008). Like many authors note that the Web lets gain useful filtered information from the crowds (Surowiecki, 2004), Twitter has become a clear way which helps us to work in this level. Some journalists have gathered new ideas, approaches, issues or perspectives thanks to opening their discussions: "A few weeks ago, for instance, @jack_welch tweeted that two events might be the 'green shoots' of a new bipartisan movement. The thoughtful pushback improved the column we went on to write about the topic" (Welch, 2009). In fact, if we compare blogs with microblogging, some authors found that Twitter is a more "interactive conversation than blogging", and "the unique conversation aspect creates a level of connectivity that is lacking in blogs" (Stevens, 2008, p. 3).

When media find new social spaces (for discussion) on the Web, some of them design ways to put its stories in these spaces. Reuters Labs contain an application called TwitterThis for sharing its news with Twitterers. Quoting the words of these laboratories, we see that "TwitterThis gives people a way to share the Reuters story they're reading with their friends on Twitter" (Labs.reuters.com, retrieved May 2009). Including a link below the headline, every reader can post their story in Twitter, using a technology called DinkyLink to shrink story URLs. Twitter gave its API (application programming interface) to the Reuters Lab people in order to undertake this project.

As Goedegebuure (2009) has argued, Twitter has become a basic tool for journalists to track witnesses and talk with them. The journalist's job is not just tracking, it is also *living* in a new public space, which involves the consequences detailed in this chapter. In addition, when a new platform has changed the complex relationship between media and sources (and audiences), at the same time the traditional bases of journalism are changing in some way. In Twitter, every source is public, and giving them the right credit is an important issue in order to maintain the credibility of journalists and visibility of sources (and new producers). In this respect, some authors point out the value of separating *Retweeting* and the traditional *Via* (O'Reilly & Milstein, 2009). The first option is related more with spreading breaking news the fastest the better and the second one is related with showing the point of view of each author after reading the original note.

With the following examples (coverages by the people and coverages by media), microblogging can show us how collective storytelling is changing journalism as we knew it. Every media has a different context due to its profile, public, goals or contents, and how to use Twitter must be integrated inside the general relations between media and audience. As Jungherr underlines, "there is no right or wrong way to Twitter. The only way to evaluate your efforts in the Twitterverse is to be clear about your purpose before your start" (2009, p. 12). Despite that this author is talking about activism campaigns, this main rule could be a good point to start twittering for media. When you know that microblogging is for something more than updating breaking news and latest headlines, you're closer to know what Twitter is for.

Coverages by the People

The following cases of coverages of citizens by Twitter are useful to understand the new complex relationship between sources and media. Besides, each one can show us several trends around formats, relations and journalistic storytelling. In a general sense and as Jungherr (2009) emphasizes, Twitter helps to spread the word all around the world, to attract the attention (of mainstream media), to coordinate actions, to profit crowd sourcing and even, to monitor partner's activities without being in the same area.

In other words, and as Catone (2008) remembers, Twitter works for news due to four reasons: it is fast in near real-time coverages, it is open (an open API architecture from the beginning) for every kind of free uses by people, it is a two-way platform which encourages feedback and finally, it fills the void of a new news cycle (Ruffini, 2008), shorter and faster than others. In some way, these features can be explained with the following examples.

Earthquake in China

Biz Stone explained some journalistic uses of Twitter with references to its emerging role as a warning in recent earthquakes. In relation to the recent grounds shaking in California, he noted that the first message in Twitter about these tremors "came nine minutes before the first Associated Press alert. So we knew early on that a shared event such as an earthquake would lead people to look at Twitter for news almost without thinking" (O'Connor, 2009). In fact, microblogging has relevant and great responses during disasters (Shklovski, Palen & Sutton, 2008).

The significance of connectivity is specially visible in cases like this. For instance, if Robert Scoble was not in China while the earthquake, how did he report it an hour before CNN? The answer is he was following several people in China at that moment, which were *twittering* "while it was going on" (Scoble, 2008). Scoble also underlines this idea about connections as resource for making news in spite of being thousands of miles away from where the news was happening: "It's amazing the kind of news you can learn by being on Twitter and the connections you can make among people across the world" (2008). When Scoble was pointing at anyone who reported something about the earthquake during the next hours, he was doing a sort of new journalistic product. Filtering and selecting messages are a good method to explain facts.

Siegler (2008) explains in a few words the importance of connectivity and the ubiquity of Twitter in this case: "before MSNBC, before the BBC, even before the United States Geological Survey had the information, Twitter was on it. How? Its users". Besides, the simple connection between users is important in itself, but it may also be important in quantitative terms if Twitter's important nodes (a sort of Tipping Points) are affected: for instance, Robert Scoble posted updates to more than 23,000 people who were following him at that moment (Siegler, 2008).

If skepticism was the dominant signal among journalists about microblogging (like all the social media on the Web in its first steps), it seems that this is changing thanks to events like the China earthquake. As Cellan-Jones (2008) said, "I was beginning to think Twitter was just another fad for people who want to share too much of their rather dull lives. Until this morning". What is changing is that the ubiquity of messages through Twitter allows people to exchange information more easily.

From the exchange of information (decentralized, open and multimedia), social and community coverage are much deeper than most of the media's coverage which are undertaken by each one. As Bradshaw (2008) points out, according to Tweetburner (links most shared on Twitter) the most shared URLs during the earthquake were about China's quake: a Google map of the location, a BBC blog post about Twitter coverage, a Twitter user's tweet in Shangai, the Earthquake Center's site, a CNN report, a picture capturing the earthquake in a office and a summarized search for the word "earthquake".

In this case, "here is crowdsourcing without the editorial management" (Bradshaw, 2008). Paul Bradshaw's article is a great example of the variety of resources and sources that can provide only the organized chaos that proposes a system like Twitter and its entire Twitterverse resources (search by tags, shared links, linked images, RT messages, etc?). As the Web From the Frontline (2008) concluded, "the time for debate [about usefulness of Twitter] is over. If it's speed you want, Twitter delivers". But it is not at all a question of speed, also it is about coordination and depth.

California Fires

California fires in October 2007 were a clear example of how local communities can make better coverages than traditional media through Twitter, getting a deeper information and being more coordinated than traditional media. In this case, as the perfect platform to get word out, Twitter became the personal media of Nate Ritter (@nateritter) to post updates about the fires. Ritter was gathering information from several sources (local television news, local radio reports, videos from the Web) and, as Kevin Poulsen says, that user began to act "as an ad hoc news aggregator" (2007). In addition to other neighbors, updates about fires from Twitter were "more frequently than most mainstream media outlets" (Poulsen, 2007).

Another neighbor, Dan Tentler (@Viss), started to publish breaking news about what he was seeing on the streets. With his camera and cell phone,

Tentler updated his Twitter account via SMS. On the other hand, the site of local news station KPBS was down due to the growth of Web traffic. Then, they decided to broadcast all news through Twitter (@kpbsnews). When the website was fixed, the online editor Leng Calog added a Twitter account and a customized Google Map about fires to their home site (Poulsen, 2007).

Meanwhile, LA Fire Department showed the need to integrate Web 2.0 services into their actions (Jungherr, 2009), Thus, its Twitter account (@LAFD) became relevant to cover rescue procedures (Glaser, 2007). In fact, LA Fire Department was trying to adopt the social media after Hurricane Katrina in August 2005. They explain the success of these tools with four reasons: they are "desirable, beneficial, justifiable and sustainable" (Havenstein, 2007). In order to get a useful number of criteria to keep connected a variety of communities, one of the most interesting reasons could be the geographical one. With Twitter Grader (twitter.grader.com), we get an ordered list by city, region or country, according to more criteria than just the number of followers. In other words, the reach and authority of the Twitter user measuring the number of followers, the power of each network of followers, the updates and few others criteria. These kinds of services are growing because of the freedom enabled by open software and mashup applications. In this way, sites like Twittervision (defined by most of the people as a "Google Maps" for Twitter) and others offer a new and radical data visualization, geo-located.

This real time posting and geo-located updates were really useful for instance in the California fires, when media gave and received data to and from people who were near the fires. While institutions like LA Fire Department were twittering the breaking news, media like LA Times created Twitter accounts just for the fires coverage (@latimesfires). The readers and Twitter users tracked the common tag "sandiegofire" by SMS or IM and received notifications whenever a tweet went out with that tag.

According to some authors, when these disasters happen people who are geographically dispersed see microblogging communities as "reconnecting with others who share their concern for the locale threatened by the hazard" (Shklovski, Palen & Sutton, 2008). At this point and as people seem to comment on the Internet, terms such as mass media or "mainstream" media are not the most appropriate to the phenomena of communication that we are witnessing: "what difference does it make if it's mainstream or not? It's very useful for situations like this, and it's actually helping people. We saw that during the San Diego fires last year as well" (Siegler, 2008).

Twitter also helped a student who was in jail in Egypt. In April 2008, during an anti-government protest, the (journalism) student James Karl Buck and his translator were arrested by the Egyptian police. Before he arrived to the police station, he sent a one-word SMS with his mobile phone: "Arrested" (@jamesbuck, April 10, 2009). From this moment, Karl's contacts in Twitter viewed the message and friends like Hossam el-Hamalawy, a blogger at UC-Berkeley, was writing "regular updates in his own blog to spread the information Buck was sending by Twitter" (Simon, 2008). By this way, several friends and contacts spread Buck's word to become his release an easier matter.

In the same line as the last case, the power of Twitter to keep people in contact and, as a result, get things is one common point. According to Siegler (2008), "news such as the American student who was arrested in Egypt but set free thanks to Twitter, are propelling the service into the spotlight. Whether that in turn it into mainstream usage, we'll see. But [...] does that really matter?" In some cases Twitter is not just part of mainstream, even it is the first step of some journalistic processes.

Plane Crash Lands in Hudson River

The airplane accident in the Hudson river (January 15, 2009) was another sign in this sense. It is normal during disasters that the first source, image or testimony appears on Twiter. The accident had no dead passengers and the pilot, Chesley Sullenberger, was considered a real heroe by the media. One of the most important pictures of this accident was provided by a witness: Janis Krums. He also wrote a message in his Twitter account: "There's a plane in the Hudson. I'm on the ferry going to pick up the people. Crazy". With this text, Krums also offered the picture. As we can see, in this case the communication is not following the traditional steps of journalistic job: the first picture, and perhaps also the first public message, was made public in a platform used just for personal publishing, and not inside mainstream media landscape, as it is considered the usual step.

This fact is highlighted by O'Connor (2009) when he talks in these terms about the first report of the rescue in the Hudson river: "[the report is] the latest evidence –if indeed it was still needed – that emerging social media are not only supplementing but supplanting the legacy mainstream media". It seems a very dramatic perspective on the survival of the media, especially considering that in this case Krums didn't do a thorough coverage of the topic.

The photo posted by Krums reached was viewed by nearly 40,000 users in four hours (O'Connor, 2009) and the image moved through social media faster than through mainstream media. Krums used Twitpic, a service for sharing photos in Twitter, and the image was disseminated by more than two thousand followers which Krums had in that moment. Afterwards, he became the protagonist of the media, granting interviews as a witness to several media such as MSNBC (Frommer, 2009).

Weeks after the Hudson accident, a plane crashed at Schiphol Airport, Amsterdam. At that time several people died and the Twitter role was very active due to the presence of witnesses. According to their Twitter profiles, @nipp and @ansgarjohn were considered as real tipping points in that coverage by media (Poulsen, 2009). In ad-

Figure 1. © 2009, Antonio Delgado Barrera. Used with permission

dition, users published a common tag (#schiphol) in order to organize the collaborative story of the Schiphol tragedy on Twitter. Tagging is a basic element offering visibility to discourses which are not inside mainstream flows, and tags are also elements to provide deeper, faster and interconnected information. In the airport case, people used freely a common tag as a service for audience. As we can see, tagging is often one of the first decisions taken by citizens who start coverage of an event.

Trial Against P2P Developer

In May 2009, many Spanish and international media began to report the trial against a P2P software designer, Pablo Soto, who was demanded by Promusicae (Spanish association of producers of music and audiovisual recordings). The association claimed $18 million for damages based on the assumption that each user of P2P tools created by Soto has downloaded at least one track without paying for it. For three days, Soto was on trial and defended himself with arguments as the following ones: "Technology is always neutral, and you cannot accuse the developer of a program because of the use made of it by its users" (Llewellyn, 2009).

Nevertheless, according to the point of this chapter the most interesting thing during the trial was the free coverage made by users and freelance reporters like Antonio Delgado (@adelgado). Delgado is a consultant and a specialist in digital media, maintains the personal blog about the new media Caspa.tv, and as a freelance he writes for media such as Soitu.es or Consumer.es, however, the most comprehensive coverage of the case was possibly made from his Twitter personal account during those three days at court.

In many situations, the power of all these kinds of coverages by citizens goes around the connection of small communities. Despite that "half of all Twitterers follow and are followed by just 10 people" (Comm, Robbins and Burge, 2009, p. 4), these micro-communities are quickly linked to journalistic sites at the same time as just one of their followers is being followed by a journalist. The main topic isn't about the number (of followers), it is about connection (among communities). In this way, journalists in Twitter create their own groups, which are made by professionals with different kind of sources. Thus, being in touch with one of these communities has a big value in terms of getting breaking news of a specialized field and dissenting views on a topic.

As we have seen, tagging has become a special useful feature of Twitter in all these cases (as if it was a big Web's metaphor). When a term is preceded by the symbol # ("hash"), it becomes a "hashtag" and is searchable for media, journalists and audiences. All these different readers get sources, promote their stories and among other features find context for the news through the hashtags. As O'Reilly and Milstein (2009) underline, managing a group chat in a particular hour, getting ideas and sharing experiences are the three main uses for tagging in microblogging.

As a result of these and other stories, the media have learned that Twitter and microblogging is ever more present in their routines. The management of interactivity, the degree of transparency and how Twitter is admitted to the media in the most natural way possible, are the unresolved issues for journalists.

People Do This, What Media Do With Twitter?

Nowadays, Twitter and microblogging are spaces for journalistic experimentation by media, but they have already showed signs where they are heading to. According to the lecturer of Digital Communication José Luis Orihuela (2009), some of the main uses of these platforms by the media are characterised for some of the following general aims: to promote diffusion, to generate conversation, live coverages and as a tool that let the newsroom as a sort of public process open. In fact, the true opportunity isn't just to generate conversation, but to spread it: "One of Twitter's many charms is that conversation can be carried on from anywhere, whether at work, at home, or while traveling" (Giustini & Wright, 2009, p. 12). This is the main idea around the following cases of coverages.

Jungherr stresses that Twitter is a critical component related to the conversation: "is a conversation tool. Keep it personal. Give your feed a voice. Don't just write when you want something from your followers. Be there for them" (2009, p. 14). From this point, the use of the tool cannot be understood without the original objective of promoting public conversation. Related to spread-

ing breaking news, Twitter also has a strong value for media based on the "secondhand posse" (Gahran, 2008). The point is the fact that follower's followers can drive traffic faster than any other media or platform. In this process, to "retweet" is the main action made by active Twitter users who love to follow media or news agencies and breaking news.

This *secondhand posse* can have a lot of interest for journalists in terms of getting feedback and give new value to their programs. For example, Rick Sanchez and CNN are the pioneers in this type of case.

Rick Sanchez and CNN

Inside the second aim (to promote feedback and get conversation), some journalists have tried to incorporate tools from microblogging in their TV programs. One of the most relevant uses in this sense is the anchor Rick Sanchez on CNN, who incorporated Twitter to his TV show to answer questions and to reply messages sent to his account (@ricksanchezcnn), showing live on television *tweets* from citizens.

According to Luckie (2008), Rick Sanchez is a great example about how journalists can provide new contents to their news and get feedback, because he "engages in conversation with many of his thousands of online followers". This is a good point (to engage in conversation and to give more value to the program, product, news, etc.), because improving digital journalism must be an action that involves not only changing technically possible.

In the first quarter of 2009, Rick Sanchez's account had more than 85.000 followers, a fact that generates the obvious question: How can digital journalists control this level of participation to achieve a journalistic product with complete sense? As Adam Hirsch (2008) points out, CNN is one of the major companies which have both early adapted to Web 2.0, but we still don't have definitive methods to the microblogging's convergence with media as television. In most cases, it is due to the asymmetry between level of participation and resources destined to manage it.

Social networks are increasingly gaining importance and presence in the routines of journalists. Therefore, the Twitter co-founder Biz Stone recalls that a reporter like Rick Sanchez was so involved thanks using the Twitter and Facebook networks. He managed to get a direct response from their audience during his live programs (O'Connor, 2009, p.3). In any case, it is important to see how Sanchez, a big supporter of using this tool as a way to detect new trends and find stories for journalists, has not forgotten that speed and strength of the social networks (like Twitter) must recall journalists that they must be responsible for checking sources and the validity of these stories: "[social media and Twitter] have been pushing us at CNN to drive the story about whether this Iran election was legitimate [...] I have read on Twitter countless reports that it wasn't. [...] not a single one of them have been able to confirm" (Reagan, 2009).

As many journalistic articles have reported (Calderón & Quesada, 2009), Twitter gives us some information about "dark governments", especially in countries such as Iran, Moldova, China or Guatemala. Even in these clear cases, it is important to not forget that social support must be maintained next to journalistic principles (as checking sources and data) to guarantee that there are true stories to back up (Kucera, 2009).

From another point of view, the credibility of the media can come from the degree of transparency that emits through your Twitter account.

Ecuadorian Newspaper HOY

Twitter as a way to open newsroom to readers is another point under discussion. The Ecuadorian newspaper HOY (Hoy.com.ec) could be a significant attempt in this sense. Following its account (@HOYonline), anyone can see which

the internal debates are in this moment. For instance, followers of this profile read on May 4, 2009 the following discussion about work of graphic reporters: "Nevertheless, the graphical chief pushes [graphic reporters] back, says that they are poor and requests them that go out to look again for a better photography" (http://tinyurl.com/HOYmay4).

Several examples of these internal (but public) discussions on HOY are how the editors debate about the Home, how they manage a football coverage or even how they think about the others media. All these cases could be defined as a sort of "information's striptease" (Vargas, 2009). In this Twitter account, newsroom staff has two main objectives. On the one hand, the first aim is to reduce the distance between those who generate information and those who consume it. On the other hand, the second aim is a consequence, to get answers about the question "What do the people want to read?" (Barahona, 2009).

The project is based on The Spokesman Review, a journal from Washington, which opened several blogs to keep connected newsrooms and audience (Ask the Editors), to make opinions a public debate (A Matter of Opinions), or, even, for covering discussions of editors (Daily Briefing). With a similar intention for opening some traditional closed journalistic debates, HOY asked the following question on February 2009: "how to replicate this experience in the newsroom today to make more transparent our journalistic exercise in front of our readers?" (Yépez, 2009).

The response was the Twitter account @ HOYonline, which is used to describe the daily routine in the newsroom. In this way, the editors want to "move towards a transparent newsroom and this is our first step" (Yépez, 2009). Related to the search for topics and news production, "is an almost inexhaustible source of information if you know who to add to your list of contacts" (Barahona, 2009). HOY is not the only media which has decided to use Twitter inside a process of transparency for newsroom. WORLD have your say, *the daily interactive show where you set the agenda*, has a Twitter feed (@BBC_WHYS) which "has the potential to further erode the gatekeeping model" (Bennett, 2009b).

On the other hand, a more advanced degree to use Twitter in the media may be to integrate it even as a permanent item on the agenda setting, something that has already happened in some newspapers.

Twitter's Metonymy in Telegraph and The Guardian

Only a few times one tool has become an *issue* for a digital newspaper. The digital English newspaper Telegraph.co.uk is one of the best examples in this sense, due to the big attention which focuses on Twitter through the Technology spaces, even as an independent section. Inside of "Science and Technology", and after "Technology", Telegraph has a deeper level of navigation in its Web site: "Twitter".

In this space, journalists are gathering news from all over the world: Oprah's followers, McCain's daughter in Twitter rant, a magistrate resigns over Twitter, etc. It's all about the same tag, platform or service. It's all about microblogging with Twitter. Close to this kind of news, Telegraph also includes services like Twitter Counter, Twitter Searcher or information about a Twitter Event (Twestival).

In a similar sense, The Guardian includes a Twitter section inside Technology. Introduction to Twitter, most recent and latest comments, related subjects and more blogs are some of the parts which can be found in this section. On the other hand, the coverage in The Guardian Web site about this tool, which is as deep as in the Telegraph's case, has replaced the part for the whole: Twitter has replaced microblogging and is a kind of metaphor of it, a sort of metonymy (the part - Twitter - for the whole - microblogging -).

These two media are clear signs of a journalistic process which could be placed in the first level of

Agenda Setting theory: Twitter becomes important (and *real*) for common people because it is kind of overexposed in media (McCombs, 2004). For example, from that moment (having knowledge of Twitter as a people's tool and not just for digital natives), it is more likely the emergence of some newspaper headlines using "Twitter" instead of more generic and vague terms such as "social networking" or "Web".

In other words, if someone gets to know more about an issue, it increases their curiosity about it. In the case of the media, this knowledge about the possibilities of Twitter is imperative if we want to improve its use as an information channel or interact with the audience. In early 2009, the newspaper The Guardian asked his followers on Twitter the reason to use this tool. The journalist Jemima Kiss (2009) collected the answers under the label "#twestion". The initiative received hundreds of responses, and some of them were especially relevant, as the following one: "@BellaGrrl: It's a fast, fun and focussed way to share information. Plus it saves those around me from hearing what's in my head" (Kiss, 2009).

Somehow in Twitter we find another channel of information that redefines privacy on the Web by making the intimate (at least part of the intimacy that we selected) public and connecting it quickly with those who want to follow us. Besides, monitoring sources of interest ("focussed") is maximum when applying the least effort. Finally, as the last comment recalls us, it can provide as much fun as appeal and benefit.

All experiments above do not apply a lot, and by the moment, the most common use is the simple integration of Twitter into Homepage by media (with embed codes).

Live Coverages at Home

Under the clear influence of microblogging and its storytelling, the journalists Pablo Mancini and Darío Gallo launched a brief project, 20Palabras. com, which published contents just during four

Figure 2. © 2009, Micromedios Digitales S.L.(Soitu.es). Used with permission

months. From this site, both authors with several correspondents overseas tried to explain the news in just twenty words. From an unenthusiastic perspective, this kind of projects could be defined by the following idea: *Writing with 20 words is not a new concept in journalism. Tweets are "Headlines"*. However, in spite of leaving doubts, another point of view suggests that sites like 20Palabras show the potential of this form of communication and a clear influence of microblogging.

However and as we have seen with the last examples, cybermedia don't have a clear model to integrate microblogging in its services. At least what they already have is the mixture of tagging and embedding codes for publishing, as the Spanish website Soitu.es did on April 2009, while it was covering G20 in the last London Summit.

We have talked about communities in touch due to fires or accidents, but we could provide a lot of cases of cultural, economic or political issues. Obama's investiture showed a few new uses of microblogging in media as well. The Spanish, journalistic Web Soitu.es (which obtained the Journalism Web Award in Excellence of Online News Association (ONA) for small journalistic sites) also changed its Home and applied a widget with Twitter users talking about Obama. During several hours, the messages from Twitter users as

well as from journalists, were in one of the most relevant places in the screen.

Indeed, it is not surprising because Twitter was the most popular tool for the media during the coverage of the summit of the G20, as Bennett (2009) points out. In several ways, a lot of media used this tool to improve its way to tell the story: The newspaper Financial Times opened a Twitter account dedicated to the summit (@g20ft), The Guardian used a page to embed all the tweets of their reporters, and other media like The Times or Sky News covered the summit using the tool CoverItLive, which is very close to the Twitter characteristics adding some advantages, such as multimedia resources or the option to manage the audience participation (Bennett, 2009).

Tagging and embed codes are Twitter rules learned quickly by the media, but these rules are just technical and not conceptual. Future research directions should go on other aspects that will help improve the quality of the collaborative coverages in a new environment like the Web.

FUTURE RESEARCH DIRECTIONS

As shown in the last cases and ideas, we have seen several fields of research in the future about relations between microblogging and media. In this sense, we must separate the following main lines: effects in journalistic coverages, the effects in narratives and the effects in relations between audiences and newsroom.

Cyberjournalism has a new work field with Twitter. No matter what will happen with this tool, microblogging will stay. For this reason, storytelling, tracking and tagging in these platforms could be considered as emerging capacities for journalists and aims in media research and high education. From this point of view, this tool can provide a sort of collaborative stories which can give to journalists the opportunity of making deeper news. As Hatcher (2009) emphasized, Twitter can help journalism to find a second level in news coverage which *die* just few minutes after they are published in paper. This author explained how his students reported about a finished story in disabled-parking spots at university properties, and how they got new data from an old story turning it even into a new public service: data about parking spot.

Actually, the point is: why journalists are using Twitter to get a deeper coverage? As Catone (2008) points out, "for reporters that aren't afraid to get down and dirty, Twitter is a golden opportunity to build a rapport with readers and gauge public opinion. It also makes readers feel more connected to the news". When some journalists do it, how do they get it? Future research should answer this issue among others questions. In fact, it would be very useful locating the *tipping points* related to the microblogging's explosion in media. In this sense, and as Strupp (2009) points out, "when did Twitter become a major factor for newspapers?" This author explains three cases which could be examples: when The New York Times' main Twitter account reached more than 880.000 followers, when Los Angeles Times implemented its 144th account and when some media (The Wall Street Journal and The Washington Post) "were forced to issue new staff guidelines for this social media in a span of two days" (2009).

At the same time, this kind of journalistic coverage can also present some disadvantages due to its speed and possible collective nature without filters. For instance, Hatcher (2009) carried out an experiment with students where he explains how some students published offensive terms which would not be accepted by a Chief in a newsroom. Therefore, these processes still have challenges in terms of filter and control of quality of the information. In the same sense, this process was explained by Catone (2008): "Sometimes, it's *too* fast. Twitter happens in moments […] for the mainstream audience, Twitter might need better filtering tools before people can really wrap their heads around it".

In addition, the twitter-style for journalists presents challenges in narratives. At this point, the only consensus may be the intention for assuming a more conversational style. Another clear idea is to recover the old journalistic axiom of writing only an idea in each paragraph. As Mauricio Jaramillo (Franco, 2008, p. 155) points out, "the limitation of characters of the format forces to that the storytelling is so demanding as the first phrase of the Lead". If, however, on the one hand, Twitter has a limitation of characters, on the other hand, a clear effect of microblogging is the possibility of pushing your messages all around the Web.

This possibility must be accompanied by the obligation of journalists to learn how to optimize the language of Twitter. It would be a great mistake to think that this only implies to be brief. As some authors suggest, from a journalistic point of view, the microblogging is primarily a narrative opportunity, because writing in 140 characters involves for instance "not to inflate sentences to dismiss the false academicism of superfluous adjectives and adverbs" (Gallo, 2009).

Social networks like Facebook or all kinds of blogs can be places where to put the feed of microblogging accounts. In relation to this point, Jungherr has a good recommendation: "Spend a little time on this by figuring out if and how you want to link your Twitter feed to others parts of your Web presence" (2009, p. 13). Narratives and presence are fragmented in the Web, and now this process can't be understood without these actions which define our digital identity. In this sense, these tools are explaining the media identity too. In relation to social networks and considering that Twitter has been called many times in this way, the words of Biz Stone should be remembered in this sense: "Twitter is social media, but NOT a social network" (O'Connor, 2009).

According to these new flows, many tools that have appeared on the Web can be useful for the journalists not just to manage identity but also to track buzz, to get sources, witnesses and breaking news. Sites like BreakingTweets.com have underlined the importance of new narratives that microblogging proposes. As the Web site shows, the "world news twitter-style" can help to change global into local, due to conversation, interaction and increasing dialogue. The point of this project is to show how people are reacting in a local area and how this phenomenon can become a global event. In this case, style of microblogging shows as a perfect way to achieve reactions and to develop a sort of *narrative of reactions*.

The next step would be to use the microblogging platform for publishing original content and not just as a simple way to import headlines from journalistic website, something that it is still the typical use in cybermedia. Taking into account this idea, the consultant of the Ecuadorian newspaper *HOY* Christian Spinosa says that "instead of doing copy and paste of breaking news for publishing via Twitter, we bring into play microblogging as tool for Journalism 2.0" (Franco, 2008, p. 159).

Next, we have the challenges and changes between audiences and the newsroom. The lack of credibility of media is a central issue in this point. When Rory O'Connor asked Biz Stone about the role of social media to solve journalism's trust problem, Stone answered with terms related to *new tools* and *crowd sources*: "We can certainly begin to get very sophisticated on credibility with new tools, and combine that with journalists

leveraging open systems such as ours to find and vet crowd sources, story leads [...]" (O'Connor, 2009). When sources and media get credibility, conversations can be maintained by them. Nobody wants to talk with someone who does not have trust. Credibility algorithms, better filtering and what role plays social media in these issues will be central points in future research of journalism.

In a similar way like "microblogging can extend our possibilities" in "all learning processes" (Ebner & Schiefner, 2008, p. 159) and to improve educational environments (Ling, 2004; Ebner & Schiefner, 2008; Wheeler, 2009), journalistic community can amplify its relations with audiences. This fact modifies some of journalism's basis. Everything is not about getting more followers or replies. We have to find general rules to transform all these new data in knowledge, and to make full sense of the journalistic job in the Web. If we are able to manage in a right way the Twitter presence, media can improve their breaking news processes (Gahran, 2008).

The point of Twitter is also related with the concept of cyberspace presence. Microblogs, as other sites like Tumblr do, allow a faster distribution of different layers of our presence on the Web. Through the fact of being interconnected, Twitter is a way to get an goal: "being *out there* (wherever *there* is) as much as possible" and "the dream is to achieve a sort of virtual omnipresence" (McFedries, 2007, p. 84). Under this point of view, microblogging is changing some rules of the digital behaviour, drawing new maps on information flows. Twitter has burst onto the Web for winning the war of attention to other social networks (Altoft, 2009). It will not be surprising if soon, for example, the mechanisms of popularity of Web sites (until now dominated by Google with the "democratic tyranny" of the PageRank) are modified by other social criteria of popularity which comes from microblogging. In fact, there are services that are moving in this direction, such as Retweetist.com ("Discovering trends, popular topics and popular people by tracking Retweets across Twitter") and DailyRT.com ("The most popular tweets on the web").

Twitter is not just a fast way for getting breaking news to media, it also lets to track trends in communities, as Biz Stone recalled in an interview: "[Twitter] it's a place where you can zoom in and out on trends and emergent topics; when you think of the entire ecosystem as an organism, that's when it begins to get really interesting" (O'Connor, 2009). From this point of view, micro-communities hyperconnected (half of all Twitter users have a small number of followers) are drawing micro trends which are the signs of groups that are causing big changes in our lives (Penn and Zalesne, 2007).

In this sense, if one of the big paradigms in journalism is to show trends, to be an active actor inside these communities is a worthy journalistic opportunity. In a different level, in a place as fast and instant as Twitter, where are the places for real and organized discussions?

CONCLUSION

As we have seen through several cases, microblogging allows sources to have a bigger life into its new role as public publishers. This fact forces the media to study a new way to make coverages: Should we consider sources in a traditional way when they are not "waiting" for media's call? It is an open question, and nowadays a temporary answer is the *embed* content.

Inside mainstream field, Twitter had several metamorphosis: from tool to *issue* (and due to this fact media have *sections*), and from publication to *space* (media have correspondents *at* Twitter). Despite microblogging and Twitter, these sources still aren't a resource in order to develop a working journalist, but they are public information that puts the media at the same level as their audience and where the point is to succeed through connectivity. From this moment on, it starts a sort of collaborative coverage.

Twitter shows a new space of conversation where journalists should be. This scenario presents an unprecedented agility to deliver multimedia resources on any story from millions of users from Twitter. If one of the obligations of a journalist is to follow the signals of a story, at first place the journalists must ascertain that there are tools to monitor that conversation (Twitterverse) to fulfill the requirement. Then, the second condition will involve being in the conversation.

We cannot point out what "useful" connections are (and it will depends on each case), but it is clear with the examples given that the power of Twitter lies in the connectivity more that in the mere publication. In other words, having many followers can be good if I want to expand my message, but from the standpoint of a journalist or media, connections with those who I follow (Following) are those that give us access to more stories, more sources and further discussions.

In that point we found one of the biggest mistakes of the media with Twitter: they want to accumulate the greatest number of followers to multiply their messages, but they are not better concerned with following multiple voices, they are not so concerned to hear. A good paradigm for this situation could be The New York Times on Twitter (@nytimes), with more than one million people as followers, while the newspaper is following just 160 people (June 15, 2009).

Speed can not sacrifice the credibility of sources. Twitter is a very big risk in this sense (Iran). Some messages are posted on Twitter hours before they appear in news agencies, and some people may not be in the first scene (Scoble), but they become useful sources for media and audience. Sources are delocalized in Twitter. It is a sort of crowdsourcing without editorial management which is becoming a new journalistic product itself.

On the other hand, geo-located updates are very useful when citizens act like news aggregators, tracking and filtering data or opinions on Twitter. These kind of coverages in some cases are deeper than traditional media (California fires). When citizens are like freelancers, the more important point is on connectivity. Trough this element, journalists can provide their products new content and value thanks to the feedback (Rick Sanchez and CNN). However it appears a problem when there is asymmetry between the level of participation and resources destined to manage it.

Microblogging not just can open newsrooms, it helps to make a more transparent journalism. At the same time, this means doing *more journalism* too. At least, the kind of journalism we need at the Web: open, interconnected, multimedia, faster and conversational.

REFERENCES

Altoft, P. (2009). *Twitter vs Digg for links and attention*. Retrieved March 25, 2009, from http://www.blogstorm.co.uk

Associated Press. (2009). *New edition of AP Stylebook adds entries and helpful features*. Retrieved June 11, 2009, from http://www.ap.org

Barahona, P. (2009). *Diario Hoy usa Twitter para acercarse a sus lectores*. Retrieved February 10, 2009, from http://palulo.ec

Bennett, D. (2009). *#G20 - Twitter dominates mainstream media coverage*. Retrieved April 1, 2009, from http://frontlineclub.com

Bennett, D. (2009b). *BBC's World have Your Say tweet editorial meeting*. Retrieved May 26, 2009, from http://mediatingconflict.blogspot.com

Bradshaw, P. (2008). *The Chinese earthquake and Twitter – crowdsourcing without managers*. Retrieved May 12, 2008, from http://onlinejournalismblog.com

Calderón, V., & Quesada, J. D. (2009). *El poder de las redes sociales*. Retrieved June 21, 2009, from http://www.elpais.com

Catone, J. (2008). *The Rise of Twitter as a Platform for Serious Discourse*. Retrieved January 30, 2008, from http://www.readwriteweb.com

Cellan-Jones, R. (2008). *Twitter and the China earthquake*. Retrieved May 12, 2008, from http://www.bbc.co.uk

Comm, J., Robbins, A., & Burge, K. (2009). *Twitter Power: How to Dominate Your Market One Tweet at a Time*. John Wiley and Sons Ltd.

Ebner, M., & Schiefner, M. (2008). Microblogging – more than fun? In I. Arnedillo, & P. Isaías (Eds.), *Proceedings of IADIS Mobile Learning Conference 2008* (pp. 155-159). Algarve, Portugal: International Association for Development of the Information Society

Encinar, J. (2009). El microblogging cambia el ecosistema de todos los blogs. Retrieved February 6, 2009, from http://www.jesusencinar.com

Franco, G. (2008). *Cómo Escribir para la Web. University of Texas*. Austin: Knight Center for Journalism in the Americas.

From the Frontline. (2008). *Twitter's quicker debate over*. Retrieved May 12, 2008, from http://www.fromthefrontline.co.uk

Frommer, D. (2009). *U.S. Airways Crash Rescue Picture: Citizen Journalism, Twitter At Work*. Retrieved January 15, 2009, from http://www.businessinsider.com

Gahran, A. (2008). *Secondhand Twitter Posse: How big is Yours, and Why Should You Care?* Retrieved July 2, 2008, from http://www.poynter.org

Gallo, D. (2009). *Por qué Twitter mejora la escritura de los nuevos periodistas*. Retrieved May 25, 2009, from http://www.blocdeperiodista.com

Gillmor, D. (2004). *We the Media. Grassroots Journalism by the People, for the People*. Sebastopol: O'Reilly.

Giustini, D. & Wright, M.D. (2009). Twitter: an introduction to microblogging for health librarians. *JCHLA - JABSC* (30), 11-17

Glaser, M. (2007). *California Wildfire Coverage by Local Media, Blogs, Twitter, Maps and More*. Retrieved October 25, 2007, from http://www.pbs.org/mediashift

Goedegebuure, D. (2009). *Twitter Rolodex for Journalists*. Retrieved March 10, 2009, from http://www.thenextcorner.net

Gonzalo, M. (2009). *Twitter no mata a ninguna blogosfera*. Retrieved June 9, 2009, from http://www.marilink.net

Hatcher, J. (2009). *Students Use Twitter to Report on Disabled-Parking Spots*. Retrieved March 10, from http://www.poynter.org

Havenstein, H. (2007). *LA Fire Department all 'a Twitter' over Web 2.0*. Retrieved August 3, 2007, from http://www.pcworld.com

Hermida, A. (2009). *Talking about Twitter as a system of journalism*. Retrieved September 9, 2009, from http://reportr.net

Hirsch, A. (2008). *CNN Heavily Promoting Twitter On Air, Making Big Moves in Social Media*. Retrieved September 4, 2008, from http://mashable.com

Java, A., Song, X., Finin, T., & Tseng, B. (2007). Why We Twitter: Understanding Microblogging Usage and Communities. In *Proceedings of the Joint 9th WEBKDD & 1st SNA-KDD Workshop*, August 12, 2007. Baltimore County: University of Maryland

Jones, S. (2003). *Encyclopedia of new media: an essential reference to communication and technology*. SAGE.

Jungherr, A. (2009). *The digiactive guide to Twitter for activism*. Retrieved April 30, 2009, from http://www.digiactive.org

Kiss, J. (2009). *What do you use Twitter for?* Retrieved February 23, 2009, from http://www.guardian.co.uk

Kucera, J. (2009). *What if Twitter is leading us all astray in Iran?* Retrieved June 15, 2009, from http://trueslant.com

Ling, R. (2004). *The Mobile Connection: The cell phone's impact on society*. San Francisco: Morgan Kaufmann.

Llewellyn, H. (2009). Spanish P2P Trial Begins. Retrieved May 21, 2009, from http://www.billboard.biz

Luckie, M. (2008). *Twitter for journalists: What you need to know*. Retrieved February 25, 2008, from http://www.10000words.net

Marques, A. (2009). Blogs, twitter e suas remediaçoes. *Journalismo & Internet. Grupo de Pesquisa Em Jornalismo On Line*. Retrieved March 23, 2009, from http://gjol.blogspot.com

Mayfield, R. (2007). *Twitter Tips the Tuna*. Retrieved March 10, 2007, from http://ross.typepad.com

McCann, U. (2008). When did we start trusting strangers? How the Internet turned us all into influencers. Retrieved December 1, 2008, from http://www.universalmccann.com

McCombs, M. (2004). *Setting the Agenda: The Mass Media and Public Opinion*. Cambridge, UK: Polity Press.

McFedries, P. (2007). Technically Speaking: All A-Twitter. *IEEE Spectrum Magazine*, 84

Middlebrook, C. (2007). *The Big Juicy Twitter Guide*. Retrieved November 2, 2007, from http://www.caroline-middlebrook.com

Nardi, B. A., Schiano, D. J., Gumbrecht, M., & Swartz, L. (2007). Why we blog. *Communications of the ACM, 47*(12), 41–46. doi:10.1145/1035134.1035163

O'Connor, R. (2009). Facebook and Twitter Are Reshaping Journalism as We Know It. Retrieved January 20, 2009, from http://www.alternet.org

O'Reilly, T. & Milstein, Sarah (2009). *The Twitter Book*. Cambridge, MA: O'Reilly Media

Orihuela, J. L. (2009). *Medios que entienden Twitter*. Retrieved April 29, 2009, from http://www.abc.es/blogs/jose-luis-orihuela

Orihuela, J. L. (2009b). *Comunidades nacionales de usuarios de Twitter*. Retrieved March 24, 2009, from http://www.ecuaderno.com

Penn, M., & Zalesne, E. (2007). *Microtrends*. London: Penguin Books.

Percival, S. (2009). *The Story (so far) of Twitter*. Retrieved June 21, 2009, from http://www.manolith.com

Perelman, Ch., & Olbrechts-Tyteca, L. (1994). *Tratado de la Argumentación. La nueva retórica*. Madrid: Gredos.

Planas, J. (2008). *¿Qué es Twitter?* Retrieved May 26, 2008, from http://joanplanas.com

Poulsen, E. (2009). *Twitter Helps Tell the Store of Amsterdam Plane Crash*. Retrieved February 26, 2009, from http://www.poynter.org

Poulsen, K. (2007). *Firsthand Reports from California Wildfires Pour Through Twitter*. October, 23, 2007, from http://www.wired.com

Reagan, G. (2009). *Ann Curry Defends Foreign Correspondents, Twitter; Rick Sanchez Defends CNN*. Retrieved June 16, 2009, from http://www.observer.com

Richardson, W. (2008). *Blogs, Wikis, Podcasts, and Other Powerful Web Tools for Classrooms*. Corwin Press.

Rowse, D. (2008). 5 ways I benefit from Twitter. Retrieved December 4, 2008, from http://www.twitip.com

Ruffini, P. (2008). *The Year of Twitter*. Retrieved January 29, 2008, from http://www.patrickruffini.com

Scoble, R. (2008). *Twittering the earthquake in China*. Retrieved May 12, 2008, from http://scobleizer.com

Shklovski, I., Palen, L., & Sutton, J. (2008). Finding community through information and communication technology in disaster response. In *Proceedings of the ACM 2008 conference on Computer supported cooperative work* (pp. 127-136). New York: Association for Computing Machinery

Sholin, R. (2009). *Welcome to ReportingOn 2.0*. Retrieved July 2, 2009, from http://blog.reportingon.com

Siegler, M. G. (2008). *Twitter is the first on the scene for a major earthquake – but who cares about that, is it mainstream yet?* Retrieved May 12, 2008, from http://digital.venturebeat.com

Simon, M. (2008). *Student "Twitter" his way out of Egyptian jail*. Retrieved April 25, 2008, from http://www.cnn.com

Smith, S. (2008). *Ultimate guide to Twitter tools and resources for journalists*. Retrieved January 18, 2008, from http://www.newmediabytes.com

Snell, S. (2008). *101 Twitter Resources*. Retrieved May 12, 2008, from http://traffikd.com

Solis, B., & Thomas, J. (2009). *Twitterverse*. Retrieved May 27, 2009, from http://www.flickr.com/photos/briansolis

Stefanov, G., & Florea, R. (2009). *Twittermap 2.0*. Retrieved January 28, 2009, from http://gramo.ro

Stevens, V. (2008). Trial by Twitter: The Rise and Slide of the Year's Most Viral Microblogging Platform. *TESL-EJ, 12*(1)

Strupp, J. (2009). *Tweets Smell of Excess? How Newsrooms Adapt to Twitter*. Retrieved June 22, 2009, from http://www.editorandpublisher.com

Surowiecki, J. (2004). *The Wisdow of Crowds*. New York: Random House.

Vargas, E. (2009). *El periodismo digital crea empleo*. Retrieved June 15, 2009, from http://www.tintadigital.org

Welch, J., & Welch, S. (2009). *Why we tweet*. Retrieved June 2, 2009, from http://www.businessweek.com

Wheeler, S. (2009). *Connected Minds, Emerging Cultures: Cybercultures in Online Learning*. IAP.

Yépez, S. (2009). *Rumbo a un diario HOY transparente con los lectores*. Retrieved February 13, 2009, from http://www.hoy.com.ec

ADDITIONAL READING

Angus, G. (2008). *Will Twitter replace RSS?* Retrieved December 11, 2008, from http://www.twitip.com

Arrington, M. (2008). *Bloggers Lose The Plot Over Twitter Search*. Retrieved December 27, 2008, from http://www.techcrunch.com

Bailey, J. (2008). *Copyright and Twitter*. Retrieved May 5, 2008, from http://www.blogherald.com

Baker, S. (2008). Why Twitter matters. *Business Week*, (May): 15.

Basu, D. (2008). *Top 20 Twitter Posts of 2008*. Retrieved December 30, 2008, from http://www.searchenginejournal.com

Brogan, C. (2008). *How I Use Twitter At Volume*. Retrieved November 11, 2008, from http://www.chrisbrogan.com

Brown, T. (2007). *This is why, this is why, this is why I Tweet*. Retrieved May 3, 2007, from http://tiffanybbrown.com

Busari, S. (2008). *Tweeting the terror: how social media reacted to Mumbai*. Retrieved November 28, 2008, from http://www.cnn.com

Campbell, I. G. (2009). *All A-Twitter about the Dalai Lama*. Retrieved February 10, 2009, from http://ssrn.com

Carlson, N. (2008). *10 things Twitters users should not do*. Retrieved May 5, 2008, from http://valleywag.gawker.com

Carvin, A. (2007). *Can Twitter Save Lives?* Retrieved March 10, 2007, from http://www.andycarvin.com

Caulfield, B., & Karmali, N. (2008). *Mumbai: Twitter's Moment*. Retrieved November 28, 2008, from http://www.forbes.com

Chitosca, M. (2007). *Emergency 2.0: Twitter helps public services speed up ahead the government en crisis situations*. Retrieved August 9, 2007, from http://www.smartmobs.com

Costa, C. (2008). *Are you twittering this?* Retrieved June 26, 2008, from http://www.pontydysgu.org

Goolsby, R. (2009). Lifting Elephants: Twitter and Blogging in Global Perspective. In H. Lin, J. Salerno & M. Young (Eds.), Social Computing and Behavioral Modeling (pp. 2-7). Springer

Green, K. (2008). *The rise of the miniblog: the founder of Twitter talks about upcoming features*. Retrieved July 9, 2008, from http://www.technologyreview.com

Grohol, J. (2009). *The Psychology of Twitter*. Retrieved February 23, 2009, from http://psychcentral.com

Heil, B., & Piskorski, M. (2009). *New Twitter Research: Men Follow Men and Nobody Tweets.* Retrieved June 1, 2009, from http://blogs.harvardbusiness.org

Horowitz, E. (2008). *Why journalists (and others) should use Twitter.* Retrieved April 9, 2008, from http://blogs.orlandosentinel.com/etan_on_tech

Howlett, D. (2007). *Benazir Bhutto assassinated: Twitter's utility.* Retrieved December 27, 2007, from http://blogs.zdnet.com/Howlett

Huberman, B.A., Romero, D.M. & Wu, F. (2009). Social networks that matter: Twitter under the microscope. *First Monday,* January (14), 1-5

Ingram, M. (2007). *Twitter: waste of time or social tool.* Retrieved December 12, 2007, from http://mathewingram.com

Kanter, B. (2007). *Twitter for Nonprofits: Waste of Time or Potentially Useful?* Retrieved March 12, 2007, from http://beth.typepad.com

Kawasaki, G. (2007). *How Twitter Made My Website Better.* Retrieved October 16, 2007, from http://blog.guykawasaki.com

Kirkpatrick, M. (2008). *How We Use Twitter for Journalism.* Retrieved April 25, 2008, from http://www.readwriteweb.com

Krishnamurthy, B., Gill, P., & Arlitt, M. (2008). A few chirps about Twitter. In *Proceedings of the first workshop on Online social networks* (pp. 19-24). New York: Association for Computing Machinery

Lawley, L. (2007). *Thoughts on Twitter.* Retrieved March 6, 2007, from http://many.corante.com

Levine, A. (2007). *Twitter Life Cycle.* Retrieved February 1, 2007, from http://cogdoghouse.wikispaces.com/TwitterCycle

Luckie, M. (2009). *Beyond Twitterfeed: Innovative uses of Twitter in newsroom.* Retrieved April 6, 2009, from http://www.10000words.net

McGiboney, M. (2009). *Twitter's tweet smell of success.* Retrieved March 18, 2009, from http://blog.nielsen.com

Mesko, B. (2008). *10 reasons why I use Twitter.* Retrieved November 1, 2008, from http://scienceroll.com

Min, A. (2009). *Shut Up and Sit Down: Singapore's Social Movements trough Twitter.* Retrieved May 28, 2009, from http://flowtv.org

Morozov, E. (2009). *Moldova's Twitter revolution is NOT a myth.* Retrieved April 10, 2009, from http://neteffect.foreignpolicy.com

Owyang, J. (2009). *The Future of Twitter: Social CRM.* Retrieved March 22, 2009, from http://www.web-strategist.com

Raven, C. (2008). *Twitter 101: Clarifying the Rules for Newbies.* Retrieved May 3, 2008, from http://shegeeks.net

Rowse, D. (2008). *5 Tips to Grow Your Twitter Presence.* Retrieved May 8, 2008, from http://www.problogger.net

Sandler, D., Mislove, A., Post, A. & Druschel, P. (2005). FeedTree: Sharing Web micronews with peer-to-peer event notification. *IPTPS,* February.

Sandler, D., & Wallach, D. (2009). *Birds of a FETHR: Open, decentralized micropublishing.* Retrieved May 5, 2009, from http://www.usenix.org

Scoble, R. (2007). *Mexico City Earthquake, reported on Twitter first.* Retrieved April 12, 2007, from http://scobleizer.com

Scola, N. (2009). *Progressives Have a Hashtag.* Retrieved January 29, 2009, from http://techpresident.com

Scola, N., & Fine, A. (2008). *Twitter: An Antidote to Election Day Voting Problems?* Retrieved October 6, 2008, from http://techpresident.com

Stone, B. (2006). *Have Your Quake And Twitter It Too.* Retrieved August 3, 2006, from http://blog.twitter.com

Thompson, C. (2007). *Clive Thompson on How Twitter Creates a Social Sixth Sense.* Retrieved June 26, 2007, from http://www.wired.com

Williams, M. (2009). *Governments use Twitter for emergency alerts, traffic notices and more.* Retrieved January 7, 2009, from http://www.govtech.com

Wilson, D. W. (2008). Monitoring technology trends with podcasts, RSS and Twitter. *Library Hi Tech News*, (25): 8–12. doi:10.1108/07419050810950001

Woodley, C. (2008). *13 Odd Ways to Use Twitter.* Retrieved May 9, 2008, from http://socialmedia-trader.com

Zetter, K. (2009). *Weak password brings 'happiness' to Twitter hacker.* Retrieved January 6, 2009, from http://blog.wired.com

KEY TERMS AND DEFINITIONS

Collaborative Journalism: Form of journalism to find, produce and review information with the audience, and a sort of journalism more developed on the Web since the so-called citizen journalist.

Collective Storytelling: Storytelling made by several authors, with different levels of implication (editors, collaborators, experts, etc.), and a deep mix between sources and writers.

Cyberjournalism: Native journalism from the Internet, which takes all the multimedia resources and ways of participation to optimize the narration of the stories.

Killer-App: Application as effective and as used by the people that leaves the rest of the market in a second level of acceptance.

Microblogging: A kind of short blogging using platforms such as Twitter, Jaiku, Plurk, Identi.ca, etc.

Twitter: Microblogging platform that enables the sharing of brief pieces of information up to a maximum of 140 characters.

Twitterverse: Set of extensions and Web applications created by developers to enhance Web user experience related to Twitter. Also the whole community of Twitter users.

Chapter 10
Articulating Tacit Knowledge in Multinational E–Collaboration on New Product Designs

Kenneth David Strang
APPC IM Research, USA & University of Central Queensland, Australia

ABSTRACT

An e-business new product development (NPD) knowledge articulation model is built from the interdisciplinary empirical and theoretical literature. The model is intended to facilitate a case study of a large multinational mobile communications services/products company (with team members in Europe, Asia and Australia). The NPD teams include subject matter experts that function as a community of practice, electronically collaborating in a virtual context. The knowledge created and shared in the NPD teams involve various unknown levels of tacit and explicit ideas, which are difficult to understand or assess. The goal of the research is to build a tacit knowledge articulation framework and measurement construct that can be used to understand how a successful (or unsuccessful) NPD team operates, in terms of knowledge innovation and productivity. Complex issues and controversies in knowledge management are examined to clarify terminology for future research.

INTRODUCTION

In new product development (NPD) for business, individual tacit knowledge must be articulated to be shared with other specialists so as to augment ideas and design new products/services (Chang & Cho, 2008; Kyriakopoulos & deRuyter, 2004; Sherman, Berkowitz, & Sounder, 2005). In the management science literature, the leading inno-vation-focused researchers argue that the ability to capture and leverage tacit knowledge is itself a competitive business advantage and it ensures organizational sustainability (Edvinsson, 1997; Hamel & Prahalad, 1994; Handy, 2001; Nonaka & Teece, 2001; Sveiby, 1997b; Teece, 2001; von Krough, Ichijo, & Takeuchi, 2000; Wiig, 2002). It takes knowledgeable subject matter expects to articulate, collaborate and transform individual tacit innovations into workable products and

DOI: 10.4018/978-1-61520-841-8.ch010

Copyright © 2011, IGI Global. Copying or distributing in print or electronic forms without written permission of IGI Global is prohibited.

services that will match consumer needs in the market (Leonard & Sensiper, 1998).

In e-business, technology can be leveraged to facilitate tacit knowledge articulation and sharing for NPD, allowing insightful people to electronically collaborate (e-collaborate) across geographic boundaries and over different time zones (Backman, Borjesson, & Setterberg, 2007; Ettlie & Elsenbach, 2007; Gordon, Tarafdar, Cook, Maksimoski, & Rogowitz, 2008; Reid & Brentani, 2004; Sawhney, Verona, & Prandelli, 2005). There are many examples of this (yet there is no attempt here to single out any particular one as being better than others). Multinational companies such as Nokia, Xerox, SAP, Apple, Microsoft and IBM are representative e-business case studies (cited in the literature and stock markets) demonstrating the capability to harness tacit knowledge in NPD across geographic and time boundaries to achieve competitive advantage and long-term sustainability (Chang & Cho, 2008; Handy, 2001; von Krough, et al., 2000).

There are two interesting trends associated with tacit knowledge sharing in the e-business economy that reveals its strategic benefit for NPD. The first is the e-collaboration of multiple stakeholders in the supply/value chain (Strang, 2008a), such as suppliers and customers interacting, providing social capital to influence NPD (Gronröos, 1994; Kavali, Tzokas, & Saren, 1999; Nonaka & Teece, 2001; von Krough, et al., 2000). The second is the concept of tacit meta-knowledge being intellectual capital, meaning that knowledge about knowledge (meta-knowledge) can be considered more valuable than the underlying information or product (Boudreau & Ramstad, 1997; Kim & Mauborgne, 1999; Stewart, 2000).

For example, in the financial market, tacit knowledge shared within and between investment analysts, can generate more profit than the explicit value increase from the knowledge about the underlying stocks. We know the exponential power of leveraging tacit knowledge from the global economic crises of 2008 because those that

could leverage the tacit meta-knowledge restructured their investments beforehand (or converted currencies for quick money market gains). In the vacation industry, the tacit knowledge for designing consumer solutions using multifaceted tours and multiple travel routes can be worth more than the combined margins on the separate package components. "The air travel industry has become two different industries: the flying industry, which is marginally profitable at best, and the information-about-flying industry, which makes money hand over fist." (Stewart, 2000, p. 15).

Nevertheless, the tacit knowledge articulation process is not well-documented for e-business NPD (Strang, 2009a). There is a lack of formal theory along with ambiguous terminology for tacit knowledge articulation in the literature (Wilson, 2002). It is argued that if there was a universal approach then there would be a generally accepted body of knowledge. Perhaps there should be more best-practices by discipline, as we find with theology across the various religions, GAAP in accounting, or PMBOK in project management.

The aim of this research is to explore tacit knowledge creation theories, in a unique context of NPD, by an online community of practice from a successful multinational e-business. (Figure 1) presents a simplified systemic model of an e-business NPD process showing the product life cycle of needs gathering through to production. The feedback loop injects new explicit and tacit knowledge into the system. NPD is just one of the many business functions (yet a critical one), that take place in most organizations (Strang, 2009a). A challenge here is to determine how knowledge articulation can take place with subject matter experts designing new products in e-business, using technology to collaborate online (across countries and cultures). The technology is considered less important (in this study), because there are numerous tools available (and emerging) that allow communities of practice to electronically collaborate (e-collaborate) for NPD, asynchronously as well as synchronously (Gordon, et al.,

Figure 1. Simplified systemic model of NPD e-collaboration in e-business

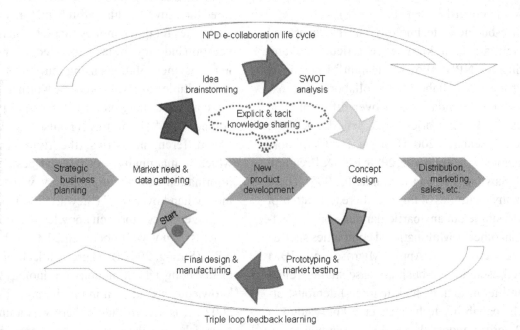

BACKGROUND

2008; Sawhney, et al., 2005). Instead it is the "how" - the underlying knowledge articulation mental-models - that are of interest.

NPD in e-business is not strictly concerned with how to manufacture components or assemble service elements into products (albeit that is often a subsequent design activity). In e-business the focus is on inventing innovative designs using explicit and tacit knowledge from decentralized subject matter experts to create products/services that will match market needs and wants (Strang, 2009a). Eventually ideas need to be transformed into services or products to be sold. Nonetheless, the scope of this research is limited to the knowledge sharing part of the NPD e-business process, as implied by the simple model in (Figure 1). The SWOT process within NPD is an acronym for analyzing strengths-weaknesses-opportunities-threats.

The genesis of many exemplary scientific and business innovations originates from the unspoken tacit knowledge of professional subject matter specialists. When Einstein received the Nobel Price for Physics in 1922 he reflected on tacit knowledge that had sparked his theory of gravitation: "I was sitting in a chair in the patent office at Bern when all of sudden a thought occurred to me: if a person falls freely he will not feel his own weight." (Einstein, A., 1922 Kyoto Address cited from: DeBono, 1967, p. 63).

Knowledge management has always played an important role in evolution and society (Fuller, 2001). Anthropology confirms that our ability to articulate and share tacit knowledge has allowed humans to evolve much quicker than other species. The world has moved through the industrial revolution and technology era, into the knowledge economy (Kim & Mauborgne, 1999). The emphasis in this knowledge economy is on collaborating to transform and combine ideas in better ways, more quickly (Brown & Duguid, 2001; Nonaka & Teece, 2001; Werbach, 2000).

Occasionally insights from the ancient philosophers inspire us for tacit knowledge creation approaches, namely Socrates and his apprentice Plato. In 1653 Aristotle (a student of Plato) offered wisdom for tacit knowledge articulation: "Write down the thoughts of the moment. Those that come unsought for are commonly the most valuable." (Grolier, 2007, p. 2387). Not surprisingly this principle is advocated as a preliminary step in the complex innovation process by contemporary knowledge creation legends (Nonaka & Teece, 2001; von Krough, et al., 2000) and by innovation research specialists (Rogers, 1995; Schön, 1983; Yin, 2003).

Despite the lack of formal theory for tacit knowledge articulation and notwithstanding the ambiguous terminology across disciplines (Wilson, 2002), it seems absurd to ignore the existing literature in favor of gathering evidence at the source by using a (blank-slate) grounded theory, or action learning approach. Consequently, the extant literature will be reviewed to define relevant tacit knowledge facets. These terms can be used to explain the espoused theory of subject matter experts using on-line NPD. The goal is to build a model that can be used to guide and assess tacit knowledge articulation by NPD subject matter experts in a multinational e-business that designs and produces mobile products and services.

In lieu of a standard methodology for tacit knowledge articulation and sharing in NPD, there are many generic theories and models explaining intellectual capital and knowledge management. There may be too much conjecture about knowledge creation (Carrillo, 2001), lacking empirical evidence with industry/discipline specific community of practice guidelines (Heaton & Taylor, 2002). Furthermore, tacit knowledge creation is often referenced differently across the overlapping disciplines. The taxonomies commonly cited include: knowledge management, intellectual capital, corporate memory, organizational learn-

ing, group idea generation, ideation, intangible assets, enterprise brainstorming, creation tension, disruptive innovation, etc. Sometimes tacit refers to a process or just a thought; sometimes it is included within the concept map of knowledge while in other literature it is not. Cross-disciplinary and cross-cultural synonyms can waste research time and camouflage novel publications (Strang, 2009b, 2009c).

Knowledge management terminology appears in most disciplines (management science, educational psychology, health sciences, engineering, project management, etc.), but there are many synonyms and conflicting perceptions (Weick, 2001; Wiig, 2002). Given the work that goes into creating international and national standards, the various standards associations were searched. Currently there is no ISO or national body of knowledge for knowledge creation. Yet there are some very basic guidelines from ISO (Rollo & Clarke, 2001) and there is a framework for knowledge management (Standards Australia, 2008), but nothing appropriate for tacit knowledge articulation in NPD. There are many online community of practices that contain a lot of interesting debate on knowledge management, such as the Knowledge Management Consortium (Wiig, 2003), which is an excellent source to examine the deeper philosophical meaning of the epistemology. There are several peer-reviewed journals that focus on knowledge management, along with research handbooks (Cortada & Woods, 2001) and books (Awad & Ghaziri, 2004; Becerra-Fernandez, Gonzalez, & Sabherwal, 2004; Wenger, McDermott, & Snyder, 2002) – all of which informed this research.

The literature on knowledge management has evolved from defining the terms (Meacham, 1983; Wiig, 2003) to discussing complex knowledge creation/sharing life cycle theories and methodologies (Becerra-Fernandez, et al., 2004). Notwithstanding theories of knowledge originated from the earlier philosophers (Socrates, Plato, Aristotle, Kant, Descartes, Dewey, etc), modern terms include: explicit, tacit, intellectual capital,

Figure 2. Generally-accepted knowledge management paradigms

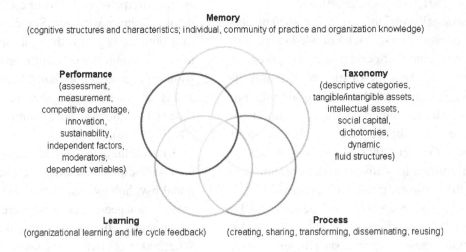

etc. (Nonaka & Teece, 2001). Knowledge has been described as complex enterprise-wide processes (O'Dell, 2000; Samaddar & Kadiyala, 2006), then expanding the individual perceptions on these processes and terms (Cabrera, Collins, & Salgado, 2006; Lesser & Prusak, 2000).

There has been a lot of research on methodologies for capturing/disseminating knowledge (Malone, 2002; Storck & Hill, 2000), followed by constructs like balanced scorecards for assessing/evaluating knowledge creation outcomes (Barchan, 2002; de Jager, 1999; Kaplan & Norton, 1992; Schuppel, Muller-Stewens, & Gomez, 1998; Sveiby, 1998). Consequently, although there is no generally-accepted comprehensive body of knowledge or meta-knowledge about 'knowledge', the widely cited literature is the best starting point. It is impossible to synthesize all publications so the emphasis is on the most relevant for tacit knowledge sharing in e-business NPD. It will make this research more applicable to other researchers and communities of practice by referencing common accessible knowledge management theories and models.

KNOWLEDGE ARTICULATION MODEL

This section begins by defining contemporary knowledge management terms, followed by a synthesis of key concepts related to tacit knowledge sharing in e-business NPD. These terms will later be used to build a model to explain e-business NPD in the case study of a mobile/wireless product/service multinational.

Generally-Accepted Knowledge Definitions

As suggested by (Figure 2), the term 'knowledge' could be described as five main paradigm views. Many domains overlap. Empirical research may encompass all of these or apply some to specific disciplines.

- **Memory**. Individual, team, community of practice or enterprise state of knowing (could be explicit or tacit or not-yet-known, includes learning and reflection at all these levels).

- **Taxonomy**. Descriptive structures with definitions to differentiate (tangible, intangible assets, resources, intellectual/social capital, explicit/tacit, facts, data, information, meta-knowledge, etc.).
- **Process**. Workflow/lifecycle to create or share, procedures to find, transform, manage and share.
- **Learning**. Comprehensive life cycle ideology, theories and feedback for organizational learning.
- **Performance**. Measurement, innovation (independent factors, moderators, dependent variables).

The remainder of this section briefly explains the meaning and relevance of these domains for NPD. Each section integrates and progressively builds on the previous, leading to a proposed measurement model.

Knowledge Memory

This paradigm refers to knowledge as memory stored and retrievable by a human or a group of humans (differentiated from artificial intelligence of computers or databases - possibly a future extension). The source(s) may include combinations of individuals, teams, communities of practice and the organization.

Cognitive psychologists categorize knowledge as declarative or procedural memory (DuBrin, 2004):

- **Declarative knowledge**. Consists of descriptions of facts, things, methods, procedures; all declarative knowledge is explicit, which can be and has been articulated into semantic memory.
- **Procedural knowledge**. Action or behavior descriptions that originate from personal experience and/or explicit knowledge, and is stored as episodic memory (two different views are common):

  - knowledge that manifests itself in the doing of something, and as such is reflected in physcio-motor or manual skills, and/or embedded in cognitive or mental skills;
  - knowledge about how to do something - this view accepts a description of the steps of a task or procedure as procedural knowledge.

In business "memory knowledge" can be held by individuals (Lank, 1997), customers (Prahlad & Ramaswamy, 2000), teams (Takeuchi, 2001), communities of practice (Wenger & Snyder, 2000) and/or organizations through their procedures, strategy or culture (Beckett, 2000; Walsh & Ungson, 1997; Zack, 1999). Memory knowledge may be a state of knowing (to know about) - be familiar with or to be aware of facts, methods, principles, techniques; a capacity for action (know how) - understand facts, methods, principles and techniques sufficient to apply them in the course of making things happen; and/or a body of knowledge (know what) - codified, captured in books, papers, formulas, procedure manuals, computer code, and so on (Nickols, 2001). Memory knowledge in business is typically differentiated from facts as "a conclusion drawn from the data and information" (Stewart, 2000, p. 69).

Several researchers such as Zack (1999, p132) extended the basic memory knowledge definition using the "W5+how" principle to include "causal knowledge (know why)", "conditional knowledge (know when)" and "relational knowledge (know [who])." Others suggest there may be memory knowledge characteristics associated with motivation (Quinn, Andersen, & Finkelstein, 1996; Teigland, 2000) as well as emotion/trust (Goleman, 1998, 2000). Anxiety (along with fear and helplessness) have also been linked with memory knowledge (Schein, 1993, pp. 86-88; Seel, 2001).

Language and national culture have always been critical psychological dimensions associated memory knowledge (Brown, 1998; Hampden-

Turner & Trompenaars, 2000; Holden, 2002; Strang, 2009c; Swierczek, 1994; Trompenaars, 1993). Language is a fundamental determinant of how humans interpret definitions (Brown, 1998); people often use shades of meaning (varying by language and culture) to explore and interpret each other's perception and sense of a phenomenon (Chomsky, 1959; Strang, 2008b, 2009c). This leads to the next critical characteristic of memory knowledge expressed as "tacit" (Polanyi, 1997, p. 136). Explicit memory refers to knowledge that is (or can be) codified while tacit means silent, "more than we can tell [...] such as face recognition from millions of faces" (Polanyi, 1997, p. 136).

There are variations and extensions to the tacit memory knowledge in the literature. Nickols (2001, p. 15) views tacit knowledge as that which cannot be articulated at all and where "the knowing is in the doing." Burton-Jones (1999) describes some kinds of tacit knowledge as "sticky" which is difficult to codify or explain so that it tends to stick to the person with that knowledge and is only transferred with a fair bit of explanation and effort.

Sharmer (2001, p. 70) expressed two additional characteristics of tacit memory knowledge: "embodied tacit knowledge" (knowledge in use) and "self-transcending knowledge" (not yet embodied knowledge). It is possible that these last two characteristics could be described as intuition – a well known phenomenon in e-business NPD (Strang, 2008a). Weick (1995, p. 112) defines tacit knowledge in use as instinct: "wise people know that they do not fully understand what is happening right now because they have never come against that precise situation before, however, they pattern match for similar situations [...] and make their judgments accordingly." Perhaps this is an innate form of knowledge?

Another form of tacit memory is "implicit knowledge" (Nickols, 2001) which is implied by or inferred from observable behavior or performance. Additionally, tacit knowledge can only be shared if the recipient individual or group is "absorptive" (Cohen & Levinthal, 1990) - ready and capable of receiving and understanding. However, certain implicit or tacit knowledge may so complex that it is "not teachable" (Davenport & Prusak, 2000, p. 70) and thus it cannot be retrieved or used other than by the holder.

Despite the difficulty of sharing or teaching tacit knowledge, organizational memory is recognized as a critical form of enterprise knowledge for corporate succession and continuity. Organizational memory includes traditional corporate knowledge, namely strategy, procedures, etc. (Hansen, Nohria, & Tierney, 2001), as well as competitive intelligence capability (Johnson, 2001), and tacit memory. Moorman and Miner (1997) suggest four dimensions of organizational memory: level, dispersion, accessibility, and content. Organizational memory is "[...] a fluid mix of framed experience, values, contextual information, and expert insight that provides a framework for evaluating and incorporating new experiences and information [...] it often becomes embedded not only in documents or repositories but also in organizational routines, processes, practices, and norms" (Davenport & Prusak, 2000, p. 5). Organizational learning often associated with, and is seen as the main source, of organizational memory (Brown, 1998, p. 16).

Communities of practice (Wenger & Snyder, 2000) are valuable sources of organizational memory. These practice communities are "informal, spontaneous, self-organized groups of people who share knowledge, solve common problems and exchange insights and frustrations" (Lesser & Prusak, 2001, p. 253). These groups are bound by informal relationships, share similar work roles and a common context, to produce social capital (memory).

Community of practice is a significant memory knowledge paradigm impacting e-business NPD. NPD teams are communities of practice (Strang, 2009a). They include subject matter specialists from anywhere (across time zones), such as designers, marketers, engineers, and so on. They are able to create and share explicit knowledge, through discussion, dialogue, drawing and/or writing, using online technology. Can NPD teams create and share tacit, implicit, knowledge-in-use, self-transcending knowledge and intuition?

Knowledge Taxonomy

Taxonomies provide an organized framework, a classification of categories and descriptions for explaining knowledge. This can facilitate understanding the content from capturing, valuing, managing and sharing knowledge. Taxonomies expand on the memory definitions because they differentiate between them. The common categories are: tangible/intangible assets, resources, intellectual/social capital, explicit/tacit, facts, data, information, and meta-knowledge. Three knowledge taxonomies are discussed: intellectual capital, action identifiers and knowledge assets. These are integrated into a matrix.

Intellectual capital has been developed as a practice (Edvinsson, 1997; Onge, 1999; Sveiby, 1997a) to classify important business knowledge memory characteristics, namely: human, structural and customer capital. Human capital "embodies the energy, talent, experience, and behavior of people" that can create an organizational culture to deliver products and services that attract customers to an organization, rather than its competitor (Stewart, 2000, p. 91). This refers to the tacit, instinct, intuition, not yet embodied memory/ capabilities, and tacit organizational memory. The human capital ideology argues to keep staff instead of other resources if cost-cutting measures are necessary. For NPD this is important because it suggests to: identify, seek out and retain talented subject matter specialists.

Structural capital is codified organizational memory and resources. It is the means by which people are connected to physical, informational and knowledge infrastructure - in order to deliver services and products that will attract customers to an organization rather than its competitor

(Stewart, 2000). Structural capital includes: databases, patents, intellectual property, organizational intelligence (collective assemblage of all intelligences that contribute towards building a shared vision, renewal process, direction for the organization), and items employees cannot take home (Liebowitz, 1999).

Customer capital is value of loyalty customers share with an organization (Onge, 1999), which enables it to continue delivering products and services that attract customers from competitors (Stewart, 2000). Loyalty can be envisaged as repeat business, co-development of products and services through development of a mutually beneficial relationship, providing feedback to an organization, as well as disseminating positive opinions about an organization to build a good reputation. In support of this, Liebowitz (1999, p. 9) declares "sharing knowledge is power." A variation of intellectual capital is "social capital": "the sum of the actual and potential resources embedded within, available through, and derived from the network of relationships possessed by an individual or social unit" (Nahapiet & Ghoshal, 1998, p. 243). Stewart (2000) insists most intellectual (social) capital does appear on the balanced sheet. In other words, this may be the intrinsic value of stocks as well as the potential within NPD communities of practice. Partnerships (either with clients, suppliers, vendors, or community groups) can be valuable sources of intellectual capital for NPD.

Returning to the discussion of self transcending memory, Scharmer (2001, p. 70) extended the concept into four action-oriented identifiers, suggesting how knowledge memory is categorized in business. The first was an action identifier referred to as delivering results that create value (performing). Next it was improving the process of performing (strategizing), then reframing the assumption of performing (mental modeling). Finally re-conceiving the identity of performing is sculpting. (Table 1) illustrates a conceptual synthesis of the four action identifiers across the

Table 1. Action identifiers across knowledge memory asset types

Action identifiers↓	Knowledge memory asset types		
	Explicit	**Tacit**	**Self transcending**
Performing	Know-what	Knowledge in use	Reflection in action
Strategizing	Know-how	Theory in use	Imagination in action
Mental modeling	Know-why	Metaphysics in use	Inspiration in action
Sculpting	Know-who	Ethics/aesthetics in use	Intuition in action

three memory knowledge types. It is likely that most of the knowledge types and action identifiers would be present in NPD team work.

The four types of knowledge assets are "experiential", "conceptual", "routine", and "systemic" (Nonaka, Toyama, & Konno, 2001, p. 29). These principles borrow upon the earlier memory definitions as well as the intellect capital taxonomy. Experiential knowledge can be human or customer capital and is primarily individual-centered - it requires a supportive environment to encourage individual knowledge sharing and development. Routine knowledge assets are primarily organization centered; they are structural and are often found as organizational memory (they may contain explicit and tacit knowledge). This requires a group or "organizational function" to create or share knowledge. Conceptual knowledge assets are human capital (sometimes customer capital) and organizational memory but tend to be decoded by human interception and are subject to human interpretation (like tacit memory). Systemic assets are structural capital, grounded in the organization, its hardware, software and groupware. NPD concepts and designs are symbolic knowledge associated with an organization's employees and, where applicable, the supply chain. Systemic brand equity in NPD is associated with customer perceived value (customer capital).

A value-added exercise is to integrate memory knowledge types with intellectual capital and knowledge asset theories. A proposed integrated matrix taxonomy is shown in (Table 2), using an

NPD perspective. A matrix such as this can be used in e-business NPD as a planning tool to guide the sharing of knowledge gathering. Starting at the top of the matrix, different team members would individually be responsible for locating explicit knowledge (from peers, organizational records and customers/partners). At the middle level, tacit knowledge is best organized by individuals first articulating ideas using knowledge and theories in use, imagination and inspiration (from peers, organizational memory and clients), then dialoguing these, using nominal brainstorming techniques. Then the bottom level of the matrix becomes useful as a guide, as the team move from mental modeling to sculpting the ideas using reflection, intuition and instinct. Often several alternative NPD designs are ranked by community of practice members (for quality and innovation potential), then by management (for economies of scale, risk and profitability).

Knowledge Process

Processes describe the way knowledge is created, transformed and shared/transferred, while borrowing upon certain memory definitions and taxonomies. As compared with methodologies, processes are separate workflows, tools and techniques in the knowledge life cycle (they are not necessarily integrated in a systematic loop). There are broad views in the literature about the knowledge management processes; the common theme is that the knowledge processes are

Table 2. Integrated intellectual knowledge taxonomy

Knowledge memory types↓	Intellectual capital		
	Human	Structural	Customer
Explicit knowledge (what, why, where, when who + how)	**Experiential** (performing), **conceptual** (organizational memory strategy)	**Routine** (organizational memory processes) & **systemic** (hardware, software)	**Experiential** (performing, surveys) **conceptual** (value & supply chain, imagination, inspires)
Tacit knowledge (knowledge in use, theory in use, meta-physics in use ethics/aesthetics in use)	**Experiential** (strategizing, meta physics in use); **conceptual** (mental modeling)	**Systemic** (conceptual system models), **mental modeling** (meta-knowledge)	**Experiential** (strategizing, ethics / aesthetics in use), **conceptual** (concept maps, value chains)
Self-transcending (intuition in action, reflection in action, imagination in action, inspiration in action, intuition in action)	**Experiential** (sculpting, embedded imagination in action, inspiration in action)	Possibly **systemic** (embedded reflection in action, intuition in action)	**Experiential** (sculpting, embedded imagination in action, inspiration in action)

discussed as systematic tools and techniques: for sourcing/capturing, organizing/transforming/storing/retrieving, and sharing/transferring.

In business, explicit knowledge is most readily captured from organizational records (techniques, performance, data mining), from communities of practice members (project histories), and from customers/suppliers (surveys, feedback). Procedural and declarative knowledge are important to capture because this is the basis for skill development, job descriptions, project management, productivity, quality, and eventually competitive advantage. The sources are often tacit behavior and occasionally they are organizational memory/intelligence (documented strategy, core competencies). Interestingly, the literature reminds us that valuable explicit intellectual capital can be researched from external sources, namely: innovation approaches and best practices (Horvath, 2001). Customers (the third relational component of intellectual capital discussed earlier) are a good source of explicit knowledge (Ulwick, 2002).

This raises another point. The primary incentive for creating knowledge in business is often to increase innovation, productivity and competitive advantage – it is recognized the best organizational resources are tacit knowledge as well as intellectual capital (Davenport & Prusak, 2000; Dixon, 2000; O'Dell & Jackson Grayson, 1998; Prusak & Cohen, 2001). Tacit knowledge (includ-

ing implicit and self-transcending memory) are considered more valuable, albeit more difficult to capture. Usually a specialist is needed (such as an engineer or analyst in a community of practice) to assist in capturing tacit or implicit knowledge (Strang, 2009a).

Tacit knowledge can be captured using a community of practice (von Krough, et al., 2000, p. 83):

- **Direct observation:** through doing so and sharing a dialogue about the observation, observers can also test beliefs about what works, what does not and speculate why that my be so;
- **Imitation:** imitate an action based upon observation;
- **Experimentation and comparison:** trying out various solutions and sharing perceptions;
- **Joint execution:** community members attempting to solve problems under the watchful and helpful support of a more experienced person.

Sharing tacit knowledge follows the general axiom that first it must be articulated (into explicit memory), before it can be communicated or transferred (Kaye, 2001). However, articulation methods go beyond verbalizing, drawing and writing - they may include body language, signals, and even shared perceptions. Storytelling is a method for sharing tacit knowledge, which involves (primarily NPD subject matter specialists) using combinations of personal stories, evidence to support their ideas, along with a visual metaphor (superimposed on an "analysis tree") that shows the structure and relationships among the ideas/phases (Forman, 2001). Storytelling permits the transfer of rich contextual knowledge details (Hansen & Kahnweiler, 1993), while empowering the community of practice members to reframe their own perceptions (not necessarily filtering out or denying cultural norms) thus enabling individuals to grasp new implied tacit knowledge not in their conscious memory (Ambrosini & Bowman, 2001; Sternberg, et al., 2000; Strang, 2009b; Swap, Leonard, Shields, & Abrams, 2001).

Other useful processes for creating and sharing tacit knowledge include sense making whereby specialists reflect on tacit, explicit and self-transcending knowledge, forming or augmenting their mental model (Senge, Kleiner, Roberts, Ross, & Smith, 1999). Additionally practice members are able to use other techniques mentioned above to share that concept. Mental models can sometimes be shared within a community of practice where members have shared experiences (Wenger, 1999).

Dixon (2000) investigated knowledge sharing and transfer using case studies of Bechtel, BP, Buckman Laboratories, Chevron, Ernst & Young, Ford, IT Texas Instruments and the US Army. She identified five types of explicit and tacit knowledge transfer processes (Dixon, 2000, p. 169):

- **Serial transfer:** the knowledge a team has learned from doing its task that can be transferred to the next time that particular team does the task in different setting.
- **Near transfer:** the explicit knowledge a team has gained from doing a frequent and repeated task that the organization would like to replicate in other teams that are doing very similar work.

- **Far transfer:** the tacit knowledge a team has gained from doing a non-routine task that the organization would like to make available to other teams that are doing similar work in another part of the organization.
- **Strategic transfer:** the collective knowledge a team needs to accomplish a strategic task that occurs infrequently but is of critical importance to the whole organization.
- **Expert transfer:** the technical knowledge a team needs that is beyond the scope of its own knowledge but can be found in the special expertise of others in the organization.

Nonaka and colleagues (2001, p. 73) describe a knowledge creating and sharing process that spirals in a four dimensional cycle of "socialization", "externalization", "combination", and "internalization" (SECI), using a community of practice. crucial in fostering creativity. Nonaka describes the community of practice as "ba" (Nonaka & Konno, 1998, p. 133), "Nippongo" in Japanese for shared interpersonal space. The SECI process is briefly enumerated below with NPD examples.

- **Socialization:** tacit to tacit (acquiring someone else's tacit knowledge through observation, imitation and practice); in NPD, knowledge is created and re-created as it is reframed, transformed through multiple perceptions then tested and challenged by all members.
- **Externalization:** tacit to explicit (conversion of acquired tacit knowledge into specifications, albeit there are some doubts this possibility since tacit knowledge has been defined as something that cannot be articulated, thus raising the question of whether such knowledge is the tacit knowledge in its original form); in NPD this is articulation through continual repeated dialogue, text, drawing, writing... and using external

information to add explicit perceptions and meanings.

- **Combination:** explicit to explicit (combining discrete pieces of explicit knowledge to form new explicit knowledge); in NPD, this is closely liked to the previous process step, whereby team members combine ideas and theories in new ways, re-using and/or revising the existing explicit knowledge such as operating procedures, manuals, information bases, product designs, etc.

- **Internalization:** explicit to tacit (the process of internalizing explicit knowledge); in NPD, self- reflection, mental modeling, and reframing are used to "make sense" of the explicit knowledge; (adapted from: Nonaka, et al., 2001).

Tools such as workflow models, diagrams, tables, text and so on, are typically used to codify tacit knowledge. Once knowledge is codified, it can be stored for later retrieval, transformation and even to be improved (these processes are often referred to as knowledge management). Technology facilitates knowledge management, in terms of organizing the memory using taxonomies, providing search engines, and also to manage the version control for changes. Technology is also useful for distribution of this knowledge. In NPD, basic e-business tools include: online discussion forums, learning management systems, email, and e-collaboration software. Additional tools include: digital imaging, voice recording, and conferencing, along with a large number of software programs for survey analysis and product design (Strang, 2008a). In NPD there is a great deal of collaboration (online and directly, depending where the community of practice members are located with respect to one another). This collaboration also takes place with the other business functions such as marketing, management, production, distribution, and finance (Strang, 2009a). If this

concept of SECI, knowledge creation-sharing, and the knowledge memory definitions were combined, the resulting model for NPD in e-business might resemble the abstract in (Figure 3). In that diagram, the word "innate" is used to represent the self-transcending, not-yet-embodied, instinct and non-human memory.

Knowledge Learning

Organizational learning as an organizational process, both intentional and unintentional, enabling the acquisition of, access to, and revision of organizational memory, thereby providing direction to organizational action (Robey, Boudreau, & Rose, 2000). Organizational learning and organizational leadership are two essential ingredients for establishing and sustaining a knowledge management life cycle (Hansen & von Oetinger, 2001). Organizational learning is necessary first to complete the systemic loop, by returning tacit and explicit feedback into the knowledge creation process (for strategy purposes). Secondly, organizational learning is takes place as knowledge is as the community of practice members create and share intellectual capital.

High quality organizational learning is often integrated with the community of practice concept, using dialogue as a process for capturing valuable tacit knowledge into the organizational memory (intellectual capital). Communities of practice (COP) are "groups of people informally bound together by shared expertise and passion for a joint enterprise" (Wenger & Snyder, 2000, p. 139). The literature contains many examples of the relevance of COPs for capturing tacit knowledge in NPD. For example, at Xerox informal (but highly focused) technical specialists solved complex and often perplexing problems by collaborating (Kikawada & Holtshouse, 2001), which was used to improve product designs. This tacit knowledge can be shared as organizational memory through dialogues, storytelling, and other processes, so

Figure 3. Knowledge articulation and e-collaboration in decentralized NPD teams

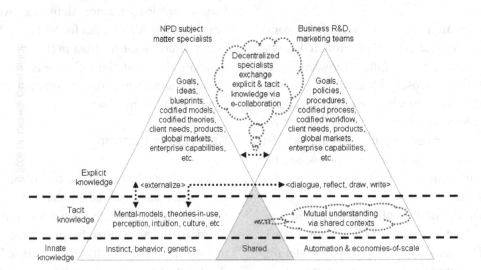

the organizational is able to "learn" (Brown & Duguid, 1991; Davenport & Prusak, 2000; Lesser & Prusak, 2001).

Organizational learning in this manner contains several feedback loops so that both the community of practice and management can capture explicit and more difficult tacit knowledge, so as to innovate and increase productivity for sustainability (the business ecology view point). Single loop learning is a basic explicit feedback process connecting results from behavior back to rules (Argyris & Schön, 1996). Double loop learning interconnects each element in the process context and goes deeper, challenging the assumptions, using reflection to find insights (tacit knowledge) of why the results occurred and how they may be improved (Argyris & Schön, 1996). Triple loop (also called a deutero process) goes even further by asking provocative questions such as: are these the right principles (McKenna, 1999) - and are there alternative ideologies philosophies or justified true perceptions of tacit knowledge (Strang, 2003).

Another important element for a knowledge articulation methodology is organizational leadership. Transformational leadership is argued to

be the most effective approach for creating and managing a knowledge methodology, as well as for inspiring a community of practice (Amabile, 1998; Nonaka, et al., 2001; Strang, 2005). Visioning, modeling, empathy, intelligence, fairness, goal setting, and humility are important traits needed for transformational leaders (Bass, 1998; Lesser & Prusak, 2000; Malhotra, 2000; McDermott & O'Dell, 2001; Nonaka, et al., 2001; Strang, 2007). Starting and implementing such a methodology essentially requires change management (a variation of organizational leadership). Nonaka (2001) suggest a "shock" is often needed to dislocate people from a sense of complacency and smugness, followed by a executive promotion of the communities of practice. Leibowitz (1999) advises to create a knowledge sharing environment using incentives or linking the employee's contribution to the knowledge repository as part of the annual job performance review. He suggests implementing the principles of the intellectual capital model to show tangible benefits, and he recommends the CEO should drive the knowledge management philosophy (Liebowitz, 1999).

Any discussion of organizational learning, communities of practice and leadership in e-business is not complete without addressing the national cultural dimensions. Holden discusses an alternative view of how global organizations can successfully develop cross-cultural competencies. He suggests a concentric model for knowledge transfer (Holden, 2002, p. 277). At its core lies a pre-established atmosphere for learning, networking and knowledge sharing. Surrounding this in concentric circles is: Participative competence - that is an ability to concurrently hold several opposing, often extreme, views in mind; interactive translation - an ability to work with others to translate concepts and knowledge from in one cultural setting (organizational or national) and point of view to another; knowledge sharing; knowledge distribution; and at the outside ring enveloping all this, an atmosphere for further knowledge-sharing.

Finally, it is necessary to return to the philosophy and ideology underlying a tacit knowledge articulation model for NPD in e-business. If the aforementioned memory definitions, taxonomies and processes are integrated, while also considering the essential NPD business function, we might have a model such as the one depicted in (Figure 4). The significant philosophy underlying that model (to differentiate from the existing knowledge management literature), is the concept of a continuum for creating, understanding, and sharing NPD community of practice ideas (explicit, tacit and innate). This is labeled in the model as falling into the three human memory domains of conscious (explicit), super-conscious (tacit) and subconscious (innate knowledge). Although knowledge artifact examples are listed in the model, these are not exhaustive, nor is there position fixed as diagrammed, since the boundaries between the three domains of articulated knowledge is inexact, thereby the same artifact could be located in alternative zones when viewed by peer community of practice members, or even if viewed by the same person at different times. In this model, the triple loop learning mechanism operates within the articulated knowledge continuum, informed

through feedback from the NPD e-business function. The outcome is the new product or services - the final component needed for this model is a measurement mechanism (discussed next).

Knowledge Performance

Performance refers to the measurement of innovation, sustainability and profitability, but for NPD knowledge articulation in e-business, intermediate dependent variables are needed to judge effectiveness. Both the independent factors as well as the dependant variables (along with any instrumental modifiers) must be isolated. Some factors may be reversed as dependent variables, and vice versa, depending on the perspective of the researchers. For example, are the number of ideas generated a factor or an outcome?

A key argument for measuring intellectual capital as a dependent variable is that human creativity produces innovation which when commercialized creates and demonstrates the quantitative value (Edvinsson, 1997; Stewart, 2000; Sveiby, 1997a).

Intellectual capital is difficult to measure, due to its tacit nature. The most critical elements are argued to be associated with human and customer capital. A possible list of NPD factors or outcome variables is:

- **Trust** ("anticipated reciprocity" or "residue of promises kept"): Likert scale rating;
- **Space** (cognitive space: share of mind around knowledge): years NPD experience;
- **Slack** (time to reflect on what you know): reflection hours per NPD project;
- **Coherence** (shared context, shared knowledge, "communities of practice"): years in COP;
- **Shared vocabulary:** number of special terms used within NPD team;
- **Symbols and signals:** number of NPD diagrams used across all projects;
- **Organizational culture:** employee satisfaction survey (Likert scales), available in

Figure 4. Knowledge articulation model for NPD e-collaboration in e-business

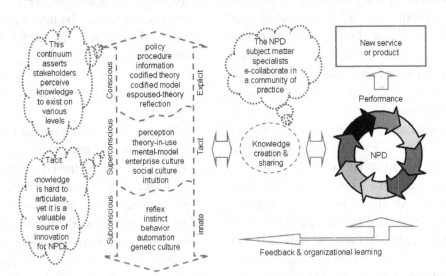

the OB/HRM literature, calculated by using an overall mean of the responses (adapted from: Liebowitz, 1999, pp. 44:86).

Another approach, which could be used in combination with the above, is to classify the most important knowledge assets (using the "Integrated intellectual knowledge taxonomy" presented in Table 2 as a framework), then assess each using a numeric scale. The scale might reflect usefulness or how easy the artifact is to share/reuse (based on perceptions surveyed from the NPD community of practice).

A measurement model has been published in the literature which closely follows the ideology of a flexible continuum for classifying knowledge (as proposed earlier in Figure 4). The "seven dimensions of knowledge" (Davenport & Prusak, 2000, p. 70) uses a taxonomy of seven knowledge memory types, each measured on a continuum (Likert scale from 0 to 4), as summarized below (with an example in Figure 5).

- **Tacit-Explicit**. An individual knowledge item could be described even if tacit yet it may lie at different locations upon the continuum (it may be precisely on one end,

or part way between); for example, finger print matching can be very tacit since a "percent match" benchmark is used;

- **Not teachable-Teachable**. Some knowledge is un-teachable in that the only way to learn is through experience. Examples of un-teachable knowledge might be emotions, faith, sports; although these examples may have underlying techniques and theory that can be taught relating to the "what", yet something "special" happens when experimenting and experiencing the actual tacit knowledge;

- **Not articulated-Articulated**. Some knowledge cannot be easily articulated. On the other hand, culinary skills may innate or super conscious - they are difficult to describe since they refer to the use of taste senses and consistency; as a further example, the Japanese invention of a bread making machine required a sustained period of apprenticeship and interaction with production engineers in an experiment to replicate the knowledge of bread making to transfer this to a machine (Nonaka & Takeuchi, 1995);

- **Not observable-Observable**. Some knowledge is not observable because it re-

Figure 5. Knowledge articulation measurement example of NPD case study

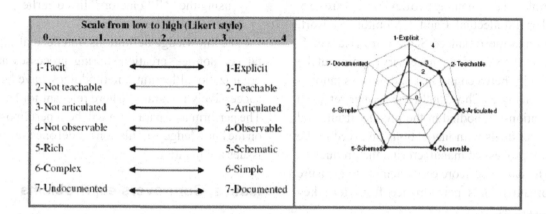

mains hidden inside the mind, such as the creative thought processes of artists, musicians and elite sportspeople and NPD subject matter specialists.

- **Rich-Schematic**. Knowledge may be schematic, easily reducible to rules and patterns, or it may be so rich in context (known only from using multiple senses) that its definition is impossible; schematic knowledge lends itself to being framed in tables, rules and other forms of clear representation, for example in case based reasoning systems (in the insurance claims industry).
- **Complex-Simple**. Complexity versus simplicity also defines ends of a knowledge item spectrum; knowledge about weather prediction (or indeed many other types of prediction) illustrates this dimension. The interaction of many different elements or dynamic sub-systems can turn predictive knowledge into a highly complex activity;
- **Undocumented-Documented**. Some knowledge is documented while other knowledge is never documented; obviously a single knowledge item can be assessed on all of the above scales.

The NPD example from Figure 5 shows a radar diagram (on right) with the zero scale of each dimension at the center, and a scoring line connecting the ratings. The case study was an NPD design "blueprint" for a mobile (cellular) phone (using e-collaboration with a multinational decentralized COP). The blueprint is clearly drawn with labels but contains a few elements that cannot be fully described in a two dimension blueprint (rated as 3 out of 4). The contents and drawing method can be taught (using CAD software), but considerable skill is needed to produce a high quality image such as the design (rated 3 out of 4). There is no question the blueprint is both articulated and observable if we focus on the paper itself and not the underlying device (rated 4 out of 4). Since the blueprint is intended to be used for assembly, it is schematic (rated 4 out of 4), but there are a few complex portions which qualify for less than total simplicity (3 out of 4). In this case the NPD team has not released the blueprint so it is not "officially" documented (but since the project is listed in the organizational program charter, we rate it 1 out of 4).

Finally, returning to the intellectual capital concept, there are obvious outcome variables that can be used to assess the success of innovation, productivity and sustainability of NPD design in e-business. The literature contains well-documented examples of this, namely two devices that are very similar: Intellectual Capital Monitor (Stewart, 2000) and the Balanced Score Card (Kaplan & Norton, 1998). First it is necessary to point out the ambiguity between product and process innovation (Chang & Cho, 2008); the former refers to innovations embodied in the product itself, and the latter deals with innovations involved in the overall process of manufacturing the product.

The balanced score card attempts to measure an organization's performance from four key perspectives:

- **Financial:** measures that are at present commonly used such as profit levels, market share etc.; these answer the question: how do we look to our shareholders? – these ratios can be calculated on an NPD project basis using variables and formulas defined in the accounting/GAAP literature;
- **Customer:** measures that can be used to report on customer satisfaction, customer experience etc.; these are concerned with the question: how do we look to our shareholders? - the can be done using many of the available client satisfaction surveys available in the HRM/OB literature;
- **Internal business process:** measures of efficiency and effectiveness of business processes, for example: throughput of a production line; OHS effectiveness in terms of lost time for injuries; quality management system measures etc.; these measures help answer the question: what must we excel at? - there are surveys available in the TQM (quality) literature to do this;
- **Innovation and learning:** measures that identify learning and innovation performance; these measures help answer the question: "can we improve and create wealth?" - this can be measured by using surveys from the organizational learning literature or by assessing the intermediate

outcomes from the NPD project (perhaps using the "NPD factors" listed earlier).

The knowledge definitions, intellectual capital taxonomies, creation/sharing processes and organizational learning methodology have been successively integrated where relevant for NPD. The performance paradigm will be superimposed on the knowledge articulation model once several issues are mentioned.

Issues, Controversies, Problems

The knowledge articulation issues are due to a lack of interdisciplinary theory as well as and failure to integrate culture and perception. The impact caused by the issues is similar despite each problem differs. Issues weaken the credibility of research and reduce the potential to improve interdisciplinary practice.

Knowledge Memory Issues

The first point concerns tacit memory controversies. Perception influences the interpretation of tacit and innate knowledge; just consider the parable of the glass being half full or half empty. On one hand many researchers follow Aristotle's view that most knowledge is derived from experience, either directly, or indirectly, by deducing new facts from those already known (Grolier, 2007). In contrast, fewer researchers discuss the instrumental impact perception has on both explicit and tacit knowledge.

The word "tacit" (Polanyi, 1966, p. 136) has been misused by some researchers. In the literature, tacit knowledge has been described as being action-oriented knowledge that could be acquired even "without" the knower being aware of its existence (e.g. on an innate or subconscious level). Tacit knowledge has been characterized as professional instinct (Sternberg, 1985; Sternberg & Horvath, 1999) yet these authors later contradict that definition. According to the alternative viewpoint, to be classified as tacit knowledge, artifacts must possess all three characteristics of being: procedural in nature, acquired with little help from others as personal experience, and relevant to the attainment of goals (Sternberg, Wagner, & Williams, 1995; Wagner & Sternberg, 1985).

Furthermore, some researchers suggest the existence of tacit knowledge memory relates to individual performance success and practical intelligence. "[Tacit knowledge is] characterized as a type of knowledge the possession of which distinguishes more from less practically successful individuals" (Sternberg, et al., 2000, p. 105). It is possible this extreme view was taken due to correlation of knowledge with performance. Nonetheless, empirical research on leadership does suggest that tacit (and innate) knowledge explains performance and follower satisfaction differences (Strang, 2005; Strang, 2007).

Many researchers such as (Nonaka, et al., 2001) cite their interpretation of tacit knowledge from the work of Polanyi, which he defined as: "knowledge is an activity which would better be described as a process of knowing." (Polanyi, 1966, p. 132). Albeit Nonaka cites Polanyi as the basis of the SECI model, tacit knowledge can articulated or made explicit during the externalization process (Nonaka, et al., 2001, p. 28), while Polanyi clearly believes all knowledge is tacit and would be difficult to articulate: "tacit knowing achieves comprehension by indwelling, and that all knowledge consists of or is rooted in such as of comprehension" (Polanyi, 1966, p. 55). Other researchers admit tacit knowledge is difficult to communicate and articulate but they assert it can be made explicit to some degree (Sternberg & Horvath, 1999; Sternberg, et al., 1995; Takeuchi, 1998; Teece, 1998).

As discussed earlier, Scharmer (2001) put forth the transcending (not yet embodied) qualification on tacit knowledge (which is described in this research as innate, Figure 4). The alternative theory is that tacit knowledge cannot be interpreted as "knowledge-not-yet-articulated" (Tsoukas, 2003),

and it was argued that tacit knowledge can never be articulated because it would no longer be tacit.

Ironically the most flexible view of tacit memory as being a continuum can be implied from the ancient philosophers. Descartes originated the *Cartesian split* concept where the act of perceiving knowledge was differentiated from the object directly perceived (Grolier, 2007), separating the tacit aspect of knowledge from the explicit object known. Kant elaborated by proposing three degrees of perception:

- exact and certain but uninformative (makes clear only what is contained in definitions) [explicit];
- experience-based (but subject to errors of perception) [somewhere between explicit and tacit];
- pure intuition, both exact and certain [innate or tacit, but mostly the latter]; (Grolier, 2007).

Knowledge Taxonomy Issues

National culture influences the articulation of tacit and explicit knowledge, beyond differences in language (Strang, 2008b, 2009b, 2009c). Eastern orthodox cultures (Buddhism, Taoism, etc.) tend to emphasize tacit aspects such as intuition, self-awareness, realism, and sensing; maintaining that only consciousness is genuinely real and that perceived objects are ultimately illusory "true beliefs"; while western cultures (Catholic, Baptist, etc.) emphasize facts, performance, explicit oriented perceptions (Nonaka & Teece, 2001; Takeuchi, 1998).

Therefore, in a multinational NPD team (that use English as a common language), there may be variations in the priority of explicit, tacit (or even innate) knowledge artifacts. Good ideas may be criticized due to cultural differences (Strang, 2009b). Furthermore, there may be gaps between the NPD team and management. There may be top down "silo" or lateral "power broker" pressures affecting knowledge classification if the organizational structure is hierarchical or if the leadership is transactional (Naito, 2001; Teece, 2001).

Furthermore, the level of analysis for intellectual capital can be misleading, as there are differences in the classification of tacit or explicit knowledge when viewed from the lens of business management versus communities of practice versus customers/supply chain partners. For example the term "design success" in NPD carries explicit and tacit attributes yet it carries different perceptions on the organizational level (profitable, economies-of-scale, regulation compliant), as compared with team (meets scope requirements of price, place, promotion, position, production) versus client advocates (meets needs and wants).

As mentioned, there are two valid attenuations of tacit and explicit NPD knowledge: the first relates to innovations being "embodied within" the product/service itself, while the second refers to the "innovative processes" underlying the product/service (Chang & Cho, 2008, p. 16). This affects the retrieval of research and best practices from the literature (as well as from organizational memory), if the object versus process attenuation is not clearly articulated. Another impact is there may be dichotomies between the attenuations placed on knowledge artifacts by the NPD team as compared to other business functions.

Knowledge Process Issues

Perceptional and cultural differences can affect individual as well as group knowledge creating, transforming and sharing processes (Strang, 2008b, 2009c). During the SECI explicit-to-tacit process, knowledge is "justified by being compared to the reality of the world" (Nonaka, et al., 2001, p. 27). Reality in this context refers to cultural norms or professional ethics. If explicit knowledge is internalized as being a justified belief in this "reality" then it is accepted; otherwise a gap of "creative tension" emerges between the "espoused" knowledge element and this "reality"

perception of it (Senge, 1990). When a knowledge gap exists this "then triggers a new cycle of knowledge creation" (Nonaka, et al., 2001).

From an organizational cultural standpoint, there may be over-reliance on transmitting explicit rather than tacit information in e-business because the communicating the former is easier and faster - especially when face-to-face or bidirectional voice contact is not available or desired (Liebowitz, 1999).

One topic that does not seem to have appeared in the knowledge management literature is the requirement and process of deleting antiquated or ineffective tacit knowledge, forgetting tacit memory (albeit there had been some research on retiring explicit knowledge artifacts). This has been mentioned in a different disciplinary context, in the organizational learning literature under the term "unfreezing" (Senge, Kleiner, Roberts, Roth, & Smith, 1999).

In terms of impact on NPD, this makes the processes unpredictable, as well as making the explicit/tacit knowledge hard to measure since the assessor could have a different perception than one or all of the community of practice members. Espoused knowledge gaps can lengthen the SECI process when a new cycle is triggered during brainstorming. Furthermore, if all NPD team members have vastly different cultures (and perceptional tendencies), this could impede the creativity and design process despite that all team members might be brilliant, experienced and creative (Strang, 2009b). This carries over to organizational knowledge assets (human and structural intellectual capital), since diversity in culture, ethics or perception affects knowledge creation and retrieval - innovative NPD knowledge could even be "purposefully" ignored (Strang, 2009b).

Knowledge Learning Issues

There are several alternative viewpoints in the literature about the role of organizational learning and communities of practice in knowledge articulation. One of the criticisms of the MIT version of organizational learning as defined by Senge comes from a scholar at nearby Harvard Business School: "discussions of learning organizations have often been reverential and utopian [...they] lack a framework for action, and thus provide little comfort to practical-minded managers." (Garvin, 1998, p. 13) and Senge (1990), studied the inner psychological factors that facilitate or block learning, Garvin (1998) focused on systemic procedure applied over the stages that encompass the knowledge life cycle. However all of these approaches focus on individual (not group) knowledge articulation techniques such as reflective learning and knowledge-in-action.

An alternative view is that tacit knowledge cannot be taught or shared so an organization cannot learn it.

Tacit knowledge refers to knowledge that usually is not openly expressed or stated [...] by our use of tacit in the present context we do not wish to imply that this knowledge is inaccessible to conscious awareness, unspeakable, or unteachable, but merely that it is not taught directly to most of us (Wagner & Sternberg, 1985, p. 439).

At an even more extreme position, it has been argued that organizational learning is not useful unless it generates organizational explicit knowledge of value to those who are able and willing to apply that knowledge in making decisions or influencing others in the organization (Miller, 1996, p. 18).

Another form of learning is also available for organization knowledge articulation and sharing: cognitive apprenticeships (Collins, Brown, & Newman, 1989). In this theory, experts mentor novices. A criticism towards cognitive-apprenticeships if that it is labor intensive (requires an subject matter expert for each novice). Furthermore, experts mentor novices to effectively apply tools and techniques, but not necessarily how to solve complex problems that have not been encountered

during training. The true value of experience is not how much mentoring a novice receives, but how well they are able to leverage experience to acquire and apply tacit knowledge (Sternberg, et al., 2000). Yet there are many unproven factors that affect explicit and tacit knowledge transfer through organizational learning and cognitive apprenticeships, such as length of time being exposed to experts, trust, culture, ethics, intelligence, experience and personality - these factors are difficult to account for in NPD teams and extremely tedious to measure in research projects.

Communities of practice members have a group identity, a subculture, and participants learn through interaction plus memorization of embedded knowledge (Wenger, 1998). On the other hand, as Nonaka and colleagues pointed out (2001), participants of the "Ba" shared context don't belong to it (no membership) - instead they relate to it, using it as a place to interrelate for creating knowledge (Nonaka, et al., 2001, p. 24). The shared "Ba" context of the SECI cycle is a place where knowledge is created (which is also the locus of control), its boundaries are fluid (changed by the participants), it is moving (with no historical element nor identity), and its membership is dynamic - composed of any combination of individuals, organizations, teams, and so on (Nonaka & Teece, 2001). An additional aspect is that Seely-Brown and Duguid emphasize the shared practice and social identity of whereby over time participants develop a common outlook and understanding of the world around them, and they share the same sort of judgment, and look to the community as place to engage in learning, rather than knowledge creation per se (Brown & Duguid, 2001). Another debatable aspect of communities is there may be some hierarchy and purposeful NPD goal-setting guidance from the organizational authority, but this might not be forthcoming with the less-structured "Ba" (Grant, 2001). Therefore, productivity could be lower in "Ba" as compared with a pure NPD community of practice format.

Communities of practice could suffer from the same interpersonal conflicts as teams do, as a result of personality differences, behaviors and/or stress. This can also manifest between individual or groups and their management (as well as with other business functions). Researchers have pointed out that communities of practice could suffer "groupthink" which can seriously hamper NPD team innovativeness (Felps, Mitchell, & Byington, 2006; Seel, 2001). In fact this led Leonard-Barton (1995) to introduce the concept of "creative abrasion" as a deliberate attempt to provide conflict within the community of practice to force members to question the status quo, reframe problems and generate fresh ideas.

Organizational leadership could even interfere with NPD team prioritization of both tacit and explicit knowledge because communities of practice operate autonomously with intrinsic and motivation. Finally, culture and learning styles differences between NPD team members and stakeholders can impact knowledge articulation and sharing (Strang, 2008b, 2009a). The risk of these issues can be reduced by making other researchers aware of this (especially if others will replicate or extend this work).

Knowledge Performance Issues

The key knowledge performance challenge concerns identifying what units of analysis to assess in terms of which independent factors and dependent variables to measure. All of the independent factors discussed in the knowledge taxonomy section are difficult to measure (Barchan, 2002). Some of these factors could be counted, such as number of explicit designs, number of tacit ideas in a storytelling session, while some of the factors could be outcomes instead of inputs (Haynes & Price, 2002). Some have only qualitative indicators, while others have no known observable or quantifiable characteristics. Tacit (and innate) factors or variables would be very difficult to quantify - researchers contend that some knowl-

edge artifacts can never be precisely articulated (Leonard & Sensiper, 1998; Tsoukas, 2003). There might be subjectivity in the assessing of any of these factors or variables (inter rater agreement issues).

This inherently exposes the controversy of "levels of analysis" for the dependent variables, which refers to what perspective is used to measure outcomes. The relevant levels of analysis would be: organization, team (community of practice), business unit, or individual. Furthermore, the same levels of analysis should be used when matching independent factors to measure dependent variables (Creswell, 2003). For example, it would not be credible in NPD research to use a community of practice member's years of experience as a factor to predict the team's experience capability (instead it would be necessary to average the experience of team members). The same factor or variable name could be measured across several of these levels, such as the example just given (subgrouped by person, team, country, culture and/or multinational business units); thus, the inherent meaning of such analysis could be multifaceted.

Finally, there is some controversy in the literature over the best construct(s) to use for measuring intellectual capital as well as organizational learning, or even if any of these devices can effectively measure what they were intended to (Mills, Platts, Bourne, & Richards, 2002; Neeley, 2002; Whitley, 2002; Wilson, 2002). It has been pointed out that the Balanced Score Card is a facsimile of the Intellectual Capital Assets structure (Wiig, 2002), yet this argument might be irrelevant as long as one of the other were effective. Generally, it is advisable to use the level of analysis closest to the input and processing point of origin. Therefore, since tacit knowledge is articulated by members in the e-business NPD community of practice, the levels of analysis should be at the NPD project team and individual levels (Strang, 2009a). Nevertheless, there are still issues in the literature over the statistical validity and reliability of the published instruments used for knowledge assessment (Haspeslagh, Noda, & Boulos, 2001; Wilson, 2002).

Solutions and Recommendations

There are ambiguities with tacit knowledge meanings, overlapping taxonomy structures, conflicting process perspectives, organizational learning controversies and tacit knowledge assessment challenges.

In terms of meanings, there has always been a philosophical disparity between researchers that take an interpretive ideology accepting phenomenological concepts, as compared with a positivist view that focuses on explicit empirical evidence (Erlandson, 2006). This philosophical polarity has also occurred in the knowledge management literature (Lee, Green, & Brennan, 2000). Much of the early and current literature adopt the interpretive perspective of tacit knowledge (Polanyi, 1966), with fewer cases applying the controversial "practical capability" meaning of (Sternberg, et al., 2000) yet there have been some interesting empirical logical positivist studies that apply an interdisciplinary view (Chang & Cho, 2008).

This "meaning of knowledge" issue may be methodological (not purely ideological in nature) because the interpretive and positivist paradigms both advocate the use of scientific research methods yet the techniques for gathering knowledge and analyzing it are different. For example, at opposite ends of the research methods continua, in action learning data is gathered from reflections and interview narratives followed by qualitative analysis to discover themes (Yin, 2003), while a correlation or explanatory approach usually gathers data using an *a priori* survey construct accompanied by factor, variance and/or regression analysis to predict cause-effect. Factor analysis can be difficult to replicate (reducing external validity) while regression will often inflate minor relationships with large samples over 500 (Strang, 2009c).

It is possible to overcome the remaining knowledge taxonomy, process ambiguity and

organizational learning obstacles by taking an interdisciplinary approach and using mixed research methods. This can be done by locating statistically validated instruments to measure the human capital factors, while best practices can be used to identify and count the knowledge artifacts and performance outcomes (Creswell, 2003; Schwalbach, 2003). Mixed methods can be used to gather corroborating qualitative and quantitative evidence from different sources and levels (Keppel & Wickens, 2004; Onwuegbuzie & Leech, 2005; Strang, 2009d; Yin, 2003), to produce an overall picture of knowledge articulation in NPD project teams. A hypothetical measurement model is shown in (Figure 6). Specific recommendations are discussed below. The "group level of analysis" will be the common denominator baseline to test the hypotheses.

The biggest challenge in viewing knowledge on a continuum is how to articulate it for research purposes (to assess it). The solution may be to use one of the knowledge processes - storytelling (in combination with other methods). To apply this idea, subject matter specialist could be asked to participate in a focus group to develop and present (transform to quasi-explicit meaning) all NPD project knowledge artifacts. As explained earlier, storytelling is a methodology (not a bedtime parent-child activity). Nevertheless it must be acknowledged there is a risk for loss of rich tacit knowledge during this proposed storytelling method for quasi-explicit knowledge articulation (Becerra-Fernandez, et al., 2004). In referring item 1 of the proposed measurement model (Figure 6), the above methodology could be used to count the quasi-explicit knowledge artifacts, grouped by taxonomy type from Table 2 on the tacit knowledge continuum of Figure 4 (along the seven knowledge dimensions in Figure 5).

Items 2, 3 and 4 of the proposed measurement model (Figure 6), could be assessed using existing *a priori* instruments (from the literature). Item 2 is proposed to measure NPD community of practice team satisfaction and organizational

Figure 6. Performance measurement model for knowledge articulation in NPD

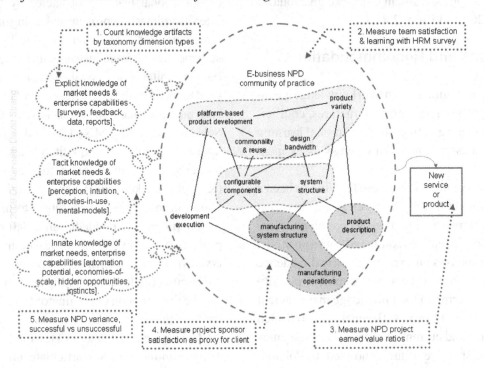

learning - both at the individual and group levels of analysis. Many instruments are available from the literature to measure individual employee satisfaction, as well as individual learning, so these can be averaged by groups to produce a composite team rating (Strang, 2009d). Item 3 can be measured by computing the project performance ratios (PMI, 2008; Strang, 2008a), on the group level of analysis. Item 4 can be assessed by adapting the e-business/NPD team constructs proposed in a number studies such as (Boddy & Macbeth, 2000; Chong, Holden, Wilhelmij, & Schmidt, 2000; Courtney, 2003; Strang, 2009a).

Finally, as a triangulation of the first four measurement items, it is proposed that a quasi-indicator of innate and tacit knowledge articulation (at the group level of analysis) can be approximated by identifying successful versus unsuccessful NPD project teams. This may seem ironic, as it implies more intelligent NPD team members should produce more innate, tacit and explicit knowledge artifacts (Sternberg, et al., 2000), yet this has been

a successful approach found in the empirical psychology literature (Creswell, 2003). This could be implemented using two statistical techniques. The first could be accomplished by treating the first two dependent variables measurements (at the group level of analysis) as independent factors, and the last two (items 3 and 4) as dependent outcomes, using MANOVA (Strang, 2009d). The second approach could be to treat all items 1 through 4 as independent factors, by merging the groups into successful versus unsuccessful classes, and then applying discriminant analysis to validate the hypothesis (Strang, 2009d).

FUTURE RESEARCH DIRECTIONS

One of the critical contributions of the proposed knowledge articulation model introduced here is the perspective of viewing and measuring knowledge on a continuum (Figure 4), complimented by proposing a triangulated mixed methods research approach to gather (and average) different perspectives (Figure 6). The philosophy here (as conceptualized in Figure 4 and 7), is that knowledge is a justified true perception on a continuum, rather than an "either or" bipolar distinction (as is commonly argued in the literature).

This itself is not a new scientific assertion since Ambrosini and Bowman (2001) as well as Edmondson and colleagues (2003) already suggested encoding knowledge as a degree of "tacitness". Furthermore it was also pointed out that ancient philosopher Kant already seemed to imply that concept. Nevertheless, this is a new proposed concept of explicit, tacit and innate knowledge being on a sub-conscious, super-conscious and conscious continuum, along with a proposed measurement model. A knowledge articulation model for e-business NPD team project innovations has never been discussed in the literature, by integrating five overlapping paradigms of: cognitive/organizational memory, intellectual capital taxonomies, creating/sharing processes, organizational learning and performance. Typically only one or two of these paradigms are encompassed within any particular empirical research study.

It is argued the growth of the knowledge economy and technology (and in light of lessons-learning from the 2008 global economic crisis), have placed a renewed emphasis on measuring knowledge. Given the increased use of e-business software, e-collaboration is becoming a common activity in NPD teams. Consequently, the interdisciplinary approach suggested here provides a more practical and positivist methodology to understand and assess knowledge articulation in e-business NPD communities of practice. Using *a priori* instruments (where applicable), and generally accepted scientific mixed methods, to test the hypothetical model (Figure 6), will provide a contribution to the empirical literature. To that end, the next phase of this project is underway to study NPD e-collaboration in a multinational mobile phone communications product/service company that has multicultural business units in several countries.

CONCLUSION

This chapter started with goal of proposing a knowledge articulation model that could be used to assess the innovative productivity of an e-business NPD community of practice team that e-collaborates across multiple cultures and countries. The relevant knowledge management literature was reviewed using a unique meta-model consisting of five paradigms: memory, taxonomies, processes, organizational learning and performance. The review was both interdisciplinary and integrative, in that explanations were grounded in multiple epistemological domains (interpretive as well as empirical), and subsequent sections built on the previous, concluding with a hypothetical knowledge articulation measurement model (Figure 6). Significant historical and contemporary knowledge management issues were revealed. A proposed solution was recommended to test the hypothetical knowledge articulation measurement model, using *a priori* instruments, best-practices and generally-accepted mixed research methods. The chapter should stand alone as a guideline for other researchers that wish to adapt or improve the theoretical models and methodologies proposed herein. Additionally, this chapter has been put into operation in a multinational mobile communications empirical case study (with the results to be published when complete).

REFERENCES

Amabile, T. M. (1998). How to kill creativity. *Harvard Business Review*, 76(5), 76–87.

Ambrosini, V., & Bowman, C. (2001). Tacit knowledge: Some suggestions for operationalization. *Journal of Management Studies, 38*(6), 811–829. doi:10.1111/1467-6486.00260

Argyris, C., & Schön, D. (1996). *Organizational learning ii: Theory, method, and practice*. Reading, MA: Addison-Wesley.

Awad, E. M., & Ghaziri, H. (2004). *Knowledge management*. Upper Saddle River, NJ: Pearson Prentice Hall.

Backman, M., Borjesson, S., & Setterberg, S. (2007). Working with concepts in the fuzzy front end: Exploring the context for innovation for different types of concepts at Volvo cars. *R & D Management, 37*(1), 17–28. doi:10.1111/j.1467-9310.2007.00455.x

Barchan, M. (2002). *How to measure intangible assets*. Knowledge Management World.

Bass, B. M. (1998). *Transformational leadership*. Mahwah, NJ: Lawrence Erlbaum Associates.

Becerra-Fernandez, I., Gonzalez, A., & Sabherwal, R. (2004). *Knowledge management: Challenges, solutions, and technologies*. Upper Saddle River, NJ: Pearson Prentice Hall.

Beckett, R. C. (2000). A characterisation of corporate as a knowledge management system. *Journal of Knowledge Management, 4*(4), 311–319. doi:10.1108/13673270010379867

Boddy, D., & Macbeth, D. (2000). Prescriptions for managing change: A survey of their effects in projects to implement collaborative working between organisations. *International Journal of Project Management, 18*(5), 297–306. doi:10.1016/S0263-7863(99)00031-9

Boudreau, J. W., & Ramstad, P. M. (1997). Measuring intellectual capital: Learning from financial history. *Human Resource Management, 36*(3). doi:10.1002/(SICI)1099-050X(199723)36:3<343::AID-HRM6>3.0.CO;2-W

Brown, A. (1998). *Organisational culture* (2nd ed.). Harlow, UK: Financial Times-Prentice Hall.

Brown, J. S., & Duguid, P. (1991). Organisational learning and communities of practice: Towards a unified view of working, learning, and innovation. *Organization Science, 2*(1), 40–57. doi:10.1287/orsc.2.1.40

Brown, J. S., & Duguid, P. (2001). Structure and spontaneity: Knowledge and organisation. In Nonaka, I., & Teece, D. (Eds.), *Managing industrial knowledge - creation, transfer and utilization* (pp. 44–67). London: Sage.

Burton-Jones, A. (1999). *Knowledge capitalism*. Oxford: Oxford University Press.

Cabrera, A., Collins, W. C., & Salgado, J. F. (2006). Determinants of individual engagement in knowledge sharing. *International Journal of Human Resource Management, 17*(2), 245–264.

Carrillo, F. J. (2001). Meta km: A program and a plea. *Journal of Knowledge and Innovation, 2*, 27–54.

Chang, D. R., & Cho, H. (2008). Organizational memory influences new product success. *Journal of Business Research, 61*, 13–23. doi:10.1016/j.jbusres.2006.05.005

Chomsky, N. (1959). Review of verbal behavior. *Language, 35*, 26–58. doi:10.2307/411334

Chong, C. W., Holden, T., Wilhelmij, P., & Schmidt, R. A. (2000). Where does knowledge management add value? *Journal of Intellectual Capital, 1*(4), 366–380. doi:10.1108/14691930010359261

Cohen, W. M., & Levinthal, D. (1990). Absorptive capacity: A new perspective on learning and innovation. *Administrative Science Quarterly, 35*(1), 128–152. doi:10.2307/2393553

Collins, A., Brown, J. S., & Newman, S. E. (1989). Cognitive apprenticeship: Teaching the crafts of reading, writing and mathematics. In Resnick, L. B. (Ed.), *Knowing, learning and instruction: Essays in honour of Robert Glaser* (pp. 453–494). Hillsdale, N. J.: Lawrence Erlbaum.

Cortada, J. W., & Woods, J. A. (Eds.). (2001). *The knowledge management yearbook 2000-2001*. NY: Butterworth-Heinemann.

Courtney, H. (2003). Decision-driven scenarios for assessing four levels of uncertainty. *Strategy and Leadership, 31*(1), 14. doi:10.1108/10878570310455015

Creswell, J. W. (2003). *Research design: Qualitative, quantitative, and mixed methods approaches* (2nd ed.). NY: Sage.

Davenport, T. H., & Prusak, L. (2000). *Working knowledge - how organizations manage what they know*. Boston: Harvard Business School Press.

de Jager, M. (1999). The kmat: Benchmarking knowledge management. *Library Management, 20*(7), 367–372. doi:10.1108/01435129910285136

DeBono, E. (1967). *New think: The use of lateral thinking in the generation of new ideas*. New York: Basic Books.

Dixon, N. M. (2000). *Common knowledge: How companies thrive by sharing what they know*. Boston: Harvard Business School Press.

DuBrin, A. J. (2004). *Applying psychology: Individual and organizational effectiveness*. Upper Saddle River, NJ: Pearson Education Ltd.

Edmondson, A. C., Winslow, A. B., Bohmer, R. M. J., & Pisano, G. P. (2003). Learning how and learning what: Effects of tacit and codified knowledge on performance improvement following technology adoption. *Decision Sciences, 34*(2), 197–224. doi:10.1111/1540-5915.02316

Edvinsson, L. (1997). Developing intellectual capital at skandia. *Long Range Planning. Elsevier Science Limited, 30*(3), 366–373.

Erlandson, P. (2006). Giving up the ghost: The control-matrix and reflection-in-action. *Reflective Practice, 7*(1), 115–124. doi:10.1080/14623940500489781

Ettlie, J. E., & Elsenbach, J. M. (2007). Modified stage-gate regimes in new product development. *Journal of Product Innovation Management, 24*(2), 20–33. doi:10.1111/j.1540-5885.2006.00230.x

Felps, W., Mitchell, T. R., & Byington, E. (2006). How, when, and why bad apples spoil the barrel: Negative group members and dysfunctional groups. *Research in Organizational Behavior, 27*, 175–222. doi:10.1016/S0191-3085(06)27005-9

Forman, J. (2001). When stories create an organization's future. In Cortada, J. W., & Woods, J. A. (Eds.), *The knowledge management yearbook 2000-2001* (pp. 231–235). NY: Butterworth-Heinemann.

Fuller, S. (2001). A critical guide to knowledge society newspeak. *Current Sociology, 49*(4), 177–201. doi:10.1177/0011392101049004010

Garvin, D. A. (1998). *Building a learning organisation, Harvard business review on knowledge management* (pp. 47–80). Boston: Harvard Business School Publishing.

Goleman, D. (1998). What makes a leader? *Harvard Business Review, 76*(6), 92–102.

Goleman, D. (2000). Leadership that gets results. *Harvard Business Review, 78*(2), 78–90.

Gordon, S., Tarafdar, M., Cook, R., Maksimoski, R., & Rogowitz, B. (2008). Improving the front end of innovation with information technology: Smart companies use it to be more effective and efficient in the early stages of the innovation process. *Research Technology Management, 51*(3), 50–59.

Grant, R. M. (2001). Knowledge and organization. In Nonaka, I., & Teece, D. (Eds.), *Managing industrial knowledge - creation, transfer and utilization* (pp. 145–165). London: Sage.

Grolier. (2007). *Encyclopedia Americana®* (Version 15). Danbury, CT: Grolier Interactive, Inc.

Gronröos, C. (1994). From marketing mix to relationship marketing: Towards a paradigm shift in marketing. *Management Decision. MCB Press, 32*(2), 4–20.

Hamel, G., & Prahalad, C. K. (1994). *Competing for the future*. Boston: Harvard Business School Press.

Hampden-Turner, C., & Trompenaars, F. (2000). *Building cross-cultural competence - how to create wealth from conflicting values*. New York: John Wiley & Sons.

Handy, C. (2001). A world of fleas and elephants. In Bennis, W., Spreitzer, G. M., & Cummings, T. G. (Eds.), *The future of leadership - today's top leadership thinkers speak to tomorrow's leaders* (pp. 29–40). San Francisco: Jossey-Bass.

Hansen, C. D., & Kahnweiler, W. M. (1993). Storytelling: An instrument for understanding the dynamics of corporate relationships. *Human Relations, 46*(12), 1391–1409. doi:10.1177/001872679304601202

Hansen, M. T., Nohria, N., & Tierney, T. (2001). What's your strategy for managing knowledge? In Cortada, J. W., & Woods, J. A. (Eds.), *The knowledge management yearbook 2000-2001* (pp. 55–69). New York: Butterworth-Heinemann.

Hansen, M. T., & von Oetinger, B. (2001). Introducing t-shaped managers - knowledge management's next generation. *Harvard Business Review, 79*(3), 107–116.

Haspeslagh, P., Noda, T., & Boulos, F. (2001). Managing for value it's not just about the numbers. *Harvard Business Review, 79*(7), 65–73.

Haynes, B., & Price, I. (2002, September). *Quantifying the complex adaptive workplace*. Paper presented at the Applying and Extending the Global Knowledge Base - CIB Working Commission 070 - Facilities Management and Maintenance, Glasgow, Scotland.

Heaton, L., & Taylor, J. R. (2002). Knowledge management and professional work. *Management Communication Quarterly, 16*(2), 210–236. doi:10.1177/089331802237235

Holden, N. J. (2002). *Cross-cultural management - a knowledge perspective*. Harlow, UK: Pearson Education.

Horvath, J. A. (2001). Working with tacit knowledge. In Cortada, J. W., & Woods, J. A. (Eds.), *The knowledge management yearbook 2000-2001* (pp. 34–51). New York: Butterworth-Heinemann.

Johnson, A. R. (2001). Competitive intelligence and competitor analysis as knowledge management applications. In Cortada, J. W., & Woods, J. A. (Eds.), *The knowledge management yearbook 2000-2001* (pp. 85–97). New York: Butterworth-Heinemann.

Kaplan, R. S., & Norton, D. P. (1992). The balanced scorecard - measures that drive performance. *Harvard Business Review, 70*(1), 171–179.

Kaplan, R. S., & Norton, D. P. (1998). *Using the balanced scorecard as a strategic management system, Harvard business review on measuring corporate performance* (pp. 183–211). Boston, MA: Harvard Business School Publishing.

Kavali, S. G., Tzokas, N. X., & Saren, M. J. (1999). Realtionship marketing as an ethical approach; philosophical and managerial considerations. *Management Decision, 37*(7), 573–581. doi:10.1108/00251749910285746

Kaye, S. (2001). Some proven ways to promote the exchange of ideas. In Cortada, J. W., & Woods, J. A. (Eds.), *The knowledge management yearbook 2000-2001* (pp. 391–398). New York: Butterworth-Heinemann.

Keppel, G., & Wickens, T. D. (2004). *Design and analysis: A researcher's handbook* (4th ed.). Upper Saddle River, NJ, USA: Pearson Prentice-Hall.

Kikawada, K., & Holtshouse, D. (2001). The knowledge perspective in the xerox group. In Nonaka, I., & Teece, D. (Eds.), *Managing industrial knowledge - creation, transfer and utilization* (pp. 283–314). London: Sage.

Kim, W. C., & Mauborgne, R. (1999). Strategy, value innovation and the knowledge economy. *Sloan Management Review, 40*(3), 41–54.

Kyriakopoulos, K., & deRuyter, K. (2004). Knowledge stocks and information flows in new product development. *Journal of Management Studies, 41*, 1469–1498. doi:10.1111/j.1467-6486.2004.00482.x

Lank, E. (1997). Leveraging invisible assets: The human factor. *Long Range Planning. Elsevier Science Limited, 30*(3), 406–412.

Lee, A., Green, W., & Brennan, M. (2000). Organisational knowledge, professional practice and the professional doctorate at work. In Carrick, J., & Rhodes, C. (Eds.), *Research and knowledge at work, perspectives, case-studies and innovative strategies* (pp. 117–136). London: Routledge.

Leonard, D., & Sensiper, D. (1998). The role of tacit knowledge in group innovation. *California Management Review, 40*(3), 112–132.

Leonard-Barton, D. (1995). *Wellsprings of knowledge - building and sustaining the sources of innovation.* Boston, MA: Harvard Business School Press.

Lesser, E., & Prusak, L. (2000). Communities of practice, social capital and organizational knowledge. In Lesser, E., Fontaine, M. A., & Slusher, J. A. (Eds.), *Knowledge and communities* (pp. 123–150). Woburn, MA: Butterworth-Heinemann. doi:10.1016/B978-0-7506-7293-1.50011-1

Lesser, E., & Prusak, L. (2001). Communities of practice, social capital and organizational knowledge. In Cortada, J. W., & Woods, J. A. (Eds.), *The knowledge management yearbook 2000-2001* (pp. 251–259). NY: Butterworth-Heinemann.

Liebowitz, J. (1999). *Building organizational intelligence: A knowledge management primer.* San Diego: CRC Press.

Malhotra, Y. (2000). Knowledge management for e-business performance: Advanced information strategy to "internet time". *Information Strategy, The Executive's Journal, 16*(4), 5–16.

Malone, D. (2002). Knowledge management; a model for organizational learning. *International Journal of Accounting Information Systems, 3*(2), 111–123. doi:10.1016/S1467-0895(02)00039-8

McDermott, R., & O'Dell, C. (2001). Overcoming cultural barriers to sharing knowledge. *Journal of Knowledge Management, 5*(1), 76–85. doi:10.1108/13673270110384428

McKenna, R. (1999). *New management.* Sydney, NSW: Irwin McGraw-Hill.

Meacham, J. A. (1983). Wisdom and the concept of knowledge. In Kuhn, D., & Meacham, J. A. (Eds.), *Contributions in human development.* Basel: Karger.

Miller, D. (1996). A preliminary typology of organizational learning: Synthesizing the literature. *Journal of Management, 22*(3), 485–505. doi:10.1177/014920639602200305

Mills, J., Platts, K., Bourne, M., & Richards, H. (2002). *Strategy and performance: Competing through competences*. Cambridge, UK: Cambridge University Press.

Nahapiet, J., & Ghoshal, S. (1998). Social capital, intellectual capital, and the organizational advantage. *Academy of Management Review, 23*(2), 242–266. doi:10.2307/259373

Naito, H. (2001). Knowledge is commitment. In Nonaka, I., & Teece, D. (Eds.), *Managing industrial knowledge - creation, transfer and utilization* (pp. 270–282). London: Sage.

Neeley, A. (2002). *Business performance measurement - theory and practice*. Cambridge, UK: Cambridge University Press.

Nickols, F. (2001). The knowledge in knowledge management. In Cortada, J. W., & Woods, J. A. (Eds.), *The knowledge management yearbook 2000-2001* (pp. 12–21). New York: Butterworth-Heinemann.

Nonaka, I., & Konno, N. (1998). The concept of ba: Building a foundation for knowledge creation. *California Management Review, 40*(3), 40–54.

Nonaka, I., & Takeuchi, H. (1995). *The knowledge-creating company*. Oxford: Oxford University Press.

Nonaka, I., & Teece, D. (Eds.). (2001). *Managing industrial knowledge - creation, transfer and utilization*. London: Sage.

Nonaka, I., Toyama, R., & Konno, N. (2001). Seci, ba, and leadership: A unified model of dynamic knowledge creation. In Nonaka, I., & Teece, D. (Eds.), *Managing industrial knowledge creation, transfer and utilization*. Thousand Oaks, CA, USA: Sage.

O'Dell, C. (2000). *Knowledge management - a guide for your journey to best-practice processes* (White Paper). Houston, Texas: Grayson, C. J., American Productivity and Quality Center.

O'Dell, C., & Jackson Grayson, J. (1998). *If only we knew what we know: The transfer of internal knowledge and best practice*. Houston, Texas: The Free Press.

Onge, H. S. (1999). Tacit knowledge: The key to the strategic alignment of intellectual capital. In M. Zack (Ed.), Knowledge and strategy (pp. pp. 223-230). Boston: Butterworth Heinemann.

Onwuegbuzie, A. J., & Leech, N. L. (2005). On becoming a pragmatic researcher: The importance of combining quantitative and qualitative research methodologies. *International Journal of Social Research Methodology, 8*(5), 375–387. doi:10.1080/13645570500402447

PMI. (2008). *A guide to the project management body of knowledge* (4th ed.). Newton Sq, PA: Project Management Institute Inc.

Polanyi, M. (1966). *The tacit dimension*. London: Routledge & Kegan Paul.

Polanyi, M. (1997). Tacit knowledge. In Prusak, L. (Ed.), *Knowledge in organizations - resources for the knowledge-based economy* (pp. 135–146). Oxford: Butterworth-Heinemann.

Prahlad, C. K., & Ramaswamy, V. (2000). Co-opting customer competence. *Harvard Business Review, 78*(1), 79–87.

Prusak, L., & Cohen, D. (2001). How to invest in social capital. *Harvard Business Review, 79*(6), 86–93.

Quinn, J. B., Andersen, P., & Finkelstein, S. (1996). Managing professional intellect: Making the most of the best. *Harvard Business Review, 74*(2), 71–80.

Reid, S. E., & Brentani, U. D. (2004). The fuzzy front end of new product development for discontinuous innovations: A theoretical model. *Journal of Product Innovation Management, 21*(3), 170–184. doi:10.1111/j.0737-6782.2004.00068.x

Robey, D., Boudreau, M.-C., & Rose, G. M. (2000). *Information technology and organizational learning: A review and assessment of research.* Accounting Management and Information Technologies.

Rogers, E. M. (1995). *Diffusion of innovation* (3rd ed.). New York: The Free Press.

Rollo, C. & Clarke, T. (2001). *International best practice - case studies in knowledge management* (Standard/Guideline HB 275 Supplement 1-2001). Sydney: Standards Australia.

Samaddar, S., & Kadiyala, S. S. (2006). An analysis of interorganizational resource sharing decisions in collaborative knowledge creation. *European Journal of Operational Research, 170*(1), 192–210. doi:10.1016/j.ejor.2004.06.024

Sawhney, M., Verona, G., & Prandelli, E. (2005). Collaborating to create: The internet as a platform for customer engagement in product innovation. *Journal of Interactive Marketing, 19*(4), 4–17. doi:10.1002/dir.20046

Scharmer, C. O. (2001). Self-transcending knowledge: Organizing around emerging realities. In Nonaka, I., & Teece, D. (Eds.), *Managing industrial knowledge - creation, transfer and utilization* (pp. 69–90). London: Sage.

Schein, E. H. (1993). How can organisations learn faster? Lessons from the green room. *Sloan Management Review,* (Winter): 85–92.

Schön, D. A. (1983). *The reflective practitioner - how professionals think in action.* Aldershot, UK: BasiAshgate ARENA.

Schuppel, J., Muller-Stewens, G., & Gomez, P. (1998). The knowledge spiral. In Krogh, G. V., Ros, J., & Kleine, D. (Eds.), *Knowing in firms: Understanding, managing and measuring knowledge* (pp. 223–239). London, UK: Sage Publications.

Schwalbach, E. M. (2003). *Value and validity in action research: A guidebook for reflective practitioners.* London: Scarecrow Press.

Seel, R. (2001). Anxiety and incompetence in the large group - a psychodynamaic perspective. *Journal of Organizational Change Management, 14*(5), 493–503. doi:10.1108/EUM0000000005878

Senge, P., Kleiner, A., Roberts, C., Roth, G., & Smith, B. (1999). *The dance of change: The challenges of sustaining momentum in learning organisations.* New York: Doubleday.

Senge, P. M. (1990). *The fifth discipline - the art & practice of the learning organization.* Sydney, Australia: Random House.

Senge, P. M., Kleiner, A., Roberts, C., Ross, R., & Smith, B. (1999). *The fifth discipline fieldbook: Strategies and tools for building a learning organization.* New York: Doubleday.

Sherman, J. D., Berkowitz, D., & Sounder, W. E. (2005). New product development performance and the interaction of cross-functional integration and knowledge management. *Journal of Product Innovation Management, 22*(3), 399–411. doi:10.1111/j.1540-5885.2005.00137.x

Standards Australia. (2008). *Knowledge management: A framework for succeeding in the knowledge era (Standard/Guideline HB 275-2001).* Sydney: Standards Australia.

Sternberg, R. J. (1985). *Beyond IQ: A triarchic theory of human intelligence.* New York: Viking.

Sternberg, R. J., Forsythe, G. B., Hedlund, J., Horvath, J. A., Wagner, R. K., & Williams, W. M. (2000). *Practical intelligence in everyday life.* New York: Cambridge University Press.

Sternberg, R. J., & Horvath, J. A. (1999). *Testing knowledge in professional practice.* Mahwah, NJ: Erlbaum.

Sternberg, R. J., Wagner, R. K., & Williams, W. M. (1995). Testing common sense. *The American Psychologist, 50*(11). doi:10.1037/0003-066X.50.11.912

Stewart, T. A. (2000). *Intellectual capital - the new wealth of organizations*. London: Nicholas Brealey Publishing.

Storck, J., & Hill, P. A. (2000). Knowledge diffusion through "strategic communities". *Sloan Management Review, 41*(2), 63–74.

Strang, K. D. (2003). Achieving organizational learning across projects. In J. Kardon (Ed.), *Proceedings of the North America global congress*. Baltimore, MD: PMI.

Strang, K. D. (2005). Examining effective and ineffective transformational project leadership. *Team Performance Management Journal, 11*(3/4), 68–103. doi:10.1108/13527590510606299

Strang, K. D. (2007). Examining effective technology project leadership traits and behaviours. *Computers in Human Behavior, 23*(2), 424–462. doi:10.1016/j.chb.2004.10.041

Strang, K. D. (2008a). Collaborative synergy and leadership in e-business. In Salmons, J., & Wilson, L. (Eds.), *Handbook of research on electronic collaboration and organizational synergy* (pp. 409–434). Hershey, PA: IGI Global.

Strang, K. D. (2008b). Quantitative online student profiling to forecast academic outcome from learning styles using dendrogram decision. *Multicultural Education & Technology Journal, 2*(4), 215–244. doi:10.1108/17504970810911043

Strang, K. D. (2009a). Assessing team member interpersonal competencies in new product development e-projects. *International Journal of Project Organisation and Management, 1*(4), 335–357. doi:10.1504/IJPOM.2009.029105

Strang, K. D. (2009b). Improving supervision of cross-cultural post graduate university students. *International Journal of Learning and Change, 4*(2), 21–42.

Strang, K. D. (2009c). Multicultural e-education: Student learning styles, culture and performance. In Song, H., & Kidd, T. (Eds.), *Handbook of research on human performance and instructional technology*. Hershey, PA: IGI Global.

Strang, K. D. (2009d). Using recursive regression to explore nonlinear relationships and interactions: A tutorial applied to a multicultural education study. *Practical Assessment. Research Evaluation, 14*(3), 1–13.

Sveiby, K. E. (1997a). *The invisible balance sheet* [Internet]. Retrieved, 2003, from www.sveiby.com/articles/InvisibleBalance.html

Sveiby, K. E. (1997b). *The new organizational wealth: Managing and measuring knowledge-based assets*. San Francisco: Berrett-Koehler Publishers, Inc.

Sveiby, K. E. (1998). *Measuring intangibles and intellectual capital - an emerging first standard* [Internet]. Retrieved, 2003, from www.sveiby.com/articles/EmergingStandard.html

Swap, W., Leonard, D., Shields, M., & Abrams, L. (2001). Using mentoring and storytelling to transfer knowledge in the workplace. *Journal of Management Information Systems, 40*(3), 95–114.

Swierczek, F. W. (1994). Culture and conflict in joint ventures in Asia. *International Journal of Project Management, 12*(1), 39–47. doi:10.1016/0263-7863(94)90008-6

Takeuchi, H. (1998). *Beyond knowledge management: Lessons from Japan* [Internet]. Retrieved from www.sveiby.com/articles/LessonsJapan.htm

Takeuchi, H. (2001). Towards a universal management concept of knowledge. In Nonaka, I., & Teece, D. (Eds.), *Managing industrial knowledge - creation, transfer and utilization* (pp. 315–329). London: Sage.

Teece, D. J. (1998). Capturing value from knowledge assets: The new economy, markets for know-how, and intangible assets. *California Management Review, 40*(3), 55–79.

Teece, D. J. (2001). Strategies for managing knowledge assets: The role of firm structure and industrial context. In Nonaka, I., & Teece, D. (Eds.), *Managing industrial knowledge - creation, transfer and utilization* (pp. 125–144). London: Sage.

Teigland, R. (2000). Communities of practice at an internet firm: Netovation vs on-time performance. In Lesser, E., Fontaine, M. A., & Slusher, J. A. (Eds.), *Knowledge and communities* (pp. 151–178). Boston: Butterworth-Heinemann. doi:10.1016/B978-0-7506-7293-1.50013-5

Trompenaars, F. (1993). *Riding the waves of culture: Understanding cultural diversity in business*. London: Economics Books.

Tsoukas, H. (Ed.). (2003). *Do we really understand tacit knowledge?* London: Blackwell.

Ulwick, A. W. (2002). Turn customer input into innovation. *Harvard Business Review, 80*(1), 91–97.

von Krough, G., Ichijo, K., & Takeuchi, H. (2000). *Enabling knowledge creation*. Oxford: Oxford University Press.

Wagner, R. K., & Sternberg, R. J. (1985). Practice intelligence in real-world pursuits: The role of tacit knowledge. *Journal of Personality and Social Psychology, 49*(2), 436–458. doi:10.1037/0022-3514.49.2.436

Walsh, J. P., & Ungson, G. R. (1997). Organizational memory. In Prusak, L. (Ed.), *Knowledge in organizations - resources for the knowledge-based economy* (pp. 147–175). Oxford: Butterworth-Heinemann.

Weick, K. E. (1995). *Sensemaking in organizations*. Thousand Oaks, CA: Sage.

Weick, K. E. (2001). *Making sense of the organization*. Oxford: Blackwell Publishers.

Wenger, E. C. (1998). *Communities of practice learning as a social system*. Systems Thinker.

Wenger, E. C. (1999). Communities of practice: The key to knowledge strategy. *The Journal of the Institute for Knowledge Management, 1*(Fall), 48–63.

Wenger, E. C., McDermott, R., & Snyder, W. M. (2002). *Cultivating communities of practice: A guide to managing knowledge*. Boston: Harvard Business School Publishing.

Wenger, E. C., & Snyder, W. M. (2000). Communities of practice: The organizational frontier. *Harvard Business Review, 78*(1), 139–145.

Werbach, K. (2000). Syndication - the emerging model for business in the internet era. *Harvard Business Review, 78*(3), 85–93.

Whitley, B. E. Jr. (2002). *Principles of research in behavioral science* (2nd ed.). New York: McGraw-Hill.

Wiig, K. M. (2002). *Knowledge management: An emerging discipline rooted in a long history*. Knowledge Research Institute. Retrieved May 21, 2006, from www.krii.com

Wiig, K. M. (2003). *Knowledge management has many facets* [internet]. Knowledge Research Institute. Retrieved March 21, 2009, from www.krii.com

Wilson, T. D. (2002). The nonsense of 'knowledge management'. *Information Research, 8*(1), 1–14.

Yin, R. K. (2003). *Case study research: Design and methods* (3rd ed.). London, UK: Sage.

Zack, M. H. (1999). Developing a knowledge strategy. *California Management Review, 41*(3), 125–145.

KEY TERMS AND DEFINITIONS

Balanced Score Card: A performance measurement device intended to represent business innovation and value from four dimensions: financial (profit levels, market share etc.); customer (satisfaction); internal business process (efficiency and effectiveness of knowledge articulation processes); innovation and learning (longer term systemic results of knowledge articulation).

Communities of Practice: "Groups of people informally bound together by shared expertise and passion for a joint enterprise" (Wenger & Snyder, 2000, p. 139); these are often informal (but highly focused) subject matter specialists, that can solve complex and perplexing problems by collaborating.

Intellectual Capital: Human (people), structural (physical, hardware, software), customers, that provide explicit and tacit knowledge to the organization.

Knowledge Articulation: Continuum: philosophy that knowledge is not necessary explicit or tacit ("black or white"), but exists as a "justified true perspective" from the viewer standpoint; it can exist on several levels of analysis, namely as organizational memory, community of practice/team capability, individual memory/capability (and possibly other levels beyond the scope of this research such as culture or political).

Organizational Learning: Memory and a systemic feedback look in e-business; leverages the power of a community of practice, along with human, structural and customer capital, to articulate knowledge that can be reused later, to improve innovation, productivity and performance at the company level.

Storytelling: A business executive or community of practice method for sharing tacit knowledge, which involves (primarily subject matter specialists) using combinations of personal stories, evidence to support their ideas, along with a visual metaphor (superimposed on an "analysis tree") that shows the structure and relationships among the ideas/phases (Forman, 2001). Storytelling permits the transfer of rich contextual knowledge details (Swap, et al., 2001), while empowering the community of practice members to reframe their own perceptions (not necessarily filtering out or denying cultural norms) thus enabling individuals to grasp new implied tacit knowledge not in their conscious memory (Ambrosini & Bowman, 2001; Hansen & Kahnweiler, 1993; Sternberg, et al., 2000; Swap, et al., 2001).

Tacit Knowledge: Characterized as "knowledge is an activity which would better be described as a process of knowing." (Polanyi, 1966, p. 132); professional instinct (Sternberg, 1985; Sternberg & Horvath, 1999); procedural in nature, acquired with little help from others as personal experience, and relevant to the attainment of goals (Sternberg, et al., 1995).

Transcending Knowledge: Scharmer (2001) put forth the transcending (not-yet-embodied) qualification on tacit knowledge (which is described in this research as innate, see Figure 4); this may be instinct, or subconscious behavior (in humans), or unobservable as economies-of-scale potential in e-businesses.

Chapter 11
Applications of a Social Software Model

Tanguy Coenen
Vrije Universiteit Brussels, Belgium

Wouter Van den Bosch
Katholieke Hogeschool Mechelen, Belgium

ABSTRACT

This paper discusses social software technologies and presents an integrated social software model that can be used to achieve collective goals. This model has grown out of a need among practitioners to identify useful social software functionalities and to find out what to do with them. As the number of social software technologies increases, the question increasingly remains what to do with them and how to apply them usefully. The model can be used within an organization, to guide it in attaining organizational goals, but it can also be used to support activities in a network of organizations or in a network of non-affiliated individuals. First, we discuss social software in general. Subsequently, we discuss a model for understanding social software data and functionality. Finally, two possible applications of the social software model are discussed: knowledge sharing and increasing social inclusion among youth.

INTRODUCTION

Social Software and Web 2.0

Around 2004, a new generation of Web-based technologies emerged, characterized by the following aspects:

- **Easy content creation interfaces**. Before, one needed to know how to program HTML pages in order to create a Web page. With the coming of new, easier interfaces, Web content could be created using WYSIWIG interfaces, making content creation by non-technical users more feasible.

- **Easy content publishing**. In order to place content on-line, there was no longer the need for an ftp-client. One could create content on-line, which would be available on the World Wide Web at once.

DOI: 10.4018/978-1-61520-841-8.ch011

Copyright © 2011, IGI Global. Copying or distributing in print or electronic forms without written permission of IGI Global is prohibited.

To name this transition, the concepts of Web 2.0 and social software emerged on the Web. This emergence was not driven by any one in particular and therefore both concepts deserve some clarification. The emergence of the term "social software" coincides with the concept of Web 2.0, indicating a move from older Web technologies to a new generation of systems. Both concepts are very similar in the technologies they denote, but differ in the emphasis they place on these technologies. To users of the Web 2.0 concept, the essence is the fact that the technologies are new compared to "1.0" systems. This was important in the light of the.com bubble of 2000-2001. The fact that a new generation of Web-based systems had arrived indicated that creating a business based on Web 1.0 technologies, which had proven to be unsustainable, was not the same as building a business on Web 2.0 technology. This idea spurred a new wave of investment in Web 2.0 technologies.

The concept of social software emphasizes the technology's support for social behavior, rather than the fact that the technology is something new, as is the case for the Web 2.0 concept. Social software allows people to do things together. In order for this to happen, it is imperative that this type of software be Web-based. Only by using the World Wide Web as a platform are different people able to interact in a way that scales as growing numbers participate in the interaction. According to Shirky (2008), a sharp drop in transaction costs for on-line communication and collaboration was spurred by the creation of easy to use Web-based technology. Through these reduced transaction costs, social software is creating new forms of social organization at a massively distributed and global scale. Indeed, it is now much easier to organize a civil protest or a party by using a social networking system like Facebook. Another advantage of the drop in transaction costs is that it has become easier to sustain relationships with people you don't know well. These so called "weak ties" are a form of social capital that can be activated to obtain certain advantages, like for example access to information. The lowering of transaction costs for communication and collaboration has also spurred a change in media-production power relations. It has placed a substantial portion of the mean of production, traditionally owned by large centralized entities like governments and media corporations, in the hands of the masses (Benkler 2006).

We believe it is more significant to focus on these new forms of social organization, than on the fact that there is a new software kid on the block. It is for this reason that this chapter focuses on social software instead of Web 2.0, although the systems denoted by both concepts are essentially the same.

On-line communities also use social software, although the nature of community support is changing. The forum-style of community support, where member of a community can post messages and answer these messages, has been around since the days of the bulletin board systems, which largely predate the world-wide Web. Communicating over such systems has proven to be highly effective, yet can be hard to set up. In recent times, community support has become something that can be created on-the-fly, in social software systems. When a need for such support is felt, the people who drive the community can us systems like Ning to set up a space with a large number of features to support the community interaction. Another option is to create a group in e.g. Facebook. The fact that most of these group spaces have a short life span, reflects the transiency nature of on-line community life. Indeed, most users have a loose affiliation to a great number of communities and participate to these communities in a fashion that is limited in time (Wellman et al 2003).

Enterprise 2.0 and Socialprise

The same parallel can be drawn between two terms in current business language: enterprise 2.0 and socialprise. Enterprise 2.0 refers to the application of Web 2.0 technologies to serve the

Figure 1. The social software functionality model

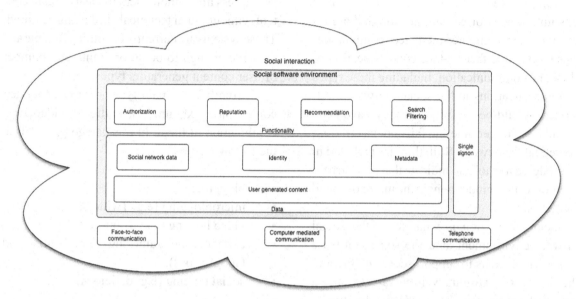

goals of the organization. However, just like Web 2.0 only denotes "something new", enterprise 2.0 is a very vague term and can mean a awful lot of things, allowing almost every software vendor to re-brand his software as such[1].

Slightly more informative is the term socialprise, which points to the application of social software to the organization. This permits new forms of social organization to serve the organizational goals. Where we will discuss organizational applications, we will therefore use the concept of socialprise. However, in order to apply this concept to the organization, it needs to be aligned with the organizational strategy. In order to allow this, we first need to create a model of social software functionality. This will permit the instantiation of the model to serve the goals of an organization or more loosely affiliated groups of people.

THE SOCIAL SOFTWARE FUNCTIONALITY MODEL

This model has been created based on our experiences with social software theory and practice.

It's purpose is to guide the practitioner in how to obtain results using social software. In a later part of this chapter, we discuss two cases, indicating how goals can be sub-divided in tasks and how these tasks can be mapped to the social software functionality model. The model in (Figure 1) presents an overview of the functionality that is currently found in social software systems. We will spend the remainder of this chapter on discussing the various components in the model.

Social Interaction

The fact that it supports and is supported by social interaction is crucial to social software. In (Figure 1), this is indicated by the cloud, surrounding the social software environment. Social interaction can be supported through face-to-face conversations or through computer-mediated communication. One could argue that computer-mediated technologies are a social software component, as they are software-based and support social interaction. However, it is chosen in this chapter to leave computer mediated communication out of the social software environment, as these technologies (e.g. email, voice-over-ip, chat) constitute modes of communication that are on par with non-computer-mediated communications modes like face-to-face communication or telephone communication. Including these types of communications in the social software environment would be awkward, as they have been around for a longer time and fall under a different theoretical framework. Still, they are included in the model as a whole, to indicate that mainstream communication modes remain the motor of social interaction.

Social interaction is what feeds the social software environment, and the social software environment exists to support social interaction. Therefore, it is absolutely necessary to take a socio-technical approach towards social software. In such an approach, both the technical and the social perspectives are considered to be first-class citizens in the discussion.

The Social Software Environment

The social software environment represents and integrated environment in which different components interact. In this section, each of these elements is discussed. In essence, the model represents a taxonomy, in which data and functionality are on the highest level of the tree. A bi-directional relationship exists between both: the data allows the functionality and the functionality creates the data.

Types of Data

User-Generated Content

One of the main characteristics of social software is the fact that it involves user generated content. Social software environments have seen a great increase in the volume of user generated content, due to the decrease in transaction costs for placing content on-line. As general tools, Content management systems such as Drupal, Joomla or Wordpress allow their users to easily create content without much technical skill being required. These systems are currently becoming flexible and versatile enough to be tailored into any number of user content generators types.

Currently[2], the main types of user generated content are text, images, audio or video or a combination of them. In this category, we place the following services:

- blogging;
- microblogging (e.g. Twitter);
- video hosting (e.g. Youtube);
- collaborative authoring (e.g. Wiki's and Google docs);
- social tagging (e.g. delicious).

User generated content is the basis of social software, as it constitutes the stuff through which on-line social interaction occurs.

Social Networking Data

Interacting in social networking systems (e.g. Facebook, mySpace, LinkedIn, etc.) generates a lot of useful data. The main type of data, created through user interaction, is the structure of the social network in which a user is operating. Who does he or she know, what is the nature of the user's relationship with the different people in the social network and how close is the relationship? This is all useful data with which to build new functionality. For example, based on social network data, applications like LinkedIn and Hoover's Connect allow people to select a person they want to talk to and then generate a path to this person through people they already know. In this way, an introduction can be arranged, which can facilitate the creation of business deals between companies.

Besides social data, social networking data also contains non-social data[3]. In a system like Facebook, the nodes in the network are not necessarily people, but also organizations, brands, movies, bands, etc. This allows the gathering of not only the social contacts of a user, but also of his or her interests and preferences. The result is a diversified graph of people and their relationships to both human and non-human entities.

Identity

In many social software applications, the user has the possibility to create a profile on which identity information is added. This can range from the rather dry descriptions of user identity, in which people answer pre-defined questions, to situations in which the user has a lot of freedom in which to express his or her identity. In the latter case, the user has the possibility to customize the type of information made available and the way it is presented, by adding images, sound and video.

All this identity information is very interesting, as it allows people to know who they talk to. Before establishing contact with a certain person, it is of the utmost importance to know who the person is, what his interest are and what you have in common. Without an insight in a user's identity, no contact will be established over social software systems.

Metadata

Different types of metadata are in use in social software environments. Identity information can be seen as a type of metadata about people. So can social networking data, although this type of data does not always pertain to a certain person, but to the relationship of a certain person with others.

In general, metadata can be applied by selecting terms from controlled ontologies. This is for example the case when people file items in databases under certain categories that are part of a taxonomy. A taxonomy is a type of ontology. Yet ontologies are designed by people and therefore only reflect the view of the designers on the world they wish to organize. More often than not, this does not reflect the way in which

others would organize this very same world. In addition, ontologies are often very expensive to create and maintain.

The alternative is the attribution of metadata that does not comply to some ontology. Using these free-tagging, social tagging or folksonomy approaches does not allow the inference that is possible when using ontologies, but on the other hand is much cheaper and always reflects the world view of the user who attributes the metadata. In addition, it is possible to generate interesting functionality by analyzing sets of tags. One example is the creation of a tag cloud that identifies a person's main interests, based on the tags he or she has attributed to on-line resources over time. In this way, a knowledge profile can be created of this person, which benefits the lookup of expertise within an organisation.

Rating or voting content is another type of metadata often found in social software systems. This can be usefull to collectively asses the quality of user generated content and with it the authors of this content, as a person who has produced much quality content can be regarded as being a high quality author.

Types of Functionality

A number of functionalities operate on the different types of social network data described in the previous section.

Authorization

In order to regulate access by different users to different content, authorization mechanisms are necessary that can handle a fine grained access regulation. This can be done, based on social networking data, which can be semantically annotated. It is for example possible to indicate that a particular person is "a colleague" or "family". Based on this information, it becomes possible to make sure that certain content is only accessed by certain groups of users.

This is particularly relevant as more stories emerge of social software being used in ways that surprise some users. One example is a court case in the United States in which a person had a car accident and then drove on without taking care of the consequences, a so called "hit and run". The driver was drunk but said it was only a one time incident. By looking up the driver's photo's on Facebook, the lawyers of the defense was able to prove that it was not a one time alcohol intoxication and that the driver has instead a partying lifestyle.

More and more, social software pundits are warning against the naive use of these technology platforms. Fine-grained authorization mechanism can give users the control they need to direct who sees what content.

Reputation

In order to promote self-organization in a social software environment, it can be beneficial to provide a way in which to build reputation within the environment. Indeed, reputation has been show to increase the likelihood that people will collaborate (Axelrod, 1997), instead of exhibiting free-rider behavior or carrying out acts of digital vandalism. This is especially true if the social network in which the system operates is relatively dense, with many relationships between users. In that case, the chances are high that if a person does something good for another person of for the community in general, this will have an impact on a future encounter with another person from this part of the social network. In a sparse network, with few connections between nodes, the chances that one will interact again with a certain individual are slim. Therefore, there may be less incentive to treat the other individual well in such a network. Reputation also travels over social networks, as people discuss the reputation of others. Still, if the social network existing among the users of a system is sparse, this reputation will not spread quickly, as relatively few users discuss reputation of others among each other. Therefore, a reputation system will have more impact if the social network among the users of the system is relatively dense. Still, reputation will automatically build and be applied in small user groups whith a dense social network. In these environments, people are likely to see each other again because of the small size of the user group and people are likely to discuss other people's reputation because of the dense social network. In such a situation, most people know each other and therefore can rely on the implicit reputation management which has been around ever since mankind developed social abilities. However, this is not the case in sparse networks, making reputation management useful as a way to promote social interaction within a system and a way to protect the system against free-rider behavior (Tucker, 2008).

Reputation systems have been deployed in different social software systems, but an approach that integrates the reputations of all the different systems in order to create a productive social software ecosystem has not been attempted to our knowledge.

Search and Filtering

In an environment in which content is created at a very high rate, it is imperative to propose good ways to quickly find relevant material. This is true for user-generated content, but also for users themselves, as talking to others is a very efficient way of sharing knowledge. Therefore, strategies that allow people to find others that have expertise in certain areas is also an interesting social software strategy. This can be done, based on the social software data generated by users. Different data manipulation techniques can be used to indicate expertise. For example, content rating, indicating quality, can be combined with content tagging, indicating topics, to produce a list of people who have produced high quality content on a certain topic.

Recommendation

Because of the availability of social network data on social and non-social relations, it becomes possible to use different types of algorithms to recommend social or non-human actors (see chapters 3,4,5 and 6 in this book). The social graph is becoming more rich and is complemented with links to non-human actors like events, TV-programs, and music. In the future, as our interactions will extend to an Internet-of-things in which physical objects will be referencable on-line, this social graph will also include physical objects like the paintings you stopped to see in a museum or the buildings you took take an interest in during a tourist trip. As the graph becomes richer, the opportunities for generating useful recommendations will increase. As anything can be a node in this graph, it will more and more become possible to obtain recommendations on a large variety of non-human nodes. These will still be features of social software, as the choices made by the people in your social network will influence the recommendations you get.

Single Sign-On

Single sign-on mechanisms allow users to log in to different systems using the same username and password combination. As such combinations can also uniquely identify user data, single sign-on also permits user profiles and social networking date to be migrated between systems.

There has recently been much critique on the "walled garden" nature of certain social software systems, in particular of the social networking flavor (*The Economist*, May 16 2008). The complaint is that different systems exist and that the effort that is invested in one system cannot be exported to other systems, requiring users to create new accounts each time they want to use a new system. Still, the response of many systems vendors has not been to make their data portable between systems. This would allow other systems to completely take

over the user generated content which established systems have painstakingly accumulated. Instead, some large social software brands like Google and Facebook have created single sign-on mechanism that allow user to use different functionalities with one username-password combination. This permits e.g. Facebook users to log in on external Web sites using their Facebooks accounts and in doing so import some Facebook functionality on the external site and easily link external site data to Facebook.

The more single sign-on mechanisms gain in popularity, the more they will have the ability to sew the very disparate social software landscape together. It is however worrying that these mechanisms are currently being pushed by commercial entities like Facebook and Google, who make claims to the user generated content they are gathering. Whereas open-source single sign-on initiatives exist, like e.g. OpenID, there is still a lack off support for such initiatives by social software system vendors that have obtained a large user base.

Now that the general social software model has been discussed, it can be applied to specific collective goals. We apply it to knowledge sharing and neighborhood effects to promote social inclusion of youth (Figure 2).

APPLYING SOCIAL SOFTWARE TO KNOWLEDGE SHARING

Issues

According to the knowledge-based theory of the firm, an important reason for the existence of organizations as entities is that they can make better use of the knowledge of their employees (Nonaka & Takeuchi, 1995). In this theory, it is plain that the sharing of knowledge is crucial to the functioning of the firm. Indeed, no individual can claim to hold the knowledge that allows them to perform all the tasks in the organization well.

Figure 2. The application of social software to knowledge sharing. The dots indicate the usage of a certain part of the model to support an issue.

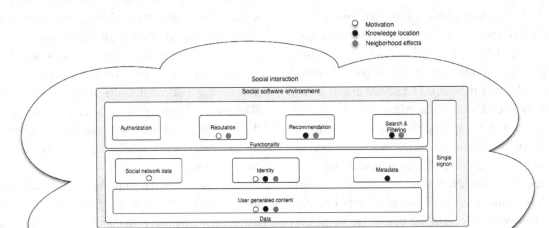

Therefore, they often need knowledge held by others in the organization. The objective of knowledge sharing is to make sure that knowledge held by individuals is distributed among other people. This poses a number of issues:

- **Knowledge location**. It is often hard to find the right knowledge to solve a particular problem. This knowledge can be embedded either in documents or in people's heads.
- **Motivation**. Not all people are readily inclined to share knowledge with others. They often feel that their knowledge is what provides their economic added value and are therefore reluctant to share it with others.

Knowledge Location

User-Generated Content

In terms of user-generated content, the main challenge is to get users to externalize their knowledge and place it on-line. Different types of content exist for different purposes. The three main containers of user-generated content that are useful to knowledge sharing in organizations are currently wiki's, blogs and microblogs. As they are mainly used at the time of writing, these types of user generated content have different characteristics in terms of velocity, deepness and structure, which are important aspects of knowledge sharing.

Velocity refers to the speed at which knowledge can travel among the users of the medium. This is much related to how people usually plug into the medium. The highest immediacy is found on microblogging platforms, where people often constantly monitor incoming new messages, using client software running in the background on their computer. Blogs generally have a lower velocity than microblogs but can still disseminate knowledge at high speed, because they are commonly accessed using RSS feed aggregators. However, a blog is typically longer that a microblog, making it more time-consuming to assimilate. People do not typically subscribe to wiki's using RSS, although it is possible to do so on many wiki platforms.

Table 1. Different user generated content platforms according to knowledge sharing parameters. Numbers indicate ranking.

	Velocity	Deepness	Structure
Wiki	3	1	1
Blog	2	2	2
Microblog	1	3	2

This, together with the fact that a wiki post is often longer than a blog or microblog post, gives it a lower velocity.

Deepness refers to the amount of elaboration of the knowledge that is embedded in the user generated content item. In terms of deepness, wiki's come first. Indeed, a wiki page on a certain topic can be as long as one wants. This is also the case for a blog entry, but the difference lies in the way in which knowledge is shared on a certain topic. In a wiki, people will collaboratively edit the page until it reaches a stage that is satisfactory to all involved parties that have access to the page. With blogs, this is different. First, people typically cannot modify someone else's blog post. A blog post is a personal artifact, not a collaborative one like a wiki. All other people can do is comment on it. Additionally, the trend seems to be to create a new blog entry when someone has something new to say on a given topic, instead of editing an older blog post. In terms of deepness, microblogs do not rate very highly, because of their 140 character limit.

Structure is also an important aspect of knowledge location, as it allows the retrieval of knowledge and shows the way different pieces of knowledge are linked together. In terms of structure, wiki's score high. Indeed, they offer different ways to categorize pages and link concepts to other concepts, resulting in a complex but usable knowledge structure. This is not the case with blogs and microblogs, where more often than not different entries are not linked to each other or categorized in any way.

Metadata

Metadata is of the utmost importance to knowledge location. Adding e.g. tags will facilitate the aggregation of documents around certain topics and the subsequent retrieval of knowledge on a certain topic Adding information on the author will provide clues on expertise within the organization. Time-related metadata provides insight on how up-to-date a document can be expected to be.

Identity

In on-line systems, identity can be represented through a user profile. This can contain free text, but can also contain automatically generated information on the documents that where written by a particular person. By aggregating metadata on the user-generated content produced by a person, an overview can be provided of a person's expertise.

Search and Filtering

Full text search of user generated content is a very useful feature, that should be present in each environment that seeks to support knowledge sharing. Yet it is also important to support search and filtering based on the tags that have been added by users in the system. In this way, it becomes possible to locate people with expertise on a certain topics. As was mentioned before, if this is combined with rating features, it even becomes possible to quantify the amount of expertise.

Recommendation

Combining the overall set of metadata related to user-generated content with the profile of a user can allow a person to obtain recommendations on knowledge that can of interest. Social networking data can also be applied to obtain social-recommendations. It is indeed likely that the relevance of content to a particular person increases as the number of peers who have accessed this content increases. Both the search and filtering, recommendation and identity functionalities can make the functioning of transactive memory systems within an organization more efficient, as explained in the following section.

Knowledge Location and Transactive Memory

A transactive memory system is defined by Wegner (1986) as the collective of individuals, their memory systems, and the communication that occurs between them. Transactive memory systems lower the need for individuals to accumulate knowledge on a great variety of topics. By dividing the learning tasks, people are able to specialize, as they will be able to obtain knowledge on certain topics from others when needed. The term transactive memory refers to the fact that people can obtain knowledge from each other by engaging in transactions. In the transactive memory system existing in a group, people develop directories, which contain knowledge on the knowledge of others, i.e. people develop a notion of who knows what.

Moreland & Myaskovsky (2000) have found that it is not necessary that people develop directories of each other's knowledge through face-to-face interaction. Group performance can also be improved if the knowledge directories are created over other mean. This means, that creating a system which provides indications on people's expertise (identity), is able to search the expertise in the organization (search and filtering) and is able to generate recommendations that will re-route knowledge in the organization (recommendation) is also likely to enable knowledge work within the organization.

Still, having pointer to other people's knowledge and ways to search this data is useless, if the people that hold the knowledge are not willing to actually share their knowledge. To share their knowledge, people need to be motivated to do so.

How this can be done by means of social software is the subject of the next section.

Motivation

Reputation

Reputation can be a very powerful way to motivate knowledge sharing in an organization. Different ways to motivate knowledge shared have been tried over time, like promotion incentives and financial bonuses. However, these have proven not to work in all cases, to be expensive and to lead people to manipulate the system in order to obtain the payoff, without giving anything of value in return (Newell, et al., 2002).

A well conceived reputation system can be a motivating element for sharing knowledge. By having the sharing of knowledge impact one's on-line reputation score, people obtain a payoff that is intangible, but of value nevertheless. Indeed, a good reputation is highly valued by many people, either for their own personal pride, or for the advantages it can get them in the future. People are more willing to do things for people with a high reputation and people with a good on-line reputation will therefore find it easier to work with others.

In addition to being a motivating aspect, reputation also acts as a deterrent. The temptation to e.g. vandalize a wiki page will be more easily resisted if this has a negative influence on one's reputation score.

However, finding a way to manage reputation that is suited to the needs of the application is not always easy and different systems have been designed over the years, like for example Slashdot's "Karma" system. To have a flexible and socially self-organizing system, it is preferable to choose an approach in which people give each other scores, either directly, or through the content which they create.

Social Networking Data

Being able to access the structure of the social network in the organization can benefit the motivation towards knowledge sharing in the organization. One of the motivational aspects of social behavior is reciprocity, or the notion that by giving something, one will obtain something in return (Blau, 1964). During direct reciprocity, the person who gives obtains something in return from the person who receives. In a situation of generalized reciprocity, the person who gives obtains something in return from a third person who belongs to the group of which the receiver is a part.

In such situation, it can be useful to have an insight in the group structure to which a person belongs. Indeed, by browsing the social network surrounding a particular person, one can get an idea of the set of people from whom a knowledge source can expect reciprocity, either on a direct or generalized way.

APPLYING SOCIAL SOFTWARE TO FOSTER SOCIAL INCLUSION BY OVERCOMING NEIGHBORHOOD EFFECTS

Neighborhood Effects

Promoting social inclusion, or undertaking affirmative action in order to reverse the social exclusion of individuals and groups in our society, has become one of Europe's focal points over the past years. Coordinated actions are being taken on a range of different levels in order to make sure that every European citizen is able to contribute to and benefit from social and economical progress. Even so, many people still find themselves at risk of being excluded from our society for a multitude of reasons.

Social exclusion goes beyond the issue of material poverty and can be seen as a multidi-mensional concept (Silver, 1994; Silver, 2007). It encompasses other forms of social disadvantages such as lack of regular and equal access to education, health care, social care and housing. Causes for exclusion too, go beyond material poverty and encompass a wide range of reasons why one might be excluded, such as discrimination against immigrants, ethnic minorities, the disabled, the elderly or ex-offenders (Hills, Grand & Piachaud, 2002).

Providing an overview of all causes and effects of social exclusion would take us beyond the scope of this chapter, yet we lift out one issue that can benefit from the use of social software tools. Research is increasingly taking neighborhood effects into account in predicting the individual disadvantage of youth (Robert, et al., 2003). Too much internal interaction in socio-economically homogeneous neighborhoods may socially isolate residents and limit information networks, thereby perpetuating the cycle of social exclusion (Tienda & Wilson, 2002). Hence, welfare organizations, working with those at risk of social exclusion, could benefit from tools that have the potential to lift people out of their usual surroundings.

Applying the Framework

Social Software tools and social networking systems in specific allow people to connect and interact with each other on-line. The difference between this medium and the real world is that location is no longer an issue. Through the on-line medium, anyone can connect to anyone, anywhere. Moreover, when interacting with others on the Internet via social software, people have considerable freedom in expressing their identity, leaving them free to decide which parts of their identity to make public or even experiment with other identities. Communicating over the Internet often make people feel less inhibited to disclose certain aspects of their identity or opinion as there is less risk for real-life repercussions (McKenna & Bargh, 2000). The use of social software in this case is interesting because it allows people at risk of social exclusion to interact with others on a medium, regardless of their situation in real life as well as grow a network of ties that can provide them with material or immaterial support.

Identity

When interacting with others on-line, be it for professional or non-professional reasons, expressing one's identity is important. We do so in the real world explicitly by telling others about ourselves but also implicitly by dressing in a certain style or associating ourselves with a particular music scene, organization or brand. These identification needs are also relevant in the on-line world (Schouten, 2008). Finegrained on-line identities allow us to find compatible matches more easily and thus are a vital component of any social software tool that wants to facilitate social interaction.

Yet the image some users of social networking sites depict of themselves does not necessarily reflect the reality. For some people these platforms offer a means to experiment with their identity in all liberty, away from the restraints of their neighborhood. Allowing this room for experimentation and creative expression of identity can be especially rewarding for youngsters who, because of their socio-economical situation, do not have such liberty in real life (Silver, 2007).

Like in real life, we choose which aspects of our identity we want to project towards others based on our relation with them. We show a different side of ourselves to our friends than we do to our boss. Social software tools should take this into account and allow for multifaceted identities that show a different side of a user's identity to different groups of other users. This in order to tap into the positive effects of being able to experiment as freely as possible with one's identity, interaction with others or expression of ideas.

User-Generated Content

When we connect with others on social networking sites, we mostly connect to people we have already met in the real world (Lampe, Ellison & Steinfield, 2006). If we want to lift people outside of their current neighborhood and have them connect to others on-line, this needs to be stimulated somehow.

Unless people have a specific need to make new connections, such as is the case on dating sites or professional networks like LinkedIn, how can we encourage the creation of new connections between users of social software? Allowing social software users to share their ideas and opinions on specific subjects with peers with the same interests or expertise, seems to be one of the ways people do connect with others they don't already know in an off-line context (Ito, et al., 2008). Shared interests or passions bring people together on-line as finding people with the same interests in the immediate neighborhood is not always that straightforward. Hence social software that allows those at risk of exclusion to form, find, join and interact with others in so-called communities of interest can be an interesting tool to employ for welfare organizations working with this target group.

For those at risk of exclusion, being able to communicate with others regardless of the reason of their exclusion can be a liberating and empowering exercise.

Reputation

We have already mentioned the power of reputation as a motor to motivate people to participate on social software platforms. For those at risk of social exclusion, positive feedback on their actions on-line can be beneficial to their self-esteem and well-being (Schouten, 2008) as well. In this case, a reputation system has to enable its users to receive feedback on their contributions within a particular community of interest by their peers.

This allows a reputation to be built based on feedback by those who matter within the context of a certain subject. In this way, the user of a social software platform could build up a reputation on a variety of topics he or she is interested in, which would probably have been impossible to achieve by purely interacting with others from within their off-line neighborhood. Feeling empowered can often be a first step towards believing that you can change your own situation.

Search and Filtering

With the early days of user-generated content generation behind us, the Internet has been flooded with information of all kinds, from a multitude of sources. Finding one's way on the Internet and finding the right information or people to interact with can be a daunting challenge. In order to use social software as a tool to encourage those at risk of social exclusion to extend their existing social network via interactions within communities of interest, users should be able to easily locate and join communities that relate to their personal field of interest. Such search methods must be facilitated by providing these groups with sufficient meta-data to make them more findable. Such meta-data can be added either explicitly by providing keywords for a group or placing it in a taxonomy or implicitly by gathering meta-data from the interactions within a group.

Recommendation

Just as an effective way to search and filter information can be useful to delve through a mass of information and possible persons of interest, a recommendation system can be another useful tool to bring the right content and contacts to the users of a social software platform. Based on a person's identity and metadata gathered from a user's interactions on a platform, suggestions can be made about both relevant information as well as other people with similar interests one could contact and share communicate with. It is the proactive nature of a recommendation system that makes it so interesting as it may uncover contacts or information one might not be on the lookout for.

CONCLUSION

The model we have described and applied in this chapter proposes a typology of social software, and through this increases the understanding in this type of systems. The model is geared towards practical application and can serve people and organizations who want to ride the Web 2.0 - social software wave but lack a framework within which to conceptualize and develop an architecture. The elements in the model are based on the long-standing experience of the authors in developing and using social software. Still, it could benefit from a more rigorous scientific approach, based on a broad overview of social-software systems.

We have discussed how the model can be applied to two very different areas of human activity: knowledge workers looking for knowledge in organizations and social workers trying to overcome social exclusion by extending the social action radius of those excluded beyond their everyday neighborhood. The diversity of the applications indicated that social software can be applied to a great many activities, as long as they have a social character.

As new types of social software systems are frequently created, the mode will probably further evolve in the coming years. Updating it will be an interesting ongoing endeavor and will result in a growing understanding of what constitutes social software.

REFERENCES

Axelrod, R. (1997). *The complexity of cooperation*. Princeton University Press.

Benkler, Y. (2006). *The wealth of networks*. New Haven, CT: Yale University Press. Retrieved from http://www.benkler.org/Benkler_Wealth_Of_Networks.pdf

Blau, P. (1964). *Exchange and Power in Social Life*. New York: Wiley.

Clay, S. (2008). *Here comes everybody: the power of organizing without organizations*. Penguin Press.

Everywhere and nowhere. (2008, May 19). *The Economist*.

Hills, J., Grand, J. L., & Piachaud, D. (2002). *Understanding Social Exclusion*. OUP Oxford.

Ito, M., Horst, H., Bittanti, M., Boyd, D., Herr-Stephenson, B., & Lange, P. (2008, November). *Living and Learning with New Media: Summary of Findings from the Digital Youth Project*.

Lampe, C., Ellison, N., & Steinfield, C. (2006). A face(book) in the crowd: social Searching vs. social browsing. In *CSCW '06: Proceedings of the 2006 20th anniversary conference on Computer supported cooperative work* (pp. 170, 167). ACM Press.

Latour, B. (2005). *Reassembling the Social: An Introduction to Actor-Network-Theory*. Clarendon Lectures in Management Studies. Oxford University Press.

McKenna, K. Y. A., & Bargh, J. A. (2000). Plan 9 From Cyberspace: The Implications of the Internet for Personality and Social Psychology. *Personality and Social Psychology Review, 4*(1), 57–75. doi:10.1207/S15327957PSPR0401_6

Moreland, R., & Myaskovsky, L. (2000). Exploring the Performance Benefits of Group Training: Transactive Memory or Improved Communication? *Organizational Behavior and Human Decision Processes, 82*(1), 117–133. doi:10.1006/obhd.2000.2891

Newell, S., Robertson, M., Scarbrough, H., & Swan, J. (2002). *Managing knowledge work*. Palgrave.

Nonaka, I., & Takeuchi, H. (1995). *The knowledge-creating company*. New York: Oxford University Press.

Sampson, R.J., Morenoff, J.D., & Gannon-Rowley, T. (2003, November 28). *Assessing Neighbourhood": Social Processes and New Directions in Research*.

Schouten, A. (2008). *Adolescents' online self-disclosure and self-presentation*. Amsterdam School of Communications Research.

Silver, H. (1994). Social Exclusion and Social Solidarity: Three Paradigms. *International Labour Review, 133*, 531–578.

Silver, H. (2007, December). *Social Exclusion: Comparative Analysis of Europe and Middle East Youth*.

Tienda, M., & Wilson, W. J. (2002). Comparative Perspectives of Urban Youth. In *Youth in Cities: A Cross National Perspective*. Cambridge: Cambridge University Press.

Tucker, E. (2008, July 21). Facebook photos judges of character. *The Washington Times*. Retrieved from http://www.washingtontimes.com/news/2008/jul/21/facebook-photos-judges-of-character/

Wellman, B., Quan-Haase, A., & Chen, W. (2003). The Social Affordances of the Internet for Networked individualism. *Journal of Computer-Mediated Communication, 8*(3).

Wenger, D. (1986). Transactive memory: A contemporary analysis of the group mind. In *Theories of group behavior* (pp. 185–205). New York: Springer-Verlag.

ENDNOTES

[1] Similarly to what happened in the late nineties, when information management vendors suddenly became knowledge management vendors.

[2] As the world wide-Web will develop further, new types of user-generated content will appear. For example, one of the imminent developments is the appearance of "Internet of things" technology that allows users to annotate real-world objects with tags, text, video or 3D computer graphics.

[3] The fact that non-social data is being discussed under the social networking data heading may seems contradictory. However, social networking data is the data which results from the interaction within social networking systems that increasingly include the addition of relationships to non-human actors. It is not be confused with social network data, which is a subset of social networking data This inclusion of non-human actors when discussing the social reflects modern sociological views like e.g. Latour's actor-network theory (Latour, 2005).

Chapter 12

People Company:
Be Part of It

Wolfgang Prinz
Fraunhofer Institute for Applied Information Technology FIT, Germany

Sabine Kolvenbach
Fraunhofer Institute for Applied Information Technology FIT, Germany

ABSTRACT

In this chapter we present results of our research on a collaborative platform that enables employees of a global company to present themselves, their business and company site in a company-wide autograph book. For the content generation the employees received an innovative technology, an application running on an Ultra-Mobile Personal Computer (UMPC) that enables users to generate video, sound, simple text, drawings, and photos. Main goal of this applied research is to bridge the gap between the various company sites, to foster working relationships and to strengthen the common understanding that each employee is part of a people company. This chapter describes the application, it presents an analysis of the generated content, the evaluation of the users' acceptance of the UMPC application and the autograph book and finally an outlook on further research activities informed by these results.

INTRODUCTION

Large distributed organizations often have the problem that, even though electronic collaboration takes place between the employees at different locations, they often do not know much about the habits, atmosphere and environment at the remote location. This fact makes it difficult to create social relationships similar to those that exist between people who work at the same location and as a consequence it becomes difficult to create and maintain communities of interest that span different company locations. This aspect motivates the research that is presented in this paper.

In 2008, the year of the Summer Olympics, a German company with 89 locations world-wide had a very special idea to address this problem: a symbolic baton travels around the earth, from company site to company site, from employee to employee, and gathers greetings, ideas, or stories which are collected step by step in an autograph book for the company. The motivation was: We

DOI: 10.4018/978-1-61520-841-8.ch012

Copyright © 2011, IGI Global. Copying or distributing in print or electronic forms without written permission of IGI Global is prohibited.

are a people company, be part of it. The relay was divided into five stages, located in different regions of the earth. The start of the relay was the summer party of the company in Berlin in July 2008. From Berlin the baton traveled to Newbury (Europe), Pittsburgh (North America), São Paulo (Latin America), and Hong Kong (Asia Pacific). Later the relay traveled around the world. Until the end of December the baton visited up to twenty-five company sites. By-and-by an autograph book grew up wherein employees present themselves and their colleagues, their business, company site and their surroundings.

The practical demand for such an application as well as the attached research goal is to enable the employees to become acquainted with the variety of the company; to enhance the dialog and cooperation between the company sites; to strengthen working relationships by overcoming organizational coherence and diversity by increasing organizational transparency (Reichling, 2005), thus making it easier to create and maintain communities of interest. With our technical approach we wanted to add to the state-of-the art organizational community sites (McCarthy, 2008) with the introduction of a mobile device as the primary tool for content generation in the actual working situation.

In the following we describe how the idea of a symbolic baton that collects messages and impressions from different employees and locations of the company was realized and how this information is presented in a Web-based autograph book. The chapter concludes with an evaluation of the collected information, the users' acceptance of the tools and an outlook on future research and design implications.

RELATED WORK ON COLLABORATION SUPPORT

Collaboration research and development in the past decade yielded in a number collaboration

and community systems. Although none of these systems matched exactly the requirement of our application we will present a brief overview on major concepts as they have provided a valuable input for the developments of the Baton application.

Since about 15 years Web based applications are available that support the coordination and cooperation of distributed teams by the provision of shared workspaces, called team rooms (Roseman, 1996; Bentley 1997). Initially these systems were developed in the research area, but quickly the ideas and concepts were employed by commercial products such as Lotus Notes and later MS-Sharepoint. These systems can be described as general purpose cooperation systems that provide a configurable collaborative working environment for many different working situations. Thus, they often provide much elaborated group management and access control services, but they focus mainly on the support of distributed working situations and less in the provision of community support interfaces for multi-media information.

In parallel to these systems a number of community and social networking applications such as Facebook, LinkedIn or XING have received a lot of attention and a growing user base. Although these systems actually raise the awareness about the importance and potential of social networking platforms within a company, they could not be applied for our purpose, since their use cannot be restricted to users of a specific organization. However, important services of such platforms like recommendation, tagging and annotation services were considered as very relevant for our Baton application.

To conclude this brief overview, we argue that many of the currently available systems provide already very useful services to realize the envisaged Baton application. Shared workspace systems provide elaborated group management and access control services, while social networking and community platforms contribute recommendation and networking services. We believe that the integration of collaborative working environments with a multi-media social networking environment will further increase the trust within the community. Thus we have applied and integrated these concepts to develop a special purpose interaction platform for a closed company based user community.

BATON APPLICATION

A main design requirement was that the baton application translates the idea of a symbolic baton into a plain technical tool. To increase the users' motivation and to achieve a high participation in the relay, the tool has to be kept easy to use, small, and intuitive, and it should run on a technical device that provides ultimate simplicity and allows a naive handling. The realization of a tangible application seems to be obvious (Brodersen, 2007). The baton should easily be handed from one employee to the next and the use of the tool should make fun. Employees that get the baton should identify themselves firstly, then compose on the fly messages and afterwards hand it to another colleague. It is important to follow these requirements to achieve a high users' acceptance since the application area consists of people of various ages and professional disciplines. Because of this demographical structure in the company, it was decided deliberately not to use blogging tools. (Koppel, 2006) states that 50% of the bloggers are 27 years old or younger, whereby only 8% of Internet users in all are bloggers (Lenhart, 2006). Most users browse the Web and look for interesting information.

We decided to run the Baton application on a UMPC (Ultra- Mobile PC) by Sony. Our intention was to combine mobility, lifestyle, and functionality in one media. The selected product weights less than 500 grams and supports full connectivity via WLAN and Bluetooth. It provides a microphone and two cameras, a front and a rear camera. The front camera is ideal to take personal photos and videos, whereby the rear camera is perfect to capture the vicinity. The touch screen enables users to control applications by finger touch or pen. By shifting the screen the selected UMPC offers a full keyboard (Figure 1).

The Baton application itself is self-explanatory with a very simple user interface. The application consists only of two forms: a login form and the main window to create the messages using different media. All interface elements like buttons and control lists are big enough to be activated by finger touch.

When the UMPC is turned on, automatically it starts the Baton application and presents the login form. First the employee selects the region, followed by the company site and then enters the business email address. After pressing the enter key or clicking the login button the application opens the form to compose messages.

The Baton application offers five different modalities to create a message: video, sound track, simple text, hand-drawing, and picture. The amount of messages per user is limited. Only one short video, one sound track, up to ten pictures, one text message, and one hand-drawing are allowed. This restriction was made to avoid any technical problems due to storage overflow.

The form to compose messages shown in (Figure 2) is divided in three areas. At the bottom five buttons to select the modality are listed side by side: video, sound, text, drawing, and photo. According to the selected modality, on the right the function buttons are vertically itemized and in the center the form displays either the current camera output, the recorded video, the last snapped photo, entered text, or drawing. While recording and playing back a video or a sound track a progress bar indicates the remaining duration.

To enter a text message the Baton application provides a simple text field in the center. In order to compose a hand-carved drawing the messages form offers a white painting area in the center, and as shown in (Figure 3), on the right two lists to select the pen color or the eraser and the pen thickness. If users use their fingers or the pen for

Figure 1. Baton Device running the Baton application

Figure 2. Baton application in video mode

painting and writing it is like crayoning and hand writing. The fifth possibility to compose messages is to capture up to ten photos.

In regular intervals the data of each baton is uploaded to a shared workspace from which the different media contributions are provided in the Web-based autograph book that is explained in the following section.

AUTOGRAPH BOOK AS A COMMUNITY SITE

The design of the autograph book is guided by three aspects: illustration of the globality of the company, representation of the relay, and an easy overview and access to the collected messages. We use the world map to visualize the world-wide distribution of the company, similar to the interac-

Figure 3. Hand-carved drawing

tive globe approach that is used in (Vyas, 2008) to share geographical locations and experiences.

An orange dot in the world map indicates a company site. The blue magnifier glasses in the map indicate that these sites have participated to the relay and gathered messages. In the middle area of the autograph book a timescale represents the timeline of the relay. The lower area of the autograph lists, on the left by default, all collected messages, grouped by the modality, and indicates the company sites, authors, and creation date. When users select a message, it is presented on the right. To filter the messages lists by origin or time, users can either select a company site by a click in the world map or select a time range by a click in the timescale.

Evaluation

In the following we evaluate the use of the Baton application and the autograph book in the company. First we analyze the contributed messages. The following diagram illustrates the use of the different modalities based on a total of 386 contributions.

It becomes apparent that photos have been very popular, followed by videos and drawings, while sounds and texts are in the minority. This demonstrates that users were more interested in the rich visual media. We identified two reasons

Figure 4. Distribution of contributions over media

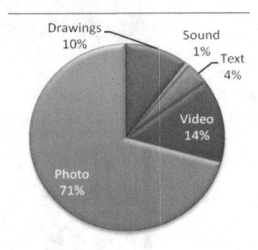

for this. One reason is the fun factor; the second reason is the form factor of the device. Writing text on the keyboard of the UMPC is a little bit tricky.

Furthermore, we analyzed the type of content provided for each modality. First all contributions were classified into categories, like location, portrait, office, message, etc. Then an intra-test was performed to increase and measure the reliability (Shrout, 1979) of this classification.

In total, 14 text messages have been contributed. Most messages (50%) were short greetings; however 30% included a local recipe, which indicates that users used the text media to transport some local flavor. The drawing feature (38 contributions) was mainly used to contribute handwritten greetings (30%), but the majority (63%) used this media to draw typical local pictures (e.g. palm trees, national flag) or small funny cartoons. A few users provided even their signature.

The variety of contributions for photos and videos is much wider. Photos were mainly used to provide portraits about individual colleagues (18%) or groups of colleagues (15%). Furthermore many users took pictures of their office or city location to provide an impression of the locality. The baton was also used to capture social employee-events which are summarized as party (38%). The high number of (sometimes funny) contributions indicates that the baton was used as an interesting high-tech toy during such an occasion. The video distribution is similar to the photo distribution. The office category (videos that show the office environment) corresponds to a photo category of colleagues. In both cases, users used the media to portrait the social or physical environment. According to the framework presented in (Moore, 2007) the contributions fit mainly into the motivation categories of altruism and collaboration (portraits of the department and environment), and self-representation (individual, group and party).

Six weeks after project start, a first evaluation of the autograph book was undertaken during the summer party of the German headquarter. The employees got a presentation of the collected messages in the autograph book on a media wall and afterwards they were able to create messages on the UMPC and access the autograph book by themselves. We noticed that the users had no problems to orient themselves on the Web site and were able to access the messages very intuitively.

In terms of user traffic and access rates, the communication department of the company states: with increasing tendency, up to 250 employees of the company worldwide visit the autograph book each day.

Recently the communications department realized a survey. The feedback indicates that the Baton application and the autograph book have been very well received and have succeeded in broadening the dialogue between employees in the different regions. For example, one of the employees reported that the tool was helpful for their everyday work. "Due to the album I know more about my colleagues in Mumbai. Before we had contact only by mail or sometimes by phone. But to see the person and to know more about her working and life conditions have improved our dialogue and cooperation." Thus the tool fulfilled our research goal of improving working relationships by the provision of a simple community site in combination with an attractive mobile

Figure 5. Analysis of photo (n=260) and video (n=53) contributions

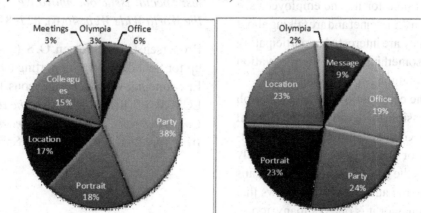

device that enables the content production in an entertaining way.

Moreover the employees in the regions are convinced by the idea of the symbolic baton. A colleague from China stated for example: "This tool improves our contact to the German head-quarter. The album underlines that we belong to one company." In this sense the baton can be regarded as a low effort approach compared to the various media-space approaches (Jancke, 2001) that enable the asynchronous linking of organizational spaces.

Regarding the contributions in the autograph book we can see that a lot of people of the region Asia / Pacific have participated. The number is higher than the number of contributions in Latin America or especially Europe, Middle East, Africa (EMEA). The reason for this is the following: since local contacts forwarded the symbolic baton into the regions, it depends on the engagement of the local contact. We notice that the contact person in Asia was more active to distribute the device than the colleague of EMEA. A further reason for this observation is the fact that people in Asia are often more open towards the use of technology and in particular mobile devices. The Baton application represents both and thus the demand for the tools was higher in Asia than in other regions of the world.

Six months after the start of the project the demand for the Baton application is still high. It is stated that there was more interest at the beginning but people still asked for it. The employees see their colleagues in the intranet and are talking about the project, so they are interested in participating as well. To see something new is the motivation to revisit the autograph book periodically.

Regarding the contributions in the autograph book it is not possible to identify special cultural differences. The German employees are present-ing themselves or their company sites mostly the same way as the Asians or South Americans for example. So, the autograph book shows that regarding the behavior it is one company, too.

CONCLUSION

Six months after the start of the project we can assess positive results. A lot of employees from all over the world participated on this project. The gathered feedback shows that the project improved the working contacts and organizational transpar-ency between the employees. With this result we have achieved the first stage of our research plan which was the introduction, the practical use and the evaluation of a mobile device for content generation and community site into a large and highly distributed working environment.

The continuous use of the system yielded new user demands for editing and collaboration support in the autograph book. The next research and development step will be the introduction of functions to increase the interactivity of the community site. Because of the high user ac-ceptance of the project, the company intends to extend the functionality of the autograph book in a subsequent project and we expect that this will finally lead to a company-wide interactive video blog (Parker, 2005).

REFERENCES

Bentley, R., Appelt, W., Busbach, U., Hinrichs, E., Kerr, D., & Sikkel, K. (1997). Basic Support for Cooperative Work on the World Wide Web. *International Journal of Human-Computer Stud-ies: Special Issue on Innovative Applications of the World Wide Web, 46*(6), 827–846.

Brodersen, Ch., & Iversen, O. S. (2007). Dressing up for School Work: Supporting a Collaborative Envrionemnt with Heterogeneous Technologies, ECSCW'07. In *Proceedings of the 10th European Conference on Computer Supported Cooperative Work* (pp. 251-270). Germany: Springer

Jancke, G., Venolia, G. D., Grudin, J., Cadiz, J. J., & Gupta, A. (2001). Linking public spaces: technical and social issues. In *Proceedings of the SIGCHI Conference on Human Factors in Computing Systems (Seattle, Washington, United States), CHI '01* (pp. 530-537). New York, NY: ACM.

Koppel, M., Schler, J., Argamon, S., & Pennebaker, J. W. (2006). Effects of age and gender on blogging. In *AAAI 2006 Spring Symposium on Computational Approaches to Analysing Weblogs*.

Lenhart, A. B., & Fox, S. (2006). *Bloggers: A portrait of the Internet's new storytellers*. Pew Internet & American Life Project.

McCarthy, J. F., Congleton, B., & Harper, F. M. (2008). The context, content & community collage: sharing personal digital media in the physical workplace. In *Proceedings of the ACM 2008 Conference on Computer Supported Cooperative Work (San Diego, CA, USA, November 08 - 12, 2008 CSCW '08* (pp. 97-106). New York: ACM.

Moore, T. D., & Serva, M. A. (2007). Understanding member motivation for contributing to different types of virtual communities: a proposed framework. In *Proceedings of the 2007 ACM SIGMIS CPR Conference on Computer Personnel Research: the Global information Technology Workforce (St. Louis, Missouri, USA, April 19 - 21, 2007) SIGMIS-CPR '07* (pp. 153-158). New York: ACM.

Parker, C., & Pfeiffer, S. (2005). Video Blogging: Content to the Max. *IEEE MultiMedia, 12*(2), 4–8. doi:10.1109/MMUL.2005.41

Reichling, T., & Veith, M. (2005). Expertise Sharing in a Heterogeneous Organisaztional Environment, ECSCW'05. In *Proceedings of the 9th European Conference on Computer Supported Cooperative Work* (pp. 325-345). Germany: Springer.

Roseman, M., & Greenberg, S. (1996). TeamRooms: Network Places for Collaboration. *Conference on Computer Supported Cooperative Work (CSCW'96)* (pp. 325-333). ACM Press.

Shrout, P. E., & Fleiss, J. L. (1979). Intraclass Correlations: Uses in Assessing Rater Reliability. *Psychological Bulletin, 86*, 420–428. doi:10.1037/0033-2909.86.2.420

Vyas, D., Eliëns, A., van de Watering, M. R., & van der Veer, G. C. (2008). Organizational probes: exploring playful interactions in work environment. In J. Abascal, I. Fajardo, & I. Oakley (Eds.), *Proceedings of the 15th European Conference on Cognitive Ergonomics: the Ergonomics of Cool interaction (Funchal, Portugal, September 16 - 19, 2008), ECCE '08, vol.* 369 (pp. 1-4). New York: ACM.

Compilation of References

Abbaci, F., Francq, P., & Delchambre, A. (2005). Query Generation for Personalized Tracking of Information. In *Proceedings of the 2005 Internation Conference on Internet Computing* (Vol. 348). Las Vegas, USA: Hamid R. Arabnia and Rose Joshua.

ACM SIGKDD (2003). Special issue on Multi-Relational Data Mining: The Current Frontiers. *ACM SIGKDD Explorations Newsletter, 5*(1).

Adomavicius, G. (2005). Toward the next generation of recommender systems: A survey of the state-of-the-art and possible extensions. *IEEE Transactions on Knowledge and Data Engineering, 17*, 734–749. doi:10.1109/TKDE.2005.99

Adomavicius, G., & Tuzhilin, A. (2005). Toward the next generation of recommender systems: A survey of the state-of-the-art and possible extensions. *IEEE Transactions on Knowledge and Data Engineering*, 734–749. doi:10.1109/TKDE.2005.99

Agaev, R., & Chebotarev, P. (2000). The matrix of maximum out forests of a digraph and its applications. *Automation and Remote Control, 61*(9), 1424–1450.

Agaev, R., & Chebotarev, P. (2001). Spanning forests of a digraph and their applications. *Automation and Remote Control, 62*(3), 443–466. doi:10.1023/A:1002862312617

Agarwal, A., & Chakrabarti, S. (2007). Learning random walks to rank nodes in graphs. In *Proceedings of the 24th International Conference on Machine Learning* (pp. 9–16).

Agarwal, R., Aggarwal, C., & Prasad, V. (1999). A Tree Projection Algorithm for Generation of Frequent Itemsets.

Journal of Parallel and Distributed Computing, 61(3), 350–371. doi:10.1006/jpdc.2000.1693

Agrawal, R., & Srikant, R. (1994, Sept. 1994). *Jorge B. Bocca and Matthias Jarke and Carlo Zaniolo.* Paper presented at the Proceedings of the 20th International Conference on Very Large Data Bases (VLDB), Santiago, Chile.

Agrawal, R., & Srikant, R. (1995, March 1995). *Mining Sequential Patterns.* Paper presented at the Proceedings of the International Conference on Data Engineering (ICDE), Taipei, Taiwan.

Aiello, G., & Alessi, M. (2007). DNK-WSD: a Distributed Approach for Knowledge Discovery in Peer to Peer Networks. In *Proceedings of the 15th EUROMICRO International Conference on Parallel, Distributed and Network-Based Processing, PDP'07* (pp. 325-332). Naples, Italy.

Aleman-Meza, B., Halaschek-Wiener, C., & Arpinar, I. B. (2005). Collective Knowledge Composition in a P2P Network. In Rivero, L. C., Doorn, J. H., & Ferraggine, V. E. (Eds.), Encyclopedia of Database Technologies and Applications (pp. 74-77). Hershey, PA: Idea Group Inc.

Altoft, P. (2009). *Twitter vs Digg for links and attention.* Retrieved March 25, 2009, from http://www.blogstorm.co.uk

Amabile, T. M. (1998). How to kill creativity. *Harvard Business Review, 76*(5), 76–87.

Ambrosini, V., & Bowman, C. (2001). Tacit knowledge: Some suggestions for operationalization. *Journal of*

Copyright © 2011, IGI Global. Copying or distributing in print or electronic forms without written permission of IGI Global is prohibited.

Management Studies, 38(6), 811–829. doi:10.1111/1467-6486.00260

Anderberg, M. R. (1973). *Cluster Analysis for Applications*. New York: Academic Press, Inc.

Anderson, C. (2004). The Long Tail. *Wired, 12*(10).

Anido, L. (2004). *Rodriguez, J., Caeiro, M., & Santos, J* (pp. 922–931). Observing Standards for Web-Based Learning from the Web.

Arenas, M., Kantere, V., Kementsietsidis, A., Kiringa, I., Miller, R. J., & Mylopoulos, J. (2003). The Hyperion Project: From Data Integration to Data Coordination. *SIGMOD Record. Special Issue on Peer-to-Peer Data Management, 32*(3), 53–58.

Argyris, C., & Schön, D. (1996). *Organizational learning ii: Theory, method, and practice*. Reading, MA: Addison-Wesley.

Armstrong, J. (2001). *Principles of Forecasting, A Handbook for Researchers and Practitioners*. Kluwer Academic.

Arthur, D., & Vassilvitskii, S. (2007). k-means++: the advantages of careful seeding. In *Proceedings of the eighteenth annual ACM-SIAM symposium on Discrete algorithms* (pp. 1027-1035). Society for Industrial and Applied Mathematics Philadelphia, PA, USA.

Associated Press. (2009). *New edition of AP Stylebook adds entries and helpful features*. Retrieved June 11, 2009, from http://www.ap.org

Asvanund, A., & Krishnan, R. (2004). Content-Based Community Formation in Hybrid Peer-to-Peer Networks. In *Proceedings of the of the SIGIR Workshop on Peer-to-Peer Information Retrieval*. Sheffield, UK.

Aumueller, D., Do, H., Massmann, S., & Rahm, E. (2005). Schema and Ontology Matching with COMA++. In *Proceedings of SIGMOD 2005 - Software Demonstration*, Baltimore, USA.

Auray, N. (2003). La régulation de la connaissance: arbitrage sur la taille et gestion aux frontières dans la communauté Debian. *Revue d'Economie Politique, 113*, 161–182.

Auray, N. (2003). Le sens du juste dans un noyau d'experts: Debian et le puritanisme civique. In S. Proulx, F. Massit-Foléa, & B. Conein (Eds.), Internet, une utopie limitée: nouvelles régulations, nouvelles solidarités (pp. 71-94). Laval: Presses de l'Université de Laval.

Avrithis, Y., Kompatsiaris, Y., Staab, S., & Vakali, A. (Eds.). (2008). *Proceedings of the CISWeb (Collective Semantics: Collective Intelligence and the Semantic Web) Workshop, located at the 5th European Semantic Web Conference ESWC 2008*. Tenerife, Spain.

Awad, E. M., & Ghaziri, H. (2004). *Knowledge management*. Upper Saddle River, NJ: Pearson Prentice Hall.

Axelrod, R. (1997). *The complexity of cooperation*. Princeton University Press.

Baader, F., Calvanese, D., McGuinness, D. L., Nardi, D., & Patel-Schneider, P. F. (Eds.). (2003). *The Description Logic Handbook: Theory, Implementation, and Applications*. Cambridge University Press.

Backman, M., Borjesson, S., & Setterberg, S. (2007). Working with concepts in the fuzzy front end: Exploring the context for innovation for different types of concepts at Volvo cars. *R & D Management, 37*(1), 17–28. doi:10.1111/j.1467-9310.2007.00455.x

Baeza-Yates, R., & Ribeiro-Neto, B. (1999). *Modern information retrieval*. Addison-Wesley.

Bagley, J. D. (1967). *The behavior of adaptive systems which employ genetic and correlation algorithms*. PhD thesis, University of Michigan.

Balabanovic, M. (1997). Content-Based, Collaborative Recommendation. *Communications of the ACM, 40*, 66–72. doi:10.1145/245108.245124

Balabanovic, M., & Shoham, Y. (1997). Fab: Content-based, collaborative recommendation. *Communications of the ACM, 40*, 66–72. doi:10.1145/245108.245124

Ball, G. H., & Hall, D. J. (1965). ISODATA, a novel method of data analysis and classification. Stanford, CA.

Barahona, P. (2009). *Diario Hoy usa Twitter para acercarse a sus lectores*. Retrieved February 10, 2009, from http://palulo.ec

Barchan, M. (2002). *How to measure intangible assets.* Knowledge Management World.

Barnett, S. (1992). *Matrices: Methods and Applications.* Oxford University Press.

Basilico, J., & Hofmann, T. (2004). Unifying collaborative and content-based filtering. In *Proceedings of the Twenty-first International Conference on Machine Learning* (pp. 65–72).

Bass, B. M. (1998). *Transformational leadership.* Mahwah, NJ: Lawrence Erlbaum Associates.

Basu, C., Hirsh, H., & Cohen, W. (1998). Recommendation as classification: Using social and content-based information in recommendation. *Recommender System Workshop, 98,* 11–15.

Becerra-Fernandez, I., Gonzalez, A., & Sabherwal, R. (2004). *Knowledge management: Challenges, solutions, and technologies.* Upper Saddle River, NJ: Pearson Prentice Hall.

Beckett, R. C. (2000). A characterisation of corporate as a knowledge management system. *Journal of Knowledge Management, 4*(4), 311–319. doi:10.1108/13673270010379867

Belkin, M., & Niyogi, P. (2001). Laplacian eigenmaps and spectral techniques for embedding and clustering. MIT Press. *Advances in Neural Information Processing Systems, 14,* 585–591.

Belkin, M., & Niyogi, P. (2003). Laplacian eigenmaps for dimensionality reduction and data representation. *Neural Computation, 15,* 1373–1396. doi:10.1162/089976603321780317

Belkin, N. J., & Croft, W. B. (1992). Information filtering and information retrieval: Two sides of the same coin. *Communications of the ACM, 35*(12), 29–38. doi:10.1145/138859.138861

Beneventano, D., Bergamaschi, S., Castano, S., De Antonellis, V., Ferrara, A., Guerra, F., et al. (2002). Semantic Integration and Query Optimization of Heterogeneous Data Sources. In *Proceedings of the Workshop on Advances in Object-Oriented Information Systems, OOIS 2002* (pp. 154-165). Montpellier, France.

Ben-Israel, A., & Greville, T. (2003). *Generalized Inverses: Theory and Applications* (2nd ed.). Springer-Verlag.

Benkler, Y. (2006). *The wealth of networks.* New Haven, CT: Yale University Press. Retrieved from http://www.benkler.org/Benkler_Wealth_Of_Networks.pdf

Bennett, D. (2009). *#G20 - Twitter dominates mainstream media coverage.* Retrieved April 1, 2009, from http://frontlineclub.com

Bennett, D. (2009). *BBC's World have Your Say tweet editorial meeting.* Retrieved May 26, 2009, from http://mediatingconflict.blogspot.com

Bentley, R., Appelt, W., Busbach, U., Hinrichs, E., Kerr, D., & Sikkel, K. (1997). Basic Support for Cooperative Work on the World Wide Web. *International Journal of Human-Computer Studies: Special Issue on Innovative Applications of the World Wide Web, 46*(6), 827–846.

Berners-Lee, T., Hendler, J., & Lassila, O. (2001). *The Semantic Web.* Scientific American.

Billsus, D., & Pazzani, M. J. (1998). Learning collaborative information filters. In *Proceedings of the 15th International Conference on Machine Learning* (pp. 46–54).

Blau, P. (1964). *Exchange and Power in Social Life.* New York: Wiley.

Blei, D. M., Ng, A. Y., & Jordan, M. I. (2003). Latent Dirichlet Allocation. *Journal of Machine Learning Research,* (3): 993–1022. doi:10.1162/jmlr.2003.3.4-5.993

Bloehdorn, S., Haase, P., Hefke, M., Sure, Y., & Tempich, C. Intelligent Community Lifecycle Support. In *Proceedings of the 5th International Conference on Knowledge Management, I-KNOW 05.* Graz, Austria.

Boddy, D., & Macbeth, D. (2000). Prescriptions for managing change: A survey of their effects in projects to implement collaborative working between organisations. *International Journal of Project Management, 18*(5), 297–306. doi:10.1016/S0263-7863(99)00031-9

Boltanski, L. (1987). *The Making of a Class: Cadres in French Society.* Cambridge: Cambridge University Press.

Boltanski, L., & Thévenot, L. (2006). *On Justification. Economies of Worth.* Princeton, NJ: Princeton University Press.

Borg, I., & Groenen, P. (1997). *Modern multidimensional scaling: Theory and applications.* Springer.

Boudreau, J. W., & Ramstad, P. M. (1997). Measuring intellectual capital: Learning from financial history. *Human Resource Management, 36*(3). doi:10.1002/(SICI)1099-050X(199723)36:3<343::AID-HRM6>3.0.CO;2-W

Bouquet, P., Serafini, L., & Zanobini, S. (2004). Peer-to-Peer Semantic Coordination. *Journal of Web Semantics, 2*(1), 81–97. doi:10.1016/j.websem.2004.07.004

Bradley, P. S., & Fayyad, U. M. (1998). Refining initial points for k-means clustering. In *Proc. 15th International Conf. on Machine Learning* (Vol. 727).

Bradshaw, P. (2008). *The Chinese earthquake and Twitter – crowdsourcing without managers.* Retrieved May 12, 2008, from http://onlinejournalismblog.com

Brand, M. (2005). A random walks perspective on maximizing satisfaction and profit. In *Proceedings of the 2005 SIAM International Conference on Data Mining.*

Brans, J., & Mareschal, B. (2002). *PROMETHEE-GAIA. Une méthodologie d'aide à la décision en présence de critères multiples.* Editions de l'Université de Bruxelles.

Breese, J., Heckerman, D., & Kadie, C. (1998). Empirical analysis of predictive algorithms for collaborative filtering. In *Proceedings of the 14th Conference on Uncertainty in Artificial Intelligence.*

Brin, S. & Page, L. (1998). The anatomy of a large-scale hypertextual Web search engine. *Computer Networks and ISDN Systems, 30*(1–7), 107–117.

Brin, S., & Page, L. (1998). The anatomy of a large-scale hypertextual Web search engine. *Computer Networks and ISDN Systems,* (33): 107–135. doi:10.1016/S0169-7552(98)00110-X

Broder, A., Glassman, S., Manasse, M., & Zweig, G. (1997, April). *Syntactic Clustering of the Web.* Paper presented at the Proceedings of the 6th International WWW Conference, Santa Clara, CA, USA.

Brodersen, Ch., & Iversen, O. S. (2007). Dressing up for School Work: Supporting a Collaborative Envrionemnt with Heterogeneous Technologies, ECSCW'07. In *Proceedings of the 10th European Conference on Computer Supported Cooperative Work* (pp. 251-270). Germany: Springer

Brown, A. (1998). *Organisational culture* (2nd ed.). Harlow, UK: Financial Times-Prentice Hall.

Brown, J. S., & Duguid, P. (1991). Organisational learning and communities of practice: Towards a unified view of working, learning, and innovation. *Organization Science, 2*(1), 40–57. doi:10.1287/orsc.2.1.40

Brown, J. S., & Duguid, P. (2001). Structure and spontaneity: Knowledge and organisation. In Nonaka, I., & Teece, D. (Eds.), *Managing industrial knowledge - creation, transfer and utilization* (pp. 44–67). London: Sage.

Burton-Jones, A. (1999). *Knowledge capitalism.* Oxford: Oxford University Press.

Cabrera, A., Collins, W. C., & Salgado, J. F. (2006). Determinants of individual engagement in knowledge sharing. *International Journal of Human Resource Management, 17*(2), 245–264.

Calderón, V., & Quesada, J. D. (2009). *El poder de las redes sociales.* Retrieved June 21, 2009, from http://www.elpais.com

Calvanese, D., De Giacomo, G., Lenzerini, M., & Rosati, R. (2004). Logical Foundations of Peer-to-Peer Data Integration. In *Proceedings of the 23th ACM SIGMOD-SIGACT-SIGART symposium on Principles of Database Systems, PODS 2004* (pp. 241-251). Paris, France.

Cao, Z., Qin, T., Liu, T.-Y., Tsai, M.-F., & Li, H. (2007). Learning to rank: From pairwise approach to listwise approach. In *Proceedings of the 24th International Conference on Machine Learning* (pp. 129–136).

Carenini, G. (2005). User-specific decision-theoretic accuracy metrics for collaborative filtering. In *Proceedings of the Intelligent User Interface Conference (IUI'05)*.

Carrillo, F. J. (2001). Meta km: A program and a plea. *Journal of Knowledge and Innovation, 2*, 27–54.

Carrington, P., Scott, J., & Wasserman, S. (2006). *Models and Methods in Social Network Analysis.* Cambridge University Press.

Castano, S., & Montanelli, S. (2005). Semantic Self-Formation of Communities of Peers. In *Proceedings of the ESWC Workshop on Ontologies in Peer-to-Peer Communities*, Heraklion, Greece.

Castano, S., De Antonellis, V., & De Capitani Di Vimercati, S. (2001). Global Viewing of Heterogeneous Data Sources. *IEEE Transactions on Knowledge and Data Engineering, 13*(2), 277–297. doi:10.1109/69.917566

Castano, S., Ferrara, A., & Messa, G. (2006). Results of the HMatch Ontology Matchmaker in OAEI 2006. In *Proceedings of the 1st International Workshop on Ontology Matching, OM 2006, Collocated with the 5th International Semantic Web Conference, ISWC 2006*, Athens, Georgia, USA.

Castano, S., Ferrara, A., & Montanelli, S. (2006). Dynamic Knowledge Discovery in Open, Distributed and Multi-Ontology Systems: Techniques and Applications. In Taniar, D., & Rahayu, J. W. (Eds.), *Web Semantics and Ontology* (pp. 226–258). Hershey, PA: Idea Group Inc.

Castano, S., Ferrara, A., & Montanelli, S. (2006). Evolving Open and Independent Ontologies. *International Journal of Metadata Semantics and Ontologies, 1*(4), 235–249. doi:10.1504/IJMSO.2006.012949

Castano, S., Ferrara, A., & Montanelli, S. (2006). Matching Ontologies in Open Networked Systems: Techniques and Applications. *Journal on Data Semantics, V*, 25–63. doi:10.1007/11617808_2

Castano, S., Ferrara, A., Lorusso, D., & Montanelli, S. (2008). Ontology Coordination: The iCoord Project Demonstration. In *Proceedings of the 27th International Conference on Conceptual Modeling, ER 2008* (pp. 512–513). Barcelona, Spain.

Catone, J. (2008). *The Rise of Twitter as a Platform for Serious Discourse.* Retrieved January 30, 2008, from http://www.readwriteweb.com

Cellan-Jones, R. (2008). *Twitter and the China earthquake.* Retrieved May 12, 2008, from http://www.bbc.co.uk

Chabert, G., Marty, J. C., Caron, B., Carron, T., Vignollet, L., & Ferraris, C. (2006). The Electronic Schoolbag, a CSCW workspace: presentation and evaluation. *AI & Society, 20*, 403–419. doi:10.1007/s00146-005-0026-1

Chan, T., Ciarlet, P., & Szeto, W. (1997). On the optimality of the median cut spectral bisection graph partitioning method. *SIAM Journal on Scientific Computing, 18*(3), 943–948. doi:10.1137/S1064827594262649

Chandra, A. K., Raghavan, P., Ruzzo, W. L., Smolensky, R., & Tiwari, P. (1989). The electrical resistance of a graph captures its commute and cover times. *Annual ACM Symposium on Theory of Computing*, (pp. 574–586).

Chang, D. R., & Cho, H. (2008). Organizational memory influences new product success. *Journal of Business Research, 61*, 13–23. doi:10.1016/j.jbusres.2006.05.005

Chebotarev, P., & Shamis, E. (1997). The matrix-forest theorem and measuring relations in small social groups. *Automation and Remote Control, 58*(9), 1505–1514.

Chebotarev, P., & Shamis, E. (1998). On a duality between metrics and s-proximities. *Automation and Remote Control, 59*(4), 608–612.

Chebotarev, P., & Shamis, E. (1998). On proximity measures for graph vertices. *Automation and Remote Control, 59*(10), 1443–1459.

Chen, T., Yang, Q., & Tang, X. (2007). Directed graph embedding. In *Proceedings of the International Joint Conference on Artificial Intelligence (IJCAI)* (pp. 2707–2712).

Chinchor, N. A. (1998). Overview of MUC-7/MET-2. In *Proceedings of the Seventh Message Understanding Conference (MUC-7)* (Vol. 1).

Chomsky, N. (1959). Review of verbal behavior. *Language, 35*, 26–58. doi:10.2307/411334

Chong, C. W., Holden, T., Wilhelmij, P., & Schmidt, R. A. (2000). Where does knowledge management add value? *Journal of Intellectual Capital, 1*(4), 366–380. doi:10.1108/14691930010359261

Chung, F. R. (1997). *Spectral graph theory*. American Mathematical Society.

Chung, F. R. (2005). Laplacians and the Cheeger inequality for directed graphs. *Annals of Combinatorics, 9*, 1–19. doi:10.1007/s00026-005-0237-z

Clay, S. (2008). *Here comes everybody: the power of organizing without organizations*. Penguin Press.

Claypool, M., Le, P., Waseda, M., & Brown, D. (2001). Implicit interest indicators. In *Proceedings of the ACM Intelligent User Interfaces Conference* (pp. 33–40).

Cohen, S., Nutt, W., & Sagiv, Y. (2006). Rewriting Queries with Arbitrary Aggregation Functions using Views. *ACM Transactions on Database Systems, 31*(2), 672–715. doi:10.1145/1138394.1138400

Cohen, W. M., & Levinthal, D. (1990). Absorptive capacity: A new perspective on learning and innovation. *Administrative Science Quarterly, 35*(1), 128–152. doi:10.2307/2393553

Cohen, W., Schapire, R., & Singer, Y. (1999). Learning to order things. *Journal of Artificial Intelligence Research, 10*, 243–270.

Collins, A., Brown, J. S., & Newman, S. E. (1989). Cognitive apprenticeship: Teaching the crafts of reading, writing and mathematics. In Resnick, L. B. (Ed.), *Knowing, learning and instruction: Essays in honour of Robert Glaser* (pp. 453–494). Hillsdale, N. J.: Lawrence Erlbaum.

Comm, J., Robbins, A., & Burge, K. (2009). *Twitter Power: How to Dominate Your Market One Tweet at a Time*. John Wiley and Sons Ltd.

Conein, B. (2004). Communautés épistémiques et réseaux cognitifs: coopération et cognition distribuée. *Revue d'Economie Politique, 113*, 141–159.

Cortada, J. W., & Woods, J. A. (Eds.). (2001). *The knowledge management yearbook 2000-2001*. NY: Butterworth-Heinemann.

Cortes, C., Mohri, M., & Rastogi, A. (2007). Magnitude-preserving ranking algorithms. In *Proceedings of the 24th International Conference onMachine Learning* (pp. 169–176).

Courtney, H. (2003). Decision-driven scenarios for assessing four levels of uncertainty. *Strategy and Leadership, 31*(1), 14. doi:10.1108/10878570310455015

Cover, T. M., & Thomas, J. A. (2006). *Elements of Information Theory* (2nd ed.). John Wiley & Sons.

Cowan, R., David, P. A., & Foray, D. (2000). The explicit economics of knowledge: Codifcation and tacitness. *Industrial and Corporate Change, 9*(2), 211–253. doi:10.1093/icc/9.2.211

Cox, T., & Cox, M. (2001). *Multidimensional scaling* (2nd ed.). Chapman and Hall.

Crespo, A., & Garcia-Molina, H. (2004). Semantic Overlay Networks for P2P Systems. In *Proceedings of the 3rd International Workshop on Agents and Peer-to-Peer Computing, P2PC 2004* (pp. 1-13). New York, NY, USA.

Creswell, J. W. (2003). *Research design: Qualitative, quantitative, and mixed methods approaches* (2nd ed.). NY: Sage.

Crouch, C., Apte, S., & Bapat, H. (2002). Using the extended vector model for XML retrieval. In *Proceedings of the 1st Workshop of the Initiative for the Evaluation of XML Retrieval (INEX)*. Dagstuhl, Germany.

Darwin, C. (1859). *On the Origin of Species*. John Murray.

Das, T., Nandi, S., & Ganguly, N. (2009). Community Formation and Search in P2P: A Robust and Self-Adjusting Algorithm. In *Proceedings of the 3rd Workshop on Intelligent Networks: Adaptation, Communication & Reconfiguration, IAMCOM 2009*, Bangalore, India.

Datta, B. N. (1995). *Numerical Linear Algebra and Application*. Brooks/Cole Publishing Company.

Davenport, T. H., & Prusak, L. (2000). *Working knowledge - how organizations manage what they know*. Boston: Harvard Business School Press.

David, P. A., & Foray, D. (2003). Economic Fundamentals of the Knowledge Society. *Policy Futures in Education, 1*(1), 20–49. doi:10.2304/pfie.2003.1.1.7

DCMI. (1999). *Dublin Core Metadata Element Set, Version 1.1: Reference Description*. (White Paper). Dublin Core Metadata Initiative.

de Jager, M. (1999). The kmat: Benchmarking knowledge management. *Library Management, 20*(7), 367–372. doi:10.1108/01435129910285136

DeBono, E. (1967). *New think: The use of lateral thinking in the generation of new ideas*. New York: Basic Books.

Delannay, N., & Verleysen, M. (2007). Collaborative filtering with interlaced generalized linear models. *European Symposium on Artificial Neural Networks*.

Deleuze, G., & Parnet, C. (2002). *Dialogues II*. New York: Columbia University Press.

Delgado, J., & Ishii, N. (1999). Memory-based weighted-majority prediction for recommender systems. In *Proceedings of the ACM SIGIR '99 Workshop Recommender Systems: Algorithms and Evaluation*.

Dempster, A. P., Laird, N. M., & Rubin, D. B. (1977). Maximum Likelihood from Incomplete Data via the EM Algorithm. *Journal of the Royal Statistical Society. Series B. Methodological, 39*(2), 1–38.

Deshpande, M., & Karypis, G. (2004). Item-based top-n recommendation algorithms. *ACM Transactions on Information Systems, 22*(1), 143–177. doi:10.1145/963770.963776

Ding, C., Jin, R., Li, T., & Simon, H. (2007). A learning framework using Green's function and kernel regularization with application to recommender system. In *Proceedings of the International Conference on Knowledge Discovery in Databases (KDD2007)* (pp. 260–269).

Dixon, N. M. (2000). *Common knowledge: How companies thrive by sharing what they know*. Boston: Harvard Business School Press.

Donetti, L., & Munoz, M. (2004). Detecting network communities: A new systematic and efficient algorithm. *Journal of Statistical Mechanics*, (2004, Oct), P10012. doi:10.1088/1742-5468/2004/10/P10012

Doyle, P. G., & Snell, J. L. (1984). *Random Walks and Electric Networks*. The Mathematical Association of America.

Dubes, R. C. (1987). How many clusters are best? -- an experiment. *Pattern Recognition, 20*(6), 645–663. doi:10.1016/0031-3203(87)90034-3

DuBrin, A. J. (2004). *Applying psychology: Individual and organizational effectiveness*. Upper Saddle River, NJ: Pearson Education Ltd.

Duda, R. O., Hart, P. E., & Stork, D. G. (2001). *Pattern classification* (2nd ed.). John Wiley & Sons.

Dunja, M. (1996). *Personal Web Watcher: design and implementation* (Technical Report No. IJS-DP_7472). Department of Intelligent Systems, J. Stefan Institute, Slovenia.

Ebner, M., & Schiefner, M. (2008). Microblogging – more than fun? In I. Arnedillo, & P. Isaías (Eds.), *Proceedings of IADIS Mobile Learning Conference 2008* (pp. 155-159). Algarve, Portugal: International Association for Development of the Information Society

Edmondson, A. C., Winslow, A. B., Bohmer, R. M. J., & Pisano, G. P. (2003). Learning how and learning what: Effects of tacit and codified knowledge on performance improvement following technology adoption. *Decision Sciences, 34*(2), 197–224. doi:10.1111/1540-5915.02316

Edvinsson, L. (1997). Developing intellectual capital at skandia. *Long Range Planning. Elsevier Science Limited, 30*(3), 366–373.

Encinar, J. (2009). El microblogging cambia el ecosistema de todos los blogs. Retrieved February 6, 2009, from http://www.jesusencinar.com

Erlandson, P. (2006). Giving up the ghost: The control-matrix and reflection-in-action. *Reflective Practice, 7*(1), 115–124. doi:10.1080/14623940500489781

Ettlie, J. E., & Elsenbach, J. M. (2007). Modified stage-gate regimes in new product development. *Journal of Product Innovation Management, 24*(2), 20–33. doi:10.1111/j.1540-5885.2006.00230.x

EU FP6 BOEMIE Project. (2006). *Bootstrapping Ontology Evolution with Multimedia Information Extraction*. Retrieved from http://www.boemie.org/

Everywhere and nowhere. (2008, May 19). *The Economist*.

Falkenauer, E. (1998). *Genetic Algorithms and Grouping Problems*. John Wiley & Sons.

Faloutsos, C., McCurley, K. S., & Tomkins, A. (2004). Fast discovery of connection subgraphs. In *Proceedings of the tenth ACM SIGKDD International Conference on Knowledge Discovery and Data Mining* (pp. 118–127).

Felps, W., Mitchell, T. R., & Byington, E. (2006). How, when, and why bad apples spoil the barrel: Negative group members and dysfunctional groups. *Research in Organizational Behavior, 27*, 175–222. doi:10.1016/S0191-3085(06)27005-9

Fiedler, M. (1975). A property of eigenvectors of non-negative symmetric matrices and its applications to graph theory. *Czechoslovak Mathematical Journal, 25*(100), 619–633.

Flake, G. W., Tarjan, R. E., & Tsioutsiouliklis, K. (2004). Graph Clustering and Minimum Cut Trees. *Internet Mathematics, 1*(4).

Fogarty, M., & Bahls, C. (2002). Information Overload: Feel the pressure? *Scientist (Philadelphia, Pa.), 16*(16).

Forman, J. (2001). When stories create an organization's future. In Cortada, J. W., & Woods, J. A. (Eds.), *The knowledge management yearbook 2000-2001* (pp. 231–235). NY: Butterworth-Heinemann.

Fouss, F., & Saerens, M. (2008). Evaluating performance of recommender systems: An experimental comparison. In *Proceedings of the 2008 IEEE/WIC/ACM International Joint Conference on Web Intelligence* (pp. 735–738).

Fouss, F., Pirotte, A., & Saerens, M. (2006). A novel way of computing similarities between nodes of a graph, with application to collaborative filtering. In *Proceedings of the Workshop on Statistical Approaches for Web Mining (ECML 2004 - SAWM)*.

Fouss, F., Pirotte, A., Renders, J.-M., & Saerens, M. (2005). A novel way of computing similarities between nodes of a graph, with application to collaborative recommendation. In *Proceedings of the 2005 IEEE/WIC/ACM International Joint Conference on Web Intelligence* (pp. 550–556).

Fouss, F., Pirotte, A., Renders, J.-M., & Saerens, M. (2007). Random walk computation of similarities between nodes of a graph, with application to collaborative recommendation. *IEEE Transactions on Knowledge and Data Engineering, 19*(3), 355–369. doi:10.1109/TKDE.2007.46

Fouss, F., Yen, L., Pirotte, A., & Saerens, M. (2006). An experimental investigation of graph kernels on a collaborative recommendation task. In *Proceedings of the 6th International Conference on Data Mining (ICDM 2006)* (pp. 863–868).

Fouss, F., Yen, L., Pirotte, A., & Saerens, M. (2007). An experimental investigation of seven kernels on two collaborative recommendation tasks.

Fox, E. A. (1983). *Extending the Boolean and Vector Space Models of Information Retrieval with P-norm Queries and Multiple Concept Types*. PhD thesis, Cornell University.

Frakes, W. B. (1992). Stemming Algorithms. In Frakes, W. B., & Baeza-Yates, R. (Eds.), *Information Retrieval: Data Structures & Algorithms* (pp. 131–160). Prentice-Hall.

Francis, W., & Kucera, H. (1982). *Frequency Analysis of English Usage*. New York: Houghton.

Franco, G. (2008). *Cómo Escribir para la Web. University of Texas*. Austin: Knight Center for Journalism in the Americas.

Francq, P. (2003). *Collaborative and structured search: an integrated approach for sharing documents among users*. PhD thesis, Université Libre de Bruxelles.

Francq, P. (2007). The GALILEI Platform: Social Browsing to Build Communities of Interests and Share Relevant Information and Expertise. In Lytras, M. D., &

Naeve, A. (Eds.), *Open source for knowledge and learning management: strategies beyond tools* (pp. 319–342). Idea Group Publishing.

Francq, P., & Delchambre, A. (2005). Using documents assessments to build communities of interests. In *Proceedings of the The 2005 Symposium on Applications and the Internet (SAINT'05)* (Vol. 327). Trento, Italy.

Francq, P., Wartel, D., Kumps, N., & Vandaele, V. (2003). *GALILEI -- Troisième Rapport Semestriel (Technical Report)*. Belgium: Université Libre de Bruxelles.

From the Frontline. (2008). *Twitter's quicker debate over*. Retrieved May 12, 2008, from http://www.fromthe-frontline.co.uk

Frommer, D. (2009). *U.S. Airways Crash Rescue Picture: Citizen Journalism, Twitter At Work*. Retrieved January 15, 2009, from http://www.businessinsider.com

Fuller, S. (2001). A critical guide to knowledge society newspeak. *Current Sociology, 49*(4), 177–201. doi:10.1177/0011392101049004010

Gahran, A. (2008). *Secondhand Twitter Posse: How big is Yours, and Why Should You Care?* Retrieved July 2, 2008, from http://www.poynter.org

Gallo, D. (2009). *Por qué Twitter mejora la escritura de los nuevos periodistas*. Retrieved May 25, 2009, from http://www.blocdeperiodista.com

Garey, M., & Johnson, D. (1979). *Computers and Intractability - A Guide to the Theory of NP-completeness*. San Francisco: W.H. Freeman Co.

Garvin, D. A. (1998). *Building a learning organisation, Harvard business review on knowledge management* (pp. 47–80). Boston: Harvard Business School Publishing.

Gibbons, A. (1985). *Algorithmic Graph Theory*. Cambridge: Cambridge University Press.

Gillmor, D. (2004). *We the Media. Grassroots Journalism by the People, for the People*. Sebastopol: O'Reilly.

Giustini, D. & Wright, M.D. (2009). Twitter: an introduction to microblogging for health librarians. *JCHLA - JABSC* (30), 11-17

Glaser, M. (2007). *California Wildfire Coverage by Local Media, Blogs, Twitter, Maps and More*. Retrieved October 25, 2007, from http://www.pbs.org/mediashift

Glover, F., & Laguna, M. (1997). *Tabu Search*. Kluwer Academic Publishers.

Glover, F., Laguna, M., Werra, D. D., & Taillard, E. (1992). Tabu Search. In *Annals of Operations Research* (*Vol. 41*). Basel, Switzerland: J.C. Baltser Pub.

Gobel, F., & Jagers, A. A. (1974). Random walks on graphs. *Stochastic Processes and their Applications, 2*, 311–336. doi:10.1016/0304-4149(74)90001-5

Goedegebuure, D. (2009). *Twitter Rolodex for Journalists*. Retrieved March 10, 2009, from http://www.thenextcorner.net

Goldberg, D. E. (1991). *Genetic Algorithms in Search*. Addison-Wesley.

Goldberg, D., Kork, B., & Deb, K. (1989). Messy genetic algorithms: motivation, analysis, and first results. *Complex Systems, 3*(5), 493–530.

Goldberg, K., Nichols, D., Oki, B. M., & Terry, D. (1992). Using collaborative filtering to weave an information tapestry. *Communications of the ACM, 35*(12), 61–70. doi:10.1145/138859.138867

Goleman, D. (1998). What makes a leader? *Harvard Business Review, 76*(6), 92–102.

Goleman, D. (2000). Leadership that gets results. *Harvard Business Review, 78*(2), 78–90.

Gonzalo, M. (2009). *Twitter no mata a ninguna blogosfera*. Retrieved June 9, 2009, from http://www.marilink.net

Gordon, S., Tarafdar, M., Cook, R., Maksimoski, R., & Rogowitz, B. (2008). Improving the front end of innovation with information technology: Smart companies use it to be more effective and efficient in the early stages of the innovation process. *Research Technology Management, 51*(3), 50–59.

Gori, M., & Pucci, A. (2006). A random-walk based scoring algorithm with application to recommender systems for large-scale e-commerce. In *Proceedings of the 12th ACM SIGKDD International Conference on Knowledge Discovery and Data Mining*.

Gori, M., & Pucci, A. (2006). Research paper recommender systems: A random-walk based approach. In *Proceedings of the 2006 IEEE/WIC/ACM International Conference on Web Intelligence*.

Grabisch, M., & Roubens, M. (2000). Application of the Choquet integral in multicriteria decision making. *Fuzzy measures and integrals, 40*, 348–374.

Grant, R. M. (2001). Knowledge and organization. In Nonaka, I., & Teece, D. (Eds.), *Managing industrial knowledge - creation, transfer and utilization* (pp. 145–165). London: Sage.

Grcar, M., & Fortuna, B. Mladenic, D., & Grobelnik, M. (2005). knn versus svm in the collaborative filtering framework. In *Proceedings of the 2005 KDD Workshop on Web Mining and Web Usage Analysis*.

Grefenstette, J. J. (Ed.). (1987). *Genetic Algorithms and Their Applications: Proceedings of the 2nd International Conference on Genetic Algorithms*.

Grolier. (2007). *Encyclopedia Americana®* (Version 15). Danbury, CT: Grolier Interactive, Inc.

Gronröos, C. (1994). From marketing mix to relationship marketing: Towards a paradigm shift in marketing. *Management Decision. MCB Press, 32*(2), 4–20.

Groot, P., van Harmelen, F., & ten Teije, A. (2000). Torture tests: a quantitative analysis for the robustness of knowledge-based systems. In *Proceedings of the European Workshop on Knowledge Acquisition, Modelling and Management (EKAW 00), LNAI Springer-Verlag* (pp. 403–418).

Gruber, T. (2008). Collective Knowledge Systems: where the Social Web meets the Semantic Web. *Journal of Web Semantics, 6*(1), 4–13.

Gu, W., & Wei, W. (2006). Automatic Community Discovery in Peer-to-Peer Systems. In *Proceedings of the 5th International Conference on Grid and Coopera-*tive Computing Workshops, GCC 2006 (pp. 110-116). Changsha, Hunan, China.

Guérin, F. (2004). Le concept de communauté: une illustration exemplaire de la production des concepts en sciences sociales? *13ème conférence de l'association internationale de management stratégique, 13*, 1-30.

Guha, S., Rastogi, R., & Shim, K. (1998). *CURE: An Efficient Clustering Algorithm for Large Database* (pp. 73–84). New York: ACM Press.

Haas, P. (1992). Introduction: Epistemic communities and international policy coordination. *International Organization, 46*, 1–37. doi:10.1017/S0020818300001442

Haase, P., Siebes, R., & Van Harmelen, F. (2008). Expertise-based Peer Selection in Peer-to-Peer Networks. *Knowledge and Information Systems, 15*(1), 75–107. doi:10.1007/s10115-006-0055-1

Halevy, A. (2001). Answering Queries using Views: A Survey. *The VLDB Journal, 10*(4), 270–294. doi:10.1007/s007780100054

Halevy, A., Rajaraman, A., & Ordille, J. (2006). Data Integration: The Teenage Years. In *Proceedings of the 32nd International Conference on Very Large Data Bases, VLDB 2006* (pp. 9-16). Seoul, Korea.

Ham, J., Lee, D., Mika, S., & Scholkopf, B. (2004). A kernel view of the dimensionality reduction of manifolds. In *Proceedings of the 21st International Conference on Machine Learning (ICML2004)*.

Hamel, G., & Prahalad, C. K. (1994). *Competing for the future*. Boston: Harvard Business School Press.

Hampden-Turner, C., & Trompenaars, F. (2000). *Building cross-cultural competence - how to create wealth from conflicting values*. New York: John Wiley & Sons.

Han, E., Karypis, G., Kumar, V., & Mobasher, B. (1998). Hypergraph Based Clustering in High-Dimensional Data Sets: A Summary of Results. *A Quarterly Bulletin of the Computer Society of the IEEE Technical Committee on Data Engineering, 21*(1), 15–22.

Han, J., & Kamber, M. (2007). *Data Mining: Concepts and Techniques*. Morgan Kaufmann.

Handy, C. (2001). A world of fleas and elephants. In Bennis, W., Spreitzer, G. M., & Cummings, T. G. (Eds.), *The future of leadership - today's top leadership thinkers speak to tomorrow's leaders* (pp. 29–40). San Francisco: Jossey-Bass.

Hansen, C. D., & Kahnweiler, W. M. (1993). Storytelling: An instrument for understanding the dynamics of corporate relationships. *Human Relations, 46*(12), 1391–1409. doi:10.1177/001872679304601202

Hansen, M. T., & von Oetinger, B. (2001). Introducing t-shaped managers - knowledge management's next generation. *Harvard Business Review, 79*(3), 107–116.

Hansen, M. T., Nohria, N., & Tierney, T. (2001). What's your strategy for managing knowledge? In Cortada, J. W., & Woods, J. A. (Eds.), *The knowledge management yearbook 2000-2001* (pp. 55–69). New York: Butterworth-Heinemann.

Harel, D., & Koren, Y. (2001). On clustering using random walks. *Proceedings of the conference on the Foundations of Software Technology and Theoretical Computer Science* (LNCS 2245, pp. 18–41).

Haspeslagh, P., Noda, T., & Boulos, F. (2001). Managing for value it's not just about the numbers. *Harvard Business Review, 79*(7), 65–73.

Hatcher, J. (2009). *Students Use Twitter to Report on Disabled-Parking Spots.* Retrieved March 10, from http://www.poynter.org

Havenstein, H. (2007). *LA Fire Department all 'a Twitter' over Web 2.0.* Retrieved August 3, 2007, from http://www.pcworld.com

Haynes, B., & Price, I. (2002, September). *Quantifying the complex adaptive workplace.* Paper presented at the Applying and Extending the Global Knowledge Base - CIB Working Commission 070 - Facilities Management and Maintenance, Glasgow, Scotland.

Heaton, L., & Taylor, J. R. (2002). Knowledge management and professional work. *Management Communication Quarterly, 16*(2), 210–236. doi:10.1177/089331802237235

Hemmings, J., & Wilkinson, J. (2003). What is a public health observatory? *Journal of Epidemiology and Community Health, 57,* 324–326. doi:10.1136/jech.57.5.324

Herlocker, J. L. (2004). Evaluating collaborative filtering recommender systems. *ACM Transactions on Information Systems, 22,* 5–53. doi:10.1145/963770.963772

Herlocker, J. L., Konstan, J. A., Borchers, A., & Riedl, J. (1999). An algorithmic framework for performing collaborative filtering (pp. 230-237).

Herlocker, J. L., Konstan, J. A., Terveen, L. G., & Riedl, J. T. (2004a). Evaluating collaborative filtering recommender systems. [TOIS]. *ACM Transactions on Information Systems, 22*(1), 5–53. doi:10.1145/963770.963772

Herlocker, J., Konstan, J., & Riedl, J. (2002). An empirical analysis of design choices in neighborhood-based collaborative filtering algorithms. *Information Retrieval, 5,* 287–310. doi:10.1023/A:1020443909834

Herlocker, J., Konstan, J., Borchers, A., & Riedl, J. (1999). An algorithmic framework for performing collaborative filtering. In *Proceedings of the international ACM SIGIR Conference on Research and Development in Information Retrieval* (pp. 230–237).

Herlocker, J., Konstan, J., Terveen, L., & Riedl, J. (2004). Evaluating collaborative filtering recommender systems. *ACM Transactions on Information Systems, 22*(1), 5–53. doi:10.1145/963770.963772

Hermida, A. (2009). *Talking about Twitter as a system of journalism.* Retrieved September 9, 2009, from http://reportr.net

Herring, S. (Ed.). (1996). *Computer-Mediated Communication. Linguistic, Social and Cross-Cultural Perspectives.* Amsterdam: John Benjamins.

Hester, S., & Eglin, P. (Eds.). (1997). *Culture in Action. Studies in Membership Categorization Analysis.* Washington: International Institute for Ethnomethodology and Conversation Analysis & University Press of America.

Hidayanto, A. N., & Bressan, S. (2007). Towards a Society of Peers: Expert and Interest Groups in Peer-to-Peer Systems. In *Proceedings of the OTM International IFIP*

Workshop On Semantic Web & Web Semantics, SWWS 2007 (pp. 487-496), Vilamoura, Portugal.

Hill, W., Stead, L., Rosenstein, M., & Furnas, G. (1995). Recommending and evaluating choices in a virtual community of use. In *Proceedings of ACM CHI'95 Conference on Human Factors in Computing Systems* (pp. 194–201).

Hills, J., Grand, J. L., & Piachaud, D. (2002). *Understanding Social Exclusion*. OUP Oxford.

Hirsch, A. (2008). *CNN Heavily Promoting Twitter On Air, Making Big Moves in Social Media*. Retrieved September 4, 2008, from http://mashable.com

Ho, N.-D., & Dooren, P. V. (2005). On the pseudo-inverse of the laplacian of a bipartite graph. *Applied Mathematics Letters*, *18*(8), 917–922. doi:10.1016/j.aml.2004.07.034

Hofmann, T. (1999, August). *Probabilistic Latent Semantic Analysis*. Paper presented at the Proceedings of the 22nd Annual ACM Conference on Research and Development in Information Retrieval, Berkeley, California, USA.

Hofmann, T. (2001). Unsupervised Learning by Probabilistic Latent Semantic Analysis. *Machine Learning Journal*, *42*(1), 177–196. doi:10.1023/A:1007617005950

Hofmann, T. (2004). Latent Semantic Models for Collaborative Filtering. *ACM Transactions on Information Systems*, *22*(1), 89–115. doi:10.1145/963770.963774

Hofmann, T., & Puzicha, J. (1999). Latent class models for collaborative filtering. In *Proceedings of the sixteenth International Joint Conference on Artificial Intelligence* (pp. 688–693).

Holden, N. J. (2002). *Cross-cultural management - a knowledge perspective*. Harlow, UK: Pearson Education.

Holland, J. H. (1975). *Adaptation in Natural and Artificial Systems*. University of Michigan Press.

Horvath, J. A. (2001). Working with tacit knowledge. In Cortada, J. W., & Woods, J. A. (Eds.), *The knowledge management yearbook 2000-2001* (pp. 34–51). New York: Butterworth-Heinemann.

Hou, J., & Zhang, Y. (2002). *Constructing Good Quality Web Page Communities*. Paper presented at the Proc. of the 13th Australasian Database Conferences (ADC2002), Melbourne, Australia.

Hou, J., & Zhang, Y. (2003a). Effectively Finding Relevant Web Pages from Linkage Information. *IEEE Transactions on Knowledge and Data Engineering*, *15*(4), 940–951. doi:10.1109/TKDE.2003.1209010

Hou, J., & Zhang, Y. (2003b). *Utilizing Hyperlink Transitivity to Improve Web Page Clustering*. Paper presented at the Proceedings of the 14th Australasian Database Conferences (ADC2003), Adelaide, Australia.

Hubert, L., & Arabie, P. (1985). Comparing partitions. *Journal of Classification*, *2*(1), 193–218. doi:10.1007/BF01908075

Ide, E. (1971). New experiments in relevance feedback. In Salton, G. (Ed.), *The SMART Retrieval System -- Experiments in Automatic Document Processing* (pp. 337–354). Englewood Cliffs, NJ: Prentice Hall Inc.

Isaacson, D., & Madsen, R. (1976). *Markov chains theory and applications*. John Wiley & Sons.

Ito, M., Horst, H., Bittanti, M., Boyd, D., Herr-Stephenson, B., & Lange, P. (2008, November). *Living and Learning with New Media: Summary of Findings from the Digital Youth Project*.

Ito, T., Shimbo, M., Kudo, T., & Matsumoto, Y. (2005). Application of kernels to link analysis. In *Proceedings of the eleventh ACM SIGKDD International Conference on Knowledge Discovery and Data Mining* (pp. 586–592).

Jain, A. K., & Dubes, R. (1988). *Algorithms for Clustering Data. Prentice-Hall advanced reference series*. Upper Saddle River, NJ: Prentice-Hall, Inc.

Jain, A. K., Murty, M. N., & Flynn, P. J. (1999). Data Clustering: A Review. *ACM Computing Surveys*, *31*(3), 264–323. doi:10.1145/331499.331504

Jancke, G., Venolia, G. D., Grudin, J., Cadiz, J. J., & Gupta, A. (2001). Linking public spaces: technical and social issues. In *Proceedings of the SIGCHI Conference on Human Factors in Computing Systems (Seattle,*

Washington, United States), CHI '01 (pp. 530-537). New York, NY: ACM.

Java, A., Song, X., Finin, T., & Tseng, B. (2007). Why We Twitter: Understanding Microblogging Usage and Communities. In *Proceedings of the Joint 9th WEBKDD & 1st SNA-KDD Workshop*, August 12, 2007. Baltimore County: University of Maryland

Ji, J., Liu, C., Yan, J., & Zhong, N. (2004). Bayesian networks structure learning and its application to personalized recommendation in a b2c portal. In *Proceedings of the IEEE/WIC/ACM International Conference on Web Intelligence.*

Jian, N., Hu, W., Cheng, G., & Qu, Y. (2005). Falcon-AO: Aligning Ontologies with Falcon. In *Proceedings of the K-CAP Workshop on Integrating Ontologies*, Banff, Canada.

Jin, R., Si, L., Zhai, C., & Callan, J. (2003). Collaborative filtering with decoupled models for preferences and ratings. In *Proceedings of the 12th International Conference on Information and Knowledge Management* (pp. 309–316).

Jin, X., Zhou, Y., & Mobasher, B. (2004, July 2004). *A Unified Approach to Personalization Based on Probabilistic Latent Semantic Models of Web Usage and Content.* Paper presented at the Proceedings of the AAAI 2004 Workshop on Semantic Web Personalization (SWP'04), San Jose.

Johnson, A. R. (2001). Competitive intelligence and competitor analysis as knowledge management applications. In Cortada, J. W., & Woods, J. A. (Eds.), *The knowledge management yearbook 2000-2001* (pp. 85–97). New York: Butterworth-Heinemann.

Jolliffe, I. (2002). *Principal components analysis* (2nd ed.). Springer-Verlag.

Jones, S. (2003). *Encyclopedia of new media: an essential reference to communication and technology.* SAGE.

Jung, J. J., & Euzenat, J. (2007). Towards Semantic Social Networks. In *Proceedings of the 4th European Semantic Web Conference, ESWC 2007* (pp. 267-280). Innsbruck, Austria.

Jungherr, A. (2009). *The digiactive guide to Twitter for activism*. Retrieved April 30, 2009, from http://www.digiactive.org

Jureta, I., Faulkner, S., Achbany, Y., & Saerens, M. (2007). Dynamic Web Service Composition within a Service-Oriented Architecture. In *IEEE International Conference on Web Services, 2007* (pp. 304-311).

Kahaner, L. (1997). *Competitive Intelligence: How to gather, analyze and use information to move your business to the top.* Touchstone.

Kandola, J., Cristianini, N., & Shawe-Taylor, J. (2002). Learning semantic similarity. *Advances in Neural Information Processing Systems, 657–664.*

Kaplan, R. S., & Norton, D. P. (1992). The balanced scorecard - measures that drive performance. *Harvard Business Review, 70*(1), 171–179.

Kaplan, R. S., & Norton, D. P. (1998). *Using the balanced scorecard as a strategic management system, Harvard business review on measuring corporate performance* (pp. 183–211). Boston, MA: Harvard Business School Publishing.

Kapur, J. N., & Kesavan, H. K. (1992). *Entropy optimization principles with applications.* Academic Press.

Karypis, G. (2001). Evaluation of item-based top-n recommendation algorithms. In *Proceedings of the tenth International Conference on Information and Knowledge Management* (pp. 247–254).

Kavali, S. G., Tzokas, N. X., & Saren, M. J. (1999). Relationship marketing as an ethical approach; philosophical and managerial considerations. *Management Decision, 37*(7), 573–581. doi:10.1108/00251749910285746

Kaye, S. (2001). Some proven ways to promote the exchange of ideas. In Cortada, J. W., & Woods, J. A. (Eds.), *The knowledge management yearbook 2000-2001* (pp. 391–398). New York: Butterworth-Heinemann.

Keen, A. (2007). *The Cult of the Amateur: How Today's Internet is Killing our Culture.* Currency.

Kelly, F. P. (1979). *Reversibility and stochastic networks.* John Wiley.

Kemeny, J. G., & Snell, J. L. (1976). *Finite Markov Chains*. Springer-Verlag.

Keppel, G., & Wickens, T. D. (2004). *Design and analysis: A researcher's handbook* (4th ed.). Upper Saddle River, NJ, USA: Pearson Prentice-Hall.

Kessler, M. M. (1963). Bibliographic coupling between scientific papers. *American Documentation, 14*(1), 10–25. doi:10.1002/asi.5090140103

Khambatti, M., Ryu, K. D., & Dasgupta, P. (2002). Efficient Discovery of Implicitly Formed Peer-to-Peer Communities. *International Journal of Parallel and Distributed Systems and Networks, 5*(4), 155–164.

Kikawada, K., & Holtshouse, D. (2001). The knowledge perspective in the xerox group. In Nonaka, I., & Teece, D. (Eds.), *Managing industrial knowledge - creation, transfer and utilization* (pp. 283–314). London: Sage.

Kim, W. C., & Mauborgne, R. (1999). Strategy, value innovation and the knowledge economy. *Sloan Management Review, 40*(3), 41–54.

Kirkpatrick, S., Gelatt, C., & Vecchi, M. (1983). Optimization by simulated annealing. *Science, 220*(4598), 671–680. doi:10.1126/science.220.4598.671

Kiss, J. (2009). *What do you use Twitter for?* Retrieved February 23, 2009, from http://www.guardian.co.uk

Klein, D. J., & Randic, M. (1993). Resistance distance. *Journal of Mathematical Chemistry, 12*, 81–95. doi:10.1007/BF01164627

Kleinberg, J. (1998). Authoritative sources in a hyperlinked environment. *Journal of the ACM, 46*(5), 604–632. doi:10.1145/324133.324140

Kondor, R. I., & Lafferty, J. (2002). Diffusion kernels on graphs and other discrete structures. In *Proceedings of the 19th International Conference on Machine Learning* (pp. 315–322).

Konstan, J. A. (1997). Applying Collaborative Filtering to Usenet News. *Communications of the ACM, 40*, 77–87. doi:10.1145/245108.245126

Konstan, J. A., Miller, B. N., Maltz, D., Herlocker, J. L., Gordon, L. R., & Riedl, J. (1997). GroupLens: applying collaborative filtering to Usenet news. *Communications of the ACM, 40*, 77–87. doi:10.1145/245108.245126

Konstan, J., Miller, B., Maltz, D., Herlocker, J., Gordon, L., & Riedl, J. (1997). Grouplens: Applying Collaborative Filtering to Usenet News. *Communications of the ACM, 40*(3), 77–87. doi:10.1145/245108.245126

Koppel, M., Schler, J., Argamon, S., & Pennebaker, J. W. (2006). Effects of age and gender on blogging. In *AAAI 2006 Spring Symposium on Computational Approaches to Analysing Weblogs*.

Kucera, J. (2009). *What if Twitter is leading us all astray in Iran?* Retrieved June 15, 2009, from http://trueslant.com

Kyriakopoulos, K., & deRuyter, K. (2004). Knowledge stocks and information flows in new product development. *Journal of Management Studies, 41*, 1469–1498. doi:10.1111/j.1467-6486.2004.00482.x

Lafon, S., & Lee, A. B. (2006). Diffusion maps and coarse-graining: A unified framework for dimensionality reduction, graph partitioning, and data set parameterization. *IEEE Transactions on Pattern Analysis and Machine Intelligence, 28*(9), 1393–1403. doi:10.1109/TPAMI.2006.184

Lagoze, C., & Van de Sompel, H. (2001). The Open Archives Initiative: Building a Low-Barrier Interoperability Framework. In *Proceedings of the first ACM/IEEE-CS Joint Conference on Digital Libraries (JCDL'01)* (pp. 54-62). New York: ACM Press.

Lampe, C., Ellison, N., & Steinfield, C. (2006). A face(book) in the crowd: social Searching vs. social browsing. In *CSCW '06: Proceedings of the 2006 20th anniversary conference on Computer supported cooperative work* (pp. 170, 167). ACM Press.

Langville, A., & Meyer, C. D. (2005). A survey of eigenvector methods for web information retrieval. *SIAM Review, 47*, 135–161. doi:10.1137/S0036144503424786

Lank, E. (1997). Leveraging invisible assets: The human factor. *Long Range Planning. Elsevier Science Limited, 30*(3), 406–412.

Latapy, M., & Pons, P. (2005). Computing communities in large networks using random walks. In *Proceedings of the 20th International Symposium on Computer and Information Sciences* (pp. 284–293).

Latour, B. (2005). *Reassembling the Social: An Introduction to Actor-Network-Theory*. Clarendon Lectures in Management Studies. Oxford University Press.

Lawrence, S., & Giles, C. L. (1999). Accessibility of Information on the Web. *Nature, 400*, 107–109. doi:10.1038/21987

Lazaro, C. (2008). *La liberté logicielle. Une ethnographie des pratiques d'échange et de coopération au sein de la communauté Debian*. Louvain-la-Neuve: Academia Bruylant.

Lazega, E. (1998). *Réseaux sociaux et structures relationnelles*. Presses Universitaires de France.

Lee, A., Green, W., & Brennan, M. (2000). Organisational knowledge, professional practice and the professional doctorate at work. In Carrick, J., & Rhodes, C. (Eds.), *Research and knowledge at work, perspectives, case-studies and innovative strategies* (pp. 117–136). London: Routledge.

Lee, J., & Verleysen, M. (2007). *Nonlinear dimensionality reduction*. Springer. doi:10.1007/978-0-387-39351-3

Lejeune, C. (2002). Indexation et organisation de la connaissance. La régulation des décisions sur un forum de discussion. *Cahiers du numérique, 3*(2), 129-144.

Lejeune, C. (2006). D'un annuaire de sites Internet à l'organisation documentaire. Une sociologie des relations sémantiques. *Cahiers de la Documentation, 3*, 12–22.

Lejeune, C. (2008). Quand le lézard s'en mêle... Ethnographie de l'indexation collective de sites Internet. *Science and Society, 75*, 101–114.

Lejeune, C. (2009). La confiance au sein des collectifs médiatisés. Une entrée par les catégorisations. *Cahiers d'ethnométhodologie, 3*.

Lejeune, C. (2010). L'organisation socio-politique des collectifs médiatisés. De quelques controverses internes à l'Open Directory Project. In Jacquemain, M., & Delwit, P. (Eds.), *Engagements actuels, actualité des engagements, Louvain-la-Neuve: Académia Bruylant*.

Lenhart, A. B., & Fox, S. (2006). *Bloggers: A portrait of the Internet's new storytellers*. Pew Internet & American Life Project.

Leonard, D., & Sensiper, D. (1998). The role of tacit knowledge in group innovation. *California Management Review, 40*(3), 112–132.

Leonard-Barton, D. (1995). *Wellsprings of knowledge - building and sustaining the sources of innovation*. Boston, MA: Harvard Business School Press.

Lesser, E., & Prusak, L. (2000). Communities of practice, social capital and organizational knowledge. In Lesser, E., Fontaine, M. A., & Slusher, J. A. (Eds.), *Knowledge and communities* (pp. 123–150). Woburn, MA: Butterworth-Heinemann. doi:10.1016/B978-0-7506-7293-1.50011-1

Lévy, P. (1994). *L'intelligence collective. Pour une anthropologie du cyberespace*. Paris: La Découverte.

Lévy, P. (1997). *Collective Intelligence: Mankind's Emerging World in Cyberspace*. Cambridge, MA: Perseus.

Lévy, P. (1998). *Becoming Virtual: Reality in the Digital Age*. Da Capo Press.

Lévy, P. (2000). Question de caractère. *Buddhaline*. Retrieved June 7, 2009, from http://www.buddhaline.net/spip.php?article322

Liebowitz, J. (1999). *Building organizational intelligence: A knowledge management primer*. San Diego: CRC Press.

Lilien, G., Smith, B., & Moorthy, K. (1992). *Marketing Models*. Prentice Hall.

Ling, R. (2004). *The Mobile Connection: The cell phone's impact on society*. San Francisco: Morgan Kaufmann.

Liu, K., Bhaduri, K., Das, K., Nguyen, P., & Kargupta, H. (2006). Client-side Web Mining for Community Formation in Peer-to-Peer Environments. *SIGKDD Explorations, 8*(2), 11–20. doi:10.1145/1233321.1233323

Llewellyn, H. (2009). Spanish P2P Trial Begins. Retrieved May 21, 2009, from http://www.billboard.biz

Löser, A., Staab, S., & Tempich, C. (2007). Semantic Social Overlay Networks. *IEEE Journal on Selected Areas in Communications*, *25*(1), 5–14. doi:10.1109/JSAC.2007.070102

Lu, S. Y., & Fu, K. S. (1978). A sentence-to-sentence clustering procedure for pattern analysis. *IEEE Transactions on Systems, Man, and Cybernetics*, *8*(5), 381–389. doi:10.1109/TSMC.1978.4309979

Luckie, M. (2008). *Twitter for journalists: What you need to know*. Retrieved February 25, 2008, from http://www.10000words.net

Luhn, H. P. (1957). A Statistical Approach to Mechanized Encoding and Searching of Literary Information. *IBM Journal of Research and Development*, *1*(4), 309–317. doi:10.1147/rd.14.0309

MacQueen, J. (1967). Some methods for classification and analysis of multivariate observations. In *Proceedings of Berkeley Symposium on mathematical statistics and probability* (Vol. 1, pp. 281-297).

Madhavan, J., Cohen, S., Dong, X. L., Halevy, A., Jeffery, S. R., Ko, D., & Yu, C. (2007). Web-Scale Data Integration: You can afford to Pay as You Go. In *Proceedings of the 3rd Biennial Conf. on Innovative Data Systems Research, CIDR 2007* (pp. 342-350). Asilomar, CA, USA.

Malhotra, Y. (2000). Knowledge management for e-business performance: Advanced information strategy to "internet time". *Information Strategy, The Executive's Journal*, *16*(4), 5–16.

Malone, D. (2002). Knowledge management; a model for organizational learning. *International Journal of Accounting Information Systems*, *3*(2), 111–123. doi:10.1016/S1467-0895(02)00039-8

Manouselis, N., & Sampson, D. (2004). *Recommendation of Quality Approaches for the European Quality Observatory* (pp. 1082–1083). IEEE Computer Society.

Mardia, K. V., Kent, J. T., & Bibby, J. M. (1979). *Multivariate Analysis*. Academic Press.

Maritza, L., Cristina, N., Perez-Alcazar, J., Garcia-Diaz, J., & Delgado, J. (2004). A comparison of several predictive algorithms for collaborative filtering on multivalued ratings. *ACM Symposium on Applied Computing* (pp. 1033–1039).

Marlin, B. (2004). *Collaborative Filtering: A Machine Learning Perspective*. University of Toronto.

Marques, A. (2009). Blogs, twitter e suas remediaçoes. *Journalismo & Internet. Grupo de Pesquisa Em Jornalismo On Line*. Retrieved March 23, 2009, from http://gjol.blogspot.com

Martello, S., & Toth, P. (1990). Lower bounds and reduction procedures for the bin packing problem. *Discrete Applied Mathematics*, *28*(1), 59–70. doi:10.1016/0166-218X(90)90094-S

Matthys, B., Falkenauer, E., Francq, P., & Delchambre, A. Robert & F., Gilson, H. (2000). An integrated system for navigation help, informational retrieval and suggestions in a hypertext structure. In Proceedings of Recherche d'Information Assistée par Ordinateur 2000 (p. 10). Paris, France.

Mayfield, R. (2007). *Twitter Tips the Tuna*. Retrieved March 10, 2007, from http://ross.typepad.com

McBrien, P., & Poulovassilis, A. (2003). Defining Peer-to-Peer Data Integration Using Both as View Rules. In *Proceedings of the 1st International Workshop on Databases, Information Systems, and Peer-to-Peer Computing, DBISP2P 2003* (pp. 91-107). Berlin, Germany.

McCann, U. (2008). When did we start trusting strangers? How the Internet turned us all into influencers. Retrieved December 1, 2008, from http://www.universalmccann.com

McCarthy, J. F., Congleton, B., & Harper, F. M. (2008). The context, content & community collage: sharing personal digital media in the physical workplace. In *Proceedings of the ACM 2008 Conference on Computer Supported Cooperative Work (San Diego, CA, USA, November 08 - 12, 2008 CSCW '08* (pp. 97-106). New York: ACM.

McCombs, M. (2004). *Setting the Agenda: The Mass Media and Public Opinion*. Cambridge, UK: Polity Press.

McDermott, R., & O'Dell, C. (2001). Overcoming cultural barriers to sharing knowledge. *Journal of Knowledge Management, 5*(1), 76–85. doi:10.1108/13673270110384428

McFedries, P. (2007). Technically Speaking: All A-Twitter. *IEEE Spectrum Magazine,* 84

McHugh, J. (1990). *Algorithmic Graph Theory.* London: Prentice Hall International.

McKenna, K. Y. A., & Bargh, J. A. (2000). Plan 9 From Cyberspace: The Implications of the Internet for Personality and Social Psychology. *Personality and Social Psychology Review, 4*(1), 57–75. doi:10.1207/S15327957PSPR0401_6

McKenna, R. (1999). *New management.* Sydney, NSW: Irwin McGraw-Hill.

McNee, S. M., Riedl, J., & Konstan, J. A. (2006). Being accurate is not enough: how accuracy metrics have hurt recommender systems. In *Proceedings of the Conference on Human Factors in Computing Systems (CHI'06)* (pp. 1097–1101).

Meacham, J. A. (1983). Wisdom and the concept of knowledge. In Kuhn, D., & Meacham, J. A. (Eds.), *Contributions in human development.* Basel: Karger.

Middlebrook, C. (2007). *The Big Juicy Twitter Guide.* Retrieved November 2, 2007, from http://www.caroline-middlebrook.com

Mikami, Y., Zavarsky, P., Rozan, M. Z., Suzuki, I., Takahashi, M., & Maki, T. (2005). *The language observatory project (LOP)* (pp. 990–991). ACM.

Miller, D. (1996). A preliminary typology of organizational learning: Synthesizing the literature. *Journal of Management, 22*(3), 485–505. doi:10.1177/014920639602200305

Milligan, G. W., & Cooper, M. C. (1986). A study of the comparability of external criteria for hierarchical cluster analysis. *Multivariate Behavioral Research, 21*(4), 441–458. doi:10.1207/s15327906mbr2104_5

Mills, J., Platts, K., Bourne, M., & Richards, H. (2002). *Strategy and performance: Competing through competences.* Cambridge, UK: Cambridge University Press.

Mobasher, B. (2004). Web Usage Mining and Personalization. In M. P. Singh (Ed.), Practical Handbook of Internet Computing (pp. 15.11-37). CRC Press.

Mobasher, B., Dai, H., Nakagawa, M., & Luo, T. (2002). Discovery and Evaluation of Aggregate Usage Profiles for Web Personalization. *Data Mining and Knowledge Discovery, 6*(1), 61–82. doi:10.1023/A:1013232803866

Mohar, B. (1992). Laplace eigenvalues of graphs – a survey. *Discrete Mathematics, 109,* 171–183. doi:10.1016/0012-365X(92)90288-Q

Montanelli, S., & Castano, S. (2008). Semantically Routing Queries in Peer-based Systems: the H-Link Approach. *The Knowledge Engineering Review, 23*(1), 51–72. doi:10.1017/S0269888907001257

Mooney, R. J. (2000). Content-based book recommending using learning for text categorization. In *Proceedings of the ACM International Conference on Digital Libraries* (pp. 195-204).

Moore, T. D., & Serva, M. A. (2007). Understanding member motivation for contributing to different types of virtual communities: a proposed framework. In *Proceedings of the 2007 ACM SIGMIS CPR Conference on Computer Personnel Research: the Global information Technology Workforce (St. Louis, Missouri, USA, April 19 - 21, 2007) SIGMIS-CPR '07* (pp. 153-158). New York: ACM.

Moreland, R., & Myaskovsky, L. (2000). Exploring the Performance Benefits of Group Training: Transactive Memory or Improved Communication? *Organizational Behavior and Human Decision Processes, 82*(1), 117–133. doi:10.1006/obhd.2000.2891

Moscovici, S. (Ed.). (1984). *Psychologie sociale.* Paris: PUF.

Motik, B., Horrocks, I., & Sattler, U. (2009). Bridging the Gap between OWL and Relational Databases. *Journal of Web Semantics, 7*(2), 74–89. doi:10.1016/j.websem.2009.02.001

Mounin, G. (1995). Introduction au problème terminologique. In *Dictionnaire de la linguistique.* Paris: PUF.

Mukherjee, C. S., & Ramakrishnan, I. V. (2008). Automated Semantic Analysis of Schematic Data. *World Wide Web Journal, 11*(4), 427–464. doi:10.1007/s11280-008-0046-0

Murthi, B., & Sarkar, S. (2003). The role of the management sciences in research on personalization. *Management Science, 49*(10), 1344–1362. doi:10.1287/mnsc.49.10.1344.17313

Murty, M. N., & Jain, A. K. (1995). Knowledge-based clustering scheme for collection management and retrieval of library books. *Pattern Recognition, 28*(7), 949–963. doi:10.1016/0031-3203(94)00173-J

Nadler, B., Lafon, S., Coifman, R., & Kevrekidis, I. (2005). Diffusion maps, spectral clustering and eigenfunctions of Fokker-Planck operators. *Advances in Neural Information Processing Systems, 18*, 955–962.

Nadler, B., Lafon, S., Coifman, R., & Kevrekidis, I. (2006). Diffusion maps, spectral clustering and reaction coordinate of dynamical systems. *Applied and Computational Harmonic Analysis, 21*, 113–127. doi:10.1016/j.acha.2005.07.004

Nahapiet, J., & Ghoshal, S. (1998). Social capital, intellectual capital, and the organizational advantage. *Academy of Management Review, 23*(2), 242–266. doi:10.2307/259373

Naito, H. (2001). Knowledge is commitment. In Nonaka, I., & Teece, D. (Eds.), *Managing industrial knowledge - creation, transfer and utilization* (pp. 270–282). London: Sage.

Nakamura, A., & Abe, N. (1998). Collaborative filtering using weighted majority prediction algorithms. In *Proceedings of the 15th International Conference on Machine Learning.*

Nanas, N., & Roeck, A. D. (2008). *Autopoiesis, the Immune System and Adaptive Information Filtering.* Natural Computing.

Nanas, N., & Vavalis, M. (2008). A Bag or a Window of Words for Information Filtering. In Arnellos, J. D. (Ed.), *Lecture Notes in Artificial Intelligence* (pp. 182–193). Springer.

Nanas, N., Uren, V., Roeck, A. D., & Domingue, J. (2003). Building and Applying a Concept Hierarchy Representation of a User Profile. In *26th Annual International ACM SIGIR Conference on Research and Development in Information Retrieval* (pp. 198-204). ACM Press.

Nanas, N., Uren, V., Roeck, A. D., & Domingue, J. (2004). Multi-Topic Information Filtering with a Single User Profile. *3rd Hellenic Conference on Artificial Intelligence* (pp. 400-409).

Nanas, N., Vavalis, M., & Houstis, E. (2009). *Personalised News and Scientific Literature Aggregation.* Information Processing and Management.

Nanas, N., Vavalis, M., & Kellis, L. (2009). Immune Learning in a Dynamic Information Environment. *8th International Conference on Artificial Immune Systems* (pp. 192-205).

Nanas, N., Vavalis, M., & Roeck, A. D. (2009). *Words, Antibodies and their Interactions.* Swarm Intelligence.

Nanas, N., Vavalis, M., Koutsaftikis, J., Kellis, L., & Houstis, E. (2009). Web Observatories: Concepts, State of the Art and Beyond. *4th Mediterranean Conference on Information Systems.*

Nardi, B. A., Schiano, D. J., Gumbrecht, M., & Swartz, L. (2007). Why we blog. *Communications of the ACM, 47*(12), 41–46. doi:10.1145/1035134.1035163

Neeley, A. (2002). *Business performance measurement - theory and practice.* Cambridge, UK: Cambridge University Press.

Newell, A., & Simon, H. (1972). *Human problem solving.* NJ: Prentice-Hall Englewood Cliffs.

Newell, S., Robertson, M., Scarbrough, H., & Swan, J. (2002). *Managing knowledge work.* Palgrave.

Newman, M. (2005). A measure of betweenness centrality based on random walks. *Social Networks, 27*(1), 39–54. doi:10.1016/j.socnet.2004.11.009

Nickols, F. (2001). The knowledge in knowledge management. In Cortada, J. W., & Woods, J. A. (Eds.), *The knowledge management yearbook 2000-2001* (pp. 12–21). New York: Butterworth-Heinemann.

Noble, B., & Daniels, J. (1988). *Applied linear algebra* (3rd ed.). Prentice-Hall.

Nonaka, I., & Konno, N. (1998). The concept of ba: Building a foundation for knowledge creation. *California Management Review, 40*(3), 40–54.

Nonaka, I., & Takeuchi, H. (1995). *The knowledge-creating company.* Oxford: Oxford University Press.

Nonaka, I., & Teece, D. (Eds.). (2001). *Managing industrial knowledge - creation, transfer and utilization.* London: Sage.

Nonaka, I., Toyama, R., & Konno, N. (2001). Seci, ba, and leadership: A unified model of dynamic knowledge creation. In Nonaka, I., & Teece, D. (Eds.), *Managing industrial knowledge creation, transfer and utilization.* Thousand Oaks, CA, USA: Sage.

Norris, J. R. (1997). *Markov Chains.* Cambridge University Press.

O'Reilly, T. & Milstein, Sarah (2009). *The Twitter Book.* Cambridge, MA: O'Reilly Media

O'Connor, M., & Herlocker, J. (2001). Clustering items for collaborative filtering. In *Proceedings of the SIGIR-2001 International Workshop on Recommender Systems.*

O'Connor, R. (2009). Facebook and Twitter are Reshaping Journalism as We Know It. Retrieved January 20, 2009, from http://www.alternet.org

O'Dell, C. (2000). *Knowledge management - a guide for your journey to best-practice processes* (White Paper). Houston, Texas: Grayson, C. J., American Productivity and Quality Center.

O'Dell, C., & Jackson Grayson, J. (1998). *If only we knew what we know: The transfer of internal knowledge and best practice.* Houston, Texas: The Free Press.

O'Mahony, M., Hurley, N., Kushmerick, N., & Silvestre, G. (2004). Collaborative recommendation: A robustness analysis. *ACM Transactions on Internet Technology, 4*(4), 344–377.

O'Reilly, T. (2005). *What is Web 2.0: Design Patterns and Business Models for the Next Generation of Software.*

Observing Standards for Web-Based Learning from the Web. (2004). *Computational Science and Its Applications ICCSA 2004.*

Onge, H. S. (1999). Tacit knowledge: The key to the strategic alignment of intellectual capital. In M. Zack (Ed.), Knowledge and strategy (pp. pp. 223-230). Boston: Butterworth Heinemann.

Onwuegbuzie, A. J., & Leech, N. L. (2005). On becoming a pragmatic researcher: The importance of combining quantitative and qualitative research methodologies. *International Journal of Social Research Methodology, 8*(5), 375–387. doi:10.1080/13645570500402447

Orihuela, J. L. (2009). *Medios que entienden Twitter.* Retrieved April 29, 2009, from http://www.abc.es/blogs/jose-luis-orihuela

Orihuela, J. L. (2009). *Comunidades nacionales de usuarios de Twitter.* Retrieved March 24, 2009, from http://www.ecuaderno.com

Otsuka, S., Toyoda, M., Hirai, J., & Kitsuregawa, M. (2004). *Extracting User Behavior by Web Communities Technology on Global Web Logs.* Paper presented at the Proc. of the 15th International Conference on Database and Expert Systems Applications (DEXA'04), Zaragoza, Spain.

Page, L., Brin, S., Motwani, R., & Winograd, T. (1998). *The PageRank citation ranking: Bringing order to the web (Tech. Rep.).* Computer System Laboratory, Stanford University.

Palmer, C., & Faloutsos, C. (2003). Electricity based external similarity of categorical attributes. In *Proceedings of the 7th Pacific-Asia Conference on Knowledge Discovery and Data Mining (PAKDD'03),* (pp. 486–500).

Pan, J.-Y., Yang, H.-J., Faloutsos, C., & Duygulu, P. (2006). Automatic multimedia cross-modal correlation discovery. *Proceedings of the 10th ACM SIGKDD International Conference on Knowledge Discovery and Data Mining, 82*(4), 331–338.

Paolillo, J. C., & Penumarthy, S. (2007). The Social Structure of Tagging Internet Video on del. icio. us. *HICSS*

2007. 40th Annual Hawaii International Conference on System Sciences (p. 85).

Papadimitriou, C., & Steiglitz, K. (1982). *Combinatorial Optimization, Algorithms and Complexity.* Englewood Cliffs, New Jersey: Prentice-Hall.

Pareto, V. (1935). The Mind and Society: A Treatise on General Sociology. New York: Harcourt Brace [1916].

Parker, C., & Pfeiffer, S. (2005). Video Blogging: Content to the Max. *IEEE MultiMedia, 12*(2), 4–8. doi:10.1109/MMUL.2005.41

Parrochia, D. (1993). *Philosophie des réseaux.* Paris: PUF.

Parzen, E. (1962). *Stochastic Processes.* Holden-Day.

Pavlov, D. X., & Pennock, D. M. (2002). A maximum entropy approach to collaborative filtering in dynamics, sparse, high-dimensional domains. In Proceedings of Neural Information Processing Systems, (pp. 1441–1448).

Pazzani, M., & Billsus, D. (1997). Learning and revising user profiles: The identification of interesting web sites. *Machine Learning, 27,* 313–331. doi:10.1023/A:1007369909943

Penn, M., & Zalesne, E. (2007). *Microtrends.* London: Penguin Books.

Percival, S. (2009). *The Story (so far) of Twitter.* Retrieved June 21, 2009, from http://www.manolith.com

Perelman, Ch., & Olbrechts-Tyteca, L. (1994). *Tratado de la Argumentación. La nueva retórica.* Madrid: Gredos.

Perkowitz, M., & Etzioni, O. (1998). *Adaptive Web Sites: Automatically Synthesizing Web Pages.* Paper presented at the Proceedings of the 15th National Conference on Artificial Intelligence, Madison, WI.

Perkowitz, M., & Etzioni, O. (1999). *Adaptive Web Sites: Conceptual Cluster Mining.* Paper presented at the Proceeding of 16th International Joint Conference on Artificial Intelligence, Stockholm, Sweden.

Pierrakos, D., Paliouras, G., Papatheodorou, C., Karkaletsis, V., & Dikaiakos, M. D. (2003). *Construction of Web Community Directories by Mining Usage Data.* Paper presented at the Proceeding of the 2nd Hellenic Data Management Symposium (HDMS'03), Athens, Greece.

Planas, J. (2008). *¿Qué es Twitter?* Retrieved May 26, 2008, from http://joanplanas.com

PMI. (2008). *A guide to the project management body of knowledge* (4th ed.). Newton Sq, PA: Project Management Institute Inc.

Polanyi, M. (1966). *The tacit dimension.* London: Routledge & Kegan Paul.

Polanyi, M. (1997). Tacit knowledge. In Prusak, L. (Ed.), *Knowledge in organizations - resources for the knowledge-based economy* (pp. 135–146). Oxford: Butterworth-Heinemann.

Pons, P., & Latapy, M. (2006). Computing communities in large networks using random walks. *Journal of Graph Algorithms and Applications, 10*(2), 191–218.

Pothen, A., Simon, H. D., & Liou, K.-P. (1990). Partitioning sparse matrices with eigenvectors of graphs. *SIAM Journal on Matrix Analysis and Applications, 11*(3), 430–452. doi:10.1137/0611030

Poulsen, E. (2009). *Twitter Helps Tell the Store of Amsterdam Plane Crash.* Retrieved February 26, 2009, from http://www.poynter.org

Poulsen, K. (2007). *Firsthand Reports from California Wildfires Pour Through Twitter.* October, 23, 2007, from http://www.wired.com

Prahlad, C. K., & Ramaswamy, V. (2000). Co-opting customer competence. *Harvard Business Review, 78*(1), 79–87.

Proulx, S., & Latzko-Toth, G. (2005). Mapping the virtual in social sciences: On the category of 'virtual community'. *The Journal of Community Informatics, 2*(1).

Prusak, L., & Cohen, D. (2001). How to invest in social capital. *Harvard Business Review, 79*(6), 86–93.

Qiu, H., & Hancock, E. R. (2005). Image segmentation using commute times. *Proceedings of the 16th British Machine Vision Conference (BMVC 2005)* (pp. 929–938).

Qiu, H., & Hancock, E. R. (2007). Clustering and embedding using commute times. *IEEE Transactions on Pattern Analysis and Machine Intelligence, 29*(11), 1873–1890. doi:10.1109/TPAMI.2007.1103

Quinn, J. B., Andersen, P., & Finkelstein, S. (1996). Managing professional intellect: Making the most of the best. *Harvard Business Review, 74*(2), 71–80.

Ramos, V., & Muge, F. (1999). Image Segmentation by Colour Cube Genetic K-Mean Clustering. In *3rd Workshop on Genetic Algorithms and Artificial Life GAAL* (pp. 319-323). Lisbon, Portugal.

Rana, O. F., & Hinze, A. (2004). Trust and Reputation in Dynamic Scientific Communities. *IEEE Distributed Systems Online, 5*(1).

Rand, W. M. (1971). Objective criteria for the evaluation of clustering methods. *Journal of the American Statistical Association, 66*, 846–850. doi:10.2307/2284239

Rashid, M., Albert, I., Cosley, D., Lam, S., McNee, S., Konstan, J., & Riedl, J. (2002). Getting to know you: Learning new user preferences in recommender systems. In *Proceedings of the 7th International Conference on Intelligence User Interfaces* (pp. 127–134).

Ray, S., & Turi, R. H. (1999). Determination of Number of Clusters in K-Means Clustering and Application in Colour Image Segmentation. In *4th International Conference on Advances in Pattern Recognition and Digital Techniques (ICAPRDT'99)* (pp. 137-143).

Raymond, E. S. (2001). *The cathedral & the Bazaar. Musings on Linux and Open Source by an Accidental Revolutionary.* Sebastopol: O'Reilly.

Reagan, G. (2009). *Ann Curry Defends Foreign Correspondents, Twitter; Rick Sanchez Defends CNN.* Retrieved June 16, 2009, from http://www.observer.com

Reichling, T., & Veith, M. (2005). Expertise Sharing in a Heterogeneous Organisaztional Environment, EC-SCW'05. In *Proceedings of the 9th European Conference on Computer Supported Cooperative Work* (pp. 325-345). Germany: Springer.

Reid, S. E., & Brentani, U. D. (2004). The fuzzy front end of new product development for discontinuous innovations: A theoretical model. *Journal of Product Innovation Management, 21*(3), 170–184. doi:10.1111/j.0737-6782.2004.00068.x

Rekiek, B. (2000). *Assembly Line Design: multiple objective grouping genetic algorithm and the balancing of mixed-model hybrid assembly line.* PhD thesis, Université libre de Bruxelles.

Resnick, P., Neophytos, I., Mitesh, S., Bergstrom, P., & Riedl, J. (1994). GroupLens: An open architecture for collaborative filtering of netnews. In *Proceedings of the Conference on Computer Supported Cooperative Work* (pp. 175–186).

Rheingold, H. (1991). *Virtual Reality. The Revolutionary Technology of Computer-Generated Artificial Worlds – And How It Promises to Transform Society.* New York: Simon & Schuster.

Rheingold, H. (1993). *The Virtual Community. Homesteading on the Electronic Frontier.* Boston, MA: Addison-Wesley.

Rheingold, H. (2000). *The Virtual Community: Homesteading on the Electronic Frontier.* MIT Press.

Rich, E. (1979). User modeling via stereotypes. *Cognitive Science, 3*(4), 329–354. doi:10.1207/s15516709cog0304_3

Richardson, W. (2008). *Blogs, Wikis, Podcasts, and Other Powerful Web Tools for Classrooms.* Corwin Press.

Robey, D., Boudreau, M.-C., & Rose, G. M. (2000). *Information technology and organizational learning: A review and assessment of research.* Accounting Management and Information Technologies.

Rocchio, J. (1971). *Relevance Feedback in Information Retrieval.*

Rocchio, J. J. (1971). Relevance feedback in information retrieval. In Salton, G. (Ed.), *The SMART Retrieval System -- Experiments in Automatic Document Processing.* Englewood Cliffs, NJ: Prentice Hall Inc.

Rogers, E. M. (1995). *Diffusion of innovation* (3rd ed.). New York: The Free Press.

Rollo, C. & Clarke, T. (2001). *International best practice - case studies in knowledge management* (Standard/Guideline HB 275 Supplement 1-2001). Sydney: Standards Australia.

Rose, E. (1960). The English record of a natural sociology. *American Sociological Review, 25*(2), 193–208. doi:10.2307/2092625

Roseman, M., & Greenberg, S. (1996). TeamRooms: Network Places for Collaboration. *Conference on Computer Supported Cooperative Work (CSCW '96)* (pp. 325-333). ACM Press.

Rosenberg, R. (1967). *Simulation of genetic populations with biochemical properties*. PhD thesis, University of Michigan.

Ross, S. (1996). *Stochastic Processes* (2nd ed.). Wiley.

Roth, V., Laub, J., Buhmann, J., & Muller, K.-R. (2002). Going metric: Denoising pairwise data. In *Proceedings of the 15th Neural Information Processing Systems conference.*

Rowse, D. (2008). 5 ways I benefit from Twitter. Retrieved December 4, 2008, from http://www.twitip.com

Ruffini, P. (2008). *The Year of Twitter*. Retrieved January 29, 2008, from http://www.patrickruffini.com

Sabou, M., D'Aquin, M., & Motta, E. (2008). Exploring the Semantic Web as Background Knowledge for Ontology Matching. *Journal on Data Semantics, XI*, 156–190. doi:10.1007/978-3-540-92148-6_6

Sacks, H. (1992). *Lectures on Conversation*. Oxford: Blackwell.

Saerens, M., Fouss, F., Yen, L., & Dupont, P. (2004). The principal components analysis of a graph, and its relationships to spectral clustering. In *Proceedings of the 15th European Conference on Machine Learning (ECML 2004)* (LNCS 3201, pp. 371-383).

Salton, G. (1968). *Automatic Information Organization and Retrieval*. New York: McGraw-Hill.

Salton, G. (1971). *The SMART Retrieval System -- Experiments in Automatic Document processing*. Englewood Cliffs, NJ: Prentice Hall Inc.

Salton, G. (1989). *Automatic Text Processing*. Addison-Wesley.

Salton, G., & McGill, M. (1983). *Modern Information Retrieval*. New York: McGraw-Hill Book Co.

Samaddar, S., & Kadiyala, S. S. (2006). An analysis of interorganizational resource sharing decisions in collaborative knowledge creation. *European Journal of Operational Research, 170*(1), 192–210. doi:10.1016/j.ejor.2004.06.024

Sampson, R.J., Morenoff, J.D., & Gannon-Rowley, T. (2003, November 28). *Assessing Neighbourhood": Social Processes and New Directions in Research.*

Sarwar, B., Karypis, G., Konstan, J., & Riedl, J. (2001). Item-based collaborative filtering recommendation algorithms. In *Proceedings of the International World Wide Web Conference* (pp. 285–295).

Sattler, U., Calvanese, D., & Molitor, R. (2003). Relationships with other Formalisms. In Description Logic Handbook (pp. 137-177).

Sawhney, M., Verona, G., & Prandelli, E. (2005). Collaborating to create: The internet as a platform for customer engagement in product innovation. *Journal of Interactive Marketing, 19*(4), 4–17. doi:10.1002/dir.20046

Schafer, B. J., Konstan, J. A., & Riedi, J. (1999). Recommender systems in e-commerce (pp. 158-166).

Scharmer, C. O. (2001). Self-transcending knowledge: Organizing around emerging realities. In Nonaka, I., & Teece, D. (Eds.), *Managing industrial knowledge - creation, transfer and utilization* (pp. 69–90). London: Sage.

Schein, A. I., Popescul, A., Ungar, L. H., & Pennock, D. M. (2005). CROC: A new evaluation criterion for recommender systems: World wide web electronic commerce, security and privacy. *Electronic Commerce Research, 1*(5), 51. doi:10.1023/B:ELEC.0000045973.51289.8c

Schein, E. H. (1993). How can organisations learn faster? Lessons from the green room. *Sloan Management Review*, (Winter): 85–92.

Schmidt-Thieme, L. (2005). Compound classification models for recommender systems. In *Proceedings of the Fifth IEEE International Conference on Data Mining* (pp. 378–385).

Scholkopf, B., & Smola, A. (2002). *Learning with kernels*. The MIT Press.

Scholkopf, B., Smola, A., & Muller, K.-R. (1998). Nonlinear component analysis as a kernel eigenvalue problem. *Neural Computation*, 5(10), 1299–1319. doi:10.1162/089976698300017467

Schön, D. A. (1983). *The reflective practitioner - how professionals think in action*. Aldershot, UK: BasiAshgate ARENA.

Schouten, A. (2008). *Adolescents' online self-disclosure and self-presentation*. Amsterdam School of Communications Research.

Schreyer, P. (1999). The Contribution of Information and Communication Technology to Output Growth. *Statistical Working Party, 99*(4).

Schuppel, J., Muller-Stewens, G., & Gomez, P. (1998). The knowledge spiral. In Krogh, G. V., Ros, J., & Kleine, D. (Eds.), *Knowing in firms: Understanding, managing and measuring knowledge* (pp. 223–239). London, UK: Sage Publications.

Schwalbach, E. M. (2003). *Value and validity in action research: A guidebook for reflective practitioners*. London: Scarecrow Press.

Scoble, R. (2008). *Twittering the earthquake in China*. Retrieved May 12, 2008, from http://scobleizer.com

Seel, R. (2001). Anxiety and incompetence in the large group - a psychodynamaic perspective. *Journal of Organizational Change Management*, 14(5), 493–503. doi:10.1108/EUM0000000005878

Senge, P. M. (1990). *The fifth discipline - the art & practice of the learning organization*. Sydney, Australia: Random House.

Senge, P. M., Kleiner, A., Roberts, C., Ross, R., & Smith, B. (1999). *The fifth discipline fieldbook: Strategies and tools for building a learning organization*. New York: Doubleday.

Senge, P., Kleiner, A., Roberts, C., Roth, G., & Smith, B. (1999). *The dance of change: The challenges of sustaining momentum in learning organisations*. New York: Doubleday.

Shardanand, U., & Maes, P. (1995). Social information filtering: Algorithms for automating 'word of mouth'. *Proceedings of the Conference on Human Factors in Computing Systems* (pp. 210–217).

Shardanand, U., & Maes, P. (1995, May 1995). *Social Information Filtering: Algorithms for Automating 'Word of Mouth'*. Paper presented at the Proceedings of the Computer-Human Interaction Conference (CHI95), Denver, CO.

Shawe-Taylor, J., & Cristianini, N. (2004). *Kernel Methods for Pattern Analysis*. Cambridge University Press.

Sherman, J. D., Berkowitz, D., & Sounder, W. E. (2005). New product development performance and the interaction of cross-functional integration and knowledge management. *Journal of Product Innovation Management*, 22(3), 399–411. doi:10.1111/j.1540-5885.2005.00137.x

Shi, J., & Malik, J. (2000). Normalised cuts and image segmentation. *IEEE Transactions on Pattern Matching and Machine Intelligence*, 22, 888–905. doi:10.1109/34.868688

Shimbo, M., & Ito, T. (2006). *Kernels as link analysis measures* (pp. 283–310). John Wiley & Sons.

Shklovski, I., Palen, L., & Sutton, J. (2008). Finding community through information and communication technology in disaster response. In *Proceedings of the ACM 2008 conference on Computer supported cooperative work* (pp. 127-136). New York: Association for Computing Machinery

Sholin, R. (2009). *Welcome to ReportingOn 2.0*. Retrieved July 2, 2009, from http://blog.reportingon.com

Shrout, P. E., & Fleiss, J. L. (1979). Intraclass Correlations: Uses in Assessing Rater Reliability. *Psychological Bulletin, 86*, 420–428. doi:10.1037/0033-2909.86.2.420

Siegler, M. G. (2008). *Twitter is the first on the scene for a major earthquake – but who cares about that, is it mainstream yet?* Retrieved May 12, 2008, from http://digital.venturebeat.com

Sigurbjörnsson, B., & Van Zwol, R. (2008). Flickr Tag Recommendation based on Collective Knowledge. In *Proceedings of the 17th International Conference on World Wide Web, WWW 2008* (pp. 327-336). Beijing, China.

Silver, H. (1994). Social Exclusion and Social Solidarity: Three Paradigms. *International Labour Review, 133*, 531–578.

Silver, H. (2007, December). *Social Exclusion: Comparative Analysis of Europe and Middle East Youth.*

Simmel, G. (1908). *Soziologie. Untersuchungen über die Formen der Vergesellschaftung.* Berlin: Duncker & Humblot.

Simon, M. (2008). *Student "Twitter" his way out of Egyptian jail.* Retrieved April 25, 2008, from http://www.cnn.com

Small, H. (1973). Co-citation in the scientific literature: a new measure of the relationship between two documents. *Journal of the American Society for Information Science American Society for Information Science, 24*(4), 265–269. doi:10.1002/asi.4630240406

Smith, S. (2008). *Ultimate guide to Twitter tools and resources for journalists.* Retrieved January 18, 2008, from http://www.newmediabytes.com

Smola, A. J., & Kondor, R. (2003). Kernels and regularization on graphs. In *Proceedings of the Conference on Learning Theory (COLT).*

Snell, S. (2008). *101 Twitter Resources.* Retrieved May 12, 2008, from http://traffikd.com

Soboroff, I., & Nicholas, C. (1999). Combining content and collaboration in text filtering. In *Proceedings of the*

IJCAI'99 Workshop on Machine Learning in Information Filtering (pp. 86–91).

Solis, B., & Thomas, J. (2009). *Twitterverse.* Retrieved May 27, 2009, from http://www.flickr.com/photos/briansolis

Specia, L., & Motta, E. (2007). Integrating Folksonomies with the Semantic Web. In *Proceedings of the 4th European Semantic Web Conference, ESWC 2007* (pp. 624-639). Innsbruck, Austria.

Srivastava, J., Cooley, R., Deshpande, M., & Tan, P. (2000). Web Usage Mining: Discovery and Applications of Usage Patterns from Web Data. *SIGKDD Explorations, 1*(2), 12–23. doi:10.1145/846183.846188

Standards Australia. (2008). *Knowledge management: A framework for succeeding in the knowledge era (Standard/Guideline HB 275-2001).* Sydney: Standards Australia.

Stefanov, G., & Florea, R. (2009). *Twittermap 2.0.* Retrieved January 28, 2009, from http://gramo.ro

Sternberg, R. J. (1985). *Beyond IQ: A triarchic theory of human intelligence.* New York: Viking.

Sternberg, R. J., & Horvath, J. A. (1999). *Testing knowledge in professional practice.* Mahwah, NJ: Erlbaum.

Sternberg, R. J., Forsythe, G. B., Hedlund, J., Horvath, J. A., Wagner, R. K., & Williams, W. M. (2000). *Practical intelligence in everyday life.* New York: Cambridge University Press.

Sternberg, R. J., Wagner, R. K., & Williams, W. M. (1995). Testing common sense. *The American Psychologist, 50*(11). doi:10.1037/0003-066X.50.11.912

Stevens, V. (2008). Trial by Twitter: The Rise and Slide of the Year's Most Viral Microblogging Platform. *TESL-EJ, 12*(1)

Stewart, T. A. (2000). *Intellectual capital - the new wealth of organizations.* London: Nicholas Brealey Publishing.

Storck, J., & Hill, P. A. (2000). Knowledge diffusion through "strategic communities". *Sloan Management Review, 41*(2), 63–74.

Strang, K. D. (2003). Achieving organizational learning across projects. In J. Kardon (Ed.), *Proceedings of the North America global congress*. Baltimore, MD: PMI.

Strang, K. D. (2005). Examining effective and ineffective transformational project leadership. *Team Performance Management Journal*, *11*(3/4), 68–103. doi:10.1108/13527590510606299

Strang, K. D. (2007). Examining effective technology project leadership traits and behaviours. *Computers in Human Behavior*, *23*(2), 424–462. doi:10.1016/j.chb.2004.10.041

Strang, K. D. (2008). Collaborative synergy and leadership in e-business. In Salmons, J., & Wilson, L. (Eds.), *Handbook of research on electronic collaboration and organizational synergy* (pp. 409–434). Hershey, PA: IGI Global.

Strang, K. D. (2008). Quantitative online student profiling to forecast academic outcome from learning styles using dendrogram decision. *Multicultural Education & Technology Journal*, *2*(4), 215–244. doi:10.1108/17504970810911043

Strang, K. D. (2009). Assessing team member interpersonal competencies in new product development e-projects. *International Journal of Project Organisation and Management*, *1*(4), 335–357. doi:10.1504/IJPOM.2009.029105

Strang, K. D. (2009). Improving supervision of cross-cultural post graduate university students. *International Journal of Learning and Change*, *4*(2), 21–42.

Strang, K. D. (2009). Multicultural e-education: Student learning styles, culture and performance. In Song, H., & Kidd, T. (Eds.), *Handbook of research on human performance and instructional technology*. Hershey, PA: IGI Global.

Strang, K. D. (2009). Using recursive regression to explore nonlinear relationships and interactions: A tutorial applied to a multicultural education study. *Practical Assessment. Research Evaluation*, *14*(3), 1–13.

Strupp, J. (2009). *Tweets Smell of Excess? How Newsrooms Adapt to Twitter*. Retrieved June 22, 2009, from http://www.editorandpublisher.com

Sunstein, C. R. (2007). *Republic.com 2.0*. Princeton, NJ: Princeton Univ Press.

Surowiecki, J. (2004). *The Wisdow of Crowds*. New York: Random House.

Sveiby, K. E. (1997). *The invisible balance sheet* [Internet]. Retrieved, 2003, from www.sveiby.com/articles/InvisibleBalance.html

Sveiby, K. E. (1997). *The new organizational wealth: Managing and measuring knowledge-based assets*. San Francisco: Berrett-Koehler Publishers, Inc.

Sveiby, K. E. (1998). *Measuring intangibles and intellectual capital - an emerging first standard* [Internet]. Retrieved, 2003, from www.sveiby.com/articles/EmergingStandard.html

Swap, W., Leonard, D., Shields, M., & Abrams, L. (2001). Using mentoring and storytelling to transfer knowledge in the workplace. *Journal of Management Information Systems*, *40*(3), 95–114.

Swierczek, F. W. (1994). Culture and conflict in joint ventures in Asia. *International Journal of Project Management*, *12*(1), 39–47. doi:10.1016/0263-7863(94)90008-6

Tajfel, H. (1972). La catégorisation sociale. In Moscovici, S. (Ed.), *Introduction à la psychologie sociale* (Vol. 1). Paris: Larousse.

Takeuchi, H. (1998). *Beyond knowledge management: Lessons from Japan* [Internet]. Retrieved from www.sveiby.com/articles/LessonsJapan.htm

Takeuchi, H. (2001). Towards a universal management concept of knowledge. In Nonaka, I., & Teece, D. (Eds.), *Managing industrial knowledge - creation, transfer and utilization* (pp. 315–329). London: Sage.

Teece, D. J. (1998). Capturing value from knowledge assets: The new economy, markets for know-how, and intangible assets. *California Management Review*, *40*(3), 55–79.

Teece, D. J. (2001). Strategies for managing knowledge assets: The role of firm structure and industrial context. In Nonaka, I., & Teece, D. (Eds.), *Managing industrial knowledge - creation, transfer and utilization* (pp. 125–144). London: Sage.

Teigland, R. (2000). Communities of practice at an internet firm: Netovation vs on-time performance. In Lesser, E., Fontaine, M. A., & Slusher, J. A. (Eds.), *Knowledge and communities* (pp. 151–178). Boston: Butterworth-Heinemann. doi:10.1016/B978-0-7506-7293-1.50013-5

Tetali, P. (1991). Random walks and the effective resistance of networks. *Journal of Theoretical Probability, 4*, 101–109. doi:10.1007/BF01046996

Thelwall, M. (2004). *Link Analysis: An Information Science Approach*. Elsevier.

Tienda, M., & Wilson, W. J. (2002). Comparative Perspectives of Urban Youth. In *Youth in Cities: A Cross National Perspective*. Cambridge: Cambridge University Press.

Tong, H., Faloutsos, C., & Pan, J.-Y. (2006). Fast random walk with restart and its applications. In *Proceedings of sixth IEEE International Conference on Data Mining (ICDM 2006)* (pp. 613–622).

Tong, H., Faloutsos, C., & Pan, J.-Y. (2008). Random walk with restart: fast solutions and applications. *Knowledge and Information Systems, 14*(3), 327–346. doi:10.1007/s10115-007-0094-2

Torvalds, L. B., & Diamond, D. (2001). *Just for Fun: The Story of an Accidental Revolutionary*. New York: Harper Business.

Trompenaars, F. (1993). *Riding the waves of culture: Understanding cultural diversity in business*. London: Economics Books.

Tsoukas, H. (Ed.). (2003). *Do we really understand tacit knowledge?* London: Blackwell.

Tucker, E. (2008, July 21). Facebook photos judges of character. *The Washington Times*. Retrieved from http://www.washingtontimes.com/news/2008/jul/21/facebook-photos-judges-of-character/

Turing, A. (1936). On computable Numbers, With an Application to the Entscheidungsproblem. *Proceedings of the London Mathematical Society, 2*(42), 230–265.

Uchyigit, G., & Clark, K. (2003). A multi-agent architecture for dynamic collaborative filtering. In *Proceedings of the 5th International Conference on Enterprise Information Systems, 4*, 363–368.

Ulwick, A. W. (2002). Turn customer input into innovation. *Harvard Business Review, 80*(1), 91–97.

Ungar, L. H., & Foster, D. P. (1998). Clustering methods for collaborative filtering. In *Proceedings of the Workshop on Recommendation Systems*.

van Laarhoven, P. J. M., & Aarts, E. H. L. (1987). *Simulated Annealing: Theory and Applications*. Springer.

Vargas, E. (2009). *El periodismo digital crea empleo*. Retrieved June 15, 2009, from http://www.tintadigital.org

von Krough, G., Ichijo, K., & Takeuchi, H. (2000). *Enabling knowledge creation*. Oxford: Oxford University Press.

von Luxburg, U. (2007). *A tutorial on spectral clustering*. Statistics and Computing.

Voulgaris, S., Gavidia, D., & Van Steen, M. (2005). CYCLON: Inexpensive Membership Management for Unstructured P2P Overlays. *Journal of Network and Systems Management, 13*(2), 197–217. doi:10.1007/s10922-005-4441-x

Vyas, D., Eliëns, A., van de Watering, M. R., & van der Veer, G. C. (2008). Organizational probes: exploring playful interactions in work environment. In J. Abascal, I. Fajardo, & I. Oakley (Eds,), *Proceedings of the 15th European Conference on Cognitive Ergonomics: the Ergonomics of Cool interaction (Funchal, Portugal, September 16 - 19, 2008), ECCE '08, vol. 369* (pp. 1-4). New York: ACM.

Wagner, R. K., & Sternberg, R. J. (1985). Practice intelligence in real-world pursuits: The role of tacit knowledge. *Journal of Personality and Social Psychology, 49*(2), 436–458. doi:10.1037/0022-3514.49.2.436

Walsh, J. P., & Ungson, G. R. (1997). Organizational memory. In Prusak, L. (Ed.), *Knowledge in organizations - resources for the knowledge-based economy* (pp. 147–175). Oxford: Butterworth-Heinemann.

Wang, Y., & Kitsuregawa, M. (2001, 3-6 December). *Use Link-based Clustering to Improve Web Search Results.* Paper presented at the Proceedings of the 2nd International Conference on Web Information Systems Engineering (WISE2001), Kyoto, Japan.

Wang, Y., & Vassileva, J. Trust-Based Community Formation in Peer-to-Peer File Sharing Networks. In *Proceedings of the IEEE/WIC/ACM International Conference on Web Intelligence, WI'04* (pp. 341-348). Beijing, China.

Wasserman, S., & Faust, K. (1994). *Social Network Analysis: Methods and Applications.* Cambridge University Press.

Weber, M. (1980). *Wirtschaft und Gesellschaft. Grundriß der verstehenden Soziologie.* Tübingen: Mohr.

Weick, K. E. (1995). *Sensemaking in organizations.* Thousand Oaks, CA: Sage.

Weick, K. E. (2001). *Making sense of the organization.* Oxford: Blackwell Publishers.

Welch, J., & Welch, S. (2009). *Why we tweet.* Retrieved June 2, 2009, from http://www.businessweek.com

Wellman, B., Quan-Haase, A., & Chen, W. (2003). The Social Affordances of the Internet for Networked individualism. *Journal of Computer-Mediated Communication, 8*(3).

Wenger, D. (1986). Transactive memory: A contemporary analysis of the group mind. In *Theories of group behavior* (pp. 185–205). New York: Springer-Verlag.

Wenger, E. (1998). Communities of practice. Learning as a social system. *Systems Thinker, 9*(5).

Wenger, E. (1998). *Communities of Practice: Learning, Meaning, and Identity.* Cambridge University Press.

Wenger, E. C. (1999). Communities of practice: The key to knowledge strategy. *The Journal of the Institute for Knowledge Management, 1*(Fall), 48–63.

Wenger, E. C., & Snyder, W. M. (2000). Communities of practice: The organizational frontier. *Harvard Business Review, 78*(1), 139–145.

Wenger, E. C., McDermott, R., & Snyder, W. M. (2002). *Cultivating communities of practice: A guide to managing knowledge.* Boston: Harvard Business School Publishing.

Werbach, K. (2000). Syndication - the emerging model for business in the internet era. *Harvard Business Review, 78*(3), 85–93.

Wheeler, S. (2009). *Connected Minds, Emerging Cultures: Cybercultures in Online Learning.* IAP.

White, S., & Smyth, P. (2003). Algorithms for estimating relative importance in networks. In *Proceedings of the ninth ACM SIGKDD International Conference on Knowledge Discovery and Data mining* (pp. 266–275).

Whitley, B. E. Jr. (2002). *Principles of research in behavioral science* (2nd ed.). New York: McGraw-Hill.

Wiig, K. M. (2002). *Knowledge management: An emerging discipline rooted in a long history.* Knowledge Research Institute. Retrieved May 21, 2006, from www.krii.com

Wiig, K. M. (2003). *Knowledge management has many facets* [internet]. Knowledge Research Institute. Retrieved March 21, 2009, from www.krii.com

Wilson, R. C., Hancock, E. R., & Luo, B. (2005). Pattern vectors from algebraic graph theory. *IEEE Transactions on Pattern Analysis and Machine Intelligence, 27,* 1112–1124. doi:10.1109/TPAMI.2005.145

Wilson, T. D. (2002). The nonsense of 'knowledge management'. *Information Research, 8*(1), 1–14.

Winkin, Y. (1981). *La nouvelle communication.* Paris: Seuil.

Xiao, J., Zhang, Y., Jia, X., & Li, T. (2001). *Measuring Similarity of Interests for Clustering Web-Users.* Paper presented at the Proceedings of the 12th Australasian Database conference (ADC2001), Queensland, Australia.

Xiong, L., & Liu, L. (2004). PeerTrust: Supporting Reputation-based Trust for Peer-to-Peer Electronic

Communities. *IEEE Transactions on Knowledge and Data Engineering*, *16*(7), 843–857. doi:10.1109/TKDE.2004.1318566

Xu, G., Zhang, Y., & Zhou, X. (2005). *A Latent Usage Approach for Clustering Web Transaction and Building User Profile*. Paper presented at the First International Conference on Advanced Data Mining and Applications (ADMA 2005), Wuhan, china.

Xu, G., Zhang, Y., & Zhou, X. (2005). *A Web Recommendation Technique Based on Probabilistic Latent Semantic Analysis*. Paper presented at the Proceeding of 6th International Conference of Web Information System Engineering (WISE' 2005), New York City, USA.

Yajima, Y., & Kuo, T.-F. (2006). Efficient formulations for 1-SVM and their application to recommendation tasks. *Journal of Computers*, *1*(3), 27–34. doi:10.4304/jcp.1.3.27-34

Yates, S. (2001). Researching Internet Interaction: Socio-linguistics and Corpus Analysis. In Wetherell, M., Taylor, S., & Yates, S. (Eds.), *Discourse as Data. A Guide for Analysis* (pp. 93–146). London: The Open University.

Yen, L., Fouss, F., Decaestecker, C., Francq, P., & Saerens, M. (2007). Graph nodes clustering based on the commute-time kernel. In *Proceedings of the 11th Pacific- Asia Conference on Knowledge Discovery and Data Mining (PAKDD 2007)* (LNAI 4426, pp. 1037–1045).

Yen, L., Mantrach, A., Shimbo, M., & Saerens, M. (2008). A family of dissimilarity measures between nodes generalizing both the shortest-path and the commute-time distances. In *Proceedings of the 14th SIGKDD International Conference on Knowledge Discovery and Data Mining* (pp. 785–793).

Yen, L., Vanvyve, D., Wouters, F., Fouss, F., Verleysen, M., & Saerens, M. (2005). Clustering using a random walk-based distance measure. In *Proceedings of the 13th European Symposium on Artificial Neural Networks (ESANN2005)* (pp. 317–324).

Yépez, S. (2009). *Rumbo a un diario HOY transparente con los lectores*. Retrieved February 13, 2009, from http://www.hoy.com.ec

Yin, R. K. (2003). *Case study research: Design and methods* (3rd ed.). London, UK: Sage.

Yu, K., Schwaighofer, A., Tresp, V., Xu, X., & Kriegel, H.-P. (2004). Probabilistic memory-based collaborative filtering. *IEEE Transactions on Knowledge and Data Engineering*, *16*(5), 56–69.

Zack, M. H. (1999). Developing a knowledge strategy. *California Management Review*, *41*(3), 125–145.

Zadeh, L. A. (1965). Fuzzy sets. *Information and Control*, *8*, 338–353. doi:10.1016/S0019-9958(65)90241-X

Zahn, C. T. (1971). Graph-theoretical methods for detecting and describing gestalt clusters. *IEEE Transactions on Computers*, *100*(20), 68–86. doi:10.1109/T-C.1971.223083

Zhang, Y., Yu, J. X., & Hou, J. (2006). *Web Communities: Analysis and Construction*. Berlin, Heidelberg: Springer.

Zhao, D., & Tang, Z. L. X. (2007). Contextual distance for data perception. In *Proceedings of the eleventh IEEE International Conference on Computer Vision (ICCV)*, *57*, 1–8.

Zhou, D., & Scholkopf, B. (2004). Learning from labeled and unlabeled data using random walks. In *Proceedings of the 26th DAGM Symposium, (Eds.) Rasmussen* (pp. 237–244).

Zhou, D., Huang, J., & Scholkopf, B. (2005). Learning from labeled and unlabeled data on a directed graph. *Proceedings of the 22nd International Conference on Machine Learning*, pages 1041–1048.

About the Contributors

Pascal Francq earned his Master's degree in applied science at the Université Libre de Bruxelles (ULB) in 1996 and his PhD in 2003. From 2003 until 2008, he held the chair in information systems and in digital information at the ULB. He decide to quit due to the lack of time and resources for its research activities, and join a research project at the Université Catholique de Louvain (UCL). His main research topic is the Internet: its technologies, its social aspects and its support as a knowledge sharing platform. Since 1998, he has been working on automatic communities detection. He is the main contributor of the open source platform GALILEI and is currently involved in research on XML document clustering and semi-automatic thesaurus building. He founded in 2009 the Paul Otlet Institute, an independent research center in information science.

* * *

Silvana Castano is full professor of Computer Science at the Università degli Studi di Milano, where she chairs the Information systems & knowledge management (ISLab) group. She received the Ph.D. degree in Computer and Automation Engineering from Politecnico di Milano. Her main research interests are in the area of databases and information systems and ontologies and Semantic Web, with focus on ontology matching and evolution, emergent semantics, knowledge discovery in open networked systems, semantic integration and interoperability. On these topics, she has been working in several national and international research projects, such as EU FP6 BOEMIE, EU FP6 INTEROP-NoE, PRIN ESTEEM, COFIN D2I, FIRB WEB-MINDS. She has been serving as PC member for several important database, information systems, and Semantic Web conferences. In 2009, she is PC co-chair of the ER 2009 conference. Since November 2008, she is the President-Elect of GRIN, the Italian association of University Professors in Informatics.

Tanguy Coenen has a broad interest in both the theoretical and practical aspects of technology and the way it applies to society at large. He has worked and is currently working on a wide array of technology-related projects. Over the years, he has developed skills both as a systems architect and programmer. As a researcher, he has been involved in theory building on social software and more specifically social networking systems.

Alfio Ferrara is assistant professor of Computer Science at the University of Milano, where he received his Ph.D. in Computer Science in 2005. His research interests include database and semi-structured data integration, Web-based information systems, ontology engineering, and knowledge representation and evolution. On these topics, he works in national and international research projects, including the

Copyright © 2011, IGI Global. Copying or distributing in print or electronic forms without written permission of IGI Global is prohibited.

recent EU FP6 BOEMIE (Bootstrapping Ontology Evolution with Multimedia Information Extraction) project, the FP6 INTEROP NoE (Interoperability Research for Networked Enterprises Applications and Software) project, and the ESTEEM (Emergent Semantics and cooperaTion in multi-knowledgE EnvironMents) PRIN project funded by the Italian Ministry of Education, University, and Research. He is also author of several articles and papers in international journals and conferences about ontology management and matching.

Francois Fouss received the MS degree in Information Systems in 2002 and the PhD degree in Management Science in 2007, both from the Université catholique de Louvain (UCL), Belgium. In 2007, he joined the Facultés Universitaires Catholiques de Mons (FUCaM) as a professor of computing science. His main research areas include data mining, machine learning, graph mining, classification, and collaborative recommendation.

Elias N. Houstis is the Director of Center of Research and Technology --Thessaly (CE.RE.TE.TH.) and a full Professor of Computer Engineering and Communications department at University of Thessaly. He has been a Professor of Computer Science and Director of the Computational Science & Engineering Program of Purdue University. He has served as acting and associate Head of the Department of Computer Sciences for several years. He participated in several European projects in the area of information technologies. Houstis is a member of several research groups in USA and Japan including ICER - The Indiana consortium for e-commerce research, NSF- Agent based modeling framework for scalable interdependent markets and organizations, Japan - NSF - Global grid computing and environments for science and technology, ICER- Indiana consortium on telemedicine. Houstis is in the editorial board of several journals. Houstis' current research interests are in the areas of portals, networking computing, enterprise systems, computational intelligence, computational finance, e-business, and e-learning. He has published several books and over 150 technical articles.

Lefteris Kellis is currently employed in the Centre of Research and Technology of Thessaly, as a member of the Laboratory for Information Systems and Services of the Mechatronics institute, and a Phd candidate at the Department of Computer & Communication Engineering at the University of Thessaly. He has a BSc in Computer Science and an MSc in Evolutionary and Adaptive Systems from the University of Sussex, UK. His research interests lie in the fields of Recommender Systems, Information Filtering and biologically inspired Artificial Intelligence. His thesis aims in achieving adaptive and distributed Information Filtering using techniques from the fields of Artificial Immune Systems, collaborative and content-based filtering.

Sabine Kolvenbach is a senior researcher at Fraunhofer FIT. In 1988 she has joined the CSCW department where she has worked in several national and EU research projects. She has managed the conceptual design and participated in the implemention of the Baton Application and Album. Her research interests are social web, web communities, cooperative task management, and group awareness.

Ioannis Koutsaftikis holds a position as a network administrator and web developer for Centre of Research and Technology --Thessaly (CE.RE.TE.TH.). Having graduated from the Computer & Communication Engineering Department at University of Thessaly, Ioannis is currently an MSc candidate at the same department. His programming skills involve working with Java, PHP, Python, C++, Javascript and are mostly focused towards web development. Ioannis' scientific interests include personalisation, collaborative filtering, web 2.0 technologies and social networking through the Internet.

Christophe Lejeune is a Researcher of Communication Sciences at the University of Brussels, Belgium. In his PhD thesis (in Sociology), he conducted participant observation of the Open Directory Project, a collective voluntary effort to index website addresses. He has also studied the regulation of discussion forums, involvement in free software and social organization of mediated collectives. His current research is focused on trust in mediated collectives and mutual help in (off-line) Linux user groups. From a methodological point of view, he is interested in the use of software in qualitative analysis. In particular, he developed the Cassandre software for textual analysis, as a module of the Hypertopic collaboratory platform.

Stefano Montanelli has a Post Doc position in Computer Science at the University of Milano, where he received his Ph.D. in Computer Science in 2006. His main research interests include database and web-based information systems, Semantic Web, ontology matching and evolution, emergent semantics and knowledge discovery in open distributed systems. On these topics, he is involved in national and international research projects, including the recent EU FP6 BOEMIE project and the ESTEEM PRIN project funded by the Italian Ministry of Education, University, and Research. He is also author of several articles and papers in international journals and conferences about P2P semantic routing and ontology-based P2P community management.

Nikolaos Nanas (www.lisys.gr/nanas) is a research fellow at the Lab for Information Systems and Services (LISyS.gr) of the Center of Research and Technology - Thessaly (CERETETH, Greece), an associate lecturer at the University of Thessaly (Greece) and a visiting research fellow at the Computing Department of the Open Univeristy (U.K.). He studied civil engineering at the Aristotle University of Thessaloniki (Greece). He received his M.S. degree in Intelligent Systems from the University of Sussex (U.K.) and his Ph.D. In Artificial Intelligence from the Knowledge Media Institute of the Open University (U.K.). His research work lies in the areas of Statistical Natural Language Processing, Adaptive Information Filtering, and Biologically Inspired Computing.

José Manuel Noguera Vivo is a lecturer in Web Journalism at Catholic University of San Antonio, Spain. Previously he was lecturer in Multimedia at SEK University (Spain), and also visiting scholar in Multimedia and Social Media at American University of Acapulco (México) and Diaconia University of Applied Sciences (Finland). He teaches postgraduate courses in Blogging and New Media at several public and private institutions. Guest speaker in V Conference of Latinoamerican Center of Journalism (Panama, 2008). Author of the book *Blogs y Medios* (Libros En Red, 2008), among other publications. Noguera maintains since April 2004 the web called La Azotea (http://laazotea.blogspot.com), a personal blog about blogging, web journalism and digital trends.

Wolfgang Prinz, PhD studied informatics at the University of Bonn and received his PhD in computer science from the University of Nottingham. He is vice chair of Fraunhofer FIT in Bonn, division manager of the Collaboration systems research department in FIT, and associate professor for cooperation systems at RWTH Aachen. He is carrying out research in the area of Cooperative Systems, Social Web and Pervasive Games. He participated in and managed several national research and international research projects and he is currently coordinator of a large European research project on collaborative work environments.

Kenneth David Strang has a Doctorate in Project Management (business research, high distinction), an MBA (honors), a BS (honors), as well as a Business Technology diploma (honors). He is a certified *Project Management Professional*® from Project Management Institute, and is a *Fellow of the Life Management Institute* (distinction, specialized in actuary statistics and pension systems), from Life Office Management Association. His research interests include: Leadership, multicultural e-learning, marketing new product development, knowledge management, and e-business project management. He designs and teaches multidisciplinary subjects in business, informatics and educational psychology, in class and online MBA programs. He supervises Phd and doctorate students. He chairs the Telstra Learning-in-Business center and he is chief researcher at an international marketing research institution.

Guandong Xu is a Research Fellow in the Center for Applied Information at Victoria University, Australia. He received his PhD in Computer Science from the School of Engineering and Science at Victoria in 2008. Prior to this, he obtained MEng and BEng degree in Computer Engineering and Science from Zhejiang University, China in 1992 and 1989, respectively. He has been employed by Wenzhou University, China as a Lecturer and Associate Professor. In 2008, he worked as a Postdoctoral Research Fellow in the Institute of Industrial Science at the University of Tokyo, which was funded by the Australian Federal Government. His research interest covers a wide range of topics including Web data management, Web information processing, Web mining, Web recommendation, data mining, machine learning, health data management and knowledge discovery, health informatics. He has had over twenty quality publications in international journals and conference proceedings in related fields. Recently he is actively engaged in a variety of research activities, such as being a PC member for international conferences and an external reviewer for international journals, and co-chairing workshops. He was the recipient of 2007 Chinese Government Award for outstanding overseas students, and was awarded the 2009 Vice-Chancellor's Citation of Research at Victoria University.

Wouter Van den Bosch works as a researcher at Memori, a research group of the University College Mechelen, since 2005. Wouter's research activities currently focus on applications of ICT and social media in such fields as knowledge management, e-government, social work and e-health. His work entails both the exploration of what new possibilities social media may bring to these fields as well as how they can best be practically implemented and embedded within organizations or institutions. Wouter also teaches a Content Management Systems class at the University College of Mechelen.

Manolis Vavalis is an Associated Professor of Computer and Communication Engineering at the University of Thessaly. He is also a Senior Researcher at the Laboratory of Information Systems and Services of the Center for Research and Technology – Thessaly (CERETETH). Before coming to Thessaly Dr. Vavalis was a faculty member in the Computer Science Department at Purdue University and in the Mathematics Department at the University of Crete. He has also been a Senior Researcher at the Foundation for Research and Technology - Hellas (FORTH) and at the Center for Research & Technology Hellas (CERTH). Dr. Vavalis conducts basic and applied research and offering undergraduate and graduate courses in the thematic areas of High Performance Scientific Computing, Knowledge Management and Information Systems.

Index

A

academicism 198

action learning approach 210

adaptive information filtering (AIF) 166, 167, 168, 169, 170, 171, 172, 178

advertisement message 145

agglomerative 108

aggregators 173, 178, 247

agreement criterion 114

Amazon 30

ambient journalism 185

amendment procedure 158

aperiodic 72

approximate multi-criteria problem 114, 122

approximation algorithms 104, 105

a priori 114, 228, 230

artificial intelligence 41

artificial neural networks 23

average commute time 70, 72, 73, 74, 75, 77, 78, 84, 88, 92

average first-passage cost 70, 72, 74, 75

average first-passage time 70, 72, 73, 74, 75, 77, 78, 79, 92

average first-passage time one-way (FPTo) 79

average first-passage time return (FPTr) 79

awareness system 185

B

baton application 7

Bayesian networks 27, 35, 48

betweenness centrality 77, 95

bipartite graph 74, 89, 94

blogosphere 2, 183, 186, 188, 189

blogs 2, 8, 64, 243

bottleneck 70

brainstorming 210, 215, 225

C

Cartesian split 224

case amplification 26

causal knowledge 212

centered kernel matrix 82, 83

centroid 50, 51, 57, 68

clustering 23, 27, 28, 39, 41, 42, 44, 45, 48, 49, 50, 51, 52, 53, 56, 57, 63

clustering algorithm 82, 106

cluster models 27

cognitive science 21

collaborative algorithms 70

collaborative approaches 22, 23, 24

collaborative filtering 3, 8, 21, 23, 25, 28, 34, 35, 36, 37, 39, 41, 47, 48, 60, 65, 66, 67

collaborative filtering systems 24

collaborative filtering tools 3, 8

collaborative platform 255

collaborative recommendation 70, 78, 84, 89, 90, 94

collaborative search 2, 4, 5, 7, 8

collective concept 135, 139, 141, 142, 149, 157, 159

collective concepts 135, 141, 142, 148, 149, 150, 157, 159

collective goals 240, 246

collective information filtering (CIF) 6, 164, 166, 167, 168, 170, 171, 172, 174, 175, 178

collective intelligence 1, 7

collective knowledge 134, 135, 136, 138, 139, 140, 141, 142, 145, 150, 151, 152, 153, 154, 156, 157, 158, 159, 163

Copyright © 2011, IGI Global. Copying or distributing in print or electronic forms without written permission of IGI Global is prohibited.

Q

R

S